CU00738504

Philo of Alexandria

THE ANCHOR YALE BIBLE REFERENCE LIBRARY
is a project of international and interfaith scope in which
Protestant, Catholic, and Jewish scholars from many countries
contribute individual volumes. The project is not sponsored by
any ecclesiastical organization and is not intended to reflect
any particular theological doctrine.

The series is committed to producing volumes in the tradition
established half a century ago by the founders of the Anchor
Bible, William Foxwell Albright and David Noel Freedman.
It aims to present the best contemporary scholarship in a way
that is accessible not only to scholars but also to the educated
nonspecialist. It is committed to work of sound philological and historical scholarship, supplemented by insight from
modern methods, such as sociological and literary criticism.

John J. Collins
General Editor

THE ANCHOR YALE BIBLE REFERENCE LIBRARY

Philo of Alexandria

An Intellectual Biography

MAREN R. NIEHOFF

 Yale
UNIVERSITY
PRESS

NEW HAVEN
AND
LONDON

Yale University Press books may be purchased in quantity for educational, business, or promotional use. For information, please e-mail sales.press@yale.edu (U.S. office) or sales@yaleup.co.uk (U.K. office).

Set in Adobe Caslon type with Bauer Bodoni display by Newgen North America.
Printed in the United States of America.

Library of Congress Control Number: 2017940024
ISBN 978-0-300-17523-3 (hardcover : alk. paper)

A catalogue record for this book is available from the British Library.

This paper meets the requirements of ANSI/NISO z39.48-1992 (Permanence of Paper).

10 9 8 7 6 5 4 3 2 1

For my parents, Ulla and Gerd Niehoff,
my husband, Udi Rosenthal,
and my daughters, Maya, Ayana, and Stav,
with much love and gratitude

In memory of
Tamar Rosenthal, my mother-in-law,
who welcomed me warmly into the family and encouraged my work

Contents

Acknowledgments, ix

1. An Intellectual Biography of Philo?, 1

PART ONE: PHILO AS AMBASSADOR AND AUTHOR
IN ROME

2. Philo's Self-Fashioning in the Historical Writings, 25
3. Power, Exile, and Religion in the Roman Empire, 47
4. Roman Philosophy and the Jews, 69

PART TWO: PHILO'S *EXPOSITION* IN A
ROMAN CONTEXT

5. Creation Theology and Monotheism, 93
6. Character and History in the *Lives* of the Biblical
   Forefathers, 109
7. Biblical Ladies in Roman Garb, 131
8. Stoic Ethics in the Service of Jewish Law, 149

PART THREE: YOUNG PHILO AMONG
ALEXANDRIAN JEWS

9. Biblical Commentary, 173

10. A Platonic Self, 192

11. An Utterly Transcendent God and His Logos, 209

12. Stoicism: Rejected, Subverted, and Advocated, 225

Epilogue: Philo at the Crossroads of Judaism, Hellenism,
and Christianity, 242

Appendix 1: Philo's Dates and Works, 245

Appendix 2: Did Philo Write an *Allegorical Commentary* on
Genesis Chapter 1?, 247

Notes, 251

Bibliography, 281

General Index, 311

Index of Ancient Sources, 320

Acknowledgments

This book had its beginning at a conversation with John Collins after I gave a lecture at Yale University in 2010. At that time the idea of writing an intellectual biography of Philo was still rather vague, and I am grateful to John for encouraging and accompanying me with singular grace and prudence. John also edited the manuscript, offering invaluable comments. Heather Gold and her team at Yale University Press promoted the production with remarkable efficiency and professionalism, rendering the preparation of the book a real pleasure. Special thanks to Jessie Dolch for her meticulous copy-editing, always in an enthusiastic spirit, and to Mary Pasti.

I have been accompanied on this journey by old and new friends who encouraged me and significantly contributed to this book. Margalit Finkelberg read all the chapters and the revised versions of some chapters with a rare combination of empathy, wisdom, and criticism. Yehuda Liebes offered insightful comments on several chapters and read with me Philo's tractate *On the Migration of Abraham*, thus enriching my understanding of his exegesis. Miriam Griffin read all the Roman chapters with utmost care and provided numerous precious comments. René Bloch, Albert Harill, Adele Yarbo Collins, and Tim Whitmarsh offered helpful comments on individual chapters. Two anonymous readers for Yale University Press offered constructive comments that considerably improved the final version of the manuscript. More generally, I thank Judith Green for hosting and guiding a reading group in Greek literature that covered, during the gestation of the book, Aurelius's *Meditations* and Philostratus's *Life of Apollonius*.

My work on the book has tremendously benefited from discussions following lectures. I recall with special gratitude the invitation by Peter Schäfer to Princeton (2008), by Carlos Lévy and Philippe

Hoffman to Paris (2010), by Steven Fraade to Yale (2010), by Francesca Calabi to Milan (2011), by Teresa Morgan to Oxford (2013), by Richard Faber and Achim Lichtenberger to Bochum (2013), by Hindy Najman to Yale (2014), by Laura Nasrallah and Shaye Cohen to Harvard (2014), by Jörg Rüpke and Eve-Marie Becker to Erfurt (2015), by Hermut Löhr to Münster (2015), by Winrich Löhr to Heidelberg (2016), and by Ciliers Breytenbach to Berlin (2016). I have also benefited from the astute questions of my students, in both the Department of Jewish Thought and the Amirim Honors Program in the Humanities at the Hebrew University of Jerusalem.

The research for this book was generously supported by the ISRAEL SCIENCE FOUNDATION (grant no. 186/11) and a grant from the Niedersachsen-Israeli Research Cooperation Program (together with Reinhard Feldmeier). Rami Schwartz helped me acquire literature and compile the bibliography. Tom Sela prepared the index. Both foundations also supported an international conference in Jerusalem, "Journeys in the Roman East: Imagined and Real," that illuminated the wider context of Philo's journey to Rome (ISRAEL SCIENCE FOUNDATION grant no. 2178/15). My sabbatical leave from the Hebrew University in 2013–2014, which I spent in Jerusalem, provided precious time to engage in undistracted work.

Thanks to Rina Talgam, my colleague in the Department of Art History, for suggesting the cover image, which is taken from the *Ara Pacis Augustae,* an altar Augustus consecrated in Rome. The southern wall of the altar depicts several groups from the imperial family, including the detail on the cover, which most likely presents the prince Drusus in conversation with his wife, Antonia. This scene expresses Augustus's ideal of the Roman couple as well as the status of the mother and wife in Roman culture. When Philo visited Rome as an ambassador, he probably saw this altar and perhaps even appreciated this particular scene. He certainly adopted the Augustan ideal of marital union. It is thus more than appropriate that this image should decorate his biography. Thanks also to Roi Sabar from the Archeology Department for providing a high-quality photograph.

The book is based on some materials that have been previously published and substantially revised. Chapter 5 is based on the article "The Emergence of Monotheistic Creation Theology," in *In the Beginning: Jewish and Christian Cosmogony in Late Antiquity,* ed. L. Jenott and S. Kattan Gribetz (Tübingen: Mohr Siebeck, 2013), 85–106; chapter 6 is based on two articles: "Philo and Plutarch as Biographers: Parallel Reactions to Roman Stoicism," *Greek, Roman, and Byzantine Studies* 52 (2012): 361–92; and "The Roman Context of Philo's Exposition," *Studia Philonica Annual* 23 (2011): 1–21. Chapter 3 contains a passage based on the article "'The Power of Ares' in Philo's *Legatio*," in *Pouvoir et puissances chez Philon d'Alexandrie,* ed. F. Calabi, O. Munnich, G. Reydams-Schils, and E. Vimercati (Turnhout: Brepols, 2016), 129–39. Chapter 4 contains a passage based on the article "The Symposium of Philo's Therapeutae: Displaying Jewish Identity in an Increasingly Roman World," *Greek, Roman, and Byzantine Studies* 50 (2010): 95–117. I thank all the editors for their kind permission to reuse the materials in this book.

This book is dedicated to my family. My parents have followed my work with great interest, making valiant efforts to get to know the Jewish tradition. My husband, Udi, has enthusiastically supported my work, even during times of physical ailment, and provided a most loving anchor to my life. My daughters have in the meantime grown up and become wonderful conversation partners, mostly on topics unconnected to Philo.

1 An Intellectual Biography of Philo?

No biography of Philo has ever been attempted, and there are good reasons for this state of affairs. Philo resists the easy grasp of a biographer because he tells us very little about his own person and virtually nothing about the circumstances of his writing activity. Vital facts, such as his upbringing in Alexandria and the sequence of his works, can therefore be only conjectured. The Jewish historian Josephus Flavius, who lived just one generation after Philo and preserved much precious information about other characters, is disappointingly brief about him. His notice merely confirms that Philo was the head of the Jewish embassy to Gaius and that he was "not inexperienced in philosophy." Christian authors began to mention Philo only later and then usually quoted or paraphrased his writings without providing additional information. The first author who offers an overall analysis of Philo's work is the church historian Eusebius (ca. 260–ca. 340 CE), who relies on a close reading of his texts, most of which are still extant.[1] While Eusebius's interpretation is remarkable and still relevant, it does not provide any additional evidence that could help us reconstruct Philo's life.

Yet Philo deserves an intellectual biography because he is an exceptionally rich and somewhat enigmatic author who has written in diverse genres and left behind one of the most voluminous oeuvres of antiquity. His intellectual achievement is impressive and innovative, worthy of being appreciated in its own right. Moreover, Philo experienced dramatic changes in his life. Although he grew up in a rather peaceful environment in Alexandria, he saw an outburst of ethnic violence in 38 CE and then became the head of the Jewish embassy to the emperor Gaius Caligula. This political responsibility took him for several years to Rome and is crucial for an appreciation of his personality and intellectual development. At a time when the eastern parts of the empire were becoming rapidly entangled with Roman structures of power and forms of discourse, Philo plays a key role in the negotiations between East and West.

Philo's significance has increasingly been recognized in recent years and is attested by a blooming of new translations, introductions, handbooks, monographs, and collections of essays. For instance, in 2015 the Hebrew translation of Philo's works available in Greek was completed, and some passages of his work were integrated into the Reform Prayer Book in Israel. At the same time two German monographs were devoted to Philo: Otto Kaiser offered a highly sympathetic introduction to him, with special attention to the *realia,* and Friederike Oertelt analyzed political aspects of Philo's image of Joseph. The year 2014 saw the publication of a handbook edited by Torrey Seland that assembles summaries of research on several key topics and addresses the question of Philo's relevance for various fields of scholarship. In 2013 Albert Geljon and David Runia's commentary on Philo's treatise *On Cultivation* appeared, as well as Francesca Calabi's Italian introduction to Philo, which pays special attention to his interpretation of Scripture and engagement with Platonic philosophy. In 2011 a French team of scholars published a large collection of articles that investigate Philo in his various cultural contexts. In 2010 a volume of the *Études Platoniciennes* was dedicated to Philo. In 2009 the *Cambridge Companion to Philo,* edited by Adam Kamesar, appeared and covered historical, philosophical, and exegetical topics, with emphasis on the state of the scholarly debate. Finally, in 2003 the French scholar Mireille Hadas-Lebel published an introduction to Philo as a thinker in the Jewish Diaspora, which was quickly translated into Hebrew and English.[2] Despite this growing interest in Philo among various academic communities, we still lack an intellectual biography that reconstructs the development of his personality and thought.

How, then, can the evident obstacles of writing an intellectual biography of Philo be overcome? I propose to meet the challenge by a comprehensive analysis of each of his series of works in its broader cultural context. Such an investigation transcends narrow specializations of research and argues that political, philosophical, theological, and literary aspects must be understood in light of each other. Philo the historian cannot be isolated from Philo the exegete. Nor can his philosophical writings be meaningfully understood without reading his work on Jewish law, which he interprets in a philosophical vein. At the same time, however, careful attention must be paid to the different genres of Philo's writings. Passages from the *Allegorical Commentary*, for example, cannot be read as if they were directly connected to the philosophical treatises. The *Questions and Answers* cannot be read as if they were a straight continuation of his *Exposition of the Law*. We rather have to understand Philo's intentions in each series of writings and ask for which purpose he used that particular literary format.[3] Who was his implied audience in each case, and what may have been the circumstances of his writing? Following these questions and adopting a comparative method, we can draw conclusions from the different texts about the cultural milieu in which each of them emerged. In each case I point to a close connection between literary genre, cultural context, and choice of philosophy.

The comparative approach leads us to properly appreciate the diversity of Philo's work, which can neither be reduced to one monolithic essence nor be judged as a case of careless eclecticism. We instead have to face the possibility of significant intellectual developments throughout Philo's long and rich career. Looking at the very few known facts of his life, we have to ask whether his journey from Alexandria to Rome, as the head of the Jewish embassy, had any visible effect on his style of writing and interpretation of Judaism.[4] Did he have different conversation partners with different backgrounds in each of these locations? Given that Philo stayed in Rome for at least three years (38–41 CE), I argue that his journey was a crucial experience, not only politically, but also intellectually. It had an immediate effect upon his choice of literary genre, Jewish identity, and philosophical orientation. Philo refashioned himself, constructing a new identity and offering new interpretations of his tradition.

Where shall our intellectual biography start? Philo's childhood can hardly be our starting point, as we know next to nothing about it. Given that he was a mature man in 38 CE when he embarked on the embassy, he must have been born around 20–10 BCE. Josephus tells us that he belonged to an eminently rich family in Alexandria, with Alexander the Alabarch as his brother. Philo's numerous references to Classical Greek literature suggest that he received a thorough Greek education. In a rare autobiographical passage he says that he went through the usual curriculum of Greek education in his "early youth" and complemented his studies by philosophy. At the same time, Philo was immersed in the Jewish Scriptures in their Greek translation, quoting many verses by heart and expecting his audience to pick up biblical allusions. Such an in-depth familiarity suggests a Jewish upbringing with extensive exposure to the Bible, yet without access to the Hebrew original.[5] Precise details of Philo's childhood, however, cannot be known as he chose to remain silent about his early years. Unlike Josephus, he did not write an autobiography, which would provide some guidelines. We must avoid reconstructing his childhood, as it is methodologically unsound to draw conclusions from our general knowledge about Alexandria to his particular life. Alexandrian culture was so diverse that we cannot know which aspects applied to Philo's infancy and youth. The only reliable evidence we have is his written work, which allows us to appreciate his perception of things as an adult. To his mature period also date the two certain events of his life: his embassy to Rome and his brief visit to the Jerusalem Temple.[6]

Our analysis opens with Philo's historical treatises because they are the only works that can be clearly dated and placed into a specific political and cultural context. The two extant treatises *On the Embassy to Gaius* and *Against Flaccus* undoubtedly belong to the mature stage of Philo's career when he served as the head of the Jewish embassy to Emperor Gaius following the ethnic violence in Alexandria. In the *Embassy* Philo mentions his travel to Rome (in the autumn of 38 CE), the ambassadors' audience with Gaius, and the new emperor Claudius, who succeeded Gaius in early 41 CE.[7] Philo therefore must have written this treatise after Gaius's assassination, when Claudius had already acceded to the throne and emended some of Gaius's political aberrations. In *Against Flaccus* Philo describes the violence Alexandrian Jews suffered during the pogrom in the summer of 38 CE. He also refers to the death of the Roman prefect Flaccus, who was arrested by Gaius's troops in the autumn of 38 CE, taken to trial in Rome, sentenced to exile on the island of Andros, and later executed by Gaius's men (39 CE).[8] This treatise, too, clearly belongs to the mature period of Philo's life, when he reflects on the political events leading to the violence in Alexandria and their implications.

To date, Philo's historical treatises mostly have been studied with a view to the question "what actually happened?" Distinguishing between Philo's rhetoric and the events themselves, generations of scholars have endeavored to reconstruct the story as it really was. Chronological questions and concern for cause and effect have dominated the debates. Building on the insights of previous scholarship, I propose to appreciate Philo's historical treatises in a more comprehensive fashion, namely, as literary texts that express his views on a wide range of topics. Events themselves are not my main concern, but Philo's interpretation of them. I ask how Philo uses events in the text to promote certain views and agendas. For example, how does he construct Jewish identity around the violence in Alexandria? What role does Rome, with its various representatives, religious cults, and institutions, play in the narrative? Moreover, I appreciate Philo's views in the context of the time when they were expressed. I ask, for example, whether other authors under Claudius shared Philo's views of Gaius. Moreover, what effect did Claudius's policies have on Philo, especially on his assumption of an intricate connection between politics, philosophy, and religion? How do his views compare with those of his late contemporary Seneca, who was exiled under Caligula and returned to fortune under Claudius? Finally, does Philo's appeal to Stoic ideas resonate with contemporary Roman Stoicism? Answering these questions, we are able to establish an intellectual profile of Philo as a mature man, taking into account his political positions, religious outlook, and intellectual preferences.

A comprehensive analysis of Philo's historical treatises provides us with a key for interpreting the other series of his writings and establishing their relative chronology. Initially, we search in the *Exposition,* the philosophical treatises, and the *Allegorical Commentary* for references to historical events. If other treatises assume a political scenario similar to that in the historical writings, they also belong to the mature stage of Philo's career. On these grounds the philosophical treatises and the *Exposition* immediately strike us as being associated with the political crisis that informs the late stage of Philo's career. The *Allegorical Commentary,* on the other hand, reflects a much more serene atmosphere. Moreover, I read the different series of Philo's writings in light of his intellectual positions in the historical works. I ask how his views compare with those expressed in the mature phase of his life. Were his ideas similar, or did Philo embrace a different approach in his other series of works? Did he address similar or different concerns and, by implication, similar or different audiences? I proceed on the assumption that works which share the values and self-positioning of the historical writings emerged in a similar historical and cultural context. They thus can be placed in the mature period of Philo's career and analyzed along similar lines. By contrast, works that significantly differ in outlook from the historical writings are identified as belonging to an earlier stage of Philo's career. I investigate them with an Alexandrian context in mind and examine to what extent they engage cultural discourses prominent in his hometown.

Following this approach, I argue that Philo's philosophical works are closely connected to his historical writings. The treatise *On the Rationality of Animals* contains a reference to an embassy in which Philo's nephew Alexander participated (*Alex.* 54). As several scholars have already suggested, this is most probably the same embassy as the one headed by Philo.[9] Alexander as a young man apparently served as a member of the Jewish embassy to Gaius, which provided him with a brilliant opportunity to meet people in high offices and prepare for his own stellar rise in the Roman administration. *On the Rationality of Animals* thus assumes the same political situation that shaped Philo's historical writings in the mature stage of his life. Philo moreover presents himself in this treatise as an aged man who shares his experience with younger family members (*Alex.* 5–8). Philo's posture on the literary level resonates with the historical writings, where he includes himself among "the aged" (*Legat.* 1). This confirms our impression of a late composition for this philosophical treatise.

In *On the Rationality of Animals* Philo presents himself as an interpreter who reaches out "not just to a few Alexandrians and Romans, the eminent or the excellent . . . gathered at a given place"; he also aims at larger crowds. He clearly speaks here about elite circles in both Alexandria and Rome, having perhaps in mind some kind of *Salonkultur* in the capital of the empire. His appeal to Theodotus at the beginning of *Every Good Man Is Free* suggests such a culture of discussion in private homes that relied on the hospitality of personal patrons. Philo may well have enjoyed the kind of literary circles in which Josephus later produced his books. Josephus addresses his patron Epaphroditus in the *Antiquities* and *Against Apion,* thanking him for his interest and support of his work. Josephus suggests that there were others "similarly wishing to learn about our people." When Philo self-consciously takes a Roman audience into account and briefly addresses Theodotus, he most likely engages such circles of Roman *Salonkultur.*[10]

While the other philosophical works do not contain historical references and could theoretically be earlier treatises, they are close in style and content to *On the Rationality of Animals.* It is likely that Philo wrote all of his philosophical dialogues at roughly the same time, because he regularly composed series of treatises rather than isolated works. As we have seen, the historical treatises belong to the mature period of his life, while no historical presentation of Alexandria before the crisis is known. Similarly, the biographies of the biblical patriarchs belong together, as Philo's internal references show, and the numerous treatises of the *Allegorical Commentary* contain cross-references that indicate their congruity. Philo's remarks on his own work suggest that in each phase of creativity he chose a particular genre, wrote several treatises in it, and then adopted a different style in a new context. This practice encourages us to assume that Philo embarked on a series of philosophical writings at roughly the same time. Moreover, these treatises share the same intellectual milieu. Philo consistently addresses themes of Stoic philosophy that resonate with distinctly Roman rather than Alexandrian discourses. The philosophical works thus are congruent with the Stoic orientation of the historical writings. Philo emerges as a thinker acutely aware of current debates in Rome who inscribes Jewish philosophy into topical discourses.

Another series of Philo's works is called the *Exposition of the Law* and contains a treatise on the creation, three extant *Lives* of biblical patriarchs, four books on Mosaic law, and two concluding treatises on virtues and rewards and punishments. This series must also belong to the later stage of Philo's career. Written as a free narrative of biblical materials rather than as a systematic commentary, it addresses a wider audience not familiar with the biblical text. Moreover, in a famous passage of *On the Special Laws* Philo positions himself in the same historical context that framed his historical and philosophical treatises, namely, the context of urgent diplomacy after the violence in Alexandria. Philo nostalgically recalls his philosophical leisure, which was abruptly disturbed by the political events:

> There was a time when I could leisurely engage in philosophy and the contemplation of the universe and its contents and enjoyed a truly beloved and blessed state of mind. I constantly associated with divine subjects and ideas, in which I rejoiced without restraint and insatiate.... But then the most grievous of mischief lay in wait for me, envy the hater of good, who suddenly assailed me and did not cease to drag me down before it had violently pressed me into the ocean of political affairs, in which I am swept away so that I cannot even raise my head above the surface. (*Spec.* 3.1–3)

Philo must be referring here to the turmoil in Alexandria, which led to his political appointment as the head of the Jewish embassy. His complaint about being driven into "the ocean of political affairs" fits precisely this transition in his life. Many scholars have already drawn the conclusion that this autobiographical reminiscence places the *Exposition* into the later part of Philo's life.[11] This conclusion can now be corroborated by further considerations. A prominent part of the *Exposition* belongs to the genre of historiography. Three of the biographies of the patriarchs are still extant, while two more are lost. Philo's choice of this genre, which had just come into vogue in Rome, shows close affinities with his historical writings while substantially differing from the *Allegorical Commentary*, in which he systematically explains the minutiae of biblical verses. Philo's choice of literary genre in the *Exposition* thus points to a composition in the late stage of his career, when he engaged in historiography. Moreover, the *Exposition* resonates intellectually with Philo's later works, which gravitate toward Stoic positions, engage Roman discourses, and tend to avoid the radical Platonic transcendentalism of the *Allegorical Commentary* from his early Alexandrian period. In the *Exposition* Philo relies on Stoic notions, such as the individual self that negotiates the circumstances of a particular life, and the idea of freedom of choice as a basic condition of ethics. His Platonism is also distinctly more Stoic than it was in his early Alexandrian period. Finally, in the *Exposition* Philo turns to an audience that is as broad as that for his historical and philosophical writings. He addresses readers who are unfamiliar with the basics of Judaism and the Jewish Scriptures but are generally keen on learning about them. In this respect, too, the *Exposition* remarkably differs from the *Allegorical Commentary*, in which Philo jumps without any introduction into a discussion of the minutiae of the biblical text and engages other, equally specialized interpreters in the Jewish community.

The *Allegorical Commentary* in its extant form offers a verse-to-verse interpretation of Gen 2:1–18:2.[12] Each treatise focuses on a cluster of consecutive verses and offers a detailed allegorical interpretation, which is often enriched by additional verses from other biblical contexts. This series is the most esoteric of Philo's works and presupposes intimate familiarity with the Scriptures as well as specialized interest in their interpretation. The *Allegorical Commentary* is most removed from the historical works in virtually every aspect: literary genre, philosophical ideas, and implied audience. Following the Alexandrian tradition of commentary culture, best known for its achievements in the field of Homer's epics, Philo offers a minute and systematic commentary of the biblical text written for an inside audience updated on the latest hermeneutical debates. He assumes the biblical text to be so intimately known that he quotes particular words without identifying speakers or explaining contexts. He freely introduces biblical expressions and weaves them into the interpretation like threads making up a colorful carpet. Philo's implied readers are Alexandrian Jews who share his religious interest and commitment to the Bible. Indicative of the early stage of his career is the fact that he introduces his allegorical method in a hesitant manner, which suggests that he has not yet established himself as a well-known authority. Philo positions himself vis-à-vis literal readers of the Bible, who are not inclined toward the allegorical approach and seem to have constituted a large part of the Alexandrian community.

The *Allegorical Commentary* shows an overall Platonic orientation and is committed to a strong form of transcendentalism, which differs from the more worldly orientation of Philo's later works. Plato's dialogues, especially the *Theaetetus,* form the backbone of Philo's Bible commentary. He often engages the lively Alexandrian discussion of that Platonic dialogue and adopts Plato's ethics, stressing the dichotomy between soul and body, which can be overcome by fleeing the world and imitating God. Philo as a young man speaks about the soul's journey to an absolutely transcendent God. His longing for the ultimately Other is often mystical and highly introverted, while his later works focus on issues of real life and perceive humans as imbedded in society. This bodiless notion of the self in the *Allegorical Commentary* has a striking equivalent on the literary level. While Philo is highly visible as an author in the historical writings, he hardly reveals himself to the reader in his early work. At the beginning of his career he is rather transcendent and avoids bodily references, such as personal experiences or historical and social realities. Neither his own person nor his environment is generally visible in these treatises, with no turmoil or political unrest yet disturbing his contemplation of the truth contained in the Jewish Scriptures. At the same time, however, the *Allegorical Commentary* already shows signs of a budding interest in Stoicism. Probably relying on some general treatises, Philo engages some ethical notions of the Stoics but remains remarkably general and translates them into Platonic categories. This initial curiosity, which goes beyond known Alexandrian discourses, prepares Philo for his intense encounter with Stoicism in Rome and enables him to embrace Stoic ethics on a much larger scale in his later writings.

The treatises called the *Questions and Answers* on Genesis and Exodus have long been recognized as congenial to the *Allegorical Commentary.* They share the latter's style of interpretation, which focuses on questions regarding particular verses and then offers an allegorical solution. Both series cover the same texts and offer similar interpretations, *Questions and Answers* extending beyond the available treatises of the *Allegorical Commentary.* Yet we must also appreciate the differences between the two series.

The *Questions and Answers* are much more simple in structure and thought, conveying ideas in the style of a handbook. This series reflects Philo's more advanced teaching activity, when he summarizes complicated arguments that he has developed in the *Allegorical Commentary*.[13] Philo has thus developed within the Jewish community of Alexandria, starting as an elitist scholar and then reaching out to broader Jewish audiences. The skills he acquires in this process serve him well upon his arrival in Rome, when he encounters even broader audiences altogether unfamiliar with Judaism.

Following these insights into the chronology of Philo's life and works, listed for easy orientation in Appendix 1, I have arranged the chapters of this book in inverse order. Part I deals with the historical and philosophical treatises, explicitly written in the context of the Jewish embassy to Gaius toward the end of Philo's career. The analysis of these works provides the intellectual tools for understanding the other series of works. Part II treats the *Exposition,* also belonging to Philo's later career, and Part III is devoted to Philo's earliest writings, the *Allegorical Commentary* and the *Questions and Answers.* In this way we move from the most known to the most opaque stage of his life, establishing initially a point of reference to which the lesser known writings can be meaningfully compared. We will follow Philo from his later Roman positions to his Alexandrian perspectives at the beginning of his career.

My overall analysis of Philo's works suggests a significant trajectory from Alexandria to Rome. He sets out as a systematic Bible commentator in Alexandria, discussing Scripture with his Jewish colleagues and offering transcendent Platonic insights resonating with Alexandrian discourses. At this early stage we see Philo engaging genres and questions that were popular among Jewish and wider pagan audiences in his hometown. He shows already a more than average interest in Stoic thought, which he nonetheless still subordinates to his overall Platonic concerns. In the Alexandrian context he makes innovative contributions to Judaism by offering for the first time a sustained philosophy of the Jewish religion, interpreting God in abstract terms and envisioning the soul's flight from the material to the spiritual realm. In the field of hermeneutics Philo ushers in a new synthesis of academic analysis on the literal level and spiritual allegory. This specifically Alexandrian interpretation of Judaism offered by the young Philo throws significant light on later intellectual developments in the Greek East, especially in Alexandria. The church father Origen, who grew up in Alexandria and later moved to Caesarea, consciously embraced his style of biblical commentary and offered minute interpretations of the literal text together with Platonic allegories. Middle Platonists and Neoplatonists as well as Alexandrian "Gnostics" adopted a theology strikingly similar to that of Philo.[14] They, too, imagined a transcendent God disconnected from the material world who can be appreciated by internal contemplation. Characteristically, these schools remained marginal in the Roman Empire, and their works were not canonized in the West.

Philo changed dramatically as a result of his journey to Rome. The embassy to Gaius Caligula became a turning point in his life, drawing him out of his contemplative mode in Alexandria into Roman politics and discourses. He became exposed to a new cultural and intellectual environment. Going to Rome meant for him getting to know new genres of writing and distinctly Roman perspectives on philosophy. The Stoic school was considerably more dominant in Rome than it was in Alexandria and prompted Philo to take a fresh look at his tradition and interpret his essentially Platonic theology in a more Stoic light. He distinguishes the Jews now from the Greeks and interprets them in Roman terms, suggesting that they embrace a code of worldly ethics based on the creation, enjoy traveling all over the empire, and are self-disciplined citizens. The *Exposition* as well as the historical and philosophical treatises are the result of this fruitful encounter with Rome. Philo became prolific at this time and offered new perspectives on Judaism, which are highly relevant in the context of the Second Sophistic and early Christianity, both of which were deeply entangled in Roman discourses. Following his visit to Rome, Philo wrote approximately half of his works in a relatively short span of time, between approximately 41 and 49 CE. This intensity of writing is not surprising given the fact that Cicero wrote more than thirty books in two years (46–44 BCE) and Seneca composed his many letters to Lucilius within three years (62–65 CE). We cannot be certain whether Philo wrote all of these later writings while physically still in Rome. It is possible that he composed some of them upon his return to Alexandria. Yet whatever the case may be, his perspective was irreversibly changed.

From Alexandria to Rome

After the Egyptian queen Cleopatra and her companion Antony lost the war against Octavian, later known as the emperor Augustus, Egypt became a Roman province. In 30 BCE Alexandria was turned into a provincial capital, with many special restrictions imposed by Rome. Deprived of royal status and officially absorbed into the Roman Empire, the city nevertheless continued to cherish its own culture and intellectual life. Some Egyptian intellectuals regretted that Alexander had died so young, hoping that he might have restricted Roman expansion. The historian and scholar Apion, who became the head of the rival Egyptian embassy to Gaius Caligula, bemoaned the demise of the Ptolemaic kingdom, trusting that Cleopatra would have had a significant and beneficial effect (Josephus, *C.Ap.* 2.60). Alexandria and Rome were thus politically and culturally connected, one submitting to the other, but also remained distinct, with more visible tensions between them than any other pair of capitals in the empire.

Recent scholarship has increasingly appreciated Rome's influence in the Greek East. Many scholars today are aware of the fact that Rome was not merely a political force that played only a minor cultural role as a receptacle of Classical Greek traditions. It has instead become clear that it set new accents in religion, philosophy, and literature. Its preferences and choices were significant, drawing attention even in the periphery. Rome's influence has recently been highlighted in the context of three fields relevant to Philo: the renaissance of Greek culture, early Christianity, and Josephus.

The study of the Greek Renaissance under the Roman Empire, called, since Philostratus's perceptive study of it, "the Second Sophistic," has recently been studied from new perspectives.[15] It has become clear that Greek culture was intricately connected to Roman structures of power. Writers such as Plutarch and Lucian cannot be properly understood without addressing the question of their involvement in Roman discourses and their effect on their construction of Greek identity. Greek authors of this period have been characterized as possessing a fragmented sense of their self and engaging in a puzzling diversity of perspectives. Plutarch and Lucian, for example, combined their local (Greek and Syrian) identities with Classical Greek *paideia* and active involvement in Roman affairs. In each act of writing they constructed a new aspect of their identity in a complex world. Even the fact that Greek authors often present themselves as mere guardians of culture, seemingly devoid of any political ambitions, resonates with Roman expectations and reflects a deep involvement in the discussions of the day.

Rome has recently become prominent in early Christian studies. Scholars have realized that long before Eusebius officially connected the church to the Roman Empire, Christian authors writing in Greek were often acutely aware of Roman discourses and made efforts to integrate the new religion into up-to-date discussions. Among the Gospel writers Luke has been identified as the author with the most visible Roman orientation. Moreover, his pointed historical style in Acts has been appreciated in the context of Roman historiography, his attention to women has been interpreted in light of Roman politics, and his portrayal of Paul has been placed into the context of contemporaneous visions of empire.[16] Moreover, Paul's letters, especially the one to the Romans, have been analyzed with a view to the *realia* and discursive structures in Rome, such as the epistolary style and greater exposure of the individual self.[17] The second-century apologist Justin Martyr has moreover come into focus as a Greek writer in Rome who engages Roman audiences and can be meaningfully compared to the Second Sophistic.[18] Broad religious phenomena, such as martyrdom and faith, also have been interpreted in a Roman context.[19] The emergence of Christianity as a distinct religion is thus intricately connected to Rome.

Josephus, too, increasingly has been appreciated as a Jewish author writing in Rome. While earlier studies focused on his sources and attempted to reconstruct the events he mentions "as they really happened," Josephus has recently emerged as a first-century author writing in Rome for Roman audiences. The implications of his Roman citizenship, his familiarity with Roman discourses, and the Roman traits of his Judaism have been studied. Moreover, his importance as a Roman historian has been highlighted, and his wide networks among Roman intellectuals have been uncovered.[20] This paradigm shift in scholarship on Josephus is highly significant for Philo, because Philo's situation as a Greek-speaking Jew going to Rome a generation earlier is in many respects strikingly similar.

Against this background of scholarly developments, it is surprising that Philo thus far has been interpreted almost exclusively in the context of Second Temple Judaism and/or Classical Greek philosophy. Scholars have been overwhelmingly concerned to figure out the precise relationship between the Jewish and the Greek components of his thought, often even assuming that these were unbridgeable contrasts, so that Philo's Jewish identity was supposedly threatened by his engagement with things Greek.[21] His references to Roman affairs in the historical writings have regularly been taken as a mere description of events that he encountered during the embassy to Gaius. The intellectual implications of Philo's stay in Rome, on the other hand, have not yet been seriously investigated. This is remarkable given the known fact that ambassadors regularly engaged in cultural activities while spending time in the imperial capital. Crates of Mallos as well as the famous Athenian ambassadors delivered public lectures, which aroused the deep aversion of the Roman aristocrat Cato. Plutarch used his trips to Rome for intensive research into historical materials for his *Parallel Lives* and acquired for this purpose a good reading knowledge of Latin. Back in Greece he stayed in contact with his Roman friends, exchanging books and imagining them as conversation partners in his dialogues.[22] Apion, the head of the Egyptian embassy to Gaius Caligula, and Chaeremon, a Stoic philosopher and most probably also a member of the Egyptian embassy, wrote treatises highly critical of the Jews and their traditions. These publications of the diplomats had such a deep impact that Josephus a generation later still felt compelled to refute them.[23] Greek-speaking ambassadors coming from the East to Rome expected to use at least some of their time in scholarly activities that would present their cultural and philosophical heritage to Roman intellectuals and broader audiences in the capital.

How can we appreciate the precise effect of Philo's embassy to Rome? The change of his personal life is obvious and has often been acknowledged, as he traveled to Rome and assumed a far more political role than previously. Yet Rome also prompted a significant intellectual development in Philo that thus far has been overlooked. This development is conspicuous even though he never mentions contacts with Roman intellectuals, not even with his late contemporary Seneca, who had partly grown up in Alexandria, spoke fluent Greek, and shared many of Philo's philosophical concerns.[24] It is initially important to note that Philo became sufficiently aware of the Latin language to use it once in his later writings in order to explain a Greek etymology. He says that the Greek term for seven (ἑπτά) must be appreciated against the background that "the Romans add the letter 'sigma,' which is left out by the Greeks" (*Opif.* 127). He uses the Latin name of the number seven, *septem,* which is reproduced here in Greek transliteration, to argue for the supposedly original root of the Greek term and to draw a connection to the notion of reverence (σεβασμός). This example, of course, proves neither Philo's immersion in Latin nor his ability to read Roman literature. It does, however, indicate his awareness of the language, at least some rudimentary knowledge of it and his conviction that his mother tongue is connected to it.

Moreover, I propose a comparative literary approach, which takes into account for the first time distinctly Roman philosophy and literature. In this respect I go beyond most studies of Roman influence on the Hellenistic East, which regularly address Roman politics and its influence on Greek speakers. Rome, however, needs to be taken seriously not only as a political power, but also as an intellectual center in its own right. A thorough study of Roman discussions on the topics Philo treated reveals a surprising congeniality. In his philosophical treatises he regularly emerges as a significant link between Cicero and Seneca. Philo's involvement in Roman culture is further corroborated by comparing his views in his later writings with those in the *Allegorical Commentary* from his early Alexandrian period. We regularly discern a striking development of views that shows Philo's intellectual openness to the new perspectives he encountered during his stay in Rome.

When Philo reached Rome in late 38 CE, he encountered a very different intellectual environment from the one he was used to in Alexandria. His home city was the capital of commentary culture in the Hellenistic world and boasted of a long tradition of scholarship and scientific research. The famous library and the Museum provided the infrastructure for intellectuals, such as Aristarchus of Samothrace and Aristophanes of Byzantium, who produced authoritative editions and systematic commentaries on Homer's epics. Platonic philosophy also flourished in Alexandria. Aristophanes in the second century BCE produced the first critical edition of Plato's works. A century later Eudorus played a decisive role in the revival of Platonism in a dogmatic mode, which replaced the Skeptic phase of the school and gave special attention to the founder's positive doctrines. In the extant fragments Eudorus shows a strong theological orientation, defining god as a wholly transcendent principle and considering humanity's imitation of him as the goal of ethics. A similar direction is taken by the anonymous commentary on the *Theaetetus,* the earliest extant running commentary on any of Plato's works, which most likely also belongs to a first-century BCE setting in Alexandria. As far as the available fragments can show, the anonymous commentator opposes Stoic concepts and harmonizes Plato's various works, stressing the certainty of knowledge and imitation of god. Another anonymous Platonic treatise most likely stems from Alexandria, albeit from a slightly later period, namely, *On the Nature of the World and the Soul,* a creative reading of Plato's *Timaeus.*[25] Alexandrian philosophy thus centered on the Platonic heritage, which it constructed as a system of theology and ethics. This type of philosophy flourished amidst highly sophisticated scholarship in the Museum, which applied Aristotelian literary approaches to the criticism of canonical texts. Evidence of

Stoic philosophy in Alexandria is mostly preserved in Philo's early writings, which still remain fairly general on Stoic matters and interpret them in a Platonic mode.

Alexandria also boasted a long Jewish tradition. The Jewish Bible was first translated here into Greek, the *Letter of Aristeas* suggesting that this translation was initiated by Demetrius, the chief librarian, who wished to acquire all worthy books known in the commonwealth. Aristeas integrates the Jewish Bible into Alexandrian discourses and ascribes to it a place of cultural prominence. This interpretation no doubt expresses self-confidence and a genuine interest in cultural dialogue with the majority culture. Alexandrian Judaism flourished over the centuries and produced an impressive and diverse literature in the Greek language. The books and fragments that have survived, thanks to Christian readers, indicate that Alexandrian Jews experimented with various literary genres, such as drama, history, and Bible commentary, while always keeping a keen eye on the Bible as a source for fashioning Jewish identity. Ezekiel produced a play on the exodus, Demetrius investigated minute details of the Scriptures with special attention to questions of historical consistency, and Aristobulus offered philosophical insights into problems of biblical anthropomorphism.[26] Philo worked in Alexandria within such a Jewish context and took up many ideas that previously had been expressed, while providing his own innovative answers. It is impossible to imagine his early work without Jewish predecessors and colleagues in Alexandria.

In Rome, by contrast, there is no evidence of a comparable Jewish community in the early first century CE. No literary works have survived, so we depend for reconstructions on some epitaphs and on Philo's own report about Jewish synagogues in the city. In Rome, as opposed to Alexandria, Philo could not connect to a rich intellectual tradition of the local Jewish community. In any case he went there as an ambassador, naturally oriented toward the larger, gentile society. While he was likely to enjoy the hospitality of Roman Jews and perhaps of prominent Jewish visitors to Rome, such as King Agrippa I, he operated mainly with a view to larger Roman audiences.[27] Socially, Philo's situation in Rome significantly differed from his earlier Alexandrian environment. This has implications for his intellectual orientation as well: while his earlier works engage in an internal Jewish discourse, his later treatises are overtly apologetic.[28]

Intellectually, Rome differed remarkably from Alexandria. Already at first sight one is struck by the different literary tastes: historiography rather than commentary characterized Rome. In contrast to Alexandria, philosophy was not practiced there in the form of interpreting the founder's writings, but rather by offering independent treatises on chosen topics. Moreover, Stoicism rather than Platonism flourished there under imperial support, encouraging practical ethics rather than theoretical contemplation. Already Cicero, who presents Greek philosophy for the first time in Latin, sets important new accents in the first century BCE. He combines a professed Platonic affiliation with Stoic ethics and Roman values, relying on numerous examples from Roman history and his own experience in politics. His attitude toward the Stoic philosopher Panaetius shows his self-perception as a pioneering Roman philosopher. While admiring Panaetius and heavily relying on him in his treatise *On Duties,* Cicero adds his own ideas, even a whole section, and criticizes some of his predecessor's judgments. Cicero offers what has rightly been described as an "essentially Roman" philosophy.[29]

When the Roman Republic was replaced by the Principate, philosophy became politically anchored in the person of Arius Didymus, a close friend of the emperor Augustus and an opponent of the Skeptical school. Arius strengthened in Rome a form of philosophy that focused on practical ethics in a Stoic mode. While other schools were marginalized, Stoicism flourished in Rome. Attalus became an influential Stoic teacher in the first century CE, inspiring Seneca and others to conceive of philosophy as a therapy of the self, aiming at the individual's daily improvement rather than pursuing theoretical contemplation or scholarship on foundational texts.[30]

Philo's late contemporary Seneca brought Stoic philosophy in Latin to a new climax, shaping it in such a recognizable way that it has often been identified as "Roman Stoicism." This form of Stoicism eclipsed many ideas of the middle phase of the school, represented mostly by Chrysippus, and revived instead notions of the founder, Zeno. Moreover, Seneca was especially concerned with the individual self as embedded in society and developed a new approach to the notion of inner freedom under political constraint. Seneca distinguished his own ethical approach from "hair-splitting" and theoretical discourses, which he associated with the Greeks and Homeric scholarship. He even seems to have implied a subtle connection between the more lenient ethics of the Aristotelian school, which he vehemently rejected, and the extravagance of Greek or "Oriental" kings. Seneca echoes Roman prejudices against Greek culture, which had been voiced from Cato onward, and constructed it as effeminate.[31]

Rome attracted many intellectuals from the Greek East. Some of them stayed, such as Arius Didymus, while others came for more limited purposes, such as embassies. Rome offered newcomers not only a platform for expressing previously conceived ideas, but also an opportunity for meeting the city's intellectuals, gaining access to new literary sources, and engaging Roman audiences on their own turf. Philo of Larissa changed his views so drastically upon arrival in Rome that he alienated his student Antiochus, who received Philo's "Roman books" in Alexandria and wrote a special treatise against them. Apion similarly arrived in the capital of the empire and formulated new slanders against the Jews, focusing on a criticism of circumcision, which he expected to resonate with Roman readers. To his original Alexandrian constituency, however, such polemics must have sounded rather odd, because the Egyptians also practiced circumcision.[32]

How does Philo fit into the picture of a lively intellectual exchange in Rome? Did he, too, engage in Roman discussions, even though he, unlike Plutarch, had not become fluent in Latin? Roman intellectuals such as Seneca were bilingual and could easily be approached in Greek. Philo may even have known Seneca from the latter's youthful stay in Alexandria with his uncle and aunt. Such a prospect is rather likely in view of the fact that Seneca's uncle was prefect in Alexandria and Philo belonged to one of the most influential families of the city, with excellent connections to the Roman elite. Philo may have met the young Seneca in Alexandria and later renewed their acquaintance when he arrived as an ambassador to Rome. Seneca published his first philosophical treatise, the *Consolation for Marcia*, precisely when Philo was in the city. Philo may well have noticed the work of a young colleague who had partly grown up in his hometown and easily would have been able to discuss the new book in his own mother tongue.[33] In addition, Philo is likely to have used bilingual assistants in Rome, as was common for eminent visitors from the Greek East. This would have helped him access Roman materials and engage in Roman discussions. As we have already seen, Philo once indicates that he aimed also at Roman audiences, most likely cultural salons, where Greek also would have been spoken.[34]

Philo and the Second Sophistic

An important factor in Philo's world that thus far has been largely overlooked is the revival of Greek culture in the Roman Empire. Scholars have increasingly become aware of the remarkable complexity of this move-

ment, stretching from Plutarch in the mid–first century to Philostratus in
the mid–third century. Living in a world governed by Rome, the Second
Sophists were more acutely aware of contemporary structures of power
than Neoplatonists, for example, who tended to withdraw from politics
during this period. The Second Sophists consciously inscribed themselves
into imperial discourses and participated in wider contemporary debates.
Most conspicuously, Plutarch wrote his *Parallel Lives,* matching Greek cultural heroes with their Roman counterparts. In his moral treatises he once
quotes Seneca for a bon mot to Nero; cites "from the excellent precepts" of
Musonius Rufus, the "Roman Socrates"; and appeals to many Roman examples. Philostratus introduces himself in the *Life of Apollonius* as a member of Julia Domna's literary circle. The empress provided him with crucial
materials for his biography and encouraged him to apply himself to the
task. Philostratus also imagines a lively encounter between his hero Apollonius and Musonius, constructing the former's image along Roman lines,
while subtly suggesting his superiority.[35] Literary concerns and fashions in
the capital of the empire thus had a visible impact on the Greek East, especially as intellectuals often visited Rome.

The Second Sophists constructed themselves as Greeks by writing on
their literary heritage with a new sense of playfulness, creativity, and irony
that differs remarkably from the often mystical seriousness of the Neoplatonists. Their identities were inevitably fissured and in a constant process of change. Several of them had mother tongues other than Greek.
Lucian, for example, had a Syrian background and continuously felt both
an insider and an outsider with regard to Greek culture, which he came
to represent and shape so energetically. For Plutarch, Philostratus, Dio of
Prusa, Galen, and others, writing was not a mere literary activity, divorced
as it were from life, but rather a creative space always entangled in contemporary structures, both intellectual and political. Their position cannot be
reduced to either pro-Roman or anti-Roman but needs to be appreciated as
a delicate product of multiple factors, including Roman discourses.[36]

Attention moreover has been drawn to the secondary nature of the
Second Sophistic. These authors constantly look back on the classical heritage, which they imitate, re-create, and playfully subvert with an ironic
smile on themselves. Philostratus offers an illuminating example. His hero
Apollonius and his companion Damis discuss the wisdom of animals that
they encounter in India. Damis recalls Euripides's line "for all humans
children are their life." Apollonius praises the line as a "wise and divinely

inspired remark" but then adds that it would have been "much wiser and truer, if it were sung in praise of all creatures." Damis quickly grasps his master's intention and suggests "rewriting the verse." He promptly offers an improved version, asserting that this it is much "better" than the original quotation from Euripides.[37] Philostratus thus shows a strong concern to ground his ideas in the Classical Greek tradition, while at the same time taking the liberty to re-create and subvert it. Previous scholarship considered the characteristic secondary status of the Second Sophistic as a fundamental weakness in comparison to classical literature. The image of the Greek renaissance, however, has significantly improved in recent years, and its high literary quality has increasingly been appreciated. The complexity of this movement, especially its ironic self-awareness and sophisticated use of diverse techniques, stems directly from its posterity. In a constant need to address both the past and the multicultural present under Roman rule, the Second Sophists became extraordinarily inventive, dynamic, and interesting.

While the authors listed by Philostratus as Second Sophists belong to the generation after Philo, their work is important for appreciating his intellectual development. Upon his arrival in Rome Philo found himself in a position strikingly similar to that of many Second Sophists. Having received Greek *paideia* and being active as a Jewish diplomat, he looked back to both the Jewish and the Greek classics, while at the same time being involved in contemporary Roman politics and culture. Philo's identity is extremely complex. His move from a particular city with a familiar culture to the central stage of the Roman Empire, with its nearly universal dimensions, new audiences, and new challenges, opened for him the possibility of intellectually experimenting in ways he had not anticipated before. His work assumed some ironic tones, poking fun at literary conventions. In many respects Philo's later writings anticipate the works of the Second Sophistic, which in turn help us to understand the wider implications of his texts.

Some scholars have already drawn attention to connections between Philo and the Second Sophistic. Wahlgren and Kim analyze linguistic features and argue that Philo's Greek shows signs of an attempt to write in a high and archaic language that anticipates the Atticizing style of the Second Sophistic.[38] The latter increasingly used classical forms of Greek in order to revive the past and distinguish their culture from lower forms of either spoken Greek or unrefined literary style, such as the one used in the New Testament. Philo emerges as an important signpost on the way to the renaissance of high Greek culture. Furthermore, Bruce Winter highlights the significance of Philo for a proper dating of the Second Sophistic. Focusing on rhetoric, he argues that Philo's attitude resonates well with the position of subsequent Greek writers, as he shares their characteristic ambiguity, both rejecting the Sophists in a Platonic spirit and relying on their rhetorical techniques.[39] In terms of his language and rhetoric, Philo thus has already been shown to anticipate the Second Sophistic.

It is time now for a comprehensive analysis of Philo in light of the Second Sophistic. My point is not merely chronological or technical. I do not simply wish to push the date of the Greek movement back to the mid–first century. More is at stake than pleading for Philo's integration into Philostratus's canon of Second Sophists.[40] I rather aim at offering new insights into Philo's texts and personality by raising questions treated in the context of the Second Sophistic. I ask whether Plutarch, Lucian, and Philostratus can help us understand Philo's construction of identity as a Greek-speaking Jew in the multicultural world of the Roman Empire. Does Philo already foreshadow the characteristic self-awareness and irony of the later Greek authors? Does he negotiate his religious and cultural traditions in a way similar to that of the Second Sophists? Can Philo's references to Alexandria, Rome, and Jerusalem, the Bible, and Homer be meaningfully compared with texts of other fissured and multilayered personalities among the Greek authors of the Roman Empire?

In many respects Philo resembles Plutarch, the first officially recognized author of the Second Sophistic. Both grew up in the Greek East under Roman rule, Philo dying a few years after Plutarch was born. Both acted as ambassadors to Rome and chose to combine a commitment to Platonic philosophy with religious observance, Philo worshiping the God of Israel and Plutarch serving as a priest of Apollo at Delphi. Furthermore, Philo and Plutarch wrote in Atticizing Greek, without yet submitting to rigorous purism, and earnestly engaged a variety of literary genres, including biography, philosophical treatises, and interpretation of canonical texts. Each of them gave special attention to the Platonic heritage, speaking venerably of its founder, while at the same time addressing contemporary Stoic philosophy and Roman culture. Both offered a new interpretation of Homer's epics, which restored their ethical value in the aftermath of

Plato's harsh criticism.[41] Reading Philo's interpretations of the Torah, his discussions of Plato's dialogues, and his general philosophical and historical treatises in light of Plutarch's parallel works will be highly rewarding.

Philo emerges as a pioneering author who anticipated important trends in Greek literature in the Roman Empire. I do not argue for Philo's historical influence on the authors of the Second Sophistic, who most probably remained ignorant of him, but rather for his significance in the first century CE.[42] Comparisons between Philo and the authors of the Second Sophistic are fruitful because he anticipates many of their concerns and shows the beginning of important developments in the Roman Empire that have considerable implications for early Christianity and subsequent Western civilization. Philo undoubtedly stood at a watershed, which prompted him to develop original and rich ideas. These deserve to be studied carefully in light of his life and his broader historical context.

PART 1

Philo as Ambassador and Author in Rome

2 Philo's Self-Fashioning in the Historical Writings

Philo is the first Jewish author who writes about contemporary politics in which he has personally participated. He offers an eyewitness account that has no parallel in biblical or postbiblical Judaism until the works of Josephus Flavius one generation later. Whereas Josephus, however, locates himself on an identifiable trajectory from aristocratic origins in Jerusalem to favored courtier in Rome, Philo's historical writings convey a peculiar sense of enigma.[1] The reader learns hardly anything about Philo as a historical figure and political actor. His upbringing in Alexandria, for example, and his current situation under the Roman emperor Claudius remain elusive. Moreover, the events he describes are strangely disconnected, not merging into a consecutive narrative, and often remain entangled with his own opinions to the degree that it is difficult to distinguish them.

The impression of enigma in Philo's historical treatises is rooted in the fact that we can hardly ever grasp the precise connection between the historical events he refers to and his own position toward them. The political events and Philo the narrator are intricately connected, although the precise nature of their relationship often remains unclear. His text is astonishingly multifaceted and playfully unreliable to the extent that the reader often wonders whether anything real is attached to the reported events or whether they are perhaps as constructed as the narrator himself. Moreover, for the first time in ancient Jewish literature Philo explicitly engages the reader's expectations and ironically subverts them. He thus positions himself more self-consciously as an author in the text than was hitherto common.

Philo offers revealing introductions to his historical treatises that address the instability of human perspectives and question literary conventions. Aware that he is embracing a new style, Philo opens the *Embassy to Gaius* with the following sigh: "How long shall we, the aged, be children grown old in our bodies through length of time, but just infants in our souls out of a lack of sense, considering the most incalculable element, fortune, to be the most persistent, but nature, the firmest element, to be the most unsteady? We change and switch our actions, as if engaged in board games, thinking that fortune's gifts are more stable than nature's, and nature's more insecure than fortune's" (*Legat.* 1). This introduction creates a sense of instability by suggesting that appearances, actions, and constructions of the self are unreliable. The physical signs of old age no longer promise wisdom, thus subverting traditional expectations. Human actions are exposed as inevitably dependent upon context. Rather than adjusting to absolute standards, people change their behavior as they change places. Even more intriguing, Philo suggests that we ourselves just play a part "as if engaged in board games." Personal identity is not fixed but is determined by the temporary roles we assume, knowing well that they are not real, but only put on for the occasion. Philo appeals to his readers with a sense of urgency, stressing that these are times when "many important questions" are being decided. He hints that nature, the one stable element in one's life, should be identified with the God of the Jews, while at the same time asserting that God cannot be known because he is too transcendent for humans to grasp. Thus even nature turns out to be a construct, a useful one, to be sure, but nevertheless not grounded in experienced reality.

In *Against Flaccus* Philo introduces himself as a narrator who consciously defies expected roles. After describing Flaccus's successful beginning as a prefect of Egypt, he imagines his reader's critical reaction: "Perhaps someone will say: my dear sir, after having decided to place a charge against the man, you have not gone through the motions of accusation, but put together great praises. Have you struck the wrong note and gone mad?" (*Flacc.* 6). Philo evokes here the atmosphere of a trial by using the verb "to place a charge," which is associated with the courtroom and immediately reminds the reader of Flaccus's historical trial in Rome. In that trial, Philo later tells us, Lampo, an Alexandrian gymnasiarch, officially played the role of "accuser," but in reality he protected Flaccus. Bribed regularly, Lampo pretended to write "the minutes of the law-suits" but instead "deleted some of the evidence and deliberately passed over it." He generally tampered with the documents, "turning the letters upside down."[2] Philo nicknames Lampo "letter starer" and parodies the conventional expert of texts, who diligently studies the minutiae of sentences, words, and letters in order to establish the original meaning. Lampo, by contrast, used his literary skills for his personal profit and "picked up money at every syllable." The pursuit of truth and justice, expected from his role at the court, has obviously been perverted.

Philo, another expert of textual criticism, decides to assume the role of accuser, translating the parodied courtroom scene into a literary genre. He has internalized Roman court procedures, which serve as a kind of palimpsest for his own writing and convey an ironic perspective on what he sets out to do. Philo not only plays creatively with courtroom scenes, but also engages in a sophisticated discussion of literary genres and narrative perspectives. He directly engages the readers, who are introduced as critical voices, accusing them of "having struck the wrong note and gone mad." This imagined charge of bias in favor of Flaccus turns out to be a clever rhetorical device that enables Philo to reflect humorously on his own writing and position himself as a violator of literary norms. While not conforming to the rules of an accusation, Philo asserts that he knows "what the sequence of an argument demands" and suggests that he will do better than simply "putting together great praises." He indicates that he will show Flaccus's villainy in a somewhat unexpected manner, namely, after enumerating his initial advantages. Philo perplexes his readers and invites them to be involved with his text without knowing precisely which genre it belongs to or which narrative perspective it conveys. Readers are encouraged to listen to the music of Philo's treatise without judging digressions from the known melody as "a wrong note." The deviant tone of Philo's music turns out to be its beauty, ever unexpected and unpredictable but always just another tune to be played.

Philo's ironic self-fashioning as an author, to use Stephen Greenblatt's term, is highly innovative in the mid–first century CE.[3] Its significance is conspicuous in view of Josephus and Lucian, who reflect on historiography at the end of the first century and in the second. Josephus introduces his first book of history, the *Jewish War*, with a remarkable provocation to his readers. He says that he will defy the "law of history" by showing compassion for his hometown and criticizing the zealots, who caused the destruction of the Temple (*J.W.* 1.11). While seemingly appealing for lenience in his readers, who are asked to pardon his transgression, Josephus in fact conveys a sense of pride. He is remarkably confident that his ironic approach is truer to historiography than conventional narratives.

An even more ironic position is adopted by Lucian in his *True Story*, which parodies historiography and exposes previous attempts as pure lies. While others pretend to tell the truth, Lucian poses as a professional liar: "I had nothing true to tell; not having had any adventures of significance, I took to lying." Yet his lying, he insists with a smile to his readers, "is more reasonable than theirs, for though I tell the truth in nothing else, I shall at least be truthful in saying that I am a liar."[4] While Lucian brought ironic self-fashioning to a new level of sophistication, Philo anticipates him as well as Josephus. He already uses implied readers as an ironic mirror to subvert literary conventions and constructs himself as a more authentic author, precisely because he defies the traditional rules of the genre. His identity as an author is put into the foreground, provocatively meeting readers and perplexing their expectations, while at the same time remaining elusive and undefined.

Mediterranean Networks and Their Limits

As we have seen, Philo hailed from Alexandria, a famous center of learning and culture in Hellenistic times, known for the largest library in the ancient world and the Museum, the earliest known form of a university. As readers of Philo, we may well be surprised that he never mentions these pearls of Ptolemaic Alexandria. Philo speaks only once about "our Alexandria," when he takes pride in its lavish architecture, especially the temple in honor of Augustus at the harbor. He describes at length the beauty of this pagan temple devoted to the Roman emperor in his role as "protector of sailors." This self-positioning as an Alexandrian is peculiar and ignores the illustrious history of this city, as if suggesting that it has come into full bloom only under Roman rule. Philo's gesture signals a strong orientation toward Rome and matches the message of the Roman emperor Claudius, who rebuilt the harbor of Ostia near Rome on the model of Alexandria, thus absorbing the symbol of Rome's grain supply. Philo evidently fashions himself in accordance with the role assigned to Alexandria by Rome as a central export center. Omitting any reference to the famous library, he also avoids the criticism of his late contemporary Seneca, who sharply criticizes it as lacking "good taste" and engaging only in "learned luxury" and ostentation.[5]

Identifying with the harbor of Alexandria, Philo expresses mobility, a significant feature of upper-class culture in the Roman period. The Romans had connected the Mediterranean world through a close network of roads and a significant improvement of sea travel. Philo suggests that crossing the Mediterranean was relatively easy, connections to Rome being frequent. He is familiar with two alternative ways of crossing the sea between Alexandria and Rome, namely, the direct route used by cargo boats and the circuitous route along the northeastern shores, which allows for breaks and acquisition of supplies. According to Philo, King Agrippa I is advised "not to undertake the voyage from Brundisium to Syria, which was long and wearisome, but to wait for the Etesian winds and take the short route through Alexandria." That this advice was historically ever given is doubtful, but Philo's reference to Mediterranean sea travel is significant because he obviously appeals to his readers' expectations. Similarly, Agrippa is said to have easily found quick Alexandrian ships in the harbor of Puteoli, which Philo calls in archaizing Greek style "Dicaercheia." Furthermore, the Roman centurion Bassus, on his way from Rome to Alexandria, is said to have taken "the swiftest sailing ships," arriving "within a few days." Philo's geographical horizons are shaped by the axis Alexandria-Rome. The capital of the Roman Empire is easily reached, his home city being closely connected. Rome plays a central role on the map of Philo's experience, much more so than for his late contemporary Paul, who is mainly oriented toward the Aegean Sea in Greece.[6]

If Philo's perception of Alexandria lacks historical roots, his family vanishes even more into the background. He mentions only two family members by name. Lysimachus, a younger member of the extended family, figures as a rather stylized discussion partner in the badly preserved dialogue *On the Rationality of Animals.* Tiberius Alexander appears in the same dialogue as Philo's nephew, who preferred political involvement to studies and participated in an embassy to Rome, presumably the same one Philo headed. Alexander is familiar with Roman customs and expresses radical ideas about the rationality of animals. His view that humans are neither uniquely endowed with reason nor protected by divine providence is deeply shocking to Philo.[7]

We require Josephus to tell us that Philo has a famous and influential brother, Alexander the Alabarch, who has excellent connections at the Roman court and the Herodian family in Judea. We learn from Josephus that Alexander administers the Egyptian estates of Antonia, mother of Claudius and grandmother of Gaius, and lends money to the Judean prince Agrippa, Antonia's protégé. Alexander later even manages to marry his son Marcus to Agrippa's daughter Berenice. Alexander is recognized for all his good services by the emperor Claudius, who calls him "an old friend." Philo's brother was thus well connected in Rome and showed his cultural commitment to the empire by choosing a Roman name for his son, a practice that some Greek intellectuals from the East rejected.[8] Why does Philo never mention this illustrious brother, whose political connections must have been useful for him? Is he perhaps silent on this matter precisely because he enjoys benefits from his brother's position that he may have preferred to earn by himself? Philo probably felt embarrassed about the fact that he received his appointment as the head of the Jewish embassy at a time when Alexander was imprisoned by Gaius and thus unavailable for the job, for which he must have been considered more suitable (Josephus, *J.A.* 19.276). Not mentioning his brother helps Philo to focus his readers' attention on his own contribution.

The limits of Philo's willingness to share autobiographical details are also visible in his vague reference to "us" receiving King Agrippa I on his visit to Alexandria in 38 CE (*Flacc.* 103). Philo gives the impression of participating in a group of Jewish leaders in the city without, however, identifying any of them and locating them in a clear historical setting. Who were these other Jewish leaders? They must have included his brother Alexander, who had lent money to Agrippa and would be Philo's natural host on his visit to Alexandria. Furthermore, between the lines of Philo's text we get the impression that upper-class facilities are at his disposal. The family possessions do not seem to have suffered during the pogrom in Alexandria, because he is able to leave shortly afterward as an ambassador to Rome, undoubtedly a responsibility with significant expenses.

One historical figure about whom Philo provides some details is the Judean king Agrippa I. Yet he too remains surprisingly enigmatic, and it is difficult to know what Philo really thinks about him. This ambiguity is all the more surprising in light of Josephus, who openly admires Agrippa's political skills and is impressed by his thorough education and extended network of friendships in Rome. Josephus credits Agrippa with two political achievements connected to Philo's embassy, namely, averting Gaius's plan to set up his statue in the Jerusalem Temple and initiating, together with his brother Herod, Claudius's famous edict settling the conflict in Alexandria. Josephus's warm attitude and wholehearted appreciation are connected to his personal friendship with Agrippa's son, King Agrippa II, who most likely provided him with materials for the account of his father in the *Antiquities*.[9]

Philo initially mentions Agrippa's arrival in Alexandria in the summer of 38 CE, when the city is already on the verge of ethnic violence. According to Philo's narrative, Agrippa had been sent by Gaius for technical reasons, judging that the journey from Rome through Alexandria to the land of Israel would be faster than the northeastern route. The historical truth of these technical justifications has often been questioned in modern scholarship and may well have surprised ancient readers, too.[10] Why, then, would Philo present them? This question is all the more pertinent as Philo explains in a different context that Flaccus, the Roman prefect in Alexandria, was Tiberius's protégé and therefore not trusted by Gaius (*Flacc.* 9–23). This displaced background information explains why Gaius sent Agrippa, his friend from his youth, to inquire about the rising ethnic tensions between Jews and Egyptians. Yet Philo curiously does not mention this evidence in the context of Agrippa's visit to Alexandria. His alternative, technical explanation creates a fractured and puzzling text.

Our sense that Philo is a multifaceted and unexpected narrator increases in the continuation of the *Embassy*. It emerges between the lines of his account that the Alexandrian Jews hardly could have hoped for a more favorable envoy from Rome than Agrippa, while Flaccus and the Egyptian nationalists had reasons to be deeply disappointed. Philo says that the prefect made efforts to hide from Agrippa his animosity toward the Jews "out of fear of him who had sent him," namely, Gaius. Philo expects the Alexandrians to show respect for Agrippa, if not on account of his role as king of Judea, but certainly in his capacity "as a member of Caesar's household." He also stresses that Agrippa is "a friend of Caesar, who had received Praetorian honors from the Roman Senate." The Egyptian party, however, mocked Agrippa in the gymnasium. All the jests, which Philo reports, refer to his role as king and friend of Rome: they placed on the head of a dummy figure a mock diadem, clothed it in royal garments, and imitated Agrippa's bodyguards, the most visible sign of his Praetorian honors (*Flacc.* 32–40). These bits of information suggest that Gaius sent Agrippa to Alexandria for political purposes, and they subvert Philo's claim about his technical considerations.

Philo is similarly ambiguous about Agrippa's diplomacy during his visit to Alexandria in the summer of 38 CE. He discloses certain aspects but hides others. According to his story, the following happened: "For when King Agrippa visited us, we told him of Flaccus' intrigues, whereupon he intervened to rectify the matter. He promised us that he would forward the decree to the emperor—which, as we later heard, is what he did indeed—with apologies for the delay, showing that we were not slow at all in understanding the duty of piety towards our benefactors and his family; that, on the contrary, we had been zealous in this respect from the very beginning, but had been deprived of the opportunity to demonstrate this zeal in time due to the governor's maliciousness."[11] Philo presents himself here as active in a group of anonymous Jewish leaders in Alexandria. Agrippa was not only told about the difficulties with Flaccus, who sided with the Alexandrian nationalists, but also checked whether he delivered the Alexandrian Jews' congratulations to Gaius. This implies that the Jewish leaders enjoyed a wide network that enabled them to solicit Agrippa's help and confirm his effective advocacy on their behalf. Philo does not mention how they "later heard" about Agrippa's trustworthiness, but readers may wonder whether his brother is once more behind the scene of Philo's text.

The political tension is caused by Flaccus's insincerity regarding the wish of the Alexandrian Jews to congratulate Gaius on his accession to the throne, as was common in the empire. They wished to send an embassy for this purpose to Rome but expected that Flaccus would not grant permission and thus suggested the compromise of a letter to be dispatched by the prefect. This, Flaccus promised to do, but he then retained the letter. We may ask how Philo and his colleagues found out about the prefect's insincerity, but there are no answers in the text. Agrippa is likely to have used his friendship with Gaius to make the necessary inquiries. Philo, however, does not credit him with this service and instead praises divine providence. Agrippa is even made to hear about the problem from the Jewish leaders in Alexandria (*Flacc.* 97–102). Is Philo's enigmatic style accidental, or does he consciously limit Agrippa's diplomacy and more generally reduce the efficiency of Mediterranean networks enjoyed by the Alexandrian Jews?

We encounter similar narrative fractures in Philo's praise of Agrippa as a reliable messenger who implements his promises to the Jewish community in Alexandria. Agrippa, he says, was concerned to establish good relations between Gaius and the Alexandrian Jews, explaining the delay of their congratulations and stressing their zealous devotion to the new emperor. Philo says nothing about the effect of Agrippa's advocacy, which probably contributed to Flaccus's recall to Rome later in 38 CE. Philo instead introduces God as the savior of the Jewish people and stresses that the "avenger of unholy men and deeds began to enter the lists against him [the prefect]" (*Flacc.* 104). This turn of Philo's story is unexpected. Why would he introduce this theological solution to his political narrative? Why does he marginalize Agrippa's intervention by placing it in the context of Flaccus's arrest, thus disconnecting his advocacy from the early stage of the conflict? Philo has transferred it to the stage when he generally highlights God's intervention. Agrippa now plays a rather more modest role in the drama of divine salvation. The Alexandrian Jews support Philo's narrative plot by recognizing God's presence behind the political scene and offering God a prayer of thanksgiving (*Flacc.* 121).

Philo's ambiguous style is visible also in the last instance of Agrippa's diplomacy mentioned, namely, his care of another letter from the Alexandrian Jews to the Roman emperor. Philo says: "We resolved to transmit to Gaius a document containing in summarized form what we had suffered and what we hoped to achieve. This document was basically an epitome of a longer supplication that we had sent to him a short time before through the hands of King Agrippa. By chance he came to stay in the city when he was about to sail to Syria regarding the kingdom that had been given to him" (*Legat.* 179). In the context of the *Embassy* Philo provides important information about Agrippa's visit to Alexandria in 38 CE that is not included in *Flaccus*, where it belongs chronologically. According to this brief note, Agrippa played a significant political role in transmitting to Rome a petition for Jewish rights in Alexandria. Mary Smallwood rightly suggests that this document must have included complaints about Flaccus's discrimination against the Jews, such as mentioned in *Flaccus* 24.[12] Agrippa mediated between the Jewish community and Gaius, circumventing Flaccus, who was known for his animosity toward the Jews and tense relationship with Gaius. At this early stage of the conflict Gaius emerges as an emperor with clear pro-Jewish tendencies. He relied on Agrippa as a close friend and ambassador, while distrusting the Roman prefect in Alexandria. Philo again reduces Agrippa's role by withholding information about the effect of his advocacy. He moreover marginalizes the importance of Agrippa's intervention by placing it in the later context of divine salvation. His narrative suggests that diplomatic efforts before the Alexandrian pogrom were doomed to failure.

Philo emerges as an unreliable narrator who consciously refashions his political experience and transforms available materials. The outcome is a text with curious dissonances that gives the impression of being disconnected and hanging in the air. Philo as a historical author projects an uprooted, Roman self who identifies with the harbor in Alexandria and Mediterranean mobility. He remains enigmatic as a narrator, obscuring his precise standpoint and withholding significant knowledge. King Agrippa plays a similar role. Appearing out of nowhere, he is hosted by anonymous figures in Alexandria and then vanishes behind the screen of divine providence. While the historical Philo obviously enjoyed Mediterranean networks, his narrative representation of them remains peculiarly limited and puzzling.

Philo's Role as Pious and Suffering Ambassador

Philo speaks about "us five ambassadors" and refers to their Egyptian counterparts as "the elders of the Alexandrians," but he says nothing about their identity and surprisingly little about their activities.[13] He writes as if the bare facts of the embassy are known to his audience, his task being to offer a broader interpretation. Philo as a narrator builds his leading role in the Jewish embassy by pointing to his experience and intellectual superiority. His exemplary maturity shows in the first meeting with Gaius, who greeted them in a friendly manner and conveyed the message that he himself would hear the case in due course. While the other ambassadors rejoice at the emperor's positive response, Philo remains skeptical and is troubled by the following thoughts:

> But as I believe to have a greater amount of good sense on account of my age and my good education, I was alarmed by the things that gave joy to them. Bestirring my own thinking power (*logismos*), I said: Why, when so many envoys have arrived from almost the whole earth, did he say that he would hear only us? What does he want? He cannot have remained ignorant of the fact that we are Jews, for whom it would be a pleasure not to be disadvantaged.... Thus thinking I was deeply disturbed and had no rest by day or night. Yet fainthearted I kept my sorrow secret, since it was not safe to express it, while another very heavy calamity suddenly and unexpectedly fell upon us—a calamity that brought danger not only to one part of the Jewish citizen-body, but collectively to the whole people. (*Legat.* 182–84)

This is one of the more personal passages in Philo's entire oeuvre, when he shares with his readers the thoughts going through his mind. Stressing his own doubts regarding Gaius's sincerity, Philo connects this scene from the initial stage of the embassy with the subsequent news about Gaius's plan to erect his own statue in the Jerusalem Temple. Philo gives the impression that immediately after the meeting with Gaius, while he was still thinking about its meaning, the bad news about the Temple reached him. According to Philo's own testimony, however, the Jewish ambassadors heard the news at a considerably later stage. In *Embassy* 185 he mentions the journeys they had in the meantime undertaken to follow Gaius, who was "spending some time round the bay [of Puteoli]." Philo thus has harmonized two events, namely, the initial meeting with Gaius in the early part of 39 CE and the subsequent announcement of his plans about the Jerusalem Temple, which most probably dates to the summer of 40 CE.[14] By fusing the two events Philo gives the impression that human diplomacy was doomed to failure from the beginning.

Philo explains his inner thoughts and shows how he relies on his education and *logismos* in order to judge external appearances more carefully than others. He prides himself in having had the "good sense" to distrust Gaius rather than accept his gestures of benevolence. This disclosure of a personal reaction to an external stimulation reflects Stoic philosophy, which is concerned with the individual as embedded in society and reacting to the outside world. While Philo does not use distinctly Stoic terminology, except the rather general notion of *logismos*, his position is close to that of the Roman philosopher Seneca, who began to publish his first works at the time of Philo's embassy. Seneca similarly treats the individual person with emphasis on his or her reaction to the outside world. Time and again he describes how he reacted to specific situations and other people by applying his rational judgment.[15]

Philo's exposition of his prudent behavior seems personal at first sight but then turns out to be rather more schematic. He doesn't say much about himself other than demonstrating a philosophical truth via his own example. This apparently personal style, which remains peculiarly detached, is also shared by Seneca. Rather than treating ethical questions in the abstract, Seneca prefers to address friends and discuss specific instances bearing on ethical questions. While often introducing experiences from life, his historical persona remains strangely elusive and detached from identifiable circumstances. In his pioneering treatise *On Anger* Seneca uses personal language and addresses his brother Novatus, while at the same time turning to a wider audience for whom his experience serves as an exemplar. Seneca thus develops his theory of the extirpation of the emotions by studying "our" inner selves and insisting that no emotion "arises without our knowledge."

On another occasion he says, "I reflected and recovered and regained my strength" through studies. Like Philo, Seneca engages in an inner dialogue, urging himself "not to be yielding up my soul." Both Seneca and Philo have integrated personal experiences into their discussions and project a narrative self of Stoic complexion in order to demonstrate the concrete truth of their positions. Seneca discloses his self in order to show that "everything depends on opinion; . . . a man is as wretched as he has convinced himself that he is." Philo tells his readers how he relies on his *logismos* in order to confront the impression of Gaius's friendly gestures, suggesting that from the beginning, this Roman emperor is "our mortal enemy."[16]

Philo describes another moment of crisis in overtly personal terms, namely, when the Jewish ambassadors hear about Gaius's plans to set up his statue in the Jerusalem Temple. We ultimately learn from Philo that Gaius's decision is a reaction to the news of Jews tearing down a pagan altar in Jamneia (in the land of Israel). Immediately after reading the tax collector Capito's account of the event, which is, according to Philo, "highly exaggerated," Gaius decides in the summer or early autumn of 40 CE to punish the Jews by erecting a colossal statue in the main sanctuary.[17] Philo, however, does not tell this story in its chronological sequence, but rather introduces the Temple issue much earlier. He constructs a dramatic scene in which the Jewish ambassadors receive the bad news from a messenger (*Legat.* 184–98).

Philo recalls a lively exchange between the unsuspecting ambassadors and the messenger, who is too shocked to break the horrifying news and needs to be encouraged to deliver his information piecemeal. Such messenger scenes are well known from classical tragedy and were introduced in the second century BCE to Jewish literature. Ezekiel the Tragedian, an Alexandrian Jew, uses the messenger in his play on the exodus to depict the battle between the Israelites and the Egyptians at the Red Sea.[18] While Ezekiel limits the messenger's role to a factual report, which solves the problem of bringing a battle onto the stage, Philo imagines a highly emotional exchange between two parties. His scene probably was inspired by Aeschylus's play *The Persians* and looks like a conscious dramatization of the embassy.[19] Both Philo and Aeschylus stress the utter surprise of the innocent listeners by making them look at "someone," who turns out to be the harbinger of the bad news. In both cases the messenger starts out by "gasping tremendously" or expressing "woes." While Aeschylus dramatizes the scene by introducing the chorus's lamentations, Philo describes in detail how the messenger collapses in tears and is unable to speak. In contrast to the messenger, the Jewish ambassadors remain composed and succeed in extracting from him the unutterable: "Our Temple is lost, Gaius has ordered a colossal statue to be set up within the inner sanctuary dedicated to himself under the name of Zeus."[20]

The ambassadors react with a consternation similar to that of the Persian king's mother in Aeschylus's play, who grasps the defeat of her son's army. She tries to orient herself in a world where only her son has survived,[21] and Philo and his fellow ambassadors similarly digest the new reality dawning on them: "Struck by his words and fixed by consternation, we could not move, but stood speechless and powerless, with our hearts melted and our bodies unnerved, while others appeared bringing the same terrible news. Afterwards we all gathered together in seclusion and bewailed the disaster personal to each and common to all and we recounted in detail such thoughts as the mind suggested, for the unfortunate man talks without end" (*Legat.* 189–90). In this scene Philo allows himself and the other ambassadors to be appropriately emotional, while also preserving decorum and expressing their plight in seclusion. Philo pays much attention to the bodily reactions of the ambassadors, which indicate primary responses not controlled by the mind. Such reactions were recognized in Stoic philosophy as compatible with the self-control of the wise man, who is generally expected to refrain from emotional expressions. Philo has created a dramatic and noble scene that illustrates the dimensions of the disaster. As much as the defeat of the Persian army at Salamis had serious political implications for the Persian king and his family, the prospective desecration of the Jerusalem Temple means a death-blow to Judaism as Philo understands it.

The messenger scene leads immediately to Philo's definition of new priorities. He stresses that the purity of the Temple is an issue of life and death that requires even martyrdom "in the defense of the laws" (*Legat.* 192). Philo moreover explains that the embassy must now give priority to the Temple issue rather than negotiate the civic rights of the Alexandrian Jews. This decision is obviously controversial, because Philo makes special efforts to justify it. He initially stresses that the Temple concerns all the Jews, while the question of Jewish rights in Alexandria is more local. Then he asks, "How can it be right and proper to struggle vainly to prove that we are Alexandrians, when over our heads hangs the danger threatening the whole of the Jewish commonwealth?" (*Legat.* 194). Philo must have used the term "Alexandrian" in the technical sense of civic rights, because the dwelling of the Jews in the city was an obvious fact requiring no proof.[22] When

Philo justifies himself for neglecting to "prove that we are Alexandrians," he seems to respond to criticism that his embassy is not sufficiently devoted to the issue of the legal status of the Alexandrian Jews. He even confronts such harsh questions as why he and his ambassadors do not resign from political life and go home (*Legat.* 195). Philo responds to such accusations of incompetence with a strong theological message: "The truly noble are always full of hope and the laws create good hopes for those who study them in depth and do not just pay lip-service. Perhaps these things are a trial of the present generation, to see how inclined it is to virtue and whether it has been trained to bear misfortune with unfaltering reason and without stumbling. All human aid vanishes—let it vanish! But let our hope in God, our Savior, who has often saved our nation from hopeless and impossible situations, remain unshaken in our souls" (*Legat.* 195–96).

In this highly personal appeal to his readers Philo develops a theology of martyrdom and presents himself as a competent leader in times of suffering. True nobility of mind and real virtue are measured by a person's willingness to endure hardship. Suffering plays a positive role in defining one's identity and prompts a more intense religiosity. The Torah plays a consoling role and inspires hope. Philo uses once more the term *logismos,* rational thinking, which has already helped him to describe his personal reaction to Gaius. Now the *logismos* is said to strengthen the mind of those who have studied and need to be reassured. The narrative about the political struggle for civil rights in Alexandria has been replaced by a theology of consolation. In the process Philo has transformed himself from diplomat to religious leader.

The highlight of Philo's story is the ambassadors' second meeting with Gaius, which enables him not only to describe the climax of the political crisis, but also to define himself as a historical actor and author in the text. His art of self-fashioning is particularly conspicuous in these scenes. Philo initially establishes his credentials as an eyewitness, stressing that he will report what "we have seen and heard" (*Legat.* 349). As he recalls it, the situation was lost from the beginning: "Entering [Gaius's presence], we immediately realized from his look and movements that we had come not to a judge but an accuser of those more hostile than our enemy" (*Legat.* 349). While Philo is eager to present Gaius as a "ruthless tyrant" on the grotesque stage of history, the worst he can say about him is that he poked fun at Jewish customs. There is an obvious tension between Philo's claim that the emperor was madly obsessed with enforcing his own worship and the relatively harmless treatment he gives to the Jews, who refuse to address him as a god. Instead of forcing them to show him divine honors, Gaius simply says that the Jews strike him as "unfortunate rather than wicked" and leaves the room.[23]

Philo further dramatizes the scene and uses the encounter with Gaius for his own theological purposes. Stressing that he and his fellow ambassadors are "seized by a profound terror" and "helpless under such befooling and reviling," Philo stages a clash of civilizations. While the issue of Alexandrian citizenship is no longer discussed, Gaius shows interest in the Jews' peculiar customs and opens the meeting by a sneering question: "Are you the god haters, who do not believe me to be a god?" Philo stresses the Jews' otherness by introducing the perspective of the Egyptian embassy, which he says rejoiced at this opening and, dancing about, invoked blessings on Gaius. Philo further writes that the emperor ridiculed Jewish food customs, asking, "Why do you refuse to eat pork?" This question, too, was enthusiastically greeted by the Egyptians, who thus confirm Judaism's unique nature and clash with Egyptian values. This image of the Egyptians reflects the historical fact that Apion, the head of the rivaling embassy, denounced the Jews on account of both their "atheism" and their abstention from pork.[24] Philo addresses only the religious and not the political points of dispute with the Egyptian diplomat, ignoring his claims about the situation of the Alexandrian Jews.

In Philo's narrative the Jewish ambassadors focus on religion and explain to the emperor that "different people have different customs" (*Legat.* 362). Philo presents the meeting between Gaius and the Jewish ambassadors as a stage for constructing Jewish difference. This scenario fits neither the context of the civic dispute in Alexandria nor the threat of a statue being placed in the Jerusalem Temple. Neither Gaius nor the ambassadors mention these topics. Most strikingly, the issue of Gaius's deification is not connected to the prospect of his statue in the Jerusalem Temple, and the subject of Jewish customs does not lead to a discussion of Alexandrian citizenship. Philo's scene is historically unlikely and primarily serves his overall theological purposes. The pillars of Jewish otherness, which he highlights—namely, monotheism, special food laws, and inherent opposition to Egyptian values—resurface in his *Exposition.* Philo declares essential features of Judaism, as he never did before in his earlier Alexandrian

writings. It is under a critical gaze from the center of Roman power that
Philo, as other Greek authors in the empire, formulates his particular ethnic
identity.[25]

Philo compares the embassy's meeting with Gaius to "mimes in theaters" (ὡς ἐν θεατρικοῖς μίμοις). Gaius and the Egyptians play a grotesque
role, corresponding to the emperor's imitations of the gods. As Philo recalls
in other passages of the *Embassy*, Gaius not only slipped on the stage and
joined in the dancing, but also, "as in a theater," put on the insignia of the
various gods, expecting to receive the reverence due to them.[26] Philo thus
unmasks Rome as a grand stage, where even the emperor does nothing but
play different parts in a mime. His own performance as an author, accentu-
ated in his self-reflective introductions and dramatic style throughout his
report, turns out to be a part played on the Roman scene. Philo not only
experiences Rome as a theatrical farce, but inscribes himself as an author in
the dramatic discourses.

Philo's self-awareness, with its implied self-irony, anticipates two
Greek writers with intimate connections to Rome, namely, Josephus and
Lucian. Josephus produces a humorous account of his first visit to Rome,
suggesting that the Jewish actor Aliturus introduced him to Poppea, the
emperor Nero's wife. The latter not only released the priests for whom he
pleaded, but even gave him "large gifts."[27] Here, too, Rome emerges as a
grotesque scene where actors and women have power and turn regular diplomatic relations upside down. Like Philo, Josephus inscribes himself into
this drama and plays his part as an author who is deeply entangled in Roman discourses. The second-century Sophist Lucian describes Rome even
more explicitly as a place of shows and theater that attracts tricksters and
deceivers. He suggests with an ironic smile that he himself was among
these, writing in a distinctly theatrical style, changing his roles, and wearing
ever more baffling apparel.[28]

Philo's notion of martyrdom in a theatrical context anticipates significant pagan and Christian voices. Seneca distinguishes himself from other
Stoics by emphasizing noble suffering. While his predecessors identified
the goal of ethics as the "good that is unalloyed, peaceful, and beyond the
reach of trouble," he considers brave endurance under torture and even
death as desirable because they bring out all the virtues more than the
"dead sea" of fortune. Socrates is admired not so much for his philosophy,
but for his willingness to meet death and drink the cup of poison. The author of Luke-Acts similarly stresses martyrdom by reinterpreting the Gos-

pel of Mark with emphasis on Jesus's noble suffering and imagining Paul's trial before the Roman emperor. In the second century martyrdom becomes a central theme in Christian discourses, ranging from Ignatius's *Letters* to the *Martyrdom of Polycarp* and the *Passion of Perpetua*. Of particular interest is Justin Martyr, because he also integrates martyrological motifs in a philosophical interpretation of religion. In his view, proper Christianity is distinguished from "Gnosticism" by its readiness to face martyrdom. Justin tells the story of his conversion as a reaction to the sight of Christian martyrs and introduces himself as someone who expects "to be fixed to the stake," perhaps by Cresence, "a lover of bravado and boasting." Interpreting Christianity in a Platonic and Stoic mode, Justin highlights the similarity between Jesus and Socrates, both of whom died a martyr's death. Justin concludes his *Second Apology* with a vivid address to the Romans, anticipating that his appeal to martyrdom will to be their taste.[29] Writing a century earlier in the context of the Jewish embassy to Gaius, Philo is already sensitive to the dramatic potential of suffering and explores it by appealing to Roman conventions. Anticipating subsequent Christian authors, he inscribes the history of his people into contemporary Roman discourses and constructs himself as a dramatic author.

What audience and what purpose does Philo's self-image serve? The key to answering this question is the fact that Philo wrote the *Embassy* during the far more relaxed reign of his successor Claudius, whom he briefly mentions as a remedy to Gaius (*Legat.* 206). Philo writes about his experience from the position of reempowered comfort. By highlighting his brave opposition to Gaius, Philo does not express a fundamental opposition to the institution of the Roman emperor, as has often been assumed, but rather inscribes himself into the current imperial ideology. It is by no means accidental that at the time of Philo's writing, Claudius advertises himself as the positive mirror image of the tyrant Gaius, who, he hastens to add, was rightly detested by the senators. The new emperor continues to stress that he would not tolerate his own worship and liberates those imprisoned by Gaius on account of *maiestas,* that is, insult to the emperor.[30]

In this congenial political climate Philo's story about Gaius's monstrosity toward the Jewish ambassadors almost reads like a self-advertisement addressed to Claudius. Philo seems to suggest that he, too, was a victim of the previous emperor on account of *maiestas* and now enjoys full freedom under Claudius. Philo's self-positioning resembles that of his contemporary Seneca, who wrote in early 44 CE a *Consolation to Polybius*. While overtly advising Polybius, Claudius's influential freedman, how to contain his grief over his brother's death, Seneca uses the opportunity to get his master's hearing and requests his own recall from exile. Indirectly appealing to Claudius, Seneca does not tire of praising him for his beneficence and blissful reversal of Gaius's policies. In his view, too, Gaius was struck by "madness" (*furor*) and proved to be "the ruin and shame of the human race."[31] Both Seneca and Philo evidently thought that it was helpful under Claudius to present his predecessor Gaius as an archvillain.

Consideration for Claudius also may have prevented Philo from addressing the issue of Alexandrian citizenship. The new emperor settled the issue of the status of the Jews in his famous *Letter to the Alexandrians* in a way that can hardly have been wholly satisfactory to the Jews. While Claudius urges the Egyptians to "behave gently and kindly towards the Jews . . . and not to dishonor any of their customs in their worship of their god," he assigns to them a role of aliens "in a city which is not their own (ἐν ἀλλοτρίᾳ πόλει)."[32] Claudius thus confirms the religious rights of the Alexandrian Jews but ignores their political or civic claims. The complexity of his position is highlighted by Josephus, who preserves a version of the edict, which asserts both religious freedom and political equality. Louis Feldman convincingly argues that Josephus has not fabricated his document, but rather preserves an earlier version drafted by King Agrippa I and his brother Herod. Claudius subsequently reconsidered its terms and limited the civic rights of the Alexandrian Jews, probably in reaction to militant Jews flocking in from Palestine and Syria.[33]

Seeing that there were two approaches to the issue of civic rights in Alexandria, an earlier and more political one associated with Agrippa and a later, more religious one reflecting Claudius's official position, it is clear that Philo's portrait of Gaius faithfully echoes imperial policies. In Philo's account Claudius's detested predecessor is criticized as tyrannical precisely in the field of Jewish customs, where Claudius is generous. Gaius's neglect of the Jews' civic rights, on the other hand, is not mentioned, most probably because Claudius, too, did not promote them. Philo moreover adopts Claudius's distinction between civic and religious rights, portraying himself as a fighter for the Jewish religion against the tyrant Gaius. He has retroactively introduced himself as someone whose aspirations to religious freedom will be fulfilled by Claudius, while relegating the issue of civic rights to the very margins of the *Embassy*. Agrippa's successful diplomacy is downplayed in the same spirit.

Philo's awareness of Claudius's policies also accounts for the rather sudden shifts we have observed in the *Embassy* from the level of human diplomacy to the realm of theology. In each case Philo's move is surprising, justified by neither the historical events nor the narrative plot. We are left with the impression that he withholds knowledge, creating a fragmented and hybrid story that conveys a peculiar sense of the dramatic figures hanging in the air. Entangled in contemporary power structures, Philo fashions himself as an enigmatic narrator, who echoes the contemporary slogan of tolerance for the Jewish religion but does not altogether control his story, leaving traces of other perspectives. Eager to play his different parts on the scene of literature, Philo is more concerned about the proper dramatic effect of each episode than overall consistency.

Philo's Self-Fashioning through Agrippa's Letter

Agrippa's letter to Gaius plays a central role in Philo's story about the threat to the Jerusalem Temple. Upon hearing about Gaius's plans to erect his statue there, Agrippa is said to have fallen into a coma and then to have written a long letter to the emperor, which Philo reproduces in fifty-three paragraphs (*Legat.* 276–329). Scholars have questioned the letter's authenticity and argued that it is too long, too Philonic in style, and too odd in the context of Agrippa's fainting to be historically true.[34] We can now add to these arguments that Philo's full "quotation" of Agrippa's letter differs from his treatment of correspondences between the emperor and his prefects. Philo never quotes such Roman letters but only briefly refers to them and paraphrases their content.[35] Regarding Agrippa, by contrast, he says that "he took a tablet and wrote thus," as if having to create a realistic setting for the king's letter (*Legat.* 276). Philo then specifies its whole content, in which he has a vested interest, even though the usual paraphrase would have been sufficient for the plot.

Philo carefully prepares the dramatic effect of the letter attributed to Agrippa by initially placing the king into the same kind of messenger scene that he previously constructed for the ambassadors. In this way he creates an ironic mirror image of himself. Philo suggests that when Agrippa "arrived to pay his respects to Gaius in the usual way, he knew absolutely nothing" about his plans to set up a statue in the Jerusalem Temple (*Legat.* 261). This scenario is highly unlikely as it implies that the king was ignorant about the event in Jamneia, which took place in his country and provoked

Gaius to adopt harsh measures. Agrippa emerges as being ignorant about news available to the ambassadors from Alexandria. His reaction to the prospect of Gaius's statue is even more surprising; Philo reports his "turning to every kind of color," shuddering with convulsions, and fainting into a coma of one and a half days (*Legat.* 266–69). Philo must have been aware of the fact that the drama of this scene would strike readers as fantastic. Its exaggeration stands in obvious contrast to the picture of the self-composed ambassadors, who reacted to the news of Gaius's plans with an appropriate balance of emotion and discipline, immediately making plans for the future and putting their trust in God.

Philo's Agrippa, like himself, is less concerned about politics than about the Jewish religion. The Jews, Philo writes in Agrippa's name, share with all other people a "passionate love for their native land and a high esteem for their own laws." They live throughout the Diaspora but turn their eyes to their "mother city." Philo's Agrippa explains the nature and importance of monotheism as well as aniconic worship. Most surprisingly, "Agrippa" praises Tiberius even though the historical king was on bad terms with that emperor because he favored Gaius from an early stage. Philo and Claudius, on the other hand, cherish Tiberius's memory.[36] Finally, "Agrippa," like Philo and his ambassadors, considers suicide if Gaius does not change his mind about the statue.

Philo has created Agrippa in his own image and playfully speaks through his letter, much like the anonymous author who invented the exchange of letters between Seneca and Paul. The Judean king not only advocates the same Jewish values as Philo, but also expresses his appreciation of Tiberius and his sense of impotence vis-à-vis Gaius. Agrippa's known friendship with Gaius is replaced by the image of their estrangement, an echo of Philo's own alienation from the emperor. Under Philo's pen Agrippa's intervention with Gaius in the Temple affair no longer achieves a reversal of the decision, mentioned by Josephus, but merely solicits an insincere politeness.[37] According to Philo, the statue would have been set up in the Jerusalem Temple if Gaius had not been assassinated and replaced by Claudius. Turning the historical Agrippa into his own mouthpiece, Philo appropriates the image of the king, who enjoyed exceptional popularity not only with Josephus, but also among Jews in general, including the rabbis.[38] Philo's Agrippa is no longer a successful, independent, and widely appreciated politician on behalf of Second Temple Jewry, but a humble extension of Philo's own religious self.

Inventing a letter by Agrippa to Gaius, Philo puts on another mask, namely, that of the Judean king, who turns out to be politically impotent but deeply pious. Given the drastic changes that Agrippa's image has undergone, Philo must have published his account after Agrippa's sudden death in 44 CE. He does not anticipate the possibility that the king can respond and publicly clarify that he neither fainted nor wrote the letter attributed to him. What has Philo gained by reshaping the memory of Agrippa and suggesting that he was politically far less effective than generally assumed? Apart from the possible pleasure of diminishing a political rival, Philo achieves a goal of highly topical significance. He has adapted Agrippa's image to Claudius's ideology, suggesting that even the foremost Jewish politician and close friend of the condemned Gaius was in fact concerned with Jewish worship and a victim of the tyrant. While the historical Agrippa must have been disappointed by Claudius's neglect of Jewish civic rights in Alexandria, for which he personally pleaded, Philo's Agrippa would have been more than happy with the emperor's protection of the Jewish religion.

Conclusion

Philo's self-fashioning in the historical writings has emerged as highly stylized and complex. Self-consciously playing with different roles, he identifies as an Alexandrian but projects an uprooted image of himself characterized by the distinctly Roman quality of mobility in the Mediterranean. Philo does not dwell on his illustrious family background, altogether skipping his influential brother Alexander. The image of King Agrippa I, who does appear in Philo's story, turns out to be enigmatic and fractured, far removed from the effective political figure known from other sources. Philo looks upon contemporary events and personalities from an intensely personal and entangled perspective, playing ironically with various narrative roles and transmitting a sense of the world as a theater.

These features of playful estrangement and emphasis on religion make sense in the context of Philo's embassy to Rome. They reflect his current situation under Claudius, which prompts him to inscribe himself into the new imperial ideology. Ironically, Philo's posture as an apolitical religious leader shows precisely his acute political awareness. Involved in political negotiations, he directly translates Claudius's new priorities into autobiographical terms, suggesting that the Jewish religion agrees with the Roman emperor. Philo's portrait of Agrippa as a leader concerned with Jewish worship reflects the same political awareness. By emphasizing religion under Gaius, Philo as a narrator regains some of the power he lost in the political arena.

Philo's self-fashioning in the historical writings significantly anticipates later Greek writers under Roman rule, who are known for projecting ironic and fractured images of themselves. Like Philo, these Greek writers are highly aware of Rome's political power and fashion themselves as representatives of Greek culture, which appears to be disconnected from politics. Just as Philo declares the Jewish religion to agree with Claudius's new policies, Greek *paideia* is shown to be compatible with the Roman Empire. Moreover, Philo's pioneering suggestion that philosophy is a form of martyrdom subsequently resurfaces in Justin Martyr and affects his construction of what would become orthodox Christianity.

3 Power, Exile, and Religion in the Roman Empire

Philo arrives in Rome at a particularly turbulent moment in history, namely, when Gaius abuses his imperial power to such an extent that he is assassinated in early 41 CE. Claudius replaces him and introduces a more moderate form of rule, promising to work with the Senate, rejecting divine honors, and amending many of Gaius's aberrations. As we saw in the previous chapter, he also issues an important edict to settle the ethnic violence in Alexandria and protects the Jewish religion against attacks from native Egyptians. At the same time, however, Claudius sends intellectuals, such as the philosopher Seneca, into exile and apparently expels in 49 CE some Jews from Rome, since they "constantly made disturbances at the instigation of Chrestus."[1] Philo briefly refers to Claudius as Caesar, thus indicating that he has written his historical treatises under this emperor. Apparently unaware of a crisis in the Jewish community around the figure of Jesus Christ, Philo must have written before 49 CE. He offers a fascinating new interpretation of Judaism in the context of the Roman Empire, which has significant implications for early Christianity and the revival of Greek culture under Roman rule, the so-called Second Sophistic.

Given the fact that Philo writes his historical treatises under Claudius, it is surprising how reticent he is about Claudius's personality and the nature of his rule. There is only one brief reference to him as emperor executing Helicon, an Egyptian agitator against the Jews who had been popular with Gaius (*Legat.* 206). In this instance Philo welcomes the change from Gaius to Claudius; otherwise, he says nothing about the emperor under whom he lives and works. This silence has led scholars to ignore Claudius in the context of Philo and read his historical treatises as if they were unfiltered reflections of Gaius's government, with no connection to the circumstances after his assassination. On this assumption Philo provides a rather faithful picture of the mad emperor, daring to speak his mind and show opposition on behalf of the Jews. However, Philo's silence about Claudius is too blatant to be taken at face value. It may indeed be rather deceptive, covering the fact that he must have been aware of current imperial policies while writing treatises on politics and religion in a Roman context.

In the previous chapter we saw how Philo styled himself as a pious and suffering ambassador precisely in the spirit of Claudius's *Letter to the Alexandrians*, which guarantees religious tolerance and provides protection against assaults from outside but denies political equality. Following this line of interpretation we have to ask how Philo's experience of this emperor shaped his views of imperial power, exile, and the Jewish religion. The Roman philosopher Seneca, Philo's contemporary, provides important insights into these issues, as he is more explicit about Claudius and indicates that it is not easy to be an intellectual in imperial Rome. Seneca's writings are thus crucial for understanding the intellectual climate in Claudian Rome and provide a key to Philo's historical works. They deserve serious attention before we can analyze Philo.

Seneca on Politics, Exile, and Philosophy under Claudius

Seneca addresses the issue of Claudius's personality in three treatises, two from the eight years of his exile on Corsica, following a controversial charge of adultery, and another, very different work, the *Apocolocyntosis*, from the time after the emperor's death in 54 CE.[2] While the first two treatises are consolations, which flatter Claudius and explain the philosophical advantages of exile, the latter expresses sarcastic criticism of the dead emperor. In the *Consolation to Polybius* Seneca turns to Claudius's influential freedman Polybius, who has lost his brother and requires advice in order to overcome his grief. Seneca overtly addresses Polybius's plight, supporting him with standard motifs of consolation, but he also has a political agenda and turns to his client's master, Claudius. The emperor is elegantly introduced as a source of comfort to Polybius. It becomes increasingly clear that Seneca is concerned about his own interests, namely, his return from exile, which depends on the emperor. Not surprisingly, Seneca praises Claudius as divinely beneficent to the empire, a healer of the human race, and, most importantly, very merciful. He stresses that Claudius has "not cast him down," but fortune treated him harshly and the emperor did his best to mitigate his fate. Seneca even says that this emperor "makes exiles live more peacefully than did princes recently under the rule of Gaius." At the same time, however, he suggests that the forthcoming triumphal procession marking Claudius's victory over Britain would be an excellent opportunity to recall him from exile and let him participate in the well-deserved celebrations. Seneca thus suppresses his anger at Claudius and declares himself as his devout supporter, praising his advantages over those of his predecessor Gaius. The latter flattery must have been especially appealing to Claudius, well known for his policy of distancing himself from Gaius's corrupt reign.[3]

In the *Consolation to Helvia*, his mother, Seneca introduces a new form of consolation in which the one suffering a wretched fate is consoling his family. He is well aware of the fact that this strategy amounts to a self-consolation and uses the suffering of exile to construct himself as a true philosopher who has learned to maintain detachment from life's hazardous circumstances. Seneca's experience of exile as a formative period resembles the autobiographical reminiscences of Diogenes of Sinope, the well-known Cynic (fourth century BCE), who insists that "it was through that [exile] ... that I came to pursue philosophy." Seneca similarly claims that "my fortune is not wretched" and "I am happy under circumstances that usually make others wretched," because "the mind can never suffer exile, since it is free, kindred to the gods and at home in every world and age." Moreover, "inside the world there can be no place of exile." Seneca models himself on Marcellus, who endured his exile "most happily" (*beatissime*) and "nobly," because he devoted himself to studying and persuaded himself that "to the wise man every place is his country."[4]

Gaius is introduced in the *Consolation to Helvia* as the ultimate Other, who combines "supreme vice and supreme power" and abuses his status for an extravagant lifestyle. The emperor Claudius, who eventually recalls Seneca from exile, plays only an implicit role, being shown the way by the negative mirror image of Julius Caesar. Seneca says that the former dictator was touched by Marcellus's heroic bearing of exile but refrained from recalling him. Julius did not anchor at Marcellus's island of exile, "because he could not bear to see a hero in disgrace," so the Senate took action and recalled him to society.[5] Seneca suggests that Marcellus is lucky in exile because his heroic bearing won him the admiration of the philosopher Brutus. At the same time, however, he subtly suggests that Claudius should adopt a philosophical approach and release him from exile. Seneca has once more suppressed his anger at the emperor and projected his criticism onto his dead predecessors.

Philosophy plays a therapeutic role in Seneca's discourse because it enables him to situate himself outside the arena of politics and create an alternative frame of reference. While Roman norms define as wretched a person who is isolated from society, lacking worldly signs of honor and positions of influence, Seneca declares himself to be in full control of his life and at the center of things that really matter. He asserts that he has lost nothing of value but has gained an opportunity to live in perfect accordance with nature, far away from the hustle of power. Following his model Marcellus, Seneca styles himself as a kind of philosophical martyr, who happily endures worldly suffering for the benefit of living by his convictions. Paradoxically, this penchant for martyrdom is politically highly effective. Seneca is not only able to identify as a philosopher and make his voice heard back home, but eventually prompts a reversal of his situation and his return to conventional society in Rome.

After Claudius's death Nero accedes to the throne at the age of sixteen, and Seneca becomes an influential minister, thanks to Nero's mother, Agrippina. One of the major publications from the early reign of the new emperor is Seneca's treatise *On Mercy*, which flatters Nero on his beneficence and generosity toward his subjects. The precarious nature of Seneca's situation in Rome can be gathered from the fact that he wrote this treatise rather soon after Nero's murder of Britannicus in 55 CE, stressing that "I would rather offend with the truth than please by flattery."[6] While caution is prudent with regard to Nero, Seneca now feels free to express criticism of the dead emperor Claudius and thus join Nero himself. He even writes a satire on Claudius, the *Apocolocyntosis*, in which he celebrates Claudius's funeral day as a day of liberation for the Roman people. Seneca declares that he is a "free man" now and invites others to "speak the truth at last." Claudius emerges from this text as a ridiculous figure, stammering and odd, but above all a disastrous ruler, given to anger and cruelty, with no vision of the empire, like a cock who is "great on his own heap." Especially important for our context is Seneca's observation that Augustus would have been appalled by this emperor because he departed from his own policies and instead followed in Gaius's footsteps, murdering many senators and knights.[7]

A clear pattern is visible in Seneca's writings. The current emperor is praised and delicately manipulated, while his predecessors, especially Gaius, become objects of open scorn, often serving as scapegoats for present plights. Moreover, there are close connections between power, exile, and philosophy. Seneca becomes known as a philosopher on account of his experience of exile, and it is his philosophical expertise that installs him in a high-ranking political position. His early philosophy focuses on the subject of suffering and overcoming emotions of misery. Philosophy is closely connected to martyrdom and offers an alternative to imperial power in Rome. It is an intellectual space, where individual identity is affirmed, at times as a compensation for lost political power, while at other times as a relatively secure haven from which current policies can be observed and sometimes even influenced.

Does the paradigm of Seneca's rhetoric apply also to Philo, who writes approximately at the time when the consolations to Polybius and Helvia are published? On the face of it, Philo is lucky to encounter in Claudius an emperor protecting the Jewish religion from assaults by the Egyptians. Claudius moreover spoke and read Greek fluently, quoting verses from Homer and even writing historical works, which he ordered to be read each year at the Museum in Alexandria.[8] The political climate of his Principate, however, seems to have been far more complex. Unlike Seneca, Philo did not live long enough to benefit from the freedom of expression after Claudius's death. Seneca's voice nevertheless alerts us to look for shadows of Claudius's presence in Philo's historical works.

Imperial Power from Philo's Point of View

At the beginning of the *Embassy* Philo makes a revealing remark about flattery. "It is the distinct quality of flattery," he says, "to pay court to success" (*Legat.* 32). Free speech is dangerous under an emperor who has just assumed supreme power. Describing Gaius's accession to the throne, Philo stresses the dramatic change of his personality and style of government, which quickly slipped from an extremely promising beginning into tyranny. The murder of Gaius's two close advisors, Macro and Silanus, signifies this shift to the worse.

According to Philo, Macro and Silanus were too outspoken in their criticism of the new emperor and paid with their lives for their courageous sincerity. Macro was Gaius's longstanding supporter and helped him gain

Tiberius's favor as well as his throne. Aware of his good services, Macro "gave outspoken admonitions without precautions" (*Legat.* 41). While conscious of a general suppression of free speech, he thought of himself as an exception to the rule. Seeing the emperor asleep at a banquet or joining vulgar dances, Macro plainly reminded him of his duties and explained the norms of proper conduct for a Roman emperor. Gaius, however, was not amused by Macro's educational zeal and ridiculed him as a "teacher of someone who no longer needs to learn" (*Legat.* 41). Considering himself to have been molded from the womb as an emperor, Gaius rejected the idea of receiving instruction. He quickly became so annoyed with his advisor that he fabricated false charges against him and forced him to commit suicide, an expression, as Philo asserts, of his criminal ingratitude.

Silanus, Gaius's son-in-law, fared no better. He, too, practiced "free speech" (παρρησία), feeling protected by both his family ties and his acknowledged competence in state affairs. He, too, hoped to improve Gaius's character and bring him up to the proper norms of government. Upset by Silanus's well-intended advice, Gaius murdered him, causing an outrage among the people, who, however, no longer dared to express their views openly and instead spoke "with a quiet voice." Philo shows a keen interest in the reaction of the masses to imperial tyranny, studying not only the spread of subversive rumors, but also the phenomenon of flattery and fearful adaptation to the political reality. Shocked by Gaius's decline, Philo observes that what people most dreaded was to recognize reality and acknowledge that Gaius was "a despot."[9]

Philo's narrative is interesting in view of two later Roman historians, namely, Suetonius, writing one generation after Philo in Latin, and Dio Cassius, who belongs to the Second Sophistic and wrote in Greek in the late second and early third centuries. They, too, discuss the political murders Gaius committed at the beginning of his rule. Suetonius, who lacks interest in constitutional questions and the republican ideal of freedom, speaks of them as expressions of Gaius's cruel character and manipulative methods. The Roman historian asserts that Gaius executed people, among them Silanus, on the basis of his own paranoia. According to Suetonius, that death was caused by the most trifling affair: suffering from seasickness, Silanus did not accompany the emperor on a boat trip during stormy weather and was on that account suspected of waiting for Gaius's death at sea in order to assume power.[10] Dio Cassius shows more interest in the constitutional features of the Principate and worries, like Philo, about its deterioration into tyranny. In his eyes, too, Gaius was cruel and bloodthirsty, murdering many innocent people. Dio mentions both Silanus and Macro, stressing that they were brought down by false accusations. Like Philo, Dio draws attention to Gaius's ingratitude toward Macro and adds his own explanation of Gaius's hatred of him: the emperor envied his talent.[11]

A comparison of these two Roman historians with Philo shows the extent of Philo's attention to Macro and Silanus. In Philo's narrative these are the only named victims of Gaius's tyranny, while Suetonius and Dio Cassius mention others as well. Moreover, only Philo introduces them as courageous characters, freely speaking their minds and instructing Gaius on the proper administration of the Roman Empire. While Suetonius and Dio portray them as inadvertently slipping into Gaius's net, Philo conceives of them as self-conscious heroes who are aware of the political risks they take for their convictions. Does Philo, a contemporary of Gaius, simply have better evidence and is therefore able to provide more reliable details? In that case we have to explain why he is so interested in the internal power struggles at the Roman court under the previous emperor, who had long been condemned by his successor. Why indeed would he dwell at such length on matters not overtly connected to the Jewish embassy to Gaius? Alternatively, we may ask whether the special features of Philo's narrative reflect present concerns under Claudius.

Let's look at Claudius's rule and see whether we recognize any element that can explain Philo's particular narrative of Gaius. The evidence we have of Gaius's rule derives from later historians writing after the emperor's death and thus who are as free as Seneca after 54 CE to speak their minds.[12] In the reports of Suetonius and Dio Cassius, and to some extent of Josephus, the following picture emerges. When Claudius assumed power in early 41 CE, he took some measures to relieve Gaius's restrictions on free speech and abolished the charge of *maiestas,* that is, insult to the emperor, "not only in the case of writings, but in the case of overt acts as well" (Dio 60.3.6). One year later, however, Claudius succumbed to paranoid suspicions and began a series of murders, which he presented as necessary measures of self-defense. The most notorious of these was the murder of Appius Silanus, his stepfather-in-law. Dio vividly describes the sudden change of Claudius's attitude toward this family member: while he "had for some time held him [Appius Silanus] in honor among those nearest and dearest to him, he suddenly killed him" (Dio 60.14.3). Both Dio and Suetonius explain that Claudius's cruelty was prompted by his wife's machinations.

A lustful adulteress, Messalina had been rejected by Silanus and was eager for revenge. She plotted to have him executed, presenting to Claudius the rather transparent pretext of a dream that she and her freedman Narcissus claimed to have had in which Silanus appeared to them on the verge of murdering Claudius. Claudius was terrified by this vision and immediately arranged for Silanus's death.[13]

Dio Cassius stresses the immense significance of Silanus's murder for the political climate in Claudian Rome: "After his death the Romans no longer cherished fair hopes of Claudius." No wonder that Seneca, looking back on this event from the safe perspective of Nero's rule, sarcastically asks "why he had Silanus killed" (*Apoc.* 8.2). Describing the climate of the tyranny under Claudius, Dio insists that "excellence no longer meant anything else but dying nobly." Martyrdom or else insincerity was the choice of the day. Dio admires the free speech of Galaesus, who says "without precaution" that if someone else had become emperor, "I would have stood behind him and kept my mouth shut."[14]

While Dio Cassius and Suetonius lived after Claudius's time and could freely express their views of this emperor's coercive policies, Philo writes during his lifetime and has to be careful. Knowing that the previous emperor Gaius is always a welcome target of public scorn, he projects the problem of free speech under tyranny onto his rule. Philo thus acts in precisely the same fashion as his contemporary Seneca, who directs his criticism to Gaius as long as Claudius is still alive. The coincidence of two victims of political persecution under two different emperors sharing the name Silanus must have encouraged such a projection. Moreover, in the case of both Gaius and Claudius the victim was a family member who previously had enjoyed special standing with the emperor. Even the motif of a wanton wife's machinations, which Dio and Suetonius adduce as an explanation for Silanus's execution, resurfaces in Philo's narrative. He uses the known relationship between Gaius and Macro's wife for some surprisingly general remarks that would describe Claudius at least as well as Macro: "A wife has a great power to paralyze and mislead her husband, especially if she is lustful, because she becomes more fawning out of a guilty conscience. The husband, unaware of the corruption of his marriage and household and taking her flattery to be unmixed good-will, is deceived. Unaware of the manipulations, he approaches his worst enemies as his dearest friends" (*Legat.* 39–40).

Dio also mentions Gaius's affair with Macro's wife, which was in his view initiated by Macro himself for reasons of political self-promotion. Dio refers to this relationship only briefly in order to highlight the cruelty of Gaius, who disregards every kind of human bond, causing even the death of his former lover and her husband.[15] In the case of Claudius, by contrast, Dio gives considerable attention to the issue of a betrayed husband. He complains about the influence of Messalina's love affairs on the emperor, not only in the case of Silanus. Dio says, for example, that everyone knew that Mnester retained his position at the theater only because he was Messalina's lover—a fact known to everybody except the emperor himself, who "alone failed to realize what was going on in the palace" (Dio 60.28.4). These rumors about Messalina's lovers must have reached Philo, too, because Dio speaks of common knowledge, which cannot have remained hidden from a well-informed contemporary. Unlike Dio, however, Philo is unable to put these criticisms into writing because Claudius is still in power. He instead projects them onto Macro. While admitting that Macro's wife has not been charged with adultery, Philo still hopes that his general reflections on the matter, conveniently formulated in the present tense, will resonate well with his readers and perhaps even be recognized as relevant to Claudius.

Having identified Claudius's shadow in Philo's story of Macro's and Silanus's deaths, let's take a fresh look at their speeches. Many years ago Erwin Goodenough suggested that Philo may have written Macro's speech as an implicit piece of advice to Claudius.[16] In his view, Philo does not present historical evidence from the period of Gaius but fabricates a speech in order to warn the new emperor that if he does not treat the Jews well, his rule will have the same disastrous end as that of his predecessor. Goodenough offers this interpretation as part of his overall argument that Philo as a Jew bravely opposed the Roman Principate but could not openly say so to a non-Jewish audience. How accurate is this interpretation of Macro's speech?

When Philo specifies Macro's admonitions to Gaius, he refrains from criticizing the political system of the Principate and focuses instead on its deterioration into tyranny. No republican sentiments about a loss of senatorial freedom under the emperors are expressed. On the contrary, both Macro and Silanus, who come from the ranks of the knights and senators, are positive heroes, precisely because they support the ideal of a good emperor. Their image matches Philo's subsequent praise of Augustus, steering the commonwealth as a "single pilot" and showing his marvelous mastery of the science of government (*Legat.* 149). Given this monarchical orientation, it is not surprising that Philo's Macro criticizes Gaius for behaving too much like everybody else: "You ought not to be like any of those present or anyone else at all." Macro approves of the Principate to such an extent that he places the "ruler of the earth and sea" far above everybody else, suggesting that he must guide humanity like a "shepherd and commander of the flock." The prime benefit of imperial rule is economic stability: agriculture flourishes and "every sea [is] safely navigated by merchant ships laden with cargoes." The ideal ruler, Philo's Macro concludes, will not exercise "coercion" but will "put forward good proposals for the benefit of his subjects and execute these plans well."[17]

All of this advice is patently out of place in the context in which Philo presents it, namely, Gaius's unsuitable behavior at dinner parties. A speech about self-discipline and control over the appetites would have been far more appropriate. Philo clearly has broader aims in mind when placing this speech on proper government into Macro's mouth. He must have written it with a view to contemporary concerns under Claudius. Philo's special mention of the emperor's beneficial contribution to safe sea trade would certainly have pleased Claudius, who was known for his efforts to keep the sea route to Alexandria open even during the winter (Suetonius, *Claud.* 18.2). Moreover, Philo's urgent appeal to rule as a benign emperor is highly relevant to Claudius in the aftermath of Silanus's murder. Like Gaius, he had become a despot after a promising beginning and was likely to enter history as an emperor who had severely disappointed the hopes for a better age.

Goodenough is thus right that Macro's speech has topical relevance in Philo's narrative and expresses his own views on politics. Some aspects of his overall argument, however, need to be qualified. There is no sign that Philo is in principle opposed to the institution of the Roman Principate and that his views were shaped by his Jewish identity. To assume that Philo is "anti-imperialist" is to apply modern values. General ethical concerns rather than constitutional or religious questions guide Philo. Through Macro's speech he expresses his expectation that the emperor should be a good ruler and exercise his supreme power for the benefit of his subjects. Philo's position resembles that of Stoic philosophers, such as Seneca, and later Greek thinkers in the Roman Empire, such as Plutarch, Lucian, and Dio Cassius. Indeed, Philo's contemporary Seneca also accepts the institution of the Roman emperor, judging each *princeps* according to his ethical merits. In his view, too, Gaius is a prime example of a bad ruler who has gone astray and serves as a warning to his successors.[18]

Moreover, it is rather unlikely that Philo directly addresses Claudius in the *Embassy*. In contrast to Seneca, who openly addresses his treatise *On Mercy* to the young Nero, Philo, as the head of a foreign embassy with no permanent post in Rome, is in no position to appeal to the Roman emperor. He probably speaks to an audience of intellectuals concerned with the problems of imperial power, hoping that they will recognize his remarks about Gaius as hints about current circumstances. Ever fond of drama, Philo adds an especially touching scene to give emphasis to his criticism. He describes at length how the young Tiberius Gemellus, Gaius's co-heir according to Tiberius's will, was forced by the emperor's henchmen to commit suicide in order to clear the way for Gaius's absolute power. Eager to follow the instructions of his foes, the poor lad desperately tries to find the right method to put an end to his wretched life (*Legat.* 28–31). No other extant historian preserves this scene, and Philo probably invented it as a strong emotional appeal to his readers, whom he urges to deplore the atrocities of tyranny at all times, including their own.

Philo has emerged as a philosophical writer with an acute political awareness. His criticism of tyranny on moral grounds is shared by other intellectuals in the Roman Empire. Philo's political involvement rather than his Jewish identity shaped his views and prompted him to write with caution, while simultaneously inscribing himself into contemporary discourses. His comments on current affairs under Claudius, projected onto his predecessor Gaius, help us understand other Greek authors in the empire, such as Dio and Plutarch, as well as their characteristic ambivalence about political involvement.

Exile Both Roman and Jewish

Exile plays a central role in Philo's discussions of politics and religion. Exile is, of course, one of the most blatant expressions of a loss of power and naturally prompts efforts to regain one's former status and find ways of reempowering oneself. In Seneca's case, we have seen that philosophy offers an opportunity for reentering public discourses, building a new identity, and eventually recovering status in Roman society. Philo is familiar with this option and shows how Gaius detested it in the case of Flaccus. The Roman prefect of Egypt was recalled to Rome, judged guilty, and sentenced to exile for reasons that Philo does not specify but interprets as a punishment for his maltreatment of the Alexandrian Jews. According to Philo, Gaius begins to think that this punishment is in reality a blessing and regrets that he did not administer the death penalty. The emperor understands that prominent exiles, such as Flaccus, are not the unfortunate and miserable creatures they ought to be according to Roman norms but have instead "secured a life of release from business, of tranquility and true liberty" (*Flacc.* 183). As if inspired by Seneca's *Consolation to Helvia*, Philo has Gaius describe exile as a "residence abroad" that enables the exiles "to enjoy the advantages of the philosophical life."[19] Gaius consequently decides to put Flaccus to death, ensuring his absolute loss of power, which can no longer be reversed by philosophy.

While Suetonius briefly mentions Gaius's murder of several exiles, because Gaius suspects that they may pray for his death, Philo explores the philosophical dimension of exile. He not only dwells on Gaius's insights into the intellectual advantages of exile, but also studies its transformative effect on Flaccus. Under his pen, the former Roman prefect becomes a highly complex character with a strong penchant for philosophy and religion. Exile is an opportunity for full individuation. On his way to the island and exposed to the mockery of onlookers, Flaccus becomes intensely aware of his changing self, using expressions such as "I am Flaccus, who until recently was governor of Alexandria," and "I Flaccus, who was born and reared in imperial Rome." He moreover asks whether the island will be for him an "exile or a new fatherland, a hapless haven or a refuge." Conventional life in Roman society now appears to him as unreal. Flaccus understands that the previous discourses of flattery and insincerity were a way "of deceiving himself," a mere phantom rather than "the truth."[20]

Flaccus's shameful solitude opens up new insights into reality and leads to a kind of conversion. He becomes "possessed as in a corybantic frenzy" and turns his eyes toward heaven, that "veritable world within a world" (*Flacc.* 169). Flaccus becomes aware of the God of Israel as the ultimate source of power in the cosmos, parallel to Philo's Abraham, who concludes from the regular movements of the stars that there must be one creator God (*Abr.* 68–80). Flaccus now turns to the God of Israel in a personal prayer and addresses him as the "king of gods and men," a unique title in Philo's work. Unlike Seneca, he never attributes the term "king" to the Roman emperors. The political terminology of monarchy thus has been transferred to the realm of the divine and is associated with the God advocated by an ethnic minority. Philo has reversed the political structures, offering an alternative source of supreme power that stems from his own religion and reflects his personal interests. He further advocates a significant reversal of conventional structures by stressing that God presided over Flaccus's trial and brought it to its morally justified conclusion even though the judges were so corrupt and incompetent that Flaccus was likely to go unpunished. Where the legal system of the Roman Empire fails, God steps in and provides justice. Flaccus stresses that belief in divine providence is the "true creed."[21] He has reached this insight in exile, far away from the illusionary façade of Roman society and power.

In Philo's story, religion plays a strikingly similar role to that of philosophy in Seneca's writings. He uses the known fact of Flaccus's lapse and punishment to present the Jewish religion as an alternative center to imperial power, where moral values matter and attain universal validity. Parallel to philosophy, it enables exiles to recognize their former lives among people as delusions and guides them to more authentic lives, which restore their dignity and self-respect. Philo encourages his readers to grasp the similar roles of religion and philosophy by introducing Gaius's insight that Flaccus uses his exile for philosophical pursuits. While both religion and philosophy provide a respite from political constraints, they pose no fundamental opposition to the institution of the Roman Principate. In fact, even political pressure such as exile is turned by religion and philosophy into a training ground for character formation. As much as Seneca writes his treatises from exile to promote himself as a philosopher back in Rome, Philo uses Flaccus's conversion to offer a powerful image of the Jewish religion to wider Roman audiences.

In one respect, however, Philo's approach differs from Seneca's. In his view the God of Israel is the ultimate savior and king, whereas this role is fulfilled by the wise man in Seneca's writings. Philo's Flaccus ultimately devotes his new self-awareness to God and inscribes himself among God's followers. Seneca, by contrast, finds salvation in the tranquility of his own mind. Overcoming the shame of exile, he discovers new resources within himself. Philo's Flaccus makes positive sense of the disaster that has befallen him by praying and atoning for his previous sins against God's people. In the case of Seneca, the process of self-finding is more gradual, whereas for Flaccus it is a rather dramatic turn with expressions of corybantic frenzy.

How are politics, exile, and religion connected for the Jews themselves? Philo stresses that during the crisis under Flaccus the Alexandrian Jews have become exiles in their own city. The Roman governor lets the Egyptians interfere with Jewish worship in the synagogues and excludes the Jews from "participation in political rights" and effectively turns them into "foreigners and aliens."[22] Their loss of civic status is most concretely expressed by the instruction to punish them by scourges in the manner of the Egyptians rather than citizens. This public disempowerment is followed by general violence in the streets of Alexandria. Jewish homes are destroyed, their inhabitants maltreated and deprived of their possessions. Even the members of the Jewish senate are helplessly exposed to public scorn, imprisonment, and humiliation.

The Jews emerge as true philosophers in the midst of this political disaster. Philo nowhere suggests that they had committed sins that caused their exile. Unlike the biblical prophets, who interpret the Babylonian exile as a punishment for Israel's sins, Philo accepts the violence in Alexandria as a given fact that demands no theological justification.[23] Assuming a distinctly political perspective, he is convinced that the Alexandrian Jews are innocent victims of whimsical Roman rulers. Moreover, their reaction to their loss of power is entirely rational and based on political thinking. Philo explores their attitude on the occasion of Flaccus's arrest, to which they initially react with suspicion, fearing that it is a calumny to test their loyalty. When additional reports confirm the truth of the news, the Alexandrian Jews go into the streets, "stretching their hands out to heaven," and lead "hymns and songs of thanksgiving to God, the guardian of human affairs." They address God as "Lord" (δεσπότης) and acknowledge his pity, compassion, and support. Most importantly, Philo makes them acknowledge a deep link between exile and religion: "Expelled as we are from all that men have created and robbed of our city . . . we have as our only habitation" the earth, sea, air, and heaven. According to Philo, the Alexandrian Jews moreover say, "We are alone of all men under the sun without a city and a home through the ill will of a governor."[24] Forced into exile from their city and local structures of political organization, the Alexandrian Jews consider themselves as citizens of the world, much like Seneca during his exile from Rome. Philo must have been painfully aware of the fact that the Alexandrian Jews have not yet regained their citizenship in Alexandria. When praising Augustus for granting full citizenship to Roman Jews, allowing them to follow their "ancestral customs," he may have wished that Claudius would speedily imitate his model emperor in this respect, too.[25]

Philo discusses the exile of the Alexandrian Jews with no reference to either atonement of sins or a return to Zion at the end of days, two prominent themes of Jewish texts from the Second Temple period in the land of Israel.[26] Instead of turning inward and gathering his community around the notion of sin, eschatological redemption, and revenge on Rome, Philo turns to a wider Roman audience and communicates the universal, philosophical value of the Jewish religion. Unlike colleagues in the land of Israel, he does not apply the paradigm of the Babylonian exile to the Alexandrian situation. Writing at a time when Claudius has already restored the religious rights of the Alexandrian Jews, Philo recalls their suffering under Flaccus and Gaius as a way of affirming current imperial policies. During their plight the Jews have shown their philosophical character, which has rendered them all the more acceptable in Roman circles. As for Seneca, exile has proved to be an interim period until the expected return to conventional society. In the case of the Alexandrian Jews, religion plays a vital role in this return to power, both as a psychological support for the community and as a concrete resource reversing the mistakes of previous Roman rulers.

The highly political and Roman nature of Philo's notions can further be appreciated by comparing his historical writings to his *Allegorical Commentary,* which he wrote in Alexandria for a Jewish audience. Philo earlier devoted a whole treatise to the *Migration of Abraham,* interpreting God's command to leave "your country and your kindred and your father's house" (Gen 12:1). Philo's reading of this biblical text is radically allegorical. Ignoring political exile, he interprets Abraham's migration as the soul's elevation from the material realm. The philosophical frame of reference is Platonic, with emphasis on the soul's flight to spirituality. This metaphorical exile is a static ideal, not a concrete plight. It is in fact a recovery of the soul's original state before it entered a human body.[27]

After his arrival in Rome, following the violence in Alexandria, Philo takes involvement in society for granted and considers exile as a painful exclusion from a specific political body. He is aware that exile affects the whole person and can be overcome by creating a philosophical or religious space until the anticipated reversal of one's situation. Philo no longer considers only the individual, torn between body and soul, but speaks about the place of the Jewish people within the Roman Empire. These new impulses in Philo's work, with their distinctly Roman orientation, are highly significant in the middle of the first century CE and anticipate important discussions among Greek intellectuals as well as early Christians. Plutarch's treatise *On Exile,* for example, expresses similar views. Like Philo, trained in Platonic philosophy and increasingly turning toward Rome, Plutarch overcomes the soul-body dichotomy and discusses exile as a painful loss of political power in a specific community. The grief of exile can be alleviated, he asserts, by adopting the right philosophical attitude. One should appreciate the freedom it entails as well as the opportunity to create a new "native city" wherever one happens to live. Relying on Stoic ideas, Plutarch insists that the whole world is home.[28]

Writing at approximately the same time as Plutarch, the author of Luke-Acts introduces political notions of exile to tell his story about the emergence of the Jesus movement from Judaism. He inscribes his religion into Roman discourses in a way strikingly similar to that of Philo. While stressing the Jewish background of Jesus and Paul, the author of Luke-Acts depicts the Jews as having lost their status in Rome. Claudius, he says, "had ordered all the Jews to leave Rome." The historicity of this note has often been questioned, Steve Mason and Tom Robinson suggesting that the claim about "all" Jews being expelled "may be the author's characteristic exaggeration." This construction of the exiled Jews matches the overall argument in Luke that the Jews are punished for their rejection of the Messiah by the destruction of their Temple, expulsion from their main city, and dispersion among the nations.[29]

The image of the Jews as exiles plays a significant role in the overall story of Luke-Acts, where Paul is cast in the role of a Jew who initially appeals to the synagogues but then succeeds as a Roman among the gentiles. An incident in Philippi illustrates the shift from Jewish stranger to Christian citizen. Paul and Silas are said to be accused by some locals of "disturbing our city" and as Jewish advocates of "customs that are not lawful for us Romans." These gentiles consider the Jews as strangers and prompt the Roman authorities to punish them by means of flogging, which is administered to noncitizens. Paul and Silas thus fare like the Alexandrian Jews during the upheaval in their city, when they were scourged in the manner of the Egyptians. Paul, however, is much swifter in reempowering himself by a miracle, which immediately converts the jailor and his family to Christianity. Then he suddenly discloses his Roman citizenship, never mentioned before in Paul's letters or Luke-Acts, and demands gestures of repair.[30] Paul's religious triumph is invested with political power and conveys a significant message about Christian status in the Roman

Empire. The harbinger of the new faith is said to be rescued by Roman administrators from hostile Jews who do not accept his message. Paul is politically victorious, enjoying a higher civic status than the Jews, who live in dispersion and exile. In this case, too, the true religion is one that helps its adherents to overcome exile and regain civic rights in the empire.

The Jewish Religion among Others in Rome

When Philo arrives in Rome in late 38 CE, he encounters a distinct religious climate, where the cult is closely connected with politics and the emperor serves as *pontifex maximus* (high priest). Political events, such as triumphal processions celebrating military victories, are invested with religious symbols and ceremonies. When Claudius accedes to the throne in 41 CE, he rejects the erection of a temple in his honor but welcomes an attitude of "piety" toward himself and his family. He scrupulously observes traditional Roman rites and subsequently abolishes the "cruel and inhuman religion of the Druids," while introducing some mystery cults.[31]

Unlike Alexandria, Rome has also been the home of philosophers of religion advocating radically historical explanations of human worship. Especially known among them is Varro, Cicero's contemporary in the first century BCE, who suggests that people regularly turn great benefactors into gods. Such human origins of religion are seen in a positive light, as part of a creative and well-functioning society. The bishop Augustine, Varro's harshest critic, subsequently regards such euhemerism as a serious threat to Christian monotheism and ridicules it.[32] Is Philo, who anticipates Augustine by roughly three centuries, familiar with the Roman scene? If so, how does he react to the intrinsic link between religion and politics?

Philo uses typically Varronian arguments to criticize Gaius's imitation of the gods and his demand to receive divine honors. It is striking that he refrains from criticizing emperor worship as such but complains that Gaius has done nothing beneficial to deserve such worship. Turning rhetorically to Gaius, who is long dead, Philo reminds his readers that the gods whom Gaius imitates in his outfit "received and still receive admiration for the benefits introduced by them and were judged worthy of worship and the highest honors." Gaius, in other words, fails to live up to the high standards of the demi-gods and gods, such as Hermes and Apollo, thus foregoing the option of divinization. Augustus, by contrast, has brought real blessings to the empire, and Philo consequently praises his "more than human nature" as well as his temple in the harbor of Alexandria.[33] Philo evidently discusses the problem of Gaius's claim to divinity from a distinctly Roman perspective, suggesting to his readers that according to their own standards, Gaius was mistaken in his religious aspirations. Readers approving of Claudius's current policies of modesty would undoubtedly agree.

Philo not only appeals to sociological interpretations of religion, but also to aspects of cultic practice in Rome. His interpretation of the Greek war god Ares, who is imitated by Gaius, discloses his knowledge and unexpected openness:

> Have we not known the power of Ares, not of the one described in myth, but of the one [grasped] by the reason that is in Nature, whom courage has taken for its own? That power keeps off evil and provides help as well as assistance to those who have been wronged, as his name perhaps suggests. It seems to me that Ares has been named thus by derivation from the [Greek] word ἀρήγειν, which means "to help" and [indicates that he is] a destroyer of wars and a creator of peace. The other one, by contrast, is an enemy of peace and a friend of war, transforming tranquility into disorder and strife. (*Legat.* 112–13)

Philo's distinction between myth and rational interpretation echoes well-known Stoic methods as well as Varro's approach to traditional religion.[34] Two diametrically opposed images of Ares are presented in the above passage, one casting him into the highly negative role of the destroyer, the other staging him as a beneficial avenger of the wronged. The negative, mythological image is based on a long Greek tradition ranging from Homer to Chrysippus and Heraclitus.[35] The positive image of Ares, on the other hand, is highly surprising in terms of Greek culture. Yet Philo naturally assumes it, expecting his readers to be familiar with it. The key to understanding Ares's positive image is Roman culture. Philo relies here on Roman traditions concerning Mars as a highly beneficial deity in Roman religion, agriculture, and politics who became amalgamated with Ares, the Greek war god. The Roman worship of Mars reached a new peak under Augustus, who devoted a temple in Rome to Mars Ultor, or "Mars the Avenger." Mars thus became a central focus of the public cult as well as a personal protector of the emperors, revenging attempts at their assassination.[36]

Philo integrates the prominent characteristics of this Roman god when explaining that Ares "keeps off evil and provides help . . . to those who have been wronged" (*Legat.* 113). He could count on his audience to draw a connection between Gaius's imitation of Ares and his special appeal to Mars in 39 CE. During Philo's visit in Rome, the emperor discovered a conspiracy against him and suspected his sisters to be involved. According to Suetonius, Gaius turned to Mars the Avenger, dedicating to him three swords that had been designed to take his life (*Gaius* 24.3). Dio Cassius also tells this story and translates Mars Ultor into the Greek term used by Philo, namely, "Ares the Helper" (Dio 59.22.7).

Philo identifies so much with this Roman image of Mars that he even provides a Greek etymology for the benevolent traits that this god has adopted. "It seems to me," he hesitantly suggests, "that Ares has been named thus by derivation from the word ἀρήγειν, which means 'to help'" (*Legat.* 113). Philo is not only familiar with new religious developments in Rome during his visit there, but also integrates them into Greek discourses. As a Greek intellectual coming to Rome, he has quickly adopted Roman perspectives, offering new impulses to Greek-speaking culture under the empire.

How does the Jewish religion fit into this thoroughly Greco-Roman picture? Philo suggests that the prevalent Stoic approach to religion, based on etymology and allegory, does not apply to the God of Israel, "who is totally untouchable and intangible" and therefore beyond the use of "proper names to begin an explanation" (*Legat.* 6). Unlike Ares, the unutterable name of the Jewish God cannot be used to analyze his nature and beneficence in the world. Moreover, Philo refrains from applying Varro's sociological notions to his own religion, avoiding the idea that the Jews have created their God in their own image. In contrast to Augustine, however, he does not consider the clash between polytheism and monotheism to be a permanent and inherent phenomenon. He rather limits the experience of a conflict between Rome and the Jewish religion to the period of the preceding emperor. Writing under Claudius, Philo is happy to offer a new interpretation of Judaism that fits well into contemporary Roman discourses.

Under Philo's pen in Rome, Judaism becomes an urban philosophy or religion that is centered in the synagogues and promotes civic virtues. Back in Alexandria, Philo expressed his Jewish identity by his hermeneutic engagement with the Jewish Scriptures. While the Greek scholars at the Museum dwelt on the minute details of their canonical texts, foremost Homer's epics, he as a Jew systematically interpreted the books of Genesis and Exodus. As we will see in chapter 9, Philo immersed himself in the biblical text, discussing textual problems and solving them by allegorical interpretations. Such scholarly study, however, was not popular in Rome, where Seneca complained that the Greeks waste their time in "laborious trifles ... on useless literary problems" (*Brev. Vit.* 13.1). Acutely aware of Roman tastes, Philo now constructs Judaism around the synagogues as training grounds for "ancestral philosophy" with laws "promoting orderly conduct" and encouraging thanksgiving to imperial benefactors.[37] This move from scholarship to philosophical religion is dramatic and indicates Philo's intellectual development upon arrival in Rome. It is perhaps not altogether surprising that the Gospel of Luke reflects a similar orientation, singling out "the scribes" as a separate and hypocritical group.[38] The author of Luke, who actively participates in Roman discourses and casts the story of Jesus into a historical mode, also seems to have adopted the typically Roman aversion to trifling scholarship. He appeals to values similar to those of the late Philo to persuade his readers of the worthiness of his religion.

Philo introduces Augustus, on whom Claudius modeled himself, to provide a Roman vision of Judaism. According to Philo, this exemplary emperor is highly aware of the urban nature of the Jewish religion and its long tradition within the city of Rome. He acknowledges the Roman citizenship of its Jewish inhabitants, while tolerating their different ancestral customs. Augustus moreover appreciates the Jewish synagogues in Rome "on the other side of the Tiber" as "meeting places" that serve important social and educational functions. Catacomb inscriptions from Rome suggest that Augustus may have been a patron of one of the oldest congregations in the capital.[39] Philo has probably used historical knowledge when putting his Roman vision of Judaism into the mouth of the emperor.

The Jerusalem Temple, which Philo never mentions in the *Allegorical Commentary*, now plays a central role in his Roman scenario. Augustus is said to have "adorned it by the costliness of votive offerings ... and ordered that for all time and continuously whole burnt sacrifices should be offered every day at his own expense to the highest God (τῷ ὑψίστῳ θεῷ). These sacrifices are carried out until now and will be maintained forever as a memorial of a truly imperial character" (*Legat.* 157). This emphasis on the Jerusalem Temple is remarkable in light of the fact that Philo in the *Allegorical Commentary* rejected the worship of God in houses "of stone and timber" and insisted that the soul is the only place suitable to receive God's presence (*Cher.* 99–100). This move from his earlier to his later position resonates well with imperial culture and Roman fondness for ritual and cult. Not only did the emperor serve as high priest, but ever since Varro's interpretation of the Roman religion, a special link is perceived between cult and religion. Not ancient texts, but ancient rites are regarded as keys to religious truth. Varro stressed that ancient Roman leaders, such as Tarquinius Rufus and Numa, expressed philosophical insights by establishing the Roman cult. Integrating Judaism into this tradition, Philo anticipates authors of the Second Sophistic. Plutarch, for example, incorporates ritual elements in his biography of King Numa, whom he interprets as a philosopher priest.[40] Philo thus inscribes the Jewish religion into a broad Roman discourse, suggesting that Augustus appreciated its ancient temple cult, which recently had been saved from Gaius's sacrilege and could now serve as an "eternal" focus of Judaism under Claudius. Insisting on the congeniality of the Jewish and the Roman religions, Philo also responds to the accusations of Apion, the head of the rivaling Egyptian embassy, who presents Judaism as a degenerated Egyptian cult with prayer houses facing the sun and Temple rites that include the worship of an ass and human sacrifice.[41]

Philo's use of the term *theos hypsistos*, highest God, inscribes Judaism into wider cultural discourses about the gods. It is implied that the Jewish God can be recognized by Romans, such as Augustus, his wife Julia Augusta, and the prefect Petronius, on the basis of their general "philosophy and piety," without their being required to devote themselves exclusively.[42] The author of Luke-Acts also uses the term *theos hypsistos* when describing a pagan perspective on Paul's commitment to the God of Israel (Acts 16:17). Here, too, the author addresses a wider audience, aiming to arouse sympathy for his religion in the context of empire.

Philo constructs Judaism as a dynamic religion that is not limited to any local community. He stresses the vast geographical spread of the Jews "in Europe and Asia," covering the whole of the Roman Empire, much like the author of Acts in his vision of Christian communities throughout the Roman world.[43] Philo, moreover, has urban models in mind and explains Jewish migration in terms of envoys sent from "the Holy City where stands the Temple of the Highest God." Jerusalem is the "metropolis," while cities of actual residence serve the Jews as homelands (*Flacc.* 46). The Jews are described as populous, eager to travel everywhere, and fond of establishing new colonies. They emerge as an energetic and enterprising people, with wide networks in the Mediterranean, much like the Romans or the early Christians in Luke-Acts.

The urban character of Judaism is complemented by the idea of its roots in nature, which enhances its mobility beyond specific local structures. In the historical writings Philo once mentions the Jewish festival of Sukkot, or the Feast of Tabernacles, which he describes as the "national feast of the autumn equinox in which it is the custom of the Jews to live in tents."[44] Philo understands the feast as part of the natural cycle of the year, autumn being the time of the harvest, when people everywhere sleep outside next to their fields and render thanks to God. Biblical explanations of the holiday, grounding it in Israel's particular history during the exodus from Egypt, are not mentioned.

Conclusion

Philo has emerged as a central author in the discourse on power, exile, and religion in first-century Rome. Highly aware of the tyrannical features of Claudius's rule, he develops a sophisticated language of projecting criticism onto Claudius's predecessor Gaius. Like his contemporary Seneca, Philo connects the loss of power, namely, exile, with philosophy, suggesting that it is a space for reasserting and refashioning one's identity. Close parallels appear between the Roman version of exile, exemplified by Flaccus, and the Jewish version of exile, exemplified by the Alexandrian Jews during the pogrom in their city. Within this distinctly Roman context Philo develops a fascinating new notion of Judaism, which he defines by nobility of mind, the Jerusalem Temple, urbanity, and civic virtues. He no longer defines Jewish identity by reference to scholarly activity on the sacred text, as he did in Alexandria, but rather in terms of distinctly Roman values. This dramatic refashioning of Judaism has significant implications for early Christianity and subsequent Greek authors in the Roman Empire.

4 Roman Philosophy and the Jews

Philo is the first Jewish author who wrote independent philosophical treatises that have come down to us. Highly aware of various schools of philosophy and their main exponents, Philo wished not only to offer a new synthesis of Judaism and pagan thought, but also to present his own views on current issues. The philosophical treatises have been rather neglected in modern scholarship, partly because some of them have survived only in an Armenian translation. Moreover, the philosophical significance of these works has thus far not been fully appreciated because they haven't been interpreted in the context of Philo's stay in Rome. As we saw in chapter 1, the philosophical works belong to the mature period of his career and need to be analyzed in light of Roman discourses. Placed on the trajectory of Roman philosophy from Cicero to Seneca, what is Philo's contribution?

This approach may surprise readers who assume that the Romans basically translated the Greek heritage into Latin without adding or challenging anything. Indeed, if Rome offered no original thought, how can Philo, who was well versed in Alexandrian philosophy, have received new inspiration during his embassy to Gaius? Rome, however, played a far more active role than is often assumed. Philo of Larissa provides an illuminating example. Arriving in Rome from Athens, he started as a devout student of the Skeptic Platonist Clitomachus but quickly accommodated to the intellectual atmosphere of the capital and wrote treatises that came as surprise to his students. His "Roman" books even provoked Antiochus to write a critical response, which unfortunately is no longer extant.[1]

Philo of Alexandria goes through a similar intellectual experience and engages Roman discourses. A first indication of his exposure to Rome is his changing perspective on Plato. While praising him in the *Allegorical Commentary* as an "excellent man, one of those admired for their wisdom," and consistently using his work in the interpretation of the Jewish Scriptures, he now sharply criticizes the *Symposium* as a voluptuous affair and even presents it as "laughable" in comparison to the frugal meals of the Jews. Philo criticizes the dialogue as conveying "myths," which seduce and deceive rather than teach the truth. Such derogatory remarks inscribe Philo into Roman discourses and allow him to distance himself from what was perceived as "Greek" licentiousness and fickleness. Josephus, writing one generation later in Rome, says that Plato had been admired by the Greeks but is now "practically mocked and satirized." Lucian, the second-century satirist, writes a *Symposium* that mocks the Platonic tradition and exposes it as decadent.[2] Moving from Alexandria to Rome, Philo thus anticipates certain trends among the Second Sophists and adopts a more critical attitude toward Plato, adding some sarcasm to his original admiration.

The Roman context of Philo's philosophical treatises is also reflected in his implied audience. He now addresses readers who are not familiar with elementary Jewish customs or Egyptian geography. The institution of the synagogue, the idea of the Sabbath, and the division of Egypt into "nomes" need to be explained. Alexandria is moreover identified as "Alexandria in Egypt," a nomenclature that reflects a typically Roman perspective. Philo describes in detail the climate near the city, which would have been known to anyone living there. Roman institutions, by contrast, are taken for granted. Philo refers to celebrations in honor of Germanicus's military victory, assuming that his readers are familiar with the details and the context.[3] His implied audience is thus neither Jewish nor Alexandrian, but primarily Roman. Which topics does Philo select for such an audience, and how does he treat them? The most conspicuous themes of the philosophical treatises are human rationality, providence, the creation, and freedom. Each of these deserves a careful analysis in light of contemporary Roman discourses.

Human Rationality

In a dialogue now extant only in Armenian, Philo addresses the question of whether animals possess the same kind of rationality as human beings. At stake is the status of humans as creatures uniquely endowed with reason and close to God. The dialogue is staged as a discussion between Lysimachus, a younger family member eager to learn, and Philo, who is deeply disturbed by a treatise of his nephew Tiberius Alexander, who expresses the view that animals are rational and morally equal to humans. Alexander's text is brought in by a servant, read aloud, and then criticized by Philo. Lysimachus plays only a marginal role, giving Philo the opportunity to expound his ideas on the controversial issue.[4]

Alexander's argument in favor of animals' rationality is based mainly on observation. He rejects the common assumption of humanity's superiority, which derives in his view merely from physical considerations, such as the fact that animals crawl on the ground and are thus physically lower than humans. Animals are wrongly denied rationality, he insists, just as women are mistakenly relegated to the margins of society. Alexander invites his readers to observe the intelligent behavior of animals and appreciate their knowledge, their ability to learn, and even their ability to choose between good and evil. Occasionally, he directly asks, "Have you not observed?" While admitting that their rationality is not perfect, Alexander insists that animals are endowed with both kinds of rationality, namely, the internal Logos of the mind and the external Logos expressed in speech. He moreover stresses that animals acquire technical skills and virtue, while many birds can even speak with a human voice. The bee, for example, is praised as having intelligence that is "hardly distinguishable from that contemplative ability of the human mind." The spider behaves like an artist, protecting its well-designed net, and the swallow raises its young with the "affection of a nurse or a mid-wife."[5]

Many examples of rational behavior in animals derive from Alexander's experience at animal shows, which he enthusiastically attended. "I saw this very thing," he says with excitement, namely, a fawn dancing and playing with a ball on the stage. "During the performance," he adds, the animal "occasionally stared fearfully at the trainer, I think afraid something may fail." Alexander is especially impressed by the elephants, who behaved in the most domesticated manner, lining up in a row and taking human food and drink on special beds. Some elephants even played the drunkard. Alexander expresses his amazement at the animal performance by stressing that "nowhere else in the world could the appearance of staggering drunks be so demonstrated." Moreover, Alexander explicitly rejects the biblical idea of humanity's exclusive creation in the image of God and stresses that "we are filled with irrational thoughts, have barren and uncultivated minds," while animals are morally excellent.[6]

Philo harshly dismisses these views as unsound, childish, and fashion-able, even saying that they are "sacrilege" and an injustice to both nature and the "sacred mind." He contrasts the inborn qualities of animals to the abil-ity of people to learn, make choices, and apply their minds to diverse tasks. In his view, animals cannot be appreciated in the way Alexander suggests because they act "neither by means of skill in the arts nor by innate reason; they have no particular accomplishment, to tell the truth, except that they work diligently." Philo argues that animals should rather be classified with plants because they do everything by dictate from nature and not as a re-sult of a conscious choice or learning. He sets humans at a fundamentally higher level because only they are capable of conceiving of God and think-ing in abstract terms.[7]

The dispute between Alexander and Philo is presented in a low philo-sophical key. In contrast to other treatises, in which Philo introduces quota-tions from known philosophical works, no school tradition is invoked here. The reader almost gets the impression that Philo spontaneously expresses his personal views in the family's living room. At the same time, however, it is clear that the matter is urgent and Philo applies himself via Alexander's book to a subject that has become fashionable. This urgency is remarkable in light of Philo's far more relaxed discussion in the *Allegorical Commen-tary*, where he explains the biblical account of humanity's creation in the image of God without relating to any controversy. He even conceives of a similarity between humans and animals in the realm of the irrational. Humans, he suggests, are blessed with additional rationality, while their impulses are as instinctive as those of the animals. At that point Philo clearly thinks of humans as superior but not fundamentally different from animals.[8]

How can the difference between the *Allegorical Commentary* and Philo's philosophical writings be explained? The topic may have attracted Philo's special attention in the later part of his career because his nephew grew up in the meantime and formed his own opinion, thus provoking Philo to reevaluate his views and assume a sharper position than previously. On this account, the dialogue is merely a family affair. The polemical fervor of Philo's response, however, suggests otherwise. Much more seems to be at stake than only persuading Alexander. Philo has written his dialogue with Alexander in order to discuss more widely circulating views. As Alexander participated most likely in Philo's embassy and thus was well known among Roman audiences, a dialogue with him could be expected to arouse interest. When looking for the intellectual context of Philo's dialogue, we notice that the topic of the animals' rationality was hotly debated in Rome, while there is no evidence of a similar discussion in Alexandria.

Cicero ushers in the discussion in Rome by presenting the belief in humanity's superiority over animals as an important aspect of Stoic theology. Balbus, Cicero's Stoic spokesman, introduces his position by reference to humans' physical nature: they are raised from the ground and stand upright, thus indicating their higher status in the creation. This is precisely the argument that Alexander in Philo's dialogue attacks as a mistaken acceptance of superficial appearances. Moreover, Balbus polemically dismisses the assumption of equality between humans and animals, suggesting, like Philo, that the man who does not recognize humanity's divine inspiration is "himself devoid of these faculties." In Cicero's dialogue this polemic is directed against the Platonists. Cotta, the Platonic spokesman, responds to Balbus's argument by stressing, like Alexander, that a person's mind is neither divinely endowed nor very exceptional.[9]

The Stoic view of animals became dominant in Rome. Cicero opens his ethical treatise *On Duties* with an emphatic assertion of humanity's superiority. Only human beings are in his view endowed with reason, memory, and speech as well as an ability to search for the truth and plan ahead. Human beings possess the necessary tools for moral behavior, which is denied to animals. Cicero's position is echoed a century later in Seneca's writings, which contain a separate epistle on the question of animal rationality. Seneca reacts here to the kind of arguments Alexander presented, namely, arguments in favor of animal rationality based on an observation of nature. Seneca explains why the bee is not as wise as has been claimed and why animals simply act out of a natural impulse rather than learning and conscious choice. The Stoic notion of humanity's exclusive rationality is confirmed by denying animals' intellectual and moral qualifications.[10]

In light of Cicero and Seneca, Philo's dialogue on the rationality of animals emerges as a significant contribution to a specifically Roman discussion. While Philo could certainly hope that his arguments would attract attention in Rome, he would have encountered little interest in his hometown of Alexandria, where the topic is not attested in the extant sources. Philo defends a known Stoic position and stresses, like Seneca, humanity's learning, self-determination, and proximity to God. The arguments he attributes to Alexander moreover resurface in Roman discussions as Platonic positions, which are of continuous concern until Seneca's work. Philo clearly assumes the majority Stoic position, while Alexander plays the role of the Platonic Other.

Philo's move from more lenient views in his earlier Alexandrian years to a strong Stoic position in his later writings illuminates the split on this issue in the following centuries. The late Philo embraces a position that became predominant in the Christian West and was forcefully defended by Justin Martyr and Augustine. Pagan Platonists, by contrast, further developed the lenient tradition visible in Philo's early writings and embraced Plato's idea of the soul's transmigration to animals. The Second Sophists Plutarch and Philostratus, for example, show genuine sympathy toward animals and appreciate their humanlike intelligence. Porphyry and Plotinus bring this position to a climax. Philo thus stands at an important threshold, leaving behind a characteristically Eastern perspective and adopting a view that was to shape the Latin West.[11]

Providence

Providence is the topic of another dialogue with Alexander that has survived in Armenian, with a good portion of the original Greek preserved by the church father Eusebius. Scholars have already investigated the possible sources of Philo's treatise, often unfortunately overlooking the distinction between his own and Alexander's voice. I take a different route and investigate the specific nature of Philo's arguments in light of their broader philosophical context. What did Philo believe to be true and why? How does he position himself in current debates, especially with regard to the known dispute between Stoics and Platonists? While Platonists generally followed the *Timaeus* and assumed the demiurge's "fatherly" maintenance of the world, they denied his care for individual humans and the details of nature. On Platonist views, god is too transcendent to be involved in the specifics of the world and humanity. The Stoics, by contrast, adopted a more immanent notion of the deity and identified a divine presence in their very lives and surroundings.[12]

Alexander challenges Philo's notion of divine providence by pointing to the "vast welter and confusion of things" in the world. There is no justice, he insists, "or do you alone not realize that good things come in abundance upon the worst and vilest of men?" In strikingly similar terms Cotta, the Platonic spokesman in Cicero's dialogue, rejects Stoic notions of providence by quoting the following poetic line: "For if they [the gods] cared for men, good men would prosper and bad men come to grief; but this is not so." Moreover, Philo's late contemporary Seneca devotes a whole treatise to the issue of divine providence. His conversation partner, Lucilius, provoked him by similar doubts: "If providence rules the world, why do many bad things happen to good men?"[13] The topic of Philo's dialogue with his nephew Alexander thus resonates with a lively discussion in Rome that focuses on the question of theodicy and divine involvement in human life.

Philo responds to Alexander's doubts by stressing God's benevolence: "God is not a tyrant," he says, "but a king invested with a kind and law-abiding sovereignty, who governs the whole heaven and earth with justice." Philo makes considerable efforts to prove divine providence in life, assuming the characteristic position of the Stoics vis-à-vis the Platonists. He distinguishes between real and apparent goods, insisting that things commonly held to be evil are not really so, because they pertain only to the external realm and have no intrinsic value. God, who ministers the world, acknowledges only real goods. A righteous person, Philo further explains, despises appearances and realizes that poverty or illness is not necessarily a bad thing. Vice versa, wicked people suffer from a bad conscience and restlessness, never attaining tranquility and happiness. Philo's argument leads to the known Stoic conclusion that all that matters is the right attitude toward what happens in the world. Circumstances are not in our control and thus beyond our moral responsibility, so it is our moral attitude that matters and constitutes the only necessary criterion for virtue and happiness. Good people can by definition not suffer from strokes of "bad luck" because they simply do not accept them as such. As Marcus Aurelius, Stoic philosopher and Roman emperor, would subsequently put it, "Everything is perception."[14]

Philo argues for divine providence also by appeal to the larger picture. He says that even things that are bad for some individuals still benefit either the world or humanity at large and are therefore consistent with divine providence. God may, for example, use strong storms or floods to purge the earth, even "if these sometimes harm sailors traveling out of season or tillers of the land." There is nothing "astonishing" about such casualties, Philo explains, because "they are only a small portion, while his care is for the whole human race." This means that people encountering unfavorable circumstances should ask themselves whether those circumstances have another side that serves the wider community and were purposely designed by God. It is implied that certain individuals are sometimes expected to offer a sacrifice for the benefit of humanity, just as athletes need to accept that the gymnasiarch may change the schedule of training for the benefit of the whole group even though that may not equally suit everyone.[15]

Toward the end of the dialogue Philo mentions "two theories" or "treatises" (λόγους) accounting for the benefit of venomous reptiles. These references indicate that he self-consciously engages current debates on the topic of divine providence and positions himself in the context of other voices in favor of God's care for the details of his creation. Philo distinguishes between those who argue for the medical usefulness of poison in healing potions and others who regard venomous animals as agents of divine punishment (*Prov.* 2.60–61). In both views, creatures that are apparently destructive turn out to fulfill a positive role in the world and reflect God's careful design. While Philo does not mention the author of these theories, they must have belonged to the Stoic school.

Philo's arguments resonate well with known Stoic positions expressed in Rome. Already Cicero's Stoic spokesman Balbus stresses "that man has been cared for by divine providence." Humans are not only constituted in a way far superior to other creatures, but also enjoy continuous divine care. In fact, the whole world, including animals, has been created with a view to their benefit for humanity, providing all the necessities. As if answering Alexander's query in Philo's dialogue, Balbus stresses that the care and providence of the immortal gods is bestowed "not only on the human race as a whole, but also on individuals (*etiam singulis*)." The proof is given by the portents of the future, which guide humans to take proper action.[16]

Seneca also addresses the topic of divine providence in response to doubts raised regarding individuals. His first argument strikingly resembles Philo's and focuses on the attitude of the righteous toward the world. Insisting that "no evil can befall a good man," Seneca argues that apparent blows of bad luck or hardship are nothing but a training ground for the righteous to strengthen virtue. One should not complain about fate but realize that "not what you endure, but how you endure it, is important." Using almost the same language as Philo, Seneca says that "things that seem to be evils are not really so." Strong and virtuous characters are regularly exposed to hardships in order to prove and perfect themselves. Philo's second argument about the larger picture also resurfaces in Seneca's writings. In his *Natural Questions* the Roman philosopher deals with many apparently harmful accidents of nature, such as earthquakes and floods, arguing that their causes often remain unknown and thus lead to perplexity. From a larger or divine perspective, however, there is nothing detrimental to them, as they serve other parts of the universe.[17]

Regarding the issue of providence, Philo emerges as deeply embedded in Roman discourses. He positions himself in the intellectual milieu of the imperial capital, assuming the prevalent Stoic position in favor of divine providence for individuals. By criticizing Alexander he dismisses the Platonic view, which serves as an important yet marginal Other in Cicero's and Seneca's discussions. The topical relevance of Philo's dialogue in Rome is all the more visible in light of the fact that Alexandrian intellectuals do not seem to have paid particular attention to this topic. No extant source from Alexandria addresses it. One may, of course, doubt the significance of this absence, given that so many ancient sources are lost. Yet the same statistics apply to Roman sources as well. Even though many of them are no longer extant, they still preserve a lively discussion about providence in Rome. Intellectuals in the capital of the empire may have been prompted to take a special interest in this question, because life under the Principate was notoriously unstable, if not dangerous. Philo, who does not discuss issues of providence in his *Allegorical Commentary,* arrives in Rome and integrates so speedily into local discourses that he devotes a whole dialogue to providence, defending the Stoic position. Philo's contribution creates an important bridge between Cicero and Seneca, presenting another signpost in the development of Roman philosophy.

Creation and Conflagration

Questions pertaining to the creation of the world occupy Philo in two of his philosophical treatises—the dialogue *On Providence* and the treatise *On the Eternity of the World.* Unfortunately, the beginning of the former is not preserved, not even in the Armenian translation, thus making it difficult to know how Philo introduces the topic of the creation. It is clear, however, that he considers the creation of the world as an important aspect of divine providence and rejects Aristotelian notions of its eternity. He moreover conceives of the creation as a shaping of preexisting material by God, the unmoved mover. Philo quotes a central passage from Plato's *Timaeus,* stressing that the Greek philosopher assumes a creator god very similar to the one described by Moses.[18] Both the Greek philosopher and the lawgiver of the Jews conceive of the creation of the world, which is from that moment onward indestructible.

Philo discusses these topics again in *On the Eternity of the World*, where he confronts various philosophical arguments against the notion of a creation. The second part of the treatise, where Philo apparently explained his own views, is lost, but the first part offers important insights into his overall approach. Throughout the treatise Philo pays special attention to the Stoics, famous for their theory of the conflagration, according to which the world is periodically created and then destroyed by fire. Philo is keen to refute this Stoic position and stresses that the idea of a conflagration contradicts the school's own assumption of providence. The liveliness of his interest is remarkable in view of the *Allegorical Commentary*, in which Philo briefly mentions the conflagration, dismissing it as a "marvelmongers' fable" (*Her.* 228). The topic has obviously become more urgent in Philo's later thought, prompting him to address it in a separate treatise and to introduce a significant amount of relevant secondary literature.

Philo is agitated by the fact that a central authority for the creation and indestructibility of the world, namely, Plato's *Timaeus*, has been interpreted wrongly and even used as a proof for the opposite view: "Some believe, producing falsifications (σοφιζόμενοι), that according to Plato the cosmos is said to be created not in the sense of possessing a beginning of creation, but rather in the sense that either, if it had been created, it would not have been formed in any other way than the one mentioned or else that its parts are observed to come into being and undergo change" (*Aet.* 14). Aristotle already had criticized some students of Plato for interpreting the *Timaeus* metaphorically, as if it were a mere image "for the purpose of instruction." Philo certainly has such interpreters in mind. Yet he also reacts to something more severe, namely, a falsification of Plato's text. This meaning of σοφίζομαι is attested by Eusebius, who justifies himself against charges "that I falsify these [previously mentioned verses]." Eusebius's suspicion is appropriate, since he has indeed manipulated the biblical text.[19] A similar text manipulation must have happened in the case of Plato's *Timaeus*. Who amended the text, and how did Philo know about it?

Alexander of Aphrodisias (third century CE) identifies the Platonic text Philo quotes, that is, *Timaeus* 27c, as a prime locus of ideological text emendation. The second-century Platonist Tauros, known as a metaphorical reader of Plato, apparently used a version of the text that perfectly suited his interpretation and implied that Plato had not advocated the creation of the world, but only temporarily entertained the notion and then dismissed it. John Dillon has suggested that Tauros himself emended the text. Yet Philo's complaint about a tampering with Plato's text points to an earlier emendation.[20]

Can such a metaphorical interpreter and emendator of the *Timaeus* be identified? Whom may Philo have known to engage in such creative hermeneutics? A very likely candidate is Thrasyllus, Philo's slightly older contemporary, who was also of Alexandrian origin and moved to Rome, where he played an influential role at Tiberius's court. Among other things, Thrasyllus was involved in editing Plato's works. Considering philosophy as a sacred rite, he was not reluctant to introduce subtle changes to the texts in order to adapt them to his own philosophical tendencies. Unfortunately, *Timaeus* 27c is not mentioned in the available fragments. Could Thrasyllus nevertheless have been responsible for this important change of the Platonic text? Thrasyllus's theory of a twofold Logos makes this prospect likely. The idea of an imminent Logos, which is the ultimate source of all existence as well as its continuous controller, would seem to support a metaphorical reading of the *Timaeus*.[21] Thrasyllus may well have emended the mythological image of the Platonic creator god, suggesting instead the more philosophical notion of a prime cause on which the cosmos is continually dependent.

The precise meaning of the *Timaeus* was the subject of a lively debate in Rome. Cicero's partial translation and explanation of this text had drawn new attention to it. While Cicero introduced in his translation a certain Stoicizing dimension, he insisted that "Plato's god in the *Timaeus* created the world," while according to Aristotle things "have always existed."[22] Cicero thus kept the Platonic and the Aristotelian traditions strictly apart and drew attention to Plato's original image of a creator god. If Thrasyllus indeed favored a metaphorical reading of the *Timaeus,* as is likely, he easily could have regarded it necessary to counter Cicero's work by circulating the "proper" version of the dialogue.

Philo engages precisely these Roman discussions and presents the different sides of the dispute. Like Cicero, he distinguishes between Aristotle's and Plato's approaches but gives more room to Stoic positions. Philo insists that the literal reading is "more truthful" to the fact that Plato "throughout the whole treatise" calls the demiurge "Father and Maker and Artificer." Philo moreover adduces Aristotle as a testimony to the original meaning of the *Timaeus*. Praising Aristotle as Plato's most excellent and reliable student, Philo draws attention to his famous criticism of Plato's theory of the creation, which is based on its literal meaning. Philo thus contributes to a lively debate in Rome that has no parallel in Alexandria.[23]

Philo's main concern throughout *On the Eternity of the World* is Stoicism. He reports that the "great mass" of Stoic philosophers assumes the conflagration of the world, which he emphatically rejects on theological grounds. If numerous worlds were created and destroyed, he argues, the creator God cannot be perfectly good and omnipotent because he would either create imperfect worlds or repeat identical creations without any apparent benefit. In Philo's view, the notion of the conflagration denies divine providence and even implies the death of the demiurge. Philo attacks especially Chrysippus (third century BCE) as the main exponent of the Stoic dogma. He introduces some lines from his treatise *On Increase* and mentions two additional aspects of his theory, in each case providing a refutation from nature. Philo stresses that this kind of philosophy is "inconsistent" with the school's own approach, because it questions providence, a pillar of Stoic theology. One generation later Plutarch, whom we have already encountered as congenial to Philo, criticizes the Stoic notion of the conflagration. He accuses especially Chrysippus of "contradicting himself" and rejects the Stoic position as impious.[24]

Among contemporary philosophers who oppose the Stoic notion of the conflagration, Philo distinguishes himself by considering the diversity of views in this school. Rather than dismissing the Stoics *tout court*, he praises some who have recognized Chrysippus's mistake and abandoned the notion of the conflagration:

> Conquered by the truth and [the arguments of] the opponents, some have changed their views, because beauty has the power to call us to her and the truth is divinely beautiful, as much as falsehood is extraordinarily ugly. Thus Boethus of Sidon and Panaetius, powerful supporters of the Stoic doctrines, in as much as they were divinely inspired, left behind the conflagrations and regenerations and deserted to a holier doctrine, namely, the indestructibility of the whole cosmos. It is also said that Diogenes in his youth subscribed to the doctrine of the conflagration, but in later years entertained doubts and considered attacking it. (*Aet.* 76–77)

Philo identifies here specific Stoic philosophers—Boethus and Panaetius of the second century BCE and their teacher Diogenes of Babylon. This specification is remarkable in view of the fact that Philo in the *Allegorical*

Commentary never mentions Stoics by name, even though he refers to Stoic notions. His attitude toward Stoicism has become visibly more differentiated, stressing the diversity of its representatives. Moreover, Philo assumes his readers' familiarity with Stoic philosophers and their interest in the details of their views. Roman readers, whom Cicero introduced to Panaetius's ideas, were especially likely to take an interest in Philo's discussion.[25]

Philo describes a kind of conversion of important Stoics, who experienced a "divine inspiration," learned the truth about the world, and adopted a "holier doctrine." He points to a significant gap between recent Stoics and the extreme views of Chrysippus, who was deserted even by his own followers. Philo stresses that the lawgiver of the Jews long ago professed the creation and indestructibility of the world, thus anticipating the enlightened Stoics (*Aet.* 19). A broad consensus emerges between the Jews, literal readers of the *Timaeus,* and enlightened Stoics. This image resonates extremely well with Roman discourses, in which Panaetius became central and eclipsed Chrysippus. Indeed, the latter's idea of the conflagration of the world became rather obsolete after Philo. Seneca, for example, does not consider the topic worthy of special attention.

Freedom

The last topic that Philo discusses at length in his later philosophical works is freedom of choice. His treatise *Every Good Man Is Free* follows upon a now lost work, *Every Bad Man Is a Slave.* Philo initially positions himself vis-à-vis those who turn wisdom into sophistry and cannot fathom an inversion of familiar notions. Such people will consider it "absurd and puzzling" to regard a man as exiled who is actively involved in the politics of his city. Vice versa, a man without a country and home is unlikely to be acknowledged as a respectable citizen. For some, Philo admits, "it is contrary to reason" to call the poor rich and a "fantastic dream" to regard those living in palaces as poor. Philo thus introduces himself as a paradoxical thinker who challenges standard views. Such a position is typically Stoic. Philo indicates as much when praising Zeno, the school's founder, as an exceptionally virtuous thinker who challenged accepted views. "Many," he expects, "will rail" at Zeno's maxim that the wise and the foolish are so far apart that they cannot talk to each other. Philo concludes that "statements considered paradoxical" always require more proofs than normative ones.[26]

Having placed himself within the Stoic tradition of paradoxical phi-losophy, Philo distinguishes between physical and mental slavery. An em-peror, who enjoys all civil liberties, may still be a slave to his own desires or fears. True freedom is in Philo's view not a physical or civic possession, but a spiritual disposition. While people "are masters of bodies, the vices and pas-sions rule over the soul," he explains. They are only free of an external force, while a man who is spiritually free "achieves liberty from the power of his passions." Philo says that nobody inquires into the first sense of freedom because cases of political liberty and its loss are clear to everyone. Personal freedom from the chains of the passions, on the other hand, still requires study (*Prob.* 17–18).

Philo defines true, inner freedom as a willing acceptance of circum-stances. While a slavish man is constantly forced to act against his own judgment, the free man or philosopher chooses to adopt the right attitude toward the world. In Philo's view, a free man "adjusts himself and his af-fairs to fit the present occasion and willingly as well as patiently holds out to the blows of fortune . . . and nobly endures all that befalls him." The key concept here is the "willing" and "noble" acceptance of fortune, which is achieved through freedom from the passions. The free person is not prompted to emotional reactions by difficult and unexpected situa-tions. Philo has already called for restraint of judgment in the context of providence and now uses this typically Stoic argument to highlight a man's freedom in situations of suffering that easily enslave the mind. He stresses the political dimension and insists that no threats, however dreadful, can subdue the truly free, who will even accept torture with indifference. The slavish person, by contrast, will be driven by a desire to live and bow down to force.[27]

Philo shares the Stoic distinction between virtue, which is the only real good, and indifferent things, which the wise will not choose. He argues that a good man cannot be compelled or enslaved because he desires only things "which have their origin in virtue and these by his very nature he cannot fail to obtain." Philo focuses the discussion of freedom on a proper orienta-tion toward those goals that are in one's power. A free person is defined as someone with a rational awareness of "what is up to us," as the Roman phi-losopher Epictetus would subsequently formulate it.[28] Philo and Epictetus agree that the choice of virtue is entirely within our power and thus offers the wise true freedom.

Philo engages a Stoic discussion in Rome that has no parallel in Alexandria and is not mentioned in the *Allegorical Commentary*. Cicero once more provides the starting point. He devotes a whole chapter of his *Stoic Paradoxes* to the double claim "that only the good man is free and that every foolish man is a slave." Cicero even quotes this paradox in the original Greek and then provides Roman examples. Like Philo, he distinguishes between social and political standing on one hand and inner freedom on the other. Freedom is defined as "the power to live as you will." This means following the things that are morally right, even if the circumstances are not favorable. According to the Stoics, Cicero explains, the good and free man is guided only by his "own will and judgment." In his treatise *On Duties* Cicero speaks again about the ideal of inner freedom, arguing that a courageous man is free from all passion and does not submit to accidents of fortune even though he is involved in society. Death is to be preferred to slavery. Cicero expresses these ideas after the Roman Republic had fallen and he personally had lost his public roles.[29]

Seneca discusses the topic of freedom in close connection with current politics and the coercion of the wise man, which he himself has experienced. He adopts a typically Stoic position and reverses everyday terms, while giving new emphasis to the choice of death. Seneca admires people who have chosen freedom and even suicide in order to maintain their integrity in the face of a despot. Practicing freedom often means "practicing death." Seneca also develops a religious notion of freedom not mentioned by Cicero, but later stressed by Epictetus, namely, the freedom to follow God. He urges his readers not to be dragged along by the events of life, but rather to accept them willingly by following God, their ultimate originator.[30]

Philo emerges as an active participant in specifically Roman discourses. He shares the paradoxical approach of the Stoics to the notion of the good man's freedom, discussing it, like Cicero and Seneca, in the context of politics. Anticipating Seneca, Philo is especially sensitive to the coercive political circumstances in the Roman Empire and stresses the freedom to choose death and follow God. For him, "in very truth only he is free who takes God as his leader." Epictetus, who taught philosophy in Rome until he was expelled by Domitian, developed these themes even further. A famous chapter of his *Discourses* treats the subject of freedom and defines the free man as one "who lives as he wills, who is subject to neither compulsion, nor hindrance, nor force." The wicked man, by contrast, is enslaved by his passions and lives in the illusion that social standing has intrinsic value. Like Philo, Epictetus stresses the freedom one gains by committing oneself to God. He prays to Zeus to "lead me on" and encourages his readers to accept willingly any of God's decrees.[31]

Philo supports his philosophical argument for true freedom with many examples from history. He is interested in expressions of freedom vis-à-vis tyrants, which he has already mentioned in his historical writings. Now the story of the Xanthians, which "is told in recent years," is adduced. Philo admires their willingness to die rather than submit to Brutus's sack of their city. Their suicide is praiseworthy because it shows that they "completed their allotted time as free men inspired by a spirit of free and noble resolution." Moreover, Philo praises the Indian philosopher Calanus as an exemplary free person. When Alexander the Great tried to force Calanus to follow him as a courtier on his expeditions, he resisted in a "most appropriate and worthy fashion." Philo admires that his "speech was full of frankness and his mind even more of freedom." Calanus "could not be enslaved," and his letter to Alexander exhibits his remarkable courage.[32]

Both of these examples resonate with Roman discourses, one of them directly referring to Roman history, the other using Alexander in a typically Roman fashion. From Cicero on, Alexander is disliked in Rome and presented as a childish Oriental king, while he continued to be appreciated in the Greek East, especially in Alexandria, as a potential threat to Rome. Philo interprets the known story about Alexander's encounter with the Indian philosophers as a conflict between Greek and Roman values. Calanus is made to write to Alexander that "we are not like the philosophers of the Greeks," who "exercised speeches for their national assemblies; with us deeds follow upon words and words accord with deeds." Philo attributes for the first time central items of Roman identity to Calanus, who advocates practical ethics in contrast to Greek rhetoric and ostentation. This image of Calanus echoes stereotypes in Rome, where already the republican Cato said that "the words of the Greeks are born on their lips, but those of the Romans in their hearts." Cato moreover dismisses Socrates as a "mighty prattler" and Carneades as a Greek philosopher seducing Roman youths to acquire "a reputation based on mere words." These stereotypes were repeated by Strabo, who spoke of the Greeks as the "most talkative of all men."[33] Philo's Calanus echoes these views and projects a distinctly Roman ideal of freedom that is based on open speech and practical ethics.

How Do the Jews Fit In?

We have already seen that Philo integrates the Jews into his discussion of human rationality. He suggests that his dispute with Alexander is not only about the status of animals, but also about the authority of the Jewish Scriptures. While Alexander departs from biblical notions of humanity's uniqueness, Philo prides himself in upholding them. Offering typically Stoic arguments for humanity's superiority, Philo suggests that the Bible is congenial to contemporary philosophy. A similar correspondence is conspicuous with regard to the creation of the world, as Philo stresses that Moses anticipated Greek philosophers by insisting on the "created and imperishable nature of the world" (*Aet.* 19). Judaism thus emerges as highly relevant to contemporary philosophical debates.

In *Every Good Man Is Free* Philo presents the Jews as a group of philosophers. He initially suggests a dependence of Stoicism on Jewish sources, as Zeno "seems to have drawn this thought from the fountain of the legislation of the Jews." The biblical story about Esau, who will be a "slave" to his brother, is interpreted as a Stoic argument about the inequality of the righteous and the wicked.[34] In this reading, Isaac's preference of Jacob no longer conveys a personal predilection supported by God, but rather reflects the brother's respective moral behavior. Esau, who will choose evil, will enslave himself. This image of the biblical figure enables Philo to inscribe the Jewish tradition into Stoic philosophy, suggesting that they convey the same message about life. He even conjectures that the biblical story inspired Zeno to formulate his own thoughts on the matter.

Philo moreover points to the Essenes as an example that "Palestinian Syria also has not failed to produce high moral excellence." This somewhat apologetic introduction immediately shows Philo's concern for the reputation of the Jews in Palestine. He wishes to place them among the virtuous men of the Greco-Roman world, whom he discusses in his treatise on freedom. The Roman historian Pliny (ca. 23–79 CE) also mentions the Essenes, praising them as "remarkable beyond all the other tribes of the world" because they renounce sexual desire and live a solitary life. If Pliny thought that the Essenes were of interest to a Roman audience, Philo must have assumed the same. Like Pliny, he starts his exposition with a geographical sketch of the area, thus integrating himself into the Roman tradition of ethnography. Philo points to the Essenes' unique devotion and stresses that they "sanctify their minds to God, living in remote places, because they are determined to avoid the wickedness of the cities." The Essenes, he further explains, are "all free" and tolerate no slaves in their midst. They also receive training in philosophy, leaving "the logical part to quibbling verbalists," while engaging "only in that part of philosophy which deals with the existence of God and the creation of the world."[35] In short, the Essenes implement Stoic ideals, which they have acquired by diligently studying "the laws of the fathers." Philo stresses the connection between biblical studies and Stoic ethics, both leading to love of virtue, belief in divine providence, and freedom from the passions. Philo concludes his description with resounding Roman compliments to the Essenes: "The philosophy, which is free from the pedantry of Greek wordiness, has produced such athletes of virtue by setting exercises for practicing laudable actions by which unenslaved liberty is firmly established" (*Prob.* 88).

The Roman contours of Philo's Essenes are confirmed by the fragments of his treatise *Hypothetica* as preserved by Eusebius. Philo presents the Essenes here as a group of philosophers who enjoy "the only real freedom," namely, freedom from the passions, and orient their lives toward worthy goods. They are "lovers of frugality" and shun luxury and private property. Philo is concerned about the enslavement of the soul by love lures and family ties, all of which the Essenes avoid. Eusebius makes an intriguing suggestion about Philo's implied audience. On grounds that can no longer be reconstructed, he says that Philo wrote his *Hypothetica* "in defense of the Jews against their accusers." If this is correct, Philo may have addressed his treatise to an audience familiar with Apion and Chaeremon, who used their embassy in Rome to write vicious accusations of the Jews. Chaeremon was moreover concerned to show that his native tradition conformed to contemporary Stoicism, describing the Egyptian priests as true philosophers who devote "their whole life to the contemplation and vision of the divine" and pursue "philosophical truth."[36] Philo's efforts in the philosophical treatises are probably aimed at countering Egyptian diplomacy and correcting current prejudices about the Jews by showing the philosophical nature of their religion.

The Therapeutae form another group of Jewish philosophers whom Philo interprets in a distinctly Roman mode. While the Essenes are said to pursue a life of action, the Therapeutae are introduced as embracing a life of "contemplation." Philo initially illustrates their philosophical lifestyle by their sober symposia, which he contrasts to others where people get drunk, assault each other in beastly fashion, and show off their material riches. Parallel to his historical writings, he introduces a distinctly ironic dimension by invoking an otherwise unknown saying by a "comic poet" who makes fun of the ravishing effect of wine. Philo presents an exaggerated picture of these Other symposiasts, who become violent and are likely to kill each other. Such images are surely meant to prompt the reader to smile at Greek excesses, which are visible even in their most classical version preserved by Plato and Xenophon. "The disciples of Moses," on the other hand, are constructed as stern philosophers who "have dedicated their own lives and themselves to knowledge and the contemplation of the acts of nature."[37] Devotion to nature, sobriety, and an earnest search for the truth are thus the Jewish and Roman alternatives to Greek frivolity.

Positioning himself vis-à-vis the Classical Greek tradition, Philo praises the Therapeutae for serving no wine at their symposia. The paradigmatic Jewish philosophers abstain from wine and consume only minimal food, such as bread and occasionally some hyssop. Philo praises their abstinence by stressing that "wine acts like a drug producing folly, and costly meals stir up that most insatiable of animals, desire." This interpretation closely conforms to the ideal of abstinence advocated by Stoic philosophers from Zeno onward. Seneca especially prides himself in having completely abstained from wine. Already in his early work *De Ira* he demands the eradication rather than moderation of pleasure, relegating sympotic excesses to the realm of Greek culture. Alexander the Great is criticized for getting so drunk at a banquet that he stabbed his best friend. Mark Antony is accused of submitting to wine and to the Egyptian queen Cleopatra, who "drove him into foreign habits and un-Roman vices." "When heavy with wine," Seneca remarks, "he thirsted for blood."[38] Philo's image of the abstemious Jewish philosophers perfectly fits this Roman rhetoric. Jews and Judaism emerge on the Roman side of a deep cultural division between philosophical restraint and Greek excess.

The discussion at the Jewish symposium also counters Greek traditions. Philo describes a highly controlled setting where a senior member of the group expounds the Bible, shunning clever rhetoric and superficial effect. The rest of the group listens silently, indicating their "praise by looks or nods." The president of the group speaks only when absolute silence prevails. His exposition is addressed not to equals, but to an audience "not similarly clear-sighted."[39] The members of the group are not expected to argue with him, as in a Classical Greek symposium, but rather to try to follow the course of his exposition. According to Philo, "they listen with ears pricked up and eyes fixed on him always in one and the same posture, indicating comprehension and acceptance by nods and glances, their praise of the speaker by cheerfulness and slightly turning their faces, their questions by a gentler movement of the head and the finger-tip of their right hand" (*Cont.* 77).

Applause and acceptance rather than open discussion characterize the Jewish symposium. Unable to argue with the speaker, the members of the group aspire only to imbibe his words. There are no traces of intellectual confrontation, frivolity, or jokes. The austere and highly educational nature of the Jewish symposium that Philo has constructed resonates with Roman discourses. Valerius Maximus, a Roman intellectual of the Tiberian age, highlights the value of a philosophical family meal. In his account the Roman symposium strikingly resembles that of Philo's Therapeutae: both assume a private setting with a clearly defined group of participants who enjoy community life beyond the meal. Both include women and cherish solemnity and decorum. The atmosphere at the Roman table is strictly hierarchical, the youth rendering respect to the elders and speaking only "sparingly and modestly" in their presence. Maximus concludes his praise of the Roman symposium by an emphatic rejection of Greek traditions, asking, "What Athens, what school of philosophy, what alien born studies should I prefer to this domestic discipline?" Philo undoubtedly would have agreed that this praise also applies to the Therapeutae. He is the first Greek-speaking author who adopts typically Roman views of the symposium, inscribing his ancestral tradition into the narrative of the empire. Plutarch expresses himself similarly in his *Table Talks*, where he raises fundamental questions about the Greek tradition of the philosophical symposium. Reflecting on Plato's canonical model, he ultimately proposes a distinctly Roman solution with a clear educational purpose and recommends that "matters of inquiry must be in themselves rather simple and easy, the topics familiar . . . so that the less intellectual guests may be neither stifled nor turned away."[40]

Conclusion

We have seen that the subjects of Philo's philosophical treatises are of lively interest in Rome, where they had been discussed since Cicero. Philo's arguments are thoroughly Stoic, while his nephew Alexander regularly defends Platonic positions. Philo emerges as a philosopher who contributes to an ongoing discussion in Rome and often adds a new dimension that anticipates Seneca. The Jews are moreover inscribed into contemporary discourses and presented as philosophers who live by both their ancestral tradition and the values of Roman Stoicism. The Jews are distinguished now from the Greeks and described by Roman notions. Philo has speedily integrated into Roman culture, which he encountered during the embassy, and shown an exceptional intellectual curiosity. His openness to Stoicism was prepared by his budding interest in this school back in Alexandria, but in Rome it increased to an unexpected extent. His versatility also must have been encouraged by the political situation in Rome, especially the rivalry with the Egyptian embassy to Gaius.

Philo's achievement is impressive, as he offers the first extant Roman interpretation of Judaism. One generation later Josephus follows in his footsteps, whether or not he is directly inspired by him. Parallel to Philo's criticism of Plato's *Symposium* and Greek "talkativeness," Josephus mocks Greek historiography and Greek culture, praising the Jews for avoiding "studied words" and committing themselves to action. Josephus moreover shares the ideal of Stoic perseverance up to death and presents the Jews as risking their lives in the defense of the Torah. Providence is a central theme throughout the *Antiquities,* where the divine presence is seen in the lives of the individual heroes. Moreover, in response to Apion Josephus sketches the principles of Judaism, highlighting, like Philo, the creation of the world and the providential demiurge. Tannaitic rabbis, too, engage Roman philosophical discourses. Tractate *Avot* in the Mishnah sets up Stoic ethics as a norm of Judaism. Leaving behind apocalyptic tendencies of the Second Temple period and avoiding Platonic flights of the soul to heaven, the rabbis of the second century CE adopt a highly this-worldly philosophy that focuses on the individual self in a providentially guided world. The rabbis in *Avot* stress practical over theoretical ethics and encourage their readers "not to be overly angry." Awareness of death is recommended as an incentive to live one's life fully, respecting both one's individual value and society. Moreover, the symposium, which the rabbis prescribe for Passover, is remarkably Roman, as it takes place in a hierarchical family setting and is ritualized around religious themes to be transmitted to the next generation. Wine is offered, but in the right measure, so the symposium does not degenerate into the Greek custom of an indulgent after-party, which is referred to by a term reverberating the Greek language (אפיקומן).[41]

Moreover, Philo's philosophy in his later treatises has implications for early Christianity, which turns in the mid–second century to philosophy in a Roman mode. Justin Martyr, writing as a Greek-speaking author in Rome, highlights strikingly similar features in the Christian religion. Directly addressing Roman readers and eager to avoid the image of Greek verbosity, Justin introduces Christ as speaking in "brief and concise words," as he was "no sophist." Moreover, the biblical creation account is highlighted and said to correspond to Plato's *Timaeus*, proving the Gnostics, who reject the creator god as evil, to be wrong. The conflagration of the world is discussed on several occasions, Justin accepting it, but not in a Stoic sense, as he hastens to explain. In his view, God is not subject to the fire but uses it to punish the wicked, thus proving that there is divine providence as well as complete freedom of choice. Finally, Justin's Roman Christians behave in the same self-disciplined manner as Philo's Therapeutae: every Sunday they study "the memoirs of the apostles or the writings of the prophets," being instructed by the president to imitate the good examples. Here, too, no messy Greek symposium is envisaged, but a dignified, hierarchical conversation with clear educational purposes.[42]

PART 2

Philo's *Exposition* in a Roman Context

5 Creation Theology and Monotheism

Philo plays an important role in the emergence of a monotheistic creed among Second Temple Jews. Probably coining the term "polytheistic doctrine" (ἡ πολύθεος δόξα), which he contrasts to the acknowledgment of one God in Judaism, Philo grounds his argument in the biblical creation account. The creation is so central to his approach that he opens the *Exposition of the Law* with a special treatise devoted to it, which is followed by the biographies of the patriarchs and four books on biblical law. The English translation of Philo's works does not preserve this original order and instead places the *Allegorical Commentary* on Genesis 2 after the treatise *On the Creation,* thus offering a running commentary on the initial chapters of Genesis. This editorial decision gravely obscures Philo's overall project in the *Exposition,* his most well-designed series of works.[1] Through numerous cross-references and signposts for the reader he stresses that the account of the creation is followed by the biographies and the books on the law. This sequence is important for Philo because he argues that Jewish monotheism and law are grounded in the creation and have already been implemented by the patriarchs.[2]

The subject of the creation also figures prominently in Philo's philosophical writings. As we saw in the previous chapter, he dedicates a whole treatise to the question of whether the world is created or eternal, stressing that, according to both Moses and Plato, God created the world and subsequently cared for it with fatherly concern. In the philosophical treatises Philo moreover pays special attention to Stoic approaches, condemning Chrysippus's idea of a conflagration, that is, a cyclical destruction of the world by fire, while praising Panaetius for adopting the idea of one everlasting creation. An important aspect of the creation is the notion of providence. Philo emphasizes that both Plato and Moses identify God's creation of the world as the basis of divine providence.

The *Exposition* further develops these ideas raised in the philosophical treatises. Most notably, Philo presents the creation as one of the three overall categories of the Bible, next to the historical narratives and the laws. Thus, one biblical chapter, Genesis, receives exceptional emphasis, much beyond its original place, and becomes a source of theological principles. Philo moreover stresses the implications of the creation for the other parts of Scripture. "The Father and Maker of the world," he explains, "was in the truest sense also its Lawgiver," so that those who observe the laws follow nature and receive the rewards outlined in the *Lives* of the biblical forefathers. Philo concludes his treatise on the creation with a catalogue of five principles. Moses, he insists, "teaches" in the creation account that "God exists and has been [from eternity]" and furthermore that he is "one." In Philo's view, the biblical creation account is the foundation of Jewish theology because it disproves atheism and the "polytheistic doctrine." The biblical story moreover demonstrates that the world is created rather than eternal, being providentially cared for by God. These articles of "piety" amount to a Jewish creation theology. Philo offers for the first time in Judaism a kind of catechism of monotheism.[3]

This theological focus on the creation of the world is striking in light of Philo's ambivalence in the *Allegorical Commentary* from his earlier Alexandrian period. The young Philo is wholeheartedly committed to Plato's early and middle dialogues, which encourage him to consider matter in highly negative terms, locating it at the opposite pole of the transcendent deity. Philo bases his theology on Exod 3:14, where God says, "I am he that is."[4] This verse suggests to him that God is defined by the Platonic category of true being as distinct from the mere appearance of material things, which are perceived by the senses rather than the mind. While Philo does not quote this verse in the *Exposition*, he mentions it three times in the *Allegorical Commentary* and provides extensive interpretation. Characteristic of Philo's approach at the beginning of his career is the following explanation: "For God alone exists in real being (ὁ θεὸς μόνος ἐν τῷ εἶναι ὑφέστηκεν). Therefore Moses will necessarily say of him 'I am he who is,' implying that others next to him do not have being according to the real sense of being, but are considered to exist only by [the criteria of] appearance" (*Det.* 160).

Inspired by Plato's *Republic*, Philo conceives of the Mosaic God as truly existing. He functions like a Platonic Idea or Form, which is grasped by the mind and enjoys unchanging being as opposed to the material elements, which are grasped by the senses and belong to the realm of becoming and appearing rather than being. In Philo's view, God is unique in his transcendence, perfect goodness, and simplicity. His essence cannot be grasped by humans, and therefore no name is attributed to him. Approaching God is accomplished by a flight from the material world. The way to the ethereal realm is shown by Plato's *Theaetetus*, a treatise enjoying special popularity among Alexandrian Platonists.[5] Philo recommends with Plato that "it is necessary to try to escape from here to there as quickly as possible. And flight is godlikeness as far as possible (ὁμοίωσις θεῷ κατὰ τὸ δυνατόν). And godlikeness is to be righteous and holy, with wisdom." In the *Allegorical Commentary* Philo follows Plato's *Theaetetus* and assumes that the created world stands at the opposite pole of God. Only someone who escapes the material realm can reach the divine. In this context Philo explicitly dismisses the Stoic proof of god from the creation, which assumes that we gain "our apprehension of the First Cause from the cosmos and its parts and the forces inherent in these." The young Philo rejects the Stoic approach because God cannot be apprehended by analogy to a builder of a house, whose essence is expressed in the construction. In his view, "those who engage in such considerations grasp God by means of a shadow, discerning the artificer through his works." Philo insists that true insight into God derives from turning inward to the soul, which God has endowed with the ability to perceive him. Given Philo's strongly transcendent orientation at the beginning of his career, it is not surprising that the creation of the world does not play a prominent role in the *Allegorical Commentary*, even though God's beneficence as a creator is mentioned.[6]

Seeing the contrast between Philo's approach in the *Allegorical Commentary* on one hand and the *Exposition* and the philosophical treatises on the other, we have to ask what prompted Philo to shift his focus from transcendence to the creation. Why does he give the creation such a central place in his later works, especially in the *Exposition*? The key to answering these questions is Philo's visit to Rome, where he encounters Stoic philosophy as a dominant factor of intellectual life. This encounter prompts him to reevaluate Plato's works and give new emphasis to one of his latest dialogues, the *Timaeus*, which provides important elements of a more immanent creation theology. We have already seen that Philo quickly became familiar with Roman culture and philosophy, addressing subjects of topical concern in the capital of the empire. We now have to examine whether and, if so, how Philo's detailed interpretation of the creation was inspired by Roman discourses.

Philo's Turn to Stoic Nature Theology

Philo opens his treatise *On the Creation* with remarks to a general audience. We are familiar with such self-positioning from his historical and philosophical writings. In the present context Philo discusses different types of lawgivers, distinguishing between those who present their legislation without any explanatory framework and those who have dressed their laws in mythologies in order to render them more appealing to their readers. Moses, he stresses, chose a better path and provides "a beautiful and most impressive introduction," namely, the creation account. This opening suggests in Philo's view a close connection between nature and biblical law: "The beginning is, as I said, most marvelous. It contains an account of the making of the world, so that the world is in harmony with the law and the law with the world and that the man who observes the law is directly a citizen of the world, orienting his actions toward the [rational] purpose of nature, in accordance with which the entire world also is administered" (*Opif.* 3).

Philo suggests that the Jewish lawgiver started his legislation with the creation account in order to alert his readers to the central function of nature as a rational and providentially guided framework of ethics. This position resonates well with Roman Stoicism, which advocates nature in the traditional Stoic sense as a personal guide to human ethics. Already Zeno, the founder of the school, and following him prominent Stoics, among them Arius Didymus, Augustus's court philosopher, had stressed that the aim of ethics is "to live in accordance with nature." Philo's late contemporary Seneca makes it a central theme of his ethics, speaking of the laws of nature and the universal bonds of humanity. Seneca also believes in nature's rational purpose, guiding everything according to a stable, yet hidden plan, which humans are invited to accept as part of their ethical orientation in life. In addition to these traditional Stoic ideas, Roman authors connected nature to a specific legislation, namely, Roman law from the Twelve Tables up to the Republic. Cicero explains the Roman constitution by reference to nature, suggesting that it is based on universal justice associated with

Jupiter. "Law," he says, "is the highest reason, implanted in nature, which commands what ought to be done and forbids the opposite." While Philo already in Alexandria had been familiar with the Stoic idea of nature, upon arrival in Rome he gives it new emphasis and highlights the link between nature, the creation, and law.[7] As if replacing Roman law by the Torah, Philo anchors his ancestral tradition in created nature.

Philo criticizes the Aristotelian notion of the world's eternity and dismisses it as an "impious falsehood." It is a grave mistake, he says, to think of God as inactive, thus severing the tie between him and the created world. The Aristotelians eliminate a powerful incentive to piety, "namely, providence, because reason proves that the Father and Maker takes care of that which has been created." Philo contrasts the abstract Aristotelian god to the highly personal demiurge, who "keenly desires" to provide for his creation and fend off any harm. It is God's responsibility to "administer and direct everything" (*Opif.* 7–11). Philo describes the nature of God's activity thus: "It is absolutely necessary that among existing things there is an active cause and a passive element and that the active cause is the absolutely pure and unadulterated intellect of the universe, superior to excellence and superior to knowledge and even superior to the good itself and the beautiful itself. But the passive element, which is of itself without soul and unmoved, when set in motion and shaped and endowed with a soul by the intellect, changed into the most perfect piece of work, this world" (*Opif.* 8–9).

Contemporary readers of Philo would easily recognize this passage as an exposition of Stoic nature philosophy. Diogenes Laertius, who summarizes Greek philosophy in the third century CE, states that the Stoics "hold that there are two principles, the active and the passive." Cicero similarly presents the physics of this school as revolving around a distinction between "the efficient cause and passive matter, which is fashioned and shaped by the efficient cause."[8] Philo's interpretation of the creation resonates well with these Stoic voices and even echoes their precise wording. Moses, he further explains, developed his notions on the basis of a philosophical education and "having been instructed in the greater and most essential parts of nature" (*Opif.* 8). Jewish theology is thus firmly inscribed into Stoic discourses prevalent in Rome. Yet Philo also preserves some aspects of his original transcendent theology and describes the mind of the universe as "superior to excellence and superior to knowledge and even superior to the good itself and the beautiful itself" (*Opif.* 8).

Philo gives special attention to Plato's *Timaeus*, which was popular in Rome and presents a rather more personal demiurge involved in the creation of the material world and taking permanent care of it. Plato wrote this dialogue toward the end of his career and thus nuanced the transcendent approach of his earlier years. Philo follows in his footsteps and advocates in his mature age a more immanent view of God by highlighting motifs from the *Timaeus*. He refers to Plato in a somewhat veiled fashion as "one of the men of old" and celebrates his idea of the creator as an ungrudging deity who extends unlimited benefits to the world. Philo often draws on the *Timaeus* and relies on such ideas as God's fatherly providence and the distinction between eternal ideas and created matter, suggesting that the demiurge used an ideal pattern to create the world. As David Runia has abundantly shown, Philo uses the Platonic dialogue as an intertext for his reading of the biblical creation account.[9]

Philo's interpretation of the *Timaeus* and his overall emphasis on the creation resonate well with Stoicism, which he intensively encountered during his embassy to Gaius. Roman Stoicism was relevant and attractive because it offered a monotheistic creation theology that reshaped some traditional Stoic ideas. Diogenes Laertius reports that the Stoics generally regard theology as part of cosmology and consider the given world as the proper starting point for humanity's contemplation of the gods. According to Diogenes, the Stoics distinguish between matter and active reason, identifying the latter with the superior God, "for he is everlasting and the artificer of each several thing throughout the whole extent [of matter]." This "dogma" (δόγμα) is said to be embraced by a great variety of Stoics, ranging from Zeno to Cleanthes, Chrysippus, and Posidonius. The Stoics consider the demiurge to be "one and the same with reason, fate, and Zeus." The one God is said to be the "seminal reason of the cosmos," creating the elements, and, most importantly, being the only deity surviving the conflagration of the world. This is so because "being the artificer of the orderly arrangement, he [Zeus] at stated periods absorbs into himself the whole substance and again creates it from himself." Chrysippus distinguishes between Zeus and the rest of the gods on account of their respective roles in the ever renewed creation of the world. "Only Zeus" is, in his view, "indestructible and everlasting," because the other gods are consumed into him during the conflagration. In his book *On the Gods* Chrysippus stresses that the regular gods "are subject to generation, while Zeus is everlasting."[10] The connection between monotheism and the creation of the cosmos is thus self-evident from a Stoic point of view. Zeus plays a unique role in the creation, whereas the other deities emerge as mere aspects of the demiurge. We have already seen that Philo rejects Chrysippus's idea of a conflagration and praises those members of the school, such as Panaetius, who abandoned it. In Rome this notion was no longer fashionable, but other elements of Stoic creation theology played a prominent role.

In Roman circles Stoic theology played a central role in the proof of god. Cicero's summary of Stoic theology closely corresponds to Philo's and stresses the special efforts the Stoics made to prove the existence of a supreme god from the creation. According to Cicero, the Stoics recognized Jupiter or Zeus as helper and "father of gods and men." Chrysippus and Cleanthes are mentioned as having deduced the existence of one divine force from the beautiful furnishing of the cosmos and the orderly movements of the stars. Chrysippus speaks of God in the singular (*deus*) and proves his existence by considering the fact that the creation of the universe vastly exceeds human powers and therefore must be attributed to one creator God. The conflagration is not mentioned in this context, as Cicero, an admirer of Panaetius, probably considers it irrelevant.[11] Rather, the discussion revolves around the notion of one demiurge. Cicero's Platonic spokesman Cotta is skeptical about Zeus's uniqueness in the creation, which can be grasped by "looking up at the sky" and by acknowledging "that some power exists whereby the heavenly bodies are governed." Cotta dismisses Stoic nature theology on the following grounds: "And so I fully agreed with the part of your discourse that dealt with nature's punctual regularity . . . ; but I could not accept your assertion that this could not have come about were it not held together by a single divine breath" (*uno divino spiritu;* Cicero, *N.D.* 3.28).

The Platonic philosopher Cotta rejects Stoic theology because of its emphasis on monotheism and divine immanence. In his view, the orderliness of the cosmos cannot be explained by reference to a single god who permeates the world like a breath. While Philo in the *Allegorical Commentary* is sympathetic to Cotta's reservations, in the *Exposition* he adopts the Stoic approach, without, however, fully accepting its implied immanence. He now stresses the importance of the creation for grasping the nature of the monotheistic God. Whereas he earlier conceived of God as essentially beyond the creation, he now identifies God primarily as the demiurge.

Following his immersion in Stoic philosophy, Philo interprets Plato's *Timaeus* with emphasis on divine immanence. He stresses that God is not "grudging a share in His own excellent nature," implying that God is so close to the world that his beneficent nature can be shared. Plato, by contrast, insists on the unbridgeable gap between the demiurge and the world. While he, too, speaks about the benevolence of the creator god, he is concerned to remind his readers that a full assimilation of the world to god is impossible. "God," he explains, "wished that all things should be good and nothing bad, as much as is possible."[12] Plato's god remains separate from the world, enjoying a perfection that is impossible in the material realm. Philo's creator God, by contrast, has become astonishingly close to humans and the world, sharing his very essence in the creation.

Philo moreover pays more attention to providence than Plato and interprets this notion in more immanent terms. Philo concludes *On the Creation* with an emphatic confirmation of divine providence: "The fifth principle is that God also takes care of the cosmos. For it is required by the laws of nature and the ordinances that the maker is always concerned about the thing made, in accordance with these [laws] parents also take care of their children" (*Opif.* 171–72). Philo assumes with Plato that God takes care of the world but expresses this idea in distinctly Stoic terms, using the key word "nature" and suggesting that God operates according to the same natural laws as human parents. God emerges as an integral part of the world he has created. Moreover, Philo introduces the idea of God's providential care for humanity, which Plato does not mention. Humans, he argues, are the beings "dearest and closest" to God. In his view, humans were created last in order to be provided with a "means of living and living well." The elements of the world are thus destined for humans and their needs. The Stoics held strikingly similar views. They, too, considered the world to have been created for the purpose of humanity. Chrysippus compared the world to a handsome mansion "built for its masters, not for mice." Another Stoic spokesman explains that "the world was created for the sake of gods and men," providing a "lavish abundance" of grain, vegetables, and fruits as well as a variety of animals for humanity.[13] Philo thus adopted Stoic motifs in order to embellish the biblical creation account, adding a dimension of immanence not found in the *Timaeus*.

Philo's emphasis on monotheism is also lacking in Plato's *Timaeus*. Although this dialogue introduces the term "Maker and Father" for the creator god, Plato clearly assumes a multiplicity of gods and assigns a somewhat marginal role to the demiurge, who relies on the eternal Ideas. Philo counters this tendency by expanding the function of the demiurge and stressing monotheistic elements. The exclusive creator God is credited with the insight that a "beautiful copy could never be produced without a beautiful paradigm," which Plato presented as a universally valid principle applying also to the creation. Philo moreover suggests that God "in as much as he is God, knew in advance" and realized the necessity of an ethereal model for the world. Philo's God is more in the center of the stage, using the ideal realm as a means of ensuring the highest quality of his creation. Most importantly, the demiurge in Philo's account "initially shaped the intelligible cosmos when he wished to create the visible world." Plato's god, by contrast, looks at a given model, which he applies to the material realm. Philo has God play a far more decisive role in the conception and concrete fashioning of the ideal world. The place where the ideal cosmos is shaped is identified with God. Philo says that it "has no other location than the divine Logos." God shapes the ideal pattern of the world as a function of his rationality.[14]

Scholars have interpreted Philo's position on the creation as the expected reaction of a Jewish thinker to the Greek world. Sometimes an intrinsic clash between Judaism and Greek polytheism is assumed. In this view, Philo inevitably offers a monotheistic interpretation of Plato's text because he as a Jew is conversant with the Bible and believes in one God, while objecting to the Greek pantheon.[15] Such a reading, however, does not do justice to the complexity of Philo's position and requires adjustment. Our analysis has shown that Philo's interpretation is highly congenial to contemporary Roman Stoicism. This school prompted him to shift his focus from utterly transcendent notions of God to the image of the demiurge. It is only in his later works and as a result of his fruitful encounter with Roman Stoicism that he recognizes the creation as a basis of monotheism. Philo has not simply remained loyal to the biblical creation account, rejecting alternative pagan views, but has instead gone through an intellectual development, exchanging a more transcendent Platonic position for the Stoic approach prevalent in Rome. He now advocates a demiurge, whose unique nature can be grasped by looking at the created cosmos. God providentially cares for the world and personally protects human beings.

Philo's ideas in the *Exposition* are likely to have evoked sympathy among his Roman readers. His creation theology resonates especially well with his late contemporary Seneca, who assumes that it is "superfluous" to show how the regularity and beauty of the cosmos prove one divine force guarding it. "Providence," he asserts, "presides over the universe and God concerns himself with us" even though he does not "guard the good man's luggage." Seneca, like Philo, preserves some more transcendental aspects of God and perceives of the deity as the pure mind of the cosmos, which is superior to matter. Seneca likewise distinguishes between *causa et materia*, identifying the former as active reason, which shapes the material elements in the process of the creation.[16] Roman readers like Seneca thus would have found Philo's creation theology highly congenial.

Creation Theology and Monotheism in Other Treatises of the *Exposition*

Philo's creation theology has significant implications for other treatises in the *Exposition*. In *On the Life of Abraham*, which follows the creation account, his creation theology is adduced to explain the hero's discovery of monotheism. Philo introduces Abraham as "eager to follow God and be obedient to the laws enacted by him." He then interprets the story of Abraham's migration from Chaldea to the land of Israel as an intellectual journey that leads to the discovery of monotheism. Philo stresses that Abraham, unlike others, who tend to cling to their family and home, was immediately ready for departure and thus showed his spiritual inclination. Abraham's journey, Philo further explains, was more in the soul than in the body, driven by a quest for the true God. Having grown up in Chaldea, Abraham was familiar with polytheism but became skeptical. While the Chaldeans "related with reverence to visible existence," not recognizing any power beyond the material realm, Abraham inferred from the orderly arrangement of the cosmos a higher, invisible force.[17] His recognition of the sole God is based on arguments from the creation: Abraham "discerned what he had not seen before, a charioteer and steersman presiding over the world and safely guiding his own work, assuming the charge and leadership of the parts in it as are worthy of divine care" (*Abr.* 70).

Philo's Abraham identifies the monotheistic God as the demiurge, who takes providential care of his work. The path to the highest religious truth is based on empirical investigation rather than theoretical contemplation or an inward search of the soul. Abraham behaves like a Stoic philosopher and relies on the creation. This Stoic orientation in the *Life* is conspicuous in comparison to the *Allegorical Commentary*, in which Abraham is said to leave behind the body in his quest for higher truth. At the beginning of his career Philo stresses that we "must think" of God as "lacking any quality, being one and indestructible and unchangeable." Abraham is seen as a pioneer "in the contemplation of divine things," because he disengages from the body and his soul strives to ascend to the sight of "him who exists." Rejecting typically Stoic views, which rely on divine immanence in the world, Philo insists that the deity is independent of the creation and not "contained" in any of its parts. Therefore, one should not contemplate the heaven, the earth, seas, and rivers but turn instead to an exploration "of yourselves only and your own nature."[18] This image of Abraham as turning inward to find God significantly differs from Philo's later story of Abraham as watching the universe and discovering God in its order.

Philo's treatise *On the Decalogue* also draws on elements of his creation theology. The first commandment, "I am the Lord, who brought you out of the land of Egypt, the house of slavery; you shall have no other gods except me," is disconnected from the historical context of the exodus and transferred to a purely philosophical realm. Philo criticizes idolatry, especially the Egyptian kind, and demands that the "highest and most august, the begetter and ruler of the great world-city" be recognized. God is praised as the cause of all the sense-perceptible elements in the world and is not identical with any of its parts. Repeating motifs from his treatise *On the Creation,* Philo stresses that the world is preserved "by the providence of its Maker" and that "there is one Cause of the world and one Ruler and King, who guides the chariot and safely steers the bark of the universe."[19] He accuses those who deny monotheism of the following error: "They among others have not even perceived of the most obvious, which a 'witless child knows,' namely, that the artificer is superior to his work, both with regard to time, as he is older than what he makes and is in a sense its father, and with regard to strength, as the active principle is more distinguished than the passive" (*Dec.* 69). Philo repeats here the typically Stoic distinction between the active and the passive element, which has already informed his account of the creation. He moreover suggests that monotheism is grasped by a proper study of the universe, which reveals the force activating all of its parts. Philo presents this view as being so obvious that even a "witless child" knows it. Monotheism, as derived from the creation, is thus what the Stoics would call a "common opinion," intuited by all without academic training or special philosophical preparation.

The creation moreover plays a prominent role in Philo's treatise *On the Special Laws,* in which he identifies "the sovereignty of God" as the first guiding principle under which several particular laws are subsumed. In this context he repeats that God is "the one Father of all," "the Maker of all," and "the Father and Ruler of all."[20] He moreover reminds his readers that Moses forbade the worship of the heaven and the stars because these are God's creations, which are in all respects inferior and secondary to the demiurge. Philo discusses at length how humans can know God, drawing attention to Moses's quest to learn about his existence and essence. While God's essence cannot be known, because he is too transcendent for human perception, Philo points to God's creation as an epistemological key. Moses cries out to God, "This cosmos has been my guide, teaching me that you are and subsist, instructing me like a son about his father and like a work about its artificer" (*Spec.* 1.41). Philo here uses remarkably anthropomorphic language to describe the connection between God and his creation. While suggesting that the father-son relationship and the image of the artificer and his work are mere similes ("like"), he argues that the material cosmos provides the key to understanding God because the product reveals aspects of its artificer.

To conclude, Philo has developed a creation theology that underlies different parts of the *Exposition*. In the first treatise *On the Creation* he establishes the centrality of the creation for Jewish theology, offering a monotheistic creed and stressing God's unique role in the cosmos. Philo's approach is inspired by Roman Stoicism and differs from his earlier writings, in which he highlights God's otherness and develops a negative theology. Once in place, creation theology becomes an integral part of Philo's discussions in the *Exposition*, informing his views of Abraham, the Decalogue, and the special laws.

Philo's Achievement

Philo's creation theology marks an important watershed in Western civilization. Within Judaism he ushers in a more philosophical approach to the creation, which subsequently receives more attention than it had during the Second Temple period. Let's initially appreciate Philo's contribution by examining some of his predecessors. The author of the book of Jubilees, while adding some embellishments to the biblical account, does not yet develop a creation theology and instead focuses on such themes as the angels, the calendar, and the Temple. Ben Sira anticipates Philo by paying special attention to the creation, praising God as the creator and specifying his works. He even recommends "looking upon the rainbow and blessing him who has made it." According to Ben Sira, the creation provides insight into God, who is "above all his works," and lays the foundation for humanity's proper attitude toward him. Ben Sira may even have been inspired by Stoic philosophy, as some of his descriptions of wisdom seem to indicate. On the whole, however, he does not go as far as Philo, who used the creation as the basis of a monotheistic creed.[21]

In Hellenistic Egypt two extant authors treat the creation, one of them too fragmented to give full insight and the other probably not earlier than Philo. Aristobulus, an Alexandrian Jew of the second century BCE, stresses that "the cosmic order was carefully created by God and permanently held together by Him." This statement reflects philosophical awareness, possibly even a familiarity with Plato's *Timaeus*. However, as far as the extant fragments can tell, Aristobulus's main theological concern is God's transcendence. The Wisdom of Solomon uses some Stoic terms, such as breath, and suggests that the world was created by God's wisdom. This author wrote in the mid–first century CE and may have been inspired by Philo. His work illustrates the philosophical tendencies of Alexandrian Judaism, which were fully developed by Philo.[22]

Philo's move from a distinctly transcendent approach, which marginalizes the creation, to a Stoic position, which emphasizes it, throws important light on subsequent intellectual developments. Judaism and orthodox Christianity adopted a perspective close to Philo's views in the *Exposition*, while pagan authors in the Greek East and "Gnostics" assumed a transcendent perspective congenial to Philo's approach in the *Allegorical Commentary*. In other words, subsequent Jews and orthodox Christians adopted the philosophical language of Rome, which Philo incorporated systematically for the first time into biblical discussions, while Greek pagans and Gnostics opted out and developed a more local, transcendent discourse.

Josephus, writing one generation after Philo in Rome and probably familiar with at least some of his works, acknowledges the importance of the creation. In his treatise *Against Apion* he sets out the main principles of Judaism for a broader, non-Jewish audience. The first principle is monotheism, followed by Temple worship, family values, self-restraint, and a humane attitude toward foreigners. These highlights of Judaism resonate well with Roman discourses, especially the emphasis on "natural" monogamy as opposed to homosexuality.[23] In the same spirit Josephus develops a philosophical notion of monotheism, stressing God's perfection and transcendence.

The key to understanding the deity is the creation. As he puts it, "We have neither seen nor conceived of anything like him and it is unholy to even imagine it. We do, however, behold his works, the light, the heaven, the earth, the sun, the water, and the creation of animals and the sprouting of fruits. God created these, neither with his hands, nor with toil, nor requiring some co-workers. Instead these things immediately came into being after he beautifully designed them" (*C.Ap.* 2.192). For Josephus, as for Philo before him, the creation is the main epistemological tool for grasping God. Through God's works humans can perceive aspects of him and worship him in the proper fashion. Divine providence is assumed even in the details of nature and not just in the overall design.

In the *Antiquities* Josephus stresses some further points that Philo previously discussed. Initially, he raises the question of why the Mosaic legislation starts with the creation of the world. Such "natural philosophy" was in his view necessary in order to familiarize humanity with God. The person who contemplates God's works and understands his nature will also imitate him, the "best of all models." God's providence is moreover said to apply especially to human beings. Humans are God's "fairest" creation, most eminently capable of imitating his perfect virtue. (*J.A.* 1.1–21). Finally, Josephus's Abraham discovers monotheism in a familiar way, namely, by observing the creation. Abraham, he says, "was thus the first who dared to declare that the creator of the universe is one and, if any other being contributed to the welfare of man, each did so by his [God's] command and not by virtue of its own power. He inferred these notions from the changes to which land and sea are subject, from the course of the sun and the moon, and from the celestial phenomena" (*J.A.* 1.155). Whether or not Josephus read Philo's *Exposition,* his portrait of Abraham resembles Philo's remarkably. According to both, the patriarch discovered monotheism by looking at the creation. Both apply Stoic notions and argue from the order of the universe, assuming humanity's centrality in the created world.[24] Josephus's account strengthens our impression of a Roman context for Philo. As Josephus writes for a Roman audience and advocates a typically Philonic creation theology, it is likely that Philo one generation earlier addressed a similar audience with Stoic inclinations.

The emerging Christian church also inscribed itself into Roman discourses and defined itself by advocating the creation as an essential creed that determines membership. The second-century apologist Justin Martyr, who probably knew some of Philo's more general treatises, such as *On the*

Creation and *On the Life of Moses,* illuminates the emergence of a Christian theology. Justin explicitly addresses Roman rulers, especially Marcus
Aurelius, and introduces Christians as those "worshiping the maker of the
universe." He is moreover proud to note that Christians advocate a creation
theology similar to Plato's doctrine in the *Timaeus.* In Justin's view, Plato
even depended on the Bible, both its Hebrew and Christian parts, and
unknowingly hinted at Jesus. Like the late Philo, Justin thus combines a
Roman orientation with monotheistic creation theology that is grounded
in Plato's work. This doctrine is identified as the proper Christian position
and contrasted to Gnostic views. Justin dismisses especially Marcion as a
heretic, who "is even now teaching men to deny that God is the maker of
all things in heaven and on earth."[25] Marcion and other Gnostics adopted a
form of theology which resembles that of the young Philo in the *Allegori-*
cal Commentary and brought the transcendent approach to its most radical conclusion. Justin, on the other hand, arrived in Rome and integrated
his particular interpretation of the Christian religion in Roman discourses.
Declaring that proper Christianity is congenial with the creation theology
popular in the imperial capital, he enlists Roman support for what would
become orthodoxy.

Celsus, a pagan Platonist probably active in Alexandria in the mid–
second century CE, further illuminates the parting of the ways. We can tell
from the extant fragments of his refutation of Christianity, which Origen
preserves in *Contra Celsus,* that he strongly criticizes Christian appropria-
tions of the *Timaeus,* which he considers as "too bound up in the flesh and
see[ing] nothing pure." Familiar with Gnostic notions of an inferior demiurge responsible for the origin of evil in the world, Celsus offers a metaphorical interpretation of Plato's vision of "the Maker and Father of this
universe" in the *Timaeus.* Speaking about "the nameless and first [being]" as
utterly abstract and distant from the material world, Celsus removes Plato's
text from Christian readings. Celsus thus thinks of the world as "uncreated
and indestructible," insisting with Aristotle that "nothing produced by matter is immortal." The biblical creation account consequently appears to him
as "most foolish."[26]

During the third and fourth centuries we see a consolidation of views
among Jews, Christians, and Greek-speaking pagans. The rabbinic Midrash
Genesis Rabbah gives new emphasis to the creation by devoting several
sections to the subject and imagining Abraham as deducing the monotheistic God from the creation. Rabbi Hoshaya, who opens the Midrash,

makes a special point of inscribing Judaism into the creation of the world. He argues that the expression "in the beginning" refers to nothing but the Torah, which God consulted when embarking on the creation (GR 1:1). The church father Origen, who moved in the third century CE from Alexandria to Caesarea, identified the creation as the first principle of the Christian faith next to a belief in God's oneness. Like Philo and Justin, he draws a connection between the demiurge of the philosophers and the biblical heritage, insisting that the creator God provided the law, the prophets, and the Gospels. Origen moreover confronted Celsus, making the creation of the world a significant point of their dispute. He claimed the *Timaeus* for his religion and argued that Jesus complements the Platonic dialogue by spreading the message of monotheism more broadly beyond the learned elite. Origen concluded rather triumphantly that pagans "pride themselves on having known God and learnt the divine truths from philosophy," yet remained polytheists, "like the most vulgar, keep[ing] on with the images and their temples and the mysteries, which are a matter of common gossip."[27]

Subsequent pagan authors are no longer known to advocate a literal creation of the world. A distinctly Greek community emerges around the metaphorical reading of the *Timaeus*. Two figures throw important light on these developments in the Greek East: the philosopher and scholar Porphyry (late third century CE) and the emperor Julian the Apostate (fourth century CE). Both criticized Christianity and wrote treatises to revive the Greek heritage. Porphyry wrote the first extant running commentary on the *Timaeus*, which has been characterized as "undoubtedly the most comprehensive and thorough of its kind." He dismissed the literal interpretation of the text as "impious" because it assumes an imperfect demiurge, either unable or unwilling to shape a perfect world. Porphyry's polemical tone suggests that he made these statements in contrast to Christian claims. Moreover, Julian refers to the *Timaeus* as "our account" of the creation, which he distinguishes from the biblical story embraced by the Christians. The *Timaeus* in its metaphorical sense has become the pagan counterpart to the book of Genesis. Not surprisingly, Sallustius, close friend of Julian and mastermind of his effort to restore the old cults in a world turned Christian, raised the notion of an eternal cosmos to the level of a pagan dogma.[28] Julian's reign, however, lasted only for a few years, and the pagan revival that he promoted was doomed to failure. The orthodox church, by contrast, triumphed and established the philosophical creation theology, which the late Philo had first developed, as the dominant view of Western civilization.

6 Character and History in the *Lives* of the Biblical Forefathers

Philo's *Exposition* contains several biographies of biblical figures that follow the treatise on the creation and refashion the known biblical stories. Philo does not comment here on particular verses, as in the *Allegorical Commentary* from his early Alexandrian period, but presents each character in a free narrative that he suggests reflects historical truth. This switch from minute Bible commentary to biography is remarkable and calls for an explanation. Why did Philo abandon the format of systematic commentary and develop an interest in personality and character? Did the embassy to Gaius, which shaped his approach to contemporary events and philosophy, also affect this change of genre?

Philo's journey to Rome indeed provides the key to understanding his biographies of the patriarchs. We have already seen that Philo's diplomatic function led him to engage contemporary Roman discourses and write in a historical mode. In the *Embassy* Philo moreover offers a first character sketch of the emperor Gaius Caligula and considers the view that he was "not naturally made for government." Philo explains Gaius's decline into tyranny and madness to be the result of the death of the previous emperor, Tiberius, whose austerity had provided a healthy check on Gaius's passions. Lacking a supervisor and role model, Gaius succumbed to Alexandrian flatterers and lost proportion. Similarly, in the treatise *Against Flaccus* Philo studies the character of the Roman prefect Flaccus, who initially succeeded thanks to his accuracy and expertise. After Gaius's accession to the throne, however, he quickly deteriorated because he had supported Gaius's rival to the throne. Flaccus saw with great concern how the new emperor killed his coregent, thus also undermining the security of his own position. Philo had written his historical accounts with a keen interest in character rather than institutions, wars, or economics. He likes to tell anecdotes in order to illustrate the protagonist's personality.[1]

Philo's biographical interests are connected to politics. Drawn out of his scholarly lifestyle in Alexandria by the riots of 38 CE, Philo becomes actively involved in the events of his time and writes historical treatises with an emphasis on influential actors and their lives. His decision to write the *Lives* of the biblical forefathers belongs to the same political context. He wrote the biographies of Abraham, Joseph, and Moses during roughly the same period as the historical works, and they are characterized by a similar style of writing. *On the Life of Moses* responds directly to detractors, most probably Apion, the head of the rival Egyptian embassy to Gaius, who presented an unfavorable image of Moses in his history of Egypt. At the same time, however, the *Lives* of the biblical forefathers extend beyond narrow political apologetics and convey a broader picture of Judaism. Philo's portraits make up a gallery of ideal ancestors of the nation who provide ethically authoritative models and appeal to Roman readers known for their appreciation of ancestors.[2]

In this chapter I investigate the three extant *Lives* of Moses, Joseph, and Abraham, also taking into account what Philo says about the lost *Lives* of Isaac and Jacob. I ask how he constructs their characters, to what extent his concerns resonate with those in the historical writings, and how he engages contemporary biographical discourses. Following our insights from the *Embassy* and *Against Flaccus*, I pay special attention to Roman conventions of writing and examine whether they were meaningful for Philo as a biographer. I moreover ask on which philosophical assumptions Philo's *Lives* are based. Was he innovative at the time, experimenting in new ways with known topics? I examine his achievement by comparison to subsequent writers such as Plutarch, Philostratus, and Luke.

The Life of Moses

Philo leaves open where precisely *On the Life of Moses* belongs within his overall work. He looks back to it on two occasions in the *Exposition*, recalling the "two treatises I wrote about the life of Moses." In both contexts Philo stresses that he wrote the *Life* in order to present Moses as an archetypical model of ethics, which he hopes his readers will emulate. In his treatise *On the Virtues* he complements the *Life* and discusses Moses's anticipation of his own death as another example of his supreme virtue. Looking back on this biography, Philo stresses apologetically that Moses was not a regular king and did not aspire to political power but had been appointed to this task by God even though he was naturally inclined toward priestly and prophetic roles. Given these cross-references, it is surprising that Philo does not define the precise relationship between the *Life of Moses* and the *Exposition.* When contemplating his achievement as a biographer, he mentions the *Lives* of Abraham, Isaac, and Jacob and says nothing about the *Life of Moses.*[3] Philo's special treatment of this *Life* may indicate that he wrote it independently of the *Exposition* as a direct response to Apion's accusations of Moses. In any case he uses the same literary term, *bios,* for all the treatises on the biblical forefathers, thus encouraging us to treat them together, while at the same time paying attention to their individual differences.

Philo introduces Moses as a character "whom some describe as the lawgiver of the Jews, others as the interpreter of the holy laws." This identification engages two different perspectives on Moses, namely, the view of general readers, who regularly speak about Moses as the lawgiver of the Jews, and the view of Jews, who refer to him from within their community in more pious language. Philo thus positions himself as someone familiar with both worlds. He speaks from the edge between the internal and the external perspectives and projects himself as a qualified mediator between the two realms, hoping "to display the notable life of the greatest and in every respect most accomplished man to those worthy not to remain ignorant of it" (*Mos.* 1.1).

Philo self-consciously constructs his implied audience. He complains about "Greek intellectuals," who refused to commemorate Moses as he was but "abused the powers which education gave them by composing in verse or prose comedies and pieces of fabulous licentiousness, to their widespread disgrace." Philo may well have had in mind public figures, such as Apion and Chaeremon, both most likely members of the Egyptian embassy to Gaius, who wrote in Greek malicious invectives against the Jews and their lawgiver Moses. By criticizing such literary activity as a shameful reversal of education, Philo signals that it is beyond discussion and negotiation. Readers holding similar views should understand that they will have to change their attitudes in order to be included in the intellectual community Philo is about to create. Philo instead aims at readers realizing that "it is necessary to fully use [one's] natural gifts to be instructed by good men and their lives." To such readers the biography of Moses will be helpful because they can benefit from his story as a model for their own lives. Occasionally, Philo anticipates a discrepancy between his own views and those of his implied readers, but he usually dismisses their potential signs of disbelief, much as Moses charismatically overcame those of the Israelites during the exodus.[4] Philo thus appeals to a sympathetic audience that is not very knowledgeable about things biblical but is open to being instructed.

Like many other biographers, Philo is concerned in the introduction to define his authority as an author. He promises that he will describe Moses "as he really was." This claim to historical truth resembles his insistence in the *Embassy* that he will report what "we have seen and heard." Regarding Moses, however, Philo is no eyewitness and has to rely on other sources. He explains to his readers that he has learned the story "from the sacred books, which he [Moses] has left behind as wonderful monuments of his wisdom, as well as from some of the nation's elders." Philo distinguishes between written and oral sources, both of which derive from his own community. Relying on "some elders of the nation," he claims authority on account of being an insider and sharing ancestral traditions. This self-positioning responds to Apion's claim that his negative account of Moses is based on a report "from the elders of the Egyptians." Philo implies that his expertise is greater than Apion's because he has access to more reliable ancestral traditions. In addition, Philo points to his own insights as a source of his biography. On such occasions he abandons his narrative posture, outlined in the introduction, and declares that he tells the story as "it appears to me" or weighs different, yet equally uncertain options of interpretation.[5] Both the scholastic nature of Philo's main source and his playful subversion of his own narrative strategy mark his work as belonging to the Hellenistic rather than the classical period.

The *Life of Moses,* Philo stresses, starts from where it is "necessary to begin," namely, the circumstances of the hero's birth.[6] Skipping the biblical information about the Israelites' situation in Egypt, Philo directly focuses his narrative on Moses. His reference to the necessary start of a *Life* indicates that he is aware of literary norms and wider discourses into which he integrates the biblical hero. He does not accidentally write in a biographical mode but consciously appeals to his readers' expectations connected with this genre. Can these literary conventions be identified? Our first look must be to Rome, because Philo spent several years there, where "writing history in terms of great individuals" was the order of the day.[7] Moreover, Roman conventions of biography, which Philo encountered during his embassy to Gaius, may explain the dramatic shift in his work from systematic Bible commentary to biography.

Cicero (first century BCE) provides the most influential theoretical framework for Roman historiography with emphasis on the personality of the protagonist. Discussing the "laws" of writing history, Cicero demands an impartial telling of the truth and special attention to "the individual actors." The historian is expected to provide the "particulars of the lives and characters of such as are outstanding in renown and dignity." Cicero's treatise *Brutus,* which he distinguishes from regular historiography, offers a sketch of the lives of famous orators, often comparing their particular qualities and methods. Cicero's outline of biographical historiography was influential in Rome and is reflected in other writers, such as Sallust and Livy.[8]

Cicero's contemporary Cornelius Nepos is the first Roman author composing separate biographies of political leaders and comparing them to their Greek counterparts. While Nepos generally remains close to the encomium and focuses on the protagonist's famous deeds, he shows already two biographical features that subsequently characterize Philo's *Lives,* namely, sketches of character and attention to the hero's gradual emergence on the political stage. Nepos writes with an overall concept of the protagonist's life and regularly introduces him by describing his family background as well as the circumstances of his entry into politics. He has an interest in the hero's *natura,* outlining his main virtues and personal characteristics. Themistocles, for example, is described as eloquent and efficient, while Alcibiades is said to be torn between his natural leadership qualities and his strong penchant for intemperance.[9]

The few scholars who have considered Nepos in the history of ancient biography have rightly remarked that his work remains rather mediocre and lacks the lively sophistication of Plutarch's *Parallel Lives.* The latter's achievement has consequently appeared to many as unprecedented. Philo, however, provides the key for a more nuanced picture of biography in the imperial period. He introduces for the first time philosophical aspects inspired by Roman Stoicism, which later resurface in other authors.[10] The background of Philo's innovation is the fact that the Stoics differed from contemporary Hellenistic schools by rejecting commentary culture and personality cult, acknowledging instead an impressive variety of exemplary figures, including philosophers from other schools, politicians, and heroes mentioned in ancient texts. Moral authority was not based on a canonical text or a particular school allegiance, but rather followed from the usefulness of the model. Such role models were depicted in real-life situations rather than in an idealized or aloof state.[11]

The Stoic philosopher Panaetius, who spent a lot of his time in Rome, played a significant role in this discourse. He powerfully argued for the self as a particular individual beyond universal rationality. This approach has rightly been distinguished from that of Plato, who divided the human soul into the impersonal categories of the rational and the material without considering the particular circumstances of individual lives. Cicero heavily relied on Panaetius's ideas and gave them a highly influential hearing in Latin. At the same time his writings continued to be available in Greek to such authors as Philo, who once mentions him. Following Panaetius, the discussion in Rome shifted from notions of universal rationality to a concern for "our own nature," "individual particularity," and "proper" characteristics. Already at birth, Cicero insists with Panaetius that people differ with regard to their physical qualities as well as their dominant traits, which subsequently determine their careers. People also differ from each other as a result of their specific family backgrounds and circumstances. These differences are so important for the evaluation of an individual person that the same deed, for example, suicide, can be a duty in the case of Cato but a fault in the case of another person.[12]

Philo's late contemporary Seneca continues this Stoic discussion of the self, adding a dimension that is of particular importance for our present inquiry. Seneca assumes a highly individuated self, which he addresses in specific situations of life. The diversity of his *Epistles* indicates his alertness to the variety of human circumstances, which demand reflection and individual appreciation. In his essay *On the Shortness of Life* Seneca proposes to extend the limitations of one's own experience by associating with figures from the past. He develops a kind of moral approach to ancient figures similar to that of Philo, recommending that his readers take great thinkers from the past, such as Zeno and Aristotle, as "their most intimate friend every day." One should become their "client" and adopt them as teachers and friends, "from whom we may seek counsel on matters great and small." Most importantly, the reader should "fashion himself in the likeness" of such great personalities.[13]

Inspired by such Roman discourses and writing at the same time as Seneca began to formulate his philosophy, Philo offers in the *Life of Moses* a sophisticated and innovative example of the biographical genre that seriously takes into account Stoic notions of the self. Philo presents for the first time the kind of philosophical biography of a political figure that is familiar to us from Plutarch. The opening of the *Life* places Moses in the wider context of biographical discourses and would have struck any educated reader in Rome as most appropriate. In addition to stressing historical truth and addressing the expectations of his readers, Philo provides details of Moses's noble family background as well as some explanations about the land of Egypt, where he grew up (*Mos.* 1.5–7). Moses emerges as an upper-class hero and is geographically contextualized according to historiographical conventions in Rome.

Philo pays special attention to the individual nature of Moses, showing its essence in early childhood and under dramatically changing circumstances. Sharing the Stoic insight that a person's physical nature is a crucial starting point of his or her individuation, Philo stresses that Moses "from the moment he was born had an appearance of more than ordinary goodliness." His beauty saved his life, as Pharaoh's daughter adopted him and the princes accepted him on account of his comely appearance. Moreover, Moses provides a first proof of his "great nature" by rejecting the delights of the Egyptian court and devoting himself to "hearing and seeing what was sure to profit the soul." Philo's Moses was naturally inclined to modesty, discipline, and learning, quickly surpassing his teachers, because his "mind was incapable of accepting any falsehood."[14]

Anecdotes become an important literary device for portraying character. Philo once explicitly formulates his concept of the anecdote: "I will describe an action he did at that time, which may appear to be small, but was performed out of no petty mind" (*Mos.* 1.51).[15] Philo points here to the inverse relation between small incident and great significance. While historians regularly describe big events, such as wars and political crises, the biographer picks private actions, which provide authentic evidence of a person's overall character. Philo's anecdotal approach in the *Life of Moses* strikingly resembles his style of writing in the historical treatises, where he once says about an incident in Alexandria that "even if it is a small thing, it is evidence of no small malice." In the *Embassy* Philo similarly studies particular cases of Gaius's behavior that indicate his mental deterioration. His falling asleep at a banquet and his joining the dancers are presented as mirrors of his personality. In both his biographies and the historical writings Philo is keen on particular incidents that illuminate the protagonist's character. This style of writing resonates well with Stoic methods of teaching philosophy. This school, more than any other, used personal examples of excellence. Seneca regularly presents known individuals in critical situations in order to illustrate a particular value. For example, he tells an "anecdote" (*fabula*) about Tullius Marcellinus's suicide, justifying his "digression" by the usefulness it will have for understanding the subject of honorable departure from life.[16]

The anecdotes Philo tells about Moses's infancy mostly pertain to his extraordinary intellectual maturity. Moses is said to have been "weaned at an earlier date than they had reckoned," to be "advanced beyond his age," and "not [to] bear himself like the mere infant that he was, nor delight in fun and laughter and sport." Later on, he applies himself so seriously to his studies that he "overtakes his teachers" and emerges as "a case rather of recollection than of learning." Philo is happy to report that Moses "devised difficult problems." None of these features of Moses are known from pre-Philonic sources. Ezekiel the Tragedian, one of his Jewish predecessors in Alexandria, mentions only briefly Moses's "royal upbringing and education." Philo takes a special interest in Moses's intellectual development and seems to have imagined the above-mentioned scenes by himself. He must have been inspired by the Septuagint translation of Exod 2:10, which says that "the child grew to maturity."[17]

Philo's anecdotes about the infant Moses remain somewhat pale because they reflect philosophical tropes. He invokes the Classical Platonic image of the recollection of the soul, which Socrates describes as the basis of all human learning. The fact that Philo singles out Moses as a student relying on recollection rather than learning from human teachers indicates that he uses the Platonic image in a loose sense, transforming it from a general human quality to a characteristic of a specific hero. Philo further embellishes the image of Moses as a precocious boy by suggesting that he "presses forward 'like the horse to a meadow,' as the proverb goes." Slightly adapting Plato's bon mot about Socrates, Philo implies that Moses had philosophical strength similar to that of Plato's role model. Moreover, the method of question and answer, which was central in many forms of learning during the Hellenistic period, is applied to Moses, whose intellectual precocity transpires in his formulation of problems.[18] All of these anecdotes are based on philosophical stereotypes that show Moses's stern nature and extraordinary intelligence. Already in his childhood he is an exceptionally spiritual person, naturally destined for his future role as philosopher king.

Philo's anecdotes become livelier in the context of Moses's ethical choices in his youth. He vividly explores Moses's reaction to Israel's plight in Egypt: "He continued to be disheartened and displeased by these events but was unable either to punish those who did wrong or to help those who suffered it. He did what he could. He assisted with words, exhorting the overseers to be moderate and loosen and alleviate the excessiveness of their orders, and the workers to bear the current situation bravely, to display a manly spirit and not to let their souls suffer together with their bodies, but to look for good to come out of the evil" (*Mos.* 1.40). Moses is described here as a person who possesses a strong sense of justice and an equally acute awareness of his limited possibilities. Seeing the overwhelming oppression of the Israelites, he chooses persuasion and encouragement as a means of improving the condition of his people. Moses's response to the circumstances of his life is rational and appropriate. His moderation turns into violent action only when some overseers go beyond their usual cruelty and become "wild beasts in human shape." This change of circumstances prompts a readjustment of behavior. Moses reacts by killing the overseer, thus provoking the final break with Pharaoh, his foster father. Philo concludes this scene by a direct authorial statement, stressing that he agrees with Moses that this action is "righteous." The idea of a change of circumstances that causes Moses's violent action has been wholly derived from Philo's imaginative reading of the biblical text, which merely says that Moses saw an Egyptian overseer beating one of the Hebrews and killed him when he believed himself to be unnoticed.[19] Philo undoubtedly wishes to justify his hero, especially in view of non-Jewish readers who may be critical of his killing of the Egyptian. He significantly does so by exploring Moses's character in changing circumstances, suggesting that his reaction was appropriate in the given context.

Moses's personality is similarly alive at the scene of the well in Median. While the biblical account simply states that Moses "stood up and helped" the shepherdesses who came to water their flocks but were harassed by some shepherds, Philo offers the following description: "Moses, seeing what had happened, as he was not far off, quickly ran up and standing by said: 'Will you not stop doing evil? Do you think the desert is a place you can take advantage of? Are you not ashamed to let your arms and elbows be idle?'" (*Mos.* 1.54). Philo has chosen Moses's intervention on behalf of shepherdesses as an exemplary scene. Hidden from the public eye, but well observed by Philo, Moses emerges as a true fighter for justice who protects the girls against men who think they can abuse the solitude of the place to promote their own interests. Philo's Moses makes an impressive speech on that occasion, asking the intruders to stop the injustice and later reminding them in God's name of their moral duties. The girls' father immediately recognizes the true significance of this incident and is "struck with admiration" for Moses's personality (*Mos.* 1.54–59). Philo implicitly encourages his readers to emulate Jethro's attitude and appreciate the anecdote as a mirror of Moses's exceptional character.

Philo moreover studies the maturation of Moses's qualities "throughout the whole of life." He surveys the increasing activity of his "good sense" and self-control, which emerge in his early ascetic tendencies, his fight for justice against the Egyptian overseers, and his escape from Egypt to Arabia. Philo is interested in the question of how a person reacts to different circumstances, especially if these represent a change for the worse. He stresses that Moses remained "zealous for the discipline and culture of his kinsmen and ancestors" and did not become "puffed up" even though he enjoyed the privileges of the Egyptian court. Philo also accompanies Moses into his exile in Arabia and constructs for him the same kind of philosophical training ground that he had assigned to Flaccus in the historical treatises. Philo speaks about Moses escaping from the "king's relentless wrath" into a "foreign land, not yet having become familiar with the native customs." Moses, he suggests, uses these dire circumstances of estrangement as an opportunity to prepare himself for his future task by "training himself for life in the highest form, the theoretical and the practical." His admirable trainer is "the reason within him," which prompts him to study philosophical doctrines and guides him on the unchanging path of nature.[20]

Moses's final appointment as the leader of the Israelites receives Philo's special attention. He tells the story of a gradual and unintended move toward involvement in politics, starting with Moses's successful shepherding and culminating in his unwilling acceptance of God's command to lead the children of Israel out of Egypt. Even though he lacks eloquence, a quality considered necessary for a public role, Moses finally declares that "he takes upon himself to be their leader on the way." Inscribing the exodus into the narrative of migration and colonization, which we have already encountered as a characteristic of the Jews in the historical treatises, Philo stresses that Moses, unlike many others, did not push himself into a position of power by means of physical force but accepted the task from the hands of

God and on account of his virtue. His rule turns out to be a form of benign monarchy for the benefit of his subjects, much like the form of government that Macro had recommended to Gaius in the historical treatises.[21]

Given Philo's lively interest in Moses's political career, which he follows through its development on the way to the land of Israel, the end of the first volume of the *Life* comes as a rather abrupt surprise. The chronological setting of the work is interrupted and Philo summarily states, "While his deeds in the realm of kingship have now been revealed, his accomplishments in the area of priesthood and legislation must be told in the following." The impersonal expression "must be told" stresses the formal nature of the switch from political biography in chronological order to topical treatment of more religious and cultural functions. Philo does not explain this move but merely suggests in a general way that the priestly and legislative roles "suit well" kingship. He is thus highly aware of the fact that he transcends the genre of biography, adding a further, unexpected dimension and another volume, which renders the *Life of Moses* an important text of the Jewish religion. Even technically Philo's *Life* goes beyond the standards of a biography, which regularly presents one life in one volume.

At the opening of the second volume of the *Life of Moses* Philo addresses again the shift from political biography to discussion of Moses's religious roles. While aware of the fact that the reader is likely to be surprised, Philo offers no real explanation. He suggests rather vaguely that he will now deal with matters "allied and consequent" to Moses's political career. In order to smooth the transition Philo introduces Plato's famous statement that a successful king will be a philosopher. Although this remark signals that a politician should be judged by spiritual standards, too, and thus seemingly supports Philo's move, it is ultimately out of place because Moses's religious rather than philosophical functions are the focus of attention. What has motivated Philo to interrupt the framework of a chronological biography and turn to religious themes, just to conclude with a biographical remark, namely, that "such was the life and such the end of Moses, king, lawgiver, high priest, and prophet"?[22]

Philo's surprising turn to religious themes in the second volume of the *Life of Moses* has to do with contemporary discourses. The intellectual atmosphere in Rome, where political leaders regularly assumed priestly roles, is significant in this context. From Augustus onward the emperors functioned as *pontifex maximus*, or high priest, exercising all-encompassing religious powers throughout the empire. As we saw in chapter 3, Varro focused his discussion of religion on the cult rather than on texts, attributing to it philosophical significance. Philo in the *Embassy* abandons his transcendent approach and interprets Judaism as an urban religion centered in the Jerusalem Temple. Augustus's praise of the Temple is introduced as a way of signaling the fundamentally Roman nature of this interpretation (*Legat.* 157). Philo's discussion of Moses as priest and prophet thus fits well into his later construction of Judaism in specifically Roman terms, which give priority to cult and religion rather than to secular politics or canonical texts.

One example will illustrate Philo's view of Moses as priest. In the context of the tabernacle, Philo explains that Moses was instructed "in all the mysteries of his priestly duties, the first of them being the building and the furnishing of the sanctuary." Philo then provides a detailed account of the tabernacle, the "portable sanctuary," by stressing the connection between cult and truth. The structure itself was based on "immaterial and invisible forms," which Moses had provided. The actual artifice "symbolically represents the realm of the mind, while what lies outside . . . represents the realm of sense." Other aspects of the building were constructed according to perfect numbers or the symbolism of the hemispheres.[23] The altar and the candlestick are of special significance in Philo's account, the incense being a symbol of thankfulness for the benefits derived from heaven and earth, and the candlestick alluding to "the movements of the luminaries" (*Mos.* 2.101–2). The tabernacle functions as the symbolic center of the universe, and the cult emerges as the substance of Judaism, with Moses as the foundational priest.

Seeing that Philo devotes virtually all of the second volume of the *Life of Moses* to such religious matters rather than to character and history, we get the impression that he repeats a move he made in the historical writings, where he consistently changed political registers into religious ones. This became especially evident in the case of King Agrippa I, whose political achievements were marginalized in favor of Philo's own mission as a religious leader in times of crisis. Such a move made sense in the context of Claudius's new policies vis-à-vis the Jews, which restricted their political rights in Alexandria while fully acknowledging their religious freedom. Philo's Moses suits this tendency. While having a brilliant record as a politician, whose life Philo is proud to present as a model for imitation, he fulfills equally important cultic functions, which strengthen the interpretation of Judaism as an apolitical, religious entity.

The Life of Joseph

When Philo introduces the figure of Joseph, he summarily looks back on the *Lives* of the three patriarchs Abraham, Isaac, and Jacob. He no longer discusses issues of historiography, as he did at the opening of the *Life of Moses*, but is instead concerned with different types of men. While Abraham represents the life "that results from teaching," Isaac exemplifies the life of the self-taught and Jacob the life of practice. Philo writes with a sense of comfort and achievement about his previous biographies, obviously having gained experience in the genre and expecting his readers to be familiar with it. His readers' continued interest in the biblical forefathers may indeed have stimulated him to write a fourth *Life*, namely, that of the politician (*Jos.* 1).

Philo uses Joseph's death to offer a kind of obituary or summary of his life. He praises his "comeliness and wisdom and power of language," showing how each of these qualities played out in the different stages of his life. The main points of Joseph's career, as Philo sets them out, are strikingly apolitical. His prominence is shown by the attraction of Potiphar's wife to his beauty, his good sense is said to have remained stable during numerous challenges, and his eloquence enabled him to persuade rather than coerce his subjects. Given the fact that Joseph was extremely successful at managing the state of Egypt as Pharaoh's viceroy, Philo easily could have highlighted his contribution to politics. In a sense he does the opposite. Whenever the biblical text speaks about his actual exercise of power, Philo uses the opportunity to teach a moral lesson. Recounting Gen 41:39–46, for example, he describes how Joseph is appointed by Pharaoh and virtually becomes the king of Egypt, but then draws a strikingly religious conclusion. "Such is the end of the pious," he says, "though they bend down, they do not altogether fall, but arise and stand upright, firm and strong, never to be upset again." Philo is clearly not interested in the political opportunities of Joseph's appointment but uses it as an example of the vindication of the righteous after a period of suffering. He conveys a message of hope and signals to his readers that one must always persist in waiting for divine providence (*Jos.* 122).

Philo moreover expands the biblical scene of Joseph's appointment by a long digression that explains Joseph's dream interpretation as a cipher for the politician facing the instability of the world and interpreting it like a dream. This general contemplation takes away the reader's attention from

Joseph's actual management of state affairs. Philo evidently likes the idea of an exemplary Jewish statesman but is rather more ambivalent about a concrete example. He may well have been concerned not to evoke the image of such Jewish politicians as Agrippa I or Tiberius Alexander, his nephew, whom Claudius appointed as procurator of Judea in 46 CE (Josephus, *J.W.* 2.220–23). Philo's *On the Life of Joseph* thus playfully transcends the genre of biography, often converting into philosophical speculation and then reverting back to the sequence of Joseph's life.

Philo envisions Joseph as visiting the inhabitants of Egypt during the famine, making a highly favorable impression on account of the "benefits that they received from him" and "the remarkable and exceptional charm of his appearance and general deportment." In Philo's view, Joseph's pleasant appeal is at least as important as his political contribution to the country, which is not specified beyond the details of the biblical story. When he mentions Joseph's position of supreme power in his meeting with his brothers in Egypt, he explores the topic for a study of character and asserts that despite the license of his position, he did not give in to vengeance. In light of this moralizing tendency, it is not surprising that Philo celebrates Joseph's cultural contribution to Egypt, where he is said to have introduced the symposium. Philo's consistent shift in the *Life of Joseph* from real politics to political theory, religion, and culture conforms to the second part of the *Life of Moses*, where Philo moves from Moses's role as king to his priestly and prophetic functions.[24]

Nevertheless, the *Life of Joseph* follows biographical conventions similar to those of the *Life of Moses*. Philo is interested in Joseph's childhood and explores the available biblical details to tell a lively story of his activities in the family (Gen 37:2–3). Joseph's character is given special attention: "So his father, who observed in him a noble mind above the ordinary, treated him with respect and special care and was fond of him more than his other sons, because he was late born and nothing conduces more to affection than this. As he himself was a lover of excellence, he fostered the fire of the child's nature by special and exceptional attentions, so that it would not only smolder, but quickly shine forth" (*Jos.* 4). Philo speaks here about Joseph's "nature" and "noble mind," indicating that he was an exceptional character from his earliest childhood onward. Philo expands the biblical story in light of biographical conventions and creates a scene that shows the development of his personality and the influence of his early mentors. Jacob plays the role of Joseph's first teacher, who recognizes and supports his son's talents. While Philo applies the same biographical techniques to the image of Joseph as he had done in the case of Moses, he is clearly more restrained. Moses is an exceptional and highly independent hero, whereas Joseph ranks above average but requires good nurture and a supporting teacher to fully develop his potential.

The theme of nature and nurture plays a prominent role throughout Joseph's *Life*, which is characterized by dramatic reversals of circumstances and invites treatment of this topic. Philo initially uses the biblical notice of the brothers' envy to study how the hero overcomes obstacles. Joseph, he stresses, confronts his brothers' envy with remarkable "innocence of manner," behaving naturally and refraining from intrigues. Not disturbed by his expulsion from the family, Joseph arrives in Potiphar's house and immediately gives "proof of the nobility and good nature of his character." Joseph then confronts the assaults of Potiphar's wife and manages to resist them because he has a strong "sense of decency and temperance, which nature and exercise had implanted in him." When Philo's Joseph reconciles with his brothers in Egypt, he assures them that he will not take revenge even though their father has just died, because "I do not change my way with the changes of times." His brothers conversely congratulate him on his ability to endure the vicissitudes of life, appreciating that he kept no "resentment at the unwelcome beginnings and the initial obstacles." Philo has rewritten the biblical account with attention to themes of Stoic philosophy, which gives special attention to the care of the self in the changing circumstances of life. He has also continued a line of thought that occupied him in his philosophical writings, when he distinguished between "a gifted nature," which one receives, and the "study and exercise" that one invests in order to beautify that nature.[25]

Adopting Stoic ethics, Philo is particularly interested in the individual's decision making in complex situations. He is no longer concerned with the body-soul dichotomy, which occupied him in the *Allegorical Commentary*, but instead assumes a rather unified soul encountering stimuli from the outside world. A good example of such character study is the scene of Joseph's first meeting with his brothers, when they do not yet recognize him. As Philo put it, "Even though he [Joseph] was young and promoted to such a high position, invested with the first office after the king, looked upon by West and East, lifted by the prime of his youth and the greatness of his power, and having an opportunity to revenge himself, could have born malice [to his brothers], yet he, on the contrary, endured his emotion with self-restraint and kept it under the control of his soul" (*Jos.* 166). Philo highlights Joseph's self-restraint by stressing other options at his disposal. It would have been perfectly understandable had Joseph taken revenge, given both his past experience and his present position. Rationality, however, prevented him from giving in to the emotions. Joseph implements the ideal of contemporary Stoic philosophy, rejecting the "first incitement" of emotion and "stopping the enemy at the frontier." While he behaved like an exemplary philosopher, his brothers had previously been "inflamed with merciless wrath" and failed to heed Reuben's advice "not to assent to anger." Philo's distinction between a good rational reaction and a bad acceptance of emotions echoes scenes from the *Embassy,* in which he described his own process of decision making. We recall that he was proud to have relied on his *logismos,* not accepting the appearances of Gaius's benevolence, while his fellow ambassadors succumbed to emotions of joy.[26]

When Philo narrates the story of Joseph's encounter with Potiphar's wife (Gen 39:6–12), he stresses his inner freedom, which enables him to resist her advances even though she is a lady of higher social rank with considerable power over his life. Joseph "was stronger than the untoward situation and burst into words suitable to a freeman and worthy of his race." In Philo's eyes it is remarkable that Joseph retained his inner freedom even though he was in the position of servant in Potiphar's house. While the freewoman is enslaved by her emotions, the servant behaves like a freeman, acting rationally and daring to speak his mind in a coercive situation. This interpretation of the biblical scene echoes Stoic philosophy, with its emphasis on freedom from the emotions. It also reminds us of the *Embassy,* in which Philo praised Macro's free speech to the Roman emperor. As we recall, there, too, the socially superior person, namely Gaius, was a slave to his emotions, while his socially inferior advisor proved himself morally stronger. Philo also devotes a whole treatise to the subject of such freedom, *Every Good Man Is Free,* in which he addresses a broader, non-Jewish audience to whom he explains that the Jews live a life of inner freedom. In the *Hypothetica* Philo describes the Essenes as a voluntary association of Jewish philosophers who lead a life free from the passions. When Philo thus says in the *Life of Joseph* that Joseph's frank speech to Potiphar's wife was "suitable to a freeman and worthy of his race," he continues a prominent theme of his later writings, which engage, as we have seen, Roman discourses.[27]

The *Life of Joseph* thus translates the general philosophical themes of Philo's later writings into concrete biographical terms, showing how Joseph as an exemplary statesman implemented Stoic ethics throughout the changing circumstances of his life. Philo shows an interest in early childhood stories and the maturation of Joseph's character, while avoiding details of his political state management. He emerges as an ideal rather than a concrete Jewish politician, extremely suitable to the narrative of the historical treatises. Given Philo's overall development, it is not surprising that Joseph's image in the *Life* strikingly differs from that in the *Allegorical Commentary*, where he figures as a symbol of material weaknesses and aspirations to honour.[28]

Philo's *Life of Joseph* must have addressed a broad, non-Jewish audience outside Alexandria because he explains that the term "nomes" refers to the various districts of Egypt—a fact that local readers undoubtedly would have known. Moreover, an Alexandrian audience hardly would have been pleased with Philo's claim that Joseph introduced the symposium to Egypt, thus attributing a well-established custom to a foreigner. The *Life of Joseph* does not seem to have been written for a Jewish audience either, because it uses Joseph's confrontation with Potiphar's wife to explain the basic ethics of Judaism. Readers raised in the Jewish tradition would not need to be told that the "children of the Hebrews" follow "laws and customs especially our own." Roman readers, by contrast, would have been delighted by Philo's question "Where is the house of the Ptolemies?" or his equally snide remark that Egypt is nowadays in slavery.[29] The biography of Joseph thus was written for an audience similar to that of the biography of Moses, both inscribing Judaism within contemporary Roman discourses, one with an emphasis on history and priesthood and the other with an emphasis on personal ethics and freedom.

The Life of Abraham

Philo opens his biography of Abraham with a disclaimer. Having placed the figure of Abraham in the context of the creation, the first heroes of the book of Genesis, and the subsequent legislation, he says, "Suitably then Moses associated the family of these three [Abraham, Isaac, and Jacob], nominally men, but in fact, as I have said, virtues, namely nature, teaching and training" (*Abr.* 54). Philo subverts here the genre of biography, stressing that this life is not about a human character, but about abstract virtues. This is indeed the only *Life* that lacks childhood anecdotes and shows no interest in the maturation of personality. To be sure, the biblical account provides no information about Abraham's childhood, but it is significant that Philo does not imagine the lacking details. He is instead concerned with types of men described in Genesis and explains the main qualities represented by Enosh, Enoch, and Noah.

Why does Philo nevertheless use the title *bios* for his work on Abraham and place it among his other biographies? One reason must be its pedagogical orientation. The heroes of the book of Genesis, especially Abraham, are ethical role models for readers. As Philo puts it, "These are men who lived blameless and good lives, whose virtues are recorded in the most Holy Scriptures, not only for their praise, but also to impel the readers and encourage them to similar zeal, for these men are endowed with life and rational laws" (*Abr.* 4). Philo envisions here the readers' moral improvement as a result of learning about past heroes. While these heroes are said to be "endowed with life and rational laws," it is their life stories that instruct the audience. Philo clarifies that he will present a positive picture of his heroes and show that virtue is within human reach. The story of Abraham's life teaches lessons of significant events that are also illuminated from an allegorical point of view. These allegorical additions do not replace the literal sense, as in the *Allegorical Commentary*, when Philo offers allegory as a solution to textual problems.

The first important event in Abraham's life, as reported in Genesis, is his prompt compliance with God's demand to "go from your country and your kindred and your father's house to the land I will show you" (Gen 12:1). Philo stresses the significance of Abraham's compliance by dwelling on the enormous difficulties connected to leaving one's home. He considers the "charms" of one's family, which naturally prevent people from moving, as well as the unbearable hardship of political banishment and the inconveniences of short-term travel for economic or diplomatic purposes. Enumerating these options, Philo contextualizes Abraham within the cultural discourses of his own time and even speaks of his migration in terms of colonization, as he had done in the context of Moses and the Jewish people in the historical treatises. Abraham emerges as a model of piety whose love for heavenly things overpowers his earthly cravings and enables him to depart from home and eventually discover the monotheistic God. Although we discussed Abraham the monotheist in the previous chapter, it is important to point out in the present context that Philo stresses Abraham's actual traveling. His character is shown in his readiness to depart promptly and take hardships upon himself—aspects not mentioned in the *Migration of Abraham* from Philo's early Alexandrian period, which dwells only on his inner personal estrangement from earthly tendencies.[30]

On the journey to Egypt Abraham gives further proof of his piety. Philo initially adds to the biblical account in Gen 12:10 that the decision to go down to Egypt during the draught in the land of Israel was well calculated. Philo's Abraham knew about the agricultural advantages of Egypt, such as the fruitful flooding of the Nile, which was of special ethnographic interest during the Hellenistic period. Philo moreover explores Abraham's character in the scene of Sarah's capture by Pharaoh. Helpless in face of Pharaoh's despotic power, Abraham "takes refuge to the last remaining championship, namely, that which comes from God" (*Abr.* 95). While Abraham in the biblical story enjoys material benefits in exchange for his wife's services to Pharaoh, Philo envisions him as a deeply concerned husband and devout hero. His piety is rewarded and his wife remains unmolested.

Abraham's "greatest deed" in Philo's view is his prompt obedience to God when told to sacrifice his son Isaac. Philo stresses that Abraham loved Isaac and appreciated his moral virtues but did not hesitate to surrender him because he was "mastered by his love for God" (*Abr.* 170). It is especially remarkable in Philo's eyes that Abraham remained "steadfast" and calm when Isaac asked him about the sacrificial victim. Abraham answered his son that God would provide a victim, while anyone else would have fallen silent or become embarrassed. Although the biblical text provides the conversation between Abraham and Isaac (Gen 22:7–8), it is Philo who turns this scene into a study of character, with an emphasis on other possible modes of action. Parallel to his other biographies, Philo studies here the individual in a complex situation with various options open to him. *On the Life of Abraham* illustrates how the virtue of piety is implemented by a past hero, who can serve as readers' role model. Philo of course does not anticipate that his readers would consider sacrificing their firstborn sons, but instead encourages them to apply similar piety in critical situations of their lives.

Philo's Achievement as a Biographer

We have seen that the most historical of Philo's biographies is the *Life of Moses*, where he makes full use of biographical conventions and themes of Roman Stoicism. It has become clear that Philo was the first Hellenistic author to offer educational *Lives* with rich insights into the personal qualities of each character. The *Lives* were a way of communicating Judaism to a broader audience ignorant of the biblical text. The patriarchs constituted a kind of national gallery of exemplary forefathers that non-Jewish readers were invited to visit.

Philo's contribution can be appreciated by comparison to subsequent authors writing in Greek under Rome. Plutarch is the most significant parallel. Like Philo, he started his career as a Platonic philosopher engaged in traditional genres of writing, ranging from dialogue, table talk, and *zetemata* to treatises on specific subjects. Coming of age under the Flavian emperors, he frequently traveled to Rome as an ambassador and philosopher, making numerous Roman friends whom he mentions in his writings. Like Philo, Plutarch began his biographical activity relatively late in life and in connection with the Roman emperors. He did not introduce some sketches of character to an otherwise historiographical treatise, but self-consciously offered biographies as distinct from regular history.[31] As he put it, "Now the accurate narration of each of these events belongs to formal history, while it is my duty not to omit such incidents as are worthy of mention in the deeds and fates of the Caesars" (*Galba* 2.3). Plutarch distinguishes here, as in his later *Parallel Lives*, between a continuous record of history and a biographical narrative focusing on exemplary incidents that illuminate character.[32] While the concept of biography is already in place, Plutarch in the extant *Lives of the Caesars* does not yet present whole lives but focuses on select periods of political significance. Like Philo in the historical writings, he treats the character of Roman politicians in decisive situations.

Plutarch's *Parallel Lives* are well known for their moral conception of biography. In the introduction to the *Life of Pericles*, where he reflects on his work in the ten preceding volumes, Plutarch stresses in a Platonic mode that art should serve the formation of character, effecting moral improvement rather than simply providing pleasure. Parallel to Philo, he sees the biography as an extremely useful form of literature that is concerned with the teaching of virtuous action. Bringing such action from the past to his readers' attention, Plutarch hopes to stir them to "imitation" and prompt them to "admire the works and strive to emulate those who performed them." Like Philo, he anticipates a sympathetic audience that is open to being instructed.[33]

The heroes of the past become alive when Plutarch inquires about them and writes down their *Lives*. He is not interested in larger state affairs and constitutions, but rather in the protagonists as exemplary personalities.

Like Philo, he uses significant anecdotes to illuminate their characters: "For it is not histories that I am writing but lives; and in the most illustrious actions there is not always a manifestation of virtue or vice. Yet a slight thing like a phrase or a jest often makes the greater revelation of character than battles where thousands fall or the greatest armaments or sieges of cities" (*Alex.* 1.2). This self-definition as a biographer has immediate implications for Plutarch. Comparing himself to a portraitist, he insists on his right to select relevant material rather than aim at a comprehensive presentation. Leaving the great contests to others, he is concerned with the "signs of the soul." Anecdotes are a favorite means to that end because the soul expresses itself most authentically in deeds hidden from the public eye. He takes a special interest in the youth of his subjects before they become well-known figures. Alexander, for example, shows his innate courage and charisma by controlling a wild horse, while Alcibiades is exceptionally handsome, devoted to Socrates, but also given to arrogance and intemperance, as shown by his reaction to a carriage blocking his way in the street.[34] Philo's *Life of Moses* clearly anticipates Plutarch's *Lives* in its anecdotal style, its overall pedagogical aim, and its *paideia,* with a Stoic sense of self and some Platonic reminiscences.

Philo's achievement is further illuminated by Philostratus, who was active in Athens around the turn of the second to the third century and describes himself as belonging to "the circle around" the empress Julia Domna, wife of Septimius Severus. His *Life of Apollonius of Tyana* is a hybrid text that combines biographical, hagiographic, and novelistic features. The eight volumes of this *Life* transcend biographical standards even more than Philo's two-volume *Life of Moses,* both pointing to broader cultural and religious purposes. Philostratus introduces himself somewhat apologetically by stressing that he will correct Apollonius's image as a magician and show his philosophical and religious virtues. His complaint about people who do not really know him, because "they single out only this or that deed," taking his relations with Eastern sages as a sign of his dilettantism, sounds like Philo's apologetics at the beginning of the *Life of Moses.* Moreover, Philostratus promises to "be accurate" and provide a most reliable account of the man as he actually was. For this purpose he specifies some of his sources, which he has gathered "from many cities," and draws special attention to the notebooks of Damis, who traveled with Apollonius. While acknowledging his clear style, Philostratus dismisses his lack of skill, thus explaining the need for his own writing. Later on he is no longer concerned with his sources, imaginatively reconstructing his hero's life, much like Philo, who promises accuracy and then freely retells the biblical account. Finally, Philostratus, like Philo, dwells on the protagonist's talents and education. While Philo formulates Moses's training in general philosophical terms, Philostratus reflects the spirit of his time by identifying specific schools of philosophy. Through the *Life of Apollonius* Philostratus offers his Greek readers a path of Greek culture in the Roman Empire, which situates them between the center of power and the East.[35]

The Gospel of Luke has increasingly been appreciated as a kind of biography and is thus of interest in the context of Philo. Luke famously opens his Gospel by distinguishing his own account from previous ones. Others may have handed down what they think they have seen, but he has made a careful investigation that guarantees the truth. This is immediately followed by the story of Jesus's exceptional birth and childhood anecdotes. The story about Jesus as a child prodigy in the Temple, "sitting among the teachers, listening to them and asking them questions," remarkably resembles Philo's anecdote about Moses among his teachers. Luke's "Life of Jesus" ends with Jesus risen from the dead, instructing his disciples, and implicitly also the readers, about his significance in history and the future tasks of his followers. Both the style of writing and the contents of this Gospel qualify as a biography of a hero who ushered in a way of life that the author recommends.[36]

Comparing Philo to these later Greek writers in the Roman Empire, we notice that he is the first author to use biographies for broader moral, cultural, and religious purposes. Through the *Lives* of the biblical patriarchs he positions himself as a Jew in contemporary Greco-Roman discourses and inscribes Judaism among the leading civilizations. His style is easily accessible and offers a splendid introduction to Judaism and Jewish values, placing the Israelite ancestors next to the Roman. While the biographical approach became popular among a variety of Greek writers in the Roman Empire, it is interesting that the rabbis avoided biographies and thus opted out of this type of discourse.[37]

7 Biblical Ladies in Roman Garb

Philo did not write separate biographies of the biblical matriarchs, but assigned them a visible role in the *Lives* of the male heroes. Sarah and the women in Moses's family loom relatively large in the biographies of Abraham and Moses, much as Cleopatra does in Plutarch's *Life of Antony*. Unlike their Egyptian counterpart, however, the biblical ladies enjoy unblemished reputations as wise and beautiful women. Their high profile is surprising in light of the *Allegorical Commentary*, written in Alexandria, in which Philo identifies the feminine with the inferior material realm. Eve, for example, is interpreted as a symbol of the "feminine" senses that cause the masculine mind to be enslaved. Sarah's menopause, mentioned in Gen 18:11, indicates that she left "all womanly things," namely, sense perception and material tendencies in the soul. After regaining her virginity, Sarah is impregnated by God, who sows his divine seed in her womb, the symbol of the human soul.[1]

In light of these allegorical interpretations in his early Alexandrian works, it is remarkable that Philo in his later *Lives* does not eliminate the women from Israel's history, but rather integrates them as positive flesh-and-blood figures. They no longer need to erase their femininity and turn into ethereal symbols in order to be appreciated. This dramatic change of Philo's views requires an explanation. Does his new interpretation of the biblical women have to do with his arrival in Rome, which had already prompted him to recast the patriarchs in a distinctly historical mode?

A first clue is provided by Philo's historical writings, which mention the only real woman in his extant oeuvre, namely, Augustus's wife Livia. He praises her in the *Embassy* for taking her husband as an "instructor in piety" and receiving a "pure training." Philo had ample opportunities in Egypt to appreciate women in public roles but never mentions any of them.[2] This silence regarding outstanding Egyptian women, such as Queen Cleopatra, must have had to do with the fact that Philo as a young man was fully integrated into Platonic discourses in Alexandria, which lacked interest in gender issues and historical women. His reference to Livia in his later historical works, on the other hand, resonates with contemporary Roman discourses. Livia was given "divine honors" by Claudius "as soon as his power was firmly established." This means that she received special public attention in Rome precisely when Philo was most likely still visiting there.[3]

Philo's interpretation of Livia engages contemporary discourses in Rome, where intellectuals took a lively interest in gender issues and the place of women in society. Livia had provoked numerous reactions. The Senate voted to call her "mother of her country" and the emperor Tiberius "son of Livia." The new emperor, however, rejected these honors and generally disliked her continuous influence in Roman politics, even warning her "not to meddle with affairs of importance and unbecoming a woman." Tacitus subsequently criticized her dominating spirit and provided a rather malicious portrait of her. Seneca, by contrast, expressed a deep appreciation for Livia. In his *Consolation for Marcia*, his earliest treatise written during Philo's years in Rome, he recommends her to Marcia and his implied readers. While generally assuming that women have a "feminine weakness of mind," Seneca praises the former empress for taking the philosopher Arius Didymus, her husband's friend, as a teacher and thus gaining rational control over her grief after her son's death. Livia is presented to Marcia as a prime role model, who can show her how to cope with the passions and mourn in a temperate way. She also demonstrates that women, if they make conscious efforts, can be as brave as men in the struggle for tranquility of mind.[4]

Both Philo and Seneca appreciate Livia as a woman willing to learn and consequently able to develop a philosophical disposition. While Seneca praises her for overcoming her grief, Philo points to her high regard for the Jewish Temple, paralleling that of her husband. Both authors assign a crucial role to her education and stress her exceptional status among the women, who, as Philo puts it, are generally "weaker and do not apprehend any mental conception apart from what their senses perceive." Moreover, both Philo and Seneca conceive of Livia as a subordinate wife, who fulfills her husband's expectations. It is through him that she acquires her intellectual training, either directly as his student or indirectly by relying on his philosopher friend. Her public influence and independence of mind, mentioned by Suetonius, are overlooked in this context (*Claud.* 4.1–7). A rather domesticated, yet positive Livia emerges.

Seeing that Philo is exposed to Roman culture and praises Livia in terms very similar to those of Seneca, we have to ask how his experience in the capital shaped his views of biblical women. To what extent is their image in the *Exposition,* especially in the *Lives* of the patriarchs, consistent with the portrait of Livia in his historical writings? Can we identify features of Roman philosophy in Philo's sketches of Sarah, Eve, and the women in Moses's family? Vice versa, are there limitations, religious or other, to his effort at integrating the biblical women into wider discourses?

Exemplary Wives

Sarah is the most prominent of the biblical women in Philo's later writings, partly thanks to the fact that her husband's biography has survived. Rebecca, Rachel, and Leah may also have fared well in the *Lives* of Isaac and Jacob, but these are unfortunately lost. Philo praises Sarah as "a wife most excellent with regard to her soul and most beautiful in her body, surpassing all the women of her time" (*Abr.* 93). The matriarch is impressive in the spiritual and the material realms, both of which Philo appreciates in the later stage of his career.

Philo uses the short biblical reference to Abraham's mourning Sarah's death in Gen 23:2 to write a lengthy encomium. In his earlier treatises from the Alexandrian period he gives this verse no attention, with the exception of *Questions and Answers on Genesis* 4.73, where he interprets Sarah's death allegorically as the demise of wisdom. Philo's new interest in the death of a beloved person and the ways of remembering her is remarkable. His excitement about this topic is so great that he abandons his narrative role as detached biographer and exclaims, "I have many praises to tell about this woman, but will mention one, which will be the clearest proof for the others as well" (*Abr.* 247). Philo identifies to such an extent with the role of the mourner that his description almost reads like an obituary of his own beloved wife. This highly personal interest in the biblical scene of mourning resonates well with contemporary Roman culture, where lengthy inscriptions on tombstones were fashionable and the remembrance of the deceased had become a subject of philosophical inquiry. Seneca's influential teacher Attalus compares the remembrance of lost relatives and friends to the "agreeably acid taste" of certain fruits, which is recommended no less than "enjoying a meal of cakes and honey."[5]

Philo praises Sarah as an exemplary wife and ideal partner who "is most suitable to his [Abraham's] heart and noble in every respect."[6] The term "most suitable to his heart" draws attention because it is absent from the biblical story and suggests a mutual relationship based on feelings and a felicitous matching of personalities. Sarah was in Philo's view dear to her husband and did not only perform marital tasks, which were appreciated for their usefulness. Unlike the biblical narrator, Philo moreover speaks about Sarah's "love for her husband," which she showed in numerous ways. She was a "real partner in life" (κοινωνὸς ὄντως βίου), "considering it right to share equally good and bad circumstances." In contrast to numerous other women, she did not "run away from misfortunes, lying in wait for pieces of good luck, but accepted her portion in both with utmost readiness as suitable and becoming of a wife" (*Abr.* 246). Philo has invested the biblical marriage with the values of marital partnership and love. This ideal developed in late republican Rome and became highly significant in various public spheres of the early empire. From Cicero and Ovid onward, love for wives and thankfulness for their partnership became literary topoi. Augustus reinforced this ideal by demanding that every citizen take a "wife who is chaste, domestic, a good housekeeper, a rearer of children … to join you in prosperity and console you in misfortune." Supporting this policy, Livia dedicated a shrine to Concordia. Seneca's loving partnership with his wife Paulina became so famous that Tacitus still spoke about it. The Roman philosopher Musonius asks one generation after Philo, "What is the chief end of marriage"? His emphatic answer is "community of life" and "perfect companionship and mutual love of husband and wife, both in health and sickness and under all circumstances." Given these distinctly Roman discourses, which have no parallel in Alexandrian sources, it is not surprising that even Josephus, not a natural feminist but deeply immersed in Roman culture, gives special attention to the mutual relationship between Jacob and Rachel. Embellishing the biblical account, Josephus stresses that Jacob is "overcome by love for the girl" and cannot act otherwise than her father requests because of his love. Once wedded to her and about to depart, he asks her and Leah whether they are ready to accompany him, thus leaving behind their family and home. Being assured of their goodwill, rather than taking it for granted, Jacob embarks on the journey. Rachel and Leah, Josephus highlights, went along out of "just kindness, which becomes wedded wives to have for their husbands."[7]

Philo especially praises Sarah's loyalty and steadfastness on the couple's journeys: "She shared with him the departure from relatives and unhesitatingly migrated from her household, shared continued and successive wanderings on foreign soil, and suffered want in famine and joined his war campaigns" (*Abr.* 245). Philo has considerably expanded the biblical text, which merely says that Abraham "took his wife" from Chaldea to the land of Israel (Gen 12:5). As we have already seen, traveling had become a favorite topic in Philo's later writings, making a prominent appearance in his conception of the Jews in the *Embassy*. The people of Israel feature as a nation of migrants, traveling from their original metropolis and founding new colonies, while the biblical patriarchs prove themselves on journeys. In the above passage Philo multiplies Abraham's journeys and discusses for the first time the contribution of a biblical matriarch. Sarah's cooperation with her husband is no longer taken for granted, as in the biblical story, but is acknowledged as a considerable effort and proof of her endurance. Sarah emerges as a personality, who takes a conscious and noble decision in support of her husband. Philo stresses that she was "unhesitating" in her commitment and "always at his side," speedily taking upon herself all the known hardships of migration.

This portrait of Sarah as a wife who courageously shares in her husband's travels shows unmistakably Roman traces. At about the same time, Seneca praises his aunt for sharing her husband's travel. She lost her "dearly beloved husband" in a shipwreck but "bore up bravely, enduring at the same time both grief and fear, and, overmastering the storm, bore his body safe to land amid the shipwreck." Seneca appreciates her behavior as one of those "outstanding deeds" of women that regularly go unnoticed. This praise is not an isolated incident, but rather part of a broader discourse. The historian Tacitus records a public debate about the question of whether wives should accompany their husbands on their journeys into the provinces. Severus Caecina opposes this idea, arguing that wives have a bad influence on their husbands and will disturb them in their public duties. This position, however, is overruled by a clear majority. Tacitus especially mentions Valerius Messalinus, who emphasizes that wives share everything with their husbands and provide the best relaxation after the men's return from stressful experiences. Moreover, the prince Drusus is quoted as pointing to Augustus as a model because he "traveled to West and East in the company of Livia."

Drusus thus justifies his need for his "dearest wife and parent of so many common children." Only in her company, he insists, will he be able to travel with "tranquility of mind" and should therefore not be torn away from her.[8]

One element in Philo's above quoted praise of Sarah is especially remarkable, namely, the motif of her "accompanying [Abraham] on war campaigns." This must be an allusion to Abraham's campaign in the north (Gen 14:13–16). Why does Philo assign such significance to this short biblical story? Moreover, why does he introduce Sarah, who is not at all mentioned in this biblical context? The hermeneutic key is once more provided by Roman culture. The princes Germanicus and Drusus were regularly accompanied by their wives on state and military affairs. Germanicus's wife even gave birth during a campaign in Germany and raised the young Gaius Caligula among the soldiers. Claudius moreover symbolically shared his military campaign in England with his wife Messalina by allowing her a prominent place in the triumphal processions.[9] Following these precedents, Philo imagines Abraham as a Roman prince who is accompanied by his courageous wife on military campaigns.

Yet Abraham and Sarah's happiness is disturbed by their lack of children. This well-known problem is easily solved by the biblical narrator in the person of Hagar, Sarah's maid, who gives birth to Abraham's first son (Gen 16:1–2). For Philo, who has stressed the loving partnership between Abraham and Sarah, this is a grave dilemma that challenges the nature of their marriage. In his retelling of the story, Sarah realizes that her sterility challenges their marriage and offers philosophical reasons for Abraham's taking an alternative mate, thus justifying a choice that otherwise may appear highly problematic. Indeed, a widower in a funerary inscription from first-century BCE Rome, known as the "Praise of Turia," rejects precisely this option in favor of his cherished partnership with his wife. The husband testifies that he was "horrified" by his wife's proposal to take a younger woman and confesses that he "went out of his mind" at the thought of losing her. Josephus, too, seems to have felt the oddity of Sarah's proposal in the context of Roman marriage ideals. While he solves the problem by relegating the initiative to God, Philo has recourse to philosophical considerations much beyond the biblical text.[10]

Philo puts into Sarah's mouth an emphatic appeal to Abraham to take Hagar as an alternative mate who will give birth to an heir:

> For a long time have we lived together, well pleased with each other, but the purpose for which we ourselves have come together and for which na-

ture has set up the partnership of husband and wife, namely, the birth of children, has not been realized and cannot be hoped to come to fulfillment in the future by me, who has grown beyond the age [of procreation]. But do not share my sterility and do not be prevented through goodwill for me from becoming what you yourself can become, a father. Envy for the other woman will not befall me, because you will not come to her out of irrational desire, but in fulfillment of the necessary law of nature. (*Abr.* 248–49)

Philo's Sarah contrasts the "natural" purpose of marriage with the couple's loving partnership. She describes her marital life thus far in tender and emotional terms as living together "well pleased with each other." Nature, on the other hand, has its "necessary law" and demands procreation, which will be achieved without involving the passions. Neither marital harmony nor procreation is based on sexual desire, but instead on rational cooperation, which leads to good feelings of care and mutual satisfaction. Ideally, partnership and procreation go together, but Sarah stresses that in cases such as theirs in which they clash, priority has to be given to nature's demand for procreation.

This appeal to nature in the context of marriage echoes contemporary Stoic discussions, which were especially prominent in imperial Rome. Stoic thinkers, in contrast to Platonists, generally advocated family life for the wise man and saw marriage and procreation as commandments of nature.[11] Arius Didymus, Augustus's philosophical advisor, makes the following emphatic recommendation: a man "will marry and father children, as these are consistent with his nature as a rational being, capable of partnership and fond of fellowship." Augustus legislated in the spirit of such philosophy against celibacy and childlessness within marriage. In Philo's own days Claudius encouraged Roman citizens to marry and beget children, even if his approach was more erratic than that of his admired predecessor. This Roman ideal of children within marriage is also advocated by Musonius, who argues in typically Stoic fashion that "marriage is manifestly in accord with nature," as humanity was purposely created in two sexes "to be united and live together and produce and rear children together."[12]

Philo uses these Stoic arguments, popular in Rome, to justify Sarah's suggestion that Abraham should have offspring from Hagar. Her proposal, which would have horrified Turia's husband, thus appears far more understandable in a Roman context. Under Philo's pen Sarah appreciates her marital partnership with Abraham but gives priority to the demands of nature, which insists on offspring even at the cost of interrupting a monogamous marriage. Sarah thus persuades Abraham on rational grounds to take Hagar. Philo has attributed this exposition of a central Jewish value, which he will further explain in *On the Special Laws*, to a woman, who transmits them to her husband.

Sarah's self-effacing love for her husband is prominent also in the story of their journey to Pharaoh, the last example Philo gives of her virtues. While the rabbis critically reacted to the biblical image of Abraham as an inconsiderate husband who enjoyed material benefits in exchange for his wife's sexual services to the Egyptian ruler, Philo interprets the incident with emphasis on the couple's harmony.[13] He stresses Abraham's helplessness before "a licentious and cruel-hearted despot" and assigns a highly cooperative role to Sarah. In his story, she prays to God, "taking refuge together with that man [Abraham] to the last remaining alliance" (*Abr.* 95). God's rescue of Sarah in Pharaoh's house thus results from the couple's common appeal. The motif of the couple's partnership in vicious circumstances renders Philo's account more egalitarian than its biblical counterpart, which does not mention Sarah's plight at all. At the same time, however, Philo confirms traditional hierarchies, assuming the wife's dutiful submission to her husband's interests. In Philo's story there is no hint, such as we find in later rabbinic literature, that Sarah may have been dissatisfied with her husband. In his view, she is a quiet and ideal wife, proving also in this most challenging incident that she is devoted to her husband and seeks help together with him. Similarly, Philo never allows Sarah to question her husband's authority or play a dominant role. He omits Sarah's insistence on Isaac as heir and her consequent expulsion of Ishmael, which is against Abraham's will in the biblical story (Gen 21:8–12). As much as Philo does not relate Livia's independence in politics, but portrays her as a dutiful student of her husband, so his Sarah, too, is a highly domesticated partner.

Philo's ideal of a wife resurfaces also in his interpretation of two other biblical women: Eve and Moses's mother. As the paradigmatic first woman of the Bible, Eve provides Philo with an opportunity to reflect on the institution of marriage. She is introduced as being "glad" about Adam's approach immediately after the creation and "shyly returns his greeting" (*Opif.* 152). Self-consciously referring to Plato's creation myth, Philo then praises marital partnership: "Love supervenes, bringing together as it were the two separate halves of one being, which have been torn apart, and fitting them into one piece. It sets up in each of them a desire for fellowship with the other for the purpose of giving birth to their like" (*Opif.* 152). This is a sophisticated play on Aristophanes's creation myth in Plato's *Symposium*, where the different kinds of love are explained by reference to the different origins of humans. Men who love other men derive from an original all-male creature, which Zeus divided into two halves, while men who love women derive from a composite creature and women who love women from an all-female original. In Plato's mind there is little doubt that the homosexual form of love is superior. He stresses that men who do not require women are the finest, having "the manliest nature" and "no natural interest in wiving and getting children" (*Symp.* 189C–192E). Well aware of this Platonic ideal, Philo presents his own and far more Stoic interpretation of marriage. Heterosexual love is the only valid option in his eyes. Adam and Eve's encounter brings the two halves together, implementing the Roman ideal of partnership and procreation. Philo radically undermines Plato's ideal of male self-sufficiency and replaces it with the image of a harmonious marriage so popular in contemporary Rome. In this new context Eve is allowed to play a far more positive role than in the *Allegorical Commentary*. Rather than imposing herself on the masculine mind, she now enables Adam to engage in a worthy and productive partnership.

Philo's new interpretation of Eve as a welcome marriage partner anticipates Plutarch, another intellectual from the Greek East who came into intimate contact with Rome. Like Philo, he was deeply immersed in the Platonic tradition and enriched it with topical Stoic notions. Plutarch opens his *Dialogue on Love* with Protogenes, who expounds the Platonic ideal of homosexual love and male sufficiency. The rest of the dialogue, however, is geared toward overcoming this position and showing the advantages of heterosexual love. Stoic arguments carry the day. Daphnaeus praises the love between women and men as "normal and natural," conducive to friendship and procreation. Plutarch stresses that the relationship between husband and wife is of much longer duration than that of homosexual couples, who do not enjoy the same sort of commitment, trust, and loyalty. Plutarch's examples of good marital partnerships significantly come from Rome. The successful Roman couples that populate his dialogue indicate that he, too, looks to the capital of the empire rather than to Plato for inspiration regarding marriage.[14] In his *Advice to the Bride and Groom* Plutarch enthusiastically praises the couple's harmony and partnership, recommending that the loving spouses unite in both their souls and bodies, an aim that requires the bride's continuous education. While Plutarch assumes a dominating role for the husband, who makes the principal decisions and

sets the tone for the relationship by his own example, he allows some egalitarian features, such as sharing property. Here, too, Plutarch draws on Roman examples and Roman law, self-consciously anchoring his views of
marriage not in Platonic philosophy, but in contemporary Roman society.[15]

Moses's mother is the third biblical woman whom Philo interprets as
a good marriage partner. While the biblical narrator briefly reports from
a male perspective that "a man from the house of Levi went and took to
wife a daughter of Levi," Philo presents Moses's parents as partners. Both
are introduced as "the best of contemporaries, members of the same tribe."
More importantly, they are connected by "mutual concord."[16] Philo's attention to the quality of their marital relationship renders his interpretation
not only more egalitarian than its biblical counterpart, but also distinctly
more Roman.

Philo thus has created three harmonious biblical couples. Biblical
women have become Roman ladies who are beloved by their husbands
and trusted for their loyalty. Sarah, the most developed of the matriarchs,
also propagates the natural purpose of marriage, namely, procreation, and
willingly shares the hardships of her husband's journeys. These flesh-and-
blood wives in Philo's later writings significantly differ from their ethereal
counterparts in the *Allegorical Commentary* and are clearly modeled on Roman ladies, such as Livia, as well as contemporary Stoic notions popular
in Rome. Philo actively engages cultural discourses that he encountered
during his embassy to Gaius. As a Jewish interpreter of the Bible he mod-
ernizes Judaism and brings it up to contemporary standards. He is far more
systematic in this respect than Josephus, who occasionally adds the motif
of romantic love but refrains from turning all biblical marriages into harmonious partnerships and developing the characters of the biblical wives.
As an author writing in Greek, Philo moreover translates Roman ideals
into Greek terms, significantly anticipating Plutarch. Political, philosophical, and religious factors combine to furnish him with his new images of
biblical wives who are no longer Platonic symbols, but rather flesh-and-
blood figures dressed in Roman garb and ready to be received in contemporary salons.

The dramatic development of Philo's position vis-à-vis biblical wives
also illuminates early Christian writings, which negotiate the place of
women from very diverse perspectives but often show a similar combination of political and religious factors. Most interesting in our context is the
author of Luke-Acts, who also writes in Greek and looks toward Roman

discourses. He mentions three couples, one Roman, one Jewish, and one Christian, who easily travel together and, in the case of Aquila and Priscilla, also share religious responsibilities in the early Christian community. More importantly, when the author of the Gospel of Luke adapts earlier materials from Mark, he adds emphasis to the women, sometimes even adding a scene with female characters, such as the one with Martha and Mary in Jesus's travelogue. Luke also rewrites the story of Jesus's birth with emphasis on the family setting and marital harmony. In his story, it is Mary who receives the message from the angel about Jesus's birth and shares it with her husband. Matthew, by contrast, suggests that Joseph receives the announcement about the birth from the Holy Spirit and then suspects his pregnant wife of adultery, even casting her out. Luke avoids marital dissonance and solves the problem by insisting that Mary was not yet pregnant at the time of the angel's announcement.[17] To the author of Luke-Acts, who also addresses broader Greco-Roman audiences, the ideal of marital partnership seems to have been important. Like Philo, he has reinterpreted received traditions and creatively adapted them to Roman values.

Devoted Mothers

Moses's mother plays a role in her son's earliest childhood that contemporary Roman readers would easily recognize as familiar. Her motherhood is immediately challenged by the need to abandon her baby, known as "exposure" in Roman society, and Philo embellishes the biblical text in response to this challenge. In the biblical story Moses's birth is set in the context of Pharaoh's measures against the Hebrews forbidding them to raise newborn males so that they will not grow too strong and become a threatening factor in Egyptian policy. The biblical narrator depicts Moses's mother with characteristic brevity. She inspects the baby upon his birth, hides him for three months, and then exposes him in order to avoid Pharaoh's violent measures (Exod 2:2–3). Deed follows upon deed, while the reader learns nothing about her feelings.

The Septuagint introduces the father into this scene, implying that he, too, inspects the newborn and hides him. Philo considerably expands this line of interpretation and points to the parents' common decision to expose their son. The decision itself is problematized. According to Philo, the parents detested the deed, which Pharaoh's policies forced upon them, and "exposed the child with tears on the banks of the river and departed moaning"

(*Mos.* 1.10). For a long time they continue to be torn by remorse and feelings of guilt. Philo considerably changes the biblical story and stresses both the extreme difficulty of exposing a child and the couple's agreement regarding it. He highlights the latter aspect because a woman doing this on her own, that is, without the father's explicit consent, would have been prosecuted under Roman law.[18] Moses's mother does not act alone, but has her husband as a full partner at her side, thus behaving legally. It is interesting that Josephus has the father alone make the decision (*J.A.* 2.218–20).

Moses's parents are furthermore committed to the ideal of raising one's children rather than exposing any of them. Philo highlights their distress when forced by external circumstances to expose Moses. Their dilemma reflects lively Roman debates. While ancient philosophers had generally accepted child exposure as a legal and morally justifiable option for parents, Roman Stoics were particularly outspoken in their criticism of the practice as a violation of nature. Seneca praises his mother, Helvia, for having raised all of her children, exposing none of them and taking pride in her pregnancies and the resulting large family (*Cons. Helv.* 16.3). Musonius even devotes a whole lecture to this topic and speaks of a religious as well as a natural duty to raise one's offspring. He moreover points to the social benefits and the high status gained by having many children. Humans, he stresses, should not be meaner than little birds, which "rear their young and find sustenance for all that are born to them" (15.4). Philo, a contemporary of Seneca, writing slightly before Musonius, shows a similar sensibility to the issue of child exposure and shows that Moses's parents abhorred the prospect but recognized that the safety of the whole family demanded this sacrifice. Their decision bespeaks an overall concern for the family rather than a lack of commitment.

Philo adds another touching scene to Moses's earliest childhood. In his narrative Moses was "breastfed at home for three months" (*Mos.* 1.9). The biblical story reports that Moses's mother nursed her son in Pharaoh's palace, as if she were an ordinary wet nurse (Exod 2:7–9). Philo introduces the motif of her breastfeeding beforehand, namely, when she is still hiding her newborn. Does Philo merely state the obvious, rendering the story more consistent, or does he convey a particular message beyond Scripture?

The fact that breastfeeding was discussed in Roman circles suggests that Philo's interpretation is not accidental. While wet nurses were common in upper-class society, Roman Stoics advocated breastfeeding as part of a simple lifestyle in accordance with nature.[19] Musonius provides useful background information in his lecture on women's studies. In his view, there is a direct connection between a woman's training in philosophy and her willingness to feed her babies by herself. A woman who is educated to overcome passions and hardships will be "prepared to nurse her children at her own breast and to serve her husband with her own hands and willing to do things which some would consider no better than slaves' work" (3.18).

Moreover, Plutarch subsequently praises his wife for having raised her children in the house and breastfed them. She even endured a surgery at her nipples for the latter purpose (*Mor.* 609d). Anticipating Plutarch and Musonius, Philo shares the ideal of a natural mother who nurses her newborns. Moses's mother emerges as a Roman matron who heeds the advice of the philosophers and does not avoid the effort of breastfeeding her newborn son. She is evidently committed to raising him and makes the decision to expose him only under extreme circumstances and with utmost emotional difficulty.

Competent Daughters

In the *Lives* of Moses and Abraham, Philo has an opportunity to speak about the youth of some biblical women, namely, Miriam, Tsippora and the shepherdesses at the well, and Sarah. In the biblical exodus story Miriam plays a significant role, observing her exposed baby brother floating on the river and encouraging Pharaoh's daughter to hire his mother as a wet nurse (Exod 2:4–8). Philo adds two small but significant details to the narrative. He initially stresses that Miriam watched Moses on the river "out of family affection," thus integrating her into the Roman ideal of a nuclear family. Though young, she shares the feelings of care for and commitment to the other family members and is an independent actor, spontaneously implementing family values. Philo's image of the active girl significantly differs from Josephus's scene, where she receives orders from her mother. Philo moreover specifies Miriam's actions in her encounter with Pharaoh's daughter, adding to the biblical account that Miriam "guessed her difficulty" when seeing the exposed Hebrew baby and "turned to ask her" whether she should bring a wet nurse. Here, too, Miriam's character is developed from within. Philo focuses the scene on her person, and the reader is invited to appreciate her initiative and sensitivity. Philo's interpretation fully emerges by comparison to Josephus, who rewrites the scene from an external perspective, stressing that Miriam "apparently came without design and from mere curiosity."[20] He looks upon her arrival through the eyes of Pharaoh's daughter, who would have attributed her approach to mere chance. Neither woman is provided with a full character.

Another group of women in Moses's *Life* deserves our attention: the seven girls who came to the well in Median to draw water for their flocks but were driven away by some male shepherds. The biblical narrator says that Moses interfered on their behalf, "stood up and helped them and watered their flock" (Exod 2:17). Philo identifies in this biblical scene an issue of gender roles among workers. He puts into the mouth of Moses a speech that assures the girls of their right to take up work usually done by the men. Accusing the shepherds of being "lumps of flesh, not men," Philo's Moses says to them, "The girls are working like youths and shirk none of their duties, while you young men live softly like girls" (*Mos.* 1.54). To be sure, Philo upholds traditional gender roles, identifying soft living with the feminine element, while true men are expected to work hard. At the same time, however, he allows for role reversals. Prompted not by the biblical text, but by his own intuition, Philo stresses the value of the girls' work and their right to use the well as professional shepherdesses.

The proto-feminist role that Philo assigns to Tsippora and her friends would be inconceivable without Roman discourses. Philo expresses such values just before they are forcefully formulated by Musonius, who generally assumes that "tasks should be assigned that are suited to the nature of each [gender], that is, the heavier tasks should be given to the stronger [i.e., the men] and the lighter ones to the weaker [i.e., the women]" (14.17). Spinning, women's traditional work, serves as an example of suitable female occupation. At the same time, Musonius, like Philo, admits that "occasionally, however, some men might more fittingly handle certain of the lighter tasks and what is generally considered women's work, and again, women might do heavier tasks which seem more appropriate for men."[21] Philo adopts a strikingly similar position on gender roles as Musonius, both accepting reversals of the "natural" division of labor. It is indeed likely that Philo was prompted by Roman discussions to interpret the biblical scene at the well in an innovative fashion.

The last biblical woman whose youth Philo discusses is Sarah. The biblical story introduces her only at a later stage as Abraham's wife, not mentioning any details of her upbringing (Gen 11:29). Philo fills in the gap and says that Sarah had been instructed "even from the cradle" in the doctrine of divine omnipotence, which explains why she understands that "everything is possible for God" and recognizes Abraham's mysterious visitors as angels. Indeed, in Philo's story it is Sarah, rather than Abraham, who "saw in the strangers before her a different and grander aspect, namely, that of prophets or angels, transformed from their spiritual or soul-like nature into human shape." To be sure, Philo does not dwell on Sarah's education as much as he does on that of Joseph and Moses; nevertheless, he is the first Jewish exegete who attributes any education to a biblical woman. In the case of Sarah he draws a consistent portrait, with religious instruction in her youth and subsequent application in the encounter with the angels. Sarah's role in the *Exposition* is especially remarkable in view of the fact that Philo never mentions her in this context in his earlier Alexandrian writings. In *Questions and Answers on Genesis* 4.2–7 he is preoccupied with the transcendent nature of God, which manifests itself in the form of three men, and assumes that Abraham, not Sarah, recognized their true identity.

Sarah's positive image in the *Exposition* resonates well with contemporary Roman discussions about women's education. Both Seneca and Musonius advocate philosophical studies for women so that they can implement their potential virtue. Seneca regrets that some husbands do not let their wives pursue proper studies and thus hamper their ability to restrain their passions and live a good life. Musonius devotes a whole lecture to the thesis "that women should study philosophy" and emphatically argues that the two sexes have been endowed with the same gifts of rationality and must therefore receive a similar training.[22] Philo's Sarah fits well into this context. Roman readers would have been delighted to learn that she received religious instruction in her childhood and put it to such good use later on. Such readers would have been equally pleased to see that the Jewish tradition has other energetic and competent daughters to boast of. Both Miriam and Tsippora and her friends at the well would have aroused interest in enlightened Roman circles open to Eastern religions.

The Adulteress

Philo declares adultery to be the "greatest of crimes" (*Jos.* 43). Given alternative vices, such as murder, this statement is surprising. Why does Philo assign adultery such a central place in the catalogue of sins? Roman culture once more provides an answer. In 2 BCE Augustus published rigorous legislation against adultery following the public scandals of his daughter Julia, who was put on trial and exiled for life. He thus hoped to set an authoritative example of enforcing family values. From then on the notion of modesty in sexual matters was a central slogan in Roman culture and literature. Philo's agenda fits well into this context. In *On the Special Laws* he pays exceptional attention to adultery, showing how Jewish values coincide with Roman preferences.[23]

Philo discusses a specific case of adultery in the *Life of Joseph*. Potiphar's wife, a mere symbol of the passions in the *Allegorical Commentary*, is now presented as a real-life figure who illustrates the gradual loss of self-control.[24] Philo is interested in the process that leads a married woman to fall in love with a young man and propose illicit sex. While the biblical text says with characteristic brevity that the woman "cast her eyes upon Joseph and said 'lie with me'" (Gen 39:7), Philo stresses that she was motivated by "love" and "doted upon the beauty of the youth and became mad by putting no restraint on her passions" (*Jos.* 40). Philo also speaks about her "lawless lust" turning into a blaze and prompting her to use violence after her verbal proposals are rejected. Several terms in Philo's description carry connotations of madness, lack of government, and raving in battle. The reader immediately gets the impression that Potiphar's wife not only proposes adulterous sex, but causes a serious disruption of society.

Philo has no sympathy for the adulteress and refrains from favorable embellishments, such as offered by the Jewish author of the *Testament of the Twelve Patriarchs*. Philo analyzes the crisis not from her perspective, but from outside, with the explicit purpose of deriving an ethical lesson from her fall. As far as Philo is concerned, her deterioration has nothing to do with an inherent dichotomy between body and soul, which Plato put in the center of his ethics. He instead offers a typically Stoic analysis with emphasis on the external trigger of the woman's passions, namely, Joseph's beauty. Philo advises her and the implied reader to exercise rational control rather than give free rein to the passions. Most importantly, the woman must respect married life and learn to prefer legitimate over adulterous unions.

Joseph's response to Potiphar's wife is remarkable for the degree of equality it assumes for men and women regarding sexuality. Philo puts the following words into Joseph's mouth: "Before the lawful union we know no intercourse with other women, but come as virgin men in marriage to virgin maidens. The end we seek is not pleasure, but the birth of lawful children" (*Jos.* 43). Philo repeats here the ideal of marriage for the purpose of procreation, which we have already encountered in the context of Sarah's sterility. In addition, he proposes an exceptionally egalitarian perspective on sexuality, which does not condemn women for sexual license while allowing men to follow their passions. Philo's Joseph instead demands commitment and abstinence from men as well.

Philo's argument resonates well with contemporary Roman philosophy, which called for equality in sexual matters, while Roman law remained conservative and protected men's license. Responding to these double standards, Seneca complains about the hypocrisy of many husbands, who consort with married women while not tolerating their own wives to have affairs. Such men, he suggests, should mind "their own chastity." Musonius makes even more stringent demands, declaring sexual intercourse "justified only when it occurs in marriage and is indulged in for the purpose of begetting children." Adultery is rejected as "most unlawful." Musonius supports his position by two arguments. Initially, he suggests, like Seneca, that husbands should not measure their wives by standards to which they themselves do not adhere. Moreover, men should not be "less moral than women or less capable of disciplining their desires."[25] Sexual restraint and premarital virginity thus become important marks of philosophically trained men and women. Philo's interpretation of Joseph's encounter with the most known adulteress of the Bible, namely, Potiphar's wife, suggests that he wholeheartedly agrees with contemporary Roman philosophers and inscribes Judaism into their moral codes.

Conclusion

Philo's refashioning of the biblical women in the *Exposition* differs significantly from his interpretation of them in the *Allegorical Commentary*, written in Alexandria. They no longer symbolize the dangerous body with its passions, best to be left behind, but rather have become exemplary wives, mothers, and daughters who play an active role in the history of Israel. This dramatic change of perspective can be explained in terms of Philo's move from Alexandria to Rome. While gender issues were not discussed in the philosophical circles of his home city, he later encountered lively philosophical discussions in Rome on the role of women in society. His new image of the biblical women in the *Exposition* closely corresponds to his view of the Roman empress Livia, whose clear-sightedness, strength, and loyalty he appreciates. The biblical women likewise become real historical figures whom Philo interprets sympathetically from within.

For Philo, the move toward historical genres of writing also implies embracing ethical values prevalent in Rome. He emancipates the women of his tradition in a way that is strikingly similar to the way that his Roman colleagues discussed new roles for their partners and daughters, while at the same time maintaining traditional hierarchies and "natural" gender divisions. Inscribing biblical women into current Roman discourses, Philo reasserts the value of his religion. The boundaries between Roman and Jewish women are to some extent blurred. Harmony prevails and no dichotomy between inherently different categories is visible. Philo thus wrote at an important juncture in the history of gender issues and reflects the tensions and developments of his time. It is significant that he eagerly adopted the new options available to him in Rome, while still refraining from novelistic motifs, as became popular in Josephus's generation.[26]

8 Stoic Ethics in the Service of Jewish Law

Philo's *Exposition* concludes with the treatises *On the Decalogue, On the Special Laws, On the Virtues,* and *On Rewards and Punishments.* No specific cases are judged here, as would be appropriate in the context of Jewish readers wishing to live by the law, but the overall meaning and ethical rationale of Jewish customs is explained. In contrast to the rabbis, Philo addresses a general audience intrigued by the otherness of Jewish life and formulates for the first time in Judaism a philosophy of law. His attention to Mosaic law in his later writings is remarkable in light of his lack of interest in the topic in his earlier Alexandrian period. In the *Allegorical Commentary* he addresses the issue of observance only once, reacting to Alexandrian Jews who argued that literal observance was no longer necessary if the allegorical meaning was implemented. In this internal Jewish debate Philo defends religious observance by stressing that the "Holy Word teaches us to consider good repute and abandon nothing of the customs fixed by divinely inspired men greater than those of our time." The authority of inspired leaders of the past guarantees the validity of Jewish law and commands adherence within a clearly defined community. Philo as a young man adopts a rather traditional position and offers only one philosophical argument, which relies on the dichotomy between body and soul. Appealing to a prominent Platonic theme in the *Allegorical Commentary,* he identifies the bodily dimension of human existence with the literal meaning and law observance, while the soul is associated with the allegorical interpretation. Both, Philo insists, must be appreciated and given expression in Jewish life.[1]

Seeing the brevity of Philo's discussion in the *Allegorical Commentary,* we have to ask how he developed a sustained interest in legal questions.

What prompted him to formulate a highly innovative philosophy of law? I argue that Philo explains the rationale of Jewish customs for a wider audience in order to meet the challenge of the embassy in Rome. This historical background is indicated in the introduction of the treatise *On the Special Laws*, which deals with circumcision, a commandment "ridiculed among many." Philo justifies circumcision by comparison with the Egyptians, who also practice it, and invites his readers to appreciate that the Jews are not the only ones "mutilating the bodies of themselves and their nearest." This appeal is apologetic, defending the Jewish ritual vis-à-vis readers suspicious about basic facts of Judaism. Philo cannot have addressed Alexandrians, given that circumcision was practiced among the Egyptians, especially the priests, and thus could not have aroused the kind of mockery he experienced. He certainly would not have to explain to Alexandrian readers that the Jews are not the only people circumcising their sons. In Rome, by contrast, circumcision was not practiced in the general population and became a ridiculed marker of the Jews. Tacitus, Horace, and Petronius did not hide their disdain. Apion, the head of the rivaling Egyptian embassy to Gaius, engaged such sentiments in Rome and "scoffed at circumcision." When Josephus a generation later addresses these issues in Rome, he notes that Apion's rhetoric does not fit his Alexandrian background.[2] Treating circumcision as the first notable custom of the Jews, Philo addresses a distinctly Roman concern and offers an explanation of the ritual that would arouse sympathy and integrate the Jews among the enlightened nations.

Philo's philosophical interpretation of Jewish law is closely connected to politics. Acutely aware of having been plunged "in the ocean of state affairs" and "civil turmoil" (*Spec.* 3.1), he arrives in Rome as a diplomat and begins to deal with the Jews' civic status and particular customs, which the rivaling Egyptian embassy had criticized. His public role prompts him to address a broader, non-Jewish audience whose opinion he hopes to shape. Philo anticipates Josephus, who arrives in Rome a generation later after the defeat of the Jewish revolt and quickly turns into a well-connected historian. Toward the end of his career Josephus writes a defense of Judaism, protecting his ancestral tradition against the accusations of various writers, mostly of Egyptian origin. Devoting almost a complete tractate to the work of Apion, Josephus offers an exposition "of the whole structure of our constitution and its individual parts." He is eager to show that "our laws" promote piety, fellowship with others, and justice. Josephus stresses that he is not about to offer a self-indulgent encomium on his nation, but rather responds to "the many and false accusations brought against us." The fairest defense, he figures, is a detailed report about the laws. Philo finds himself in a strikingly similar situation in Rome, directly facing Apion's slanders, which would still occupy Josephus one generation later. As the Egyptian diplomat criticizes Jewish "Temple rituals and other customs," Philo offers an exposition of the Jewish religion for a broad Roman audience. His implied readers resemble Josephus's audience and are probably intellectuals in Roman salons, sympathetic toward Judaism and willing to learn more about the controversial religion.[3] Philo appeals to such readers, attempting to show that the Jewish religion is not a degeneration of Egyptian cults, but rather a philosophy of life congenial to Roman values. The Jews are not, as Apion suggests, hostile to Greek culture and non-Jewish *paideia*, but live according to principles shared by the Greco-Roman world.

The Ten Commandments as Heads of Jewish Law

In his treatise *On the Decalogue* Philo develops an innovative notion of Jewish law that has been recognized as a breakthrough in ancient Judaism. Although the Ten Commandments probably had been used in liturgical contexts from the first century BCE onward, Philo is the first extant author identifying them as "heads" of the whole of Mosaic legislation. He stresses that "those [laws] revealed in his [God's] own person and by himself alone are both laws and heads (κεφάλαια) of the particular laws, while those given through the prophet all belong to the former category." Moreover, the "ten words" or "exhortations" are in his view "generic laws," which "allude" to a variety of congenial precepts. The particular laws are identified as "dependent species," which are "contained" or "implied" in the leading principles. Even ritual laws are associated with broader moral concepts.[4]

Philo's distinction of the Decalogue may to some extent have been inspired by its unique role in the Bible. Unlike other collections of biblical law, the Decalogue establishes the covenant between God and Israel and contains timeless instructions for every Israelite without reference to particular circumstances. Moreover, the number ten is typological, as Philo enthusiastically points out, and the tenth commandment is altogether unique because it prescribes things not to be desired and thus treats pure intention rather than its practical consequences. These special features of the Decalogue point to fundamental questions of ethics and naturally prompt philosophical contemplation.[5] Philo, however, is the first known reader of the Decalogue who explores this philosophical potential and identifies it as the basis of Jewish law, thus providing a universal, ethical interpretation of Judaism. His approach draws special attention because other authors of the Second Temple period take different routes. The book of Jubilees, for example, refers only to the most particularistic of the Ten Commandments, namely, Shabbat observance. Instead of providing a universal perspective on the Jewish tradition, the author regularly connects general precepts to specific events in Israelite history and renders them more particularistic than they originally were. Similarly, the various legal documents from Qumran stress divine revelation and authority, which are mediated through inspired leaders and translated into stringent, sectarian precepts.[6]

Alexandrian Jews, on the other hand, had already moved in a philosophical direction. Aristobulus (second century BCE) speaks about Jewish law as "set up with a view to piety, justice, self-control, and other qualities that are truly good." While the extant fragments of Aristobulus's work shed no light on the details of his thought, it is clear that he associates the Torah with universal standards of virtue and extracts Jewish law from the realm of God's personal will. The *Letter of Aristeas* (second century BCE) moreover says that "to live well means to keep the customs," stressing that each law "has a profound reason for it." Aristeas is concerned to show the objective value of Jewish law, which can be appreciated by anyone committed to moral education.[7] As far as the extant fragments can tell, however, Philo's predecessors in Alexandria neither highlighted the Decalogue nor developed a systematic philosophy of Jewish law.

Philo's philosophical interpretation of the Decalogue defines intrinsic qualities of Judaism. Assuming that the Ten Commandments are broader principles, Philo stresses that they "run through the whole of the legislation." Even the most minute or ritual regulations are anchored in overall philosophical principles and open "broad highroads, which lead to one end, namely, the undisturbed journey of the soul ever desiring the best." In this view, all the biblical laws serve educational purposes and aim at spiritual elevation. Philo highlights the ethical dimension by insisting, against Scripture, that no punishment is envisaged for the transgression of the Ten Commandments. God purposely refrained from threats, he explains, "so that people will choose the best, not involuntarily, but out of a willing consciousness, not using fear as their senseless counselor, but the good sense of reason."[8] The laws, including the most particular and ritual ones, are invested with an aspect of moral choice, which transforms them from commandments that demand obedience into ethical advice that is heeded on account of its intrinsic good.

Philo's approach must be appreciated in the context of Stoic philosophy in Rome. Cicero already describes Stoic ethics as a system that attributes utmost importance to free choice. The morally good is chosen for its own sake, without consideration of either punishment or reward. Cicero more- over says that for the Stoics the law, even in its most specific form, is rooted in philosophy and reflects universal right reason. The Stoic definition of the ethical function of law sounds remarkably similar to Philo's: "The law ought to be a reformer of vice and an incentive to virtue; the doctrine of living may be derived from it."[9]

Seneca devotes an important epistle to the question of how ethical principles are related to particular precepts. This issue is contextualized in an ongoing Stoic discussion. Seneca initially positions himself vis-à-vis Aristo, who argued that precepts amount to old wives' advice and are there- fore useless for the philosopher. Cleanthes, the second head of the Stoic school, by contrast, considered precepts to be beneficial provided that they are grounded in philosophical principles or "heads" (*capita*). Since Clean- thes's original Greek text is no longer extant, we cannot be sure which term he used, but it is highly likely that is was Philo's term, namely, *kephalaia* (κεφάλαια). Seneca follows Cleanthes and affirms the importance of pre- cepts, stressing that nature does not teach us our duty in each particular case. Human beings require specific instructions, derived from nature, in order to realize what is appropriate in specific situations. In Seneca's view, precepts do not coerce, "but plead," and they are effective if they are "often with you."[10]

These Roman discussions, which have no parallel in Alexandria, ex- plain the background to Philo's approach. To be sure, Seneca indicates that the Stoics discussed the tension between philosophical principles and particular precepts at least from Cleanthes onward. Philo thus could have been inspired by Cleanthes's work during the early Alexandrian stage of his career. In the *Allegorical Commentary* he once even mentions the idea of the Ten Commandments as "heads" of the particular laws.[11] This reference, however, remains isolated and does not lead to a broader interpretation of the Decalogue and its central role in Jewish ethics. At this stage Philo has no serious interest in questions pertaining to the philosophy of law. Only after his arrival in Rome does he apply himself to a detailed study of the Decalogue and its philosophical significance for Judaism as a whole. He now uses key terms and ideas that resonate well with Roman Stoicism and are ultimately based on Cleanthes's approach. Philo thus appeals to readers in the capital of the empire and hopes to persuade them that Mosaic law is not an idiosyncratic, foreign system with strange practices, but rather a philosophy of life that relies on familiar assumptions and points Jews toward broadly recognized virtues.

Philo's interpretation of the Decalogue has significant implications for Early Christianity. Paul wrote his letter to the Romans a few years after Philo's *Exposition* and expresses strikingly similar ideas. He engages the same notion of particular laws being "summed up" in an overarching principle, using a verb connected to "head," namely, *anakephalaiomai* (ἀνακεφαλαιόω). According to Paul, the four ethical commandments of the Decalogue are summed up in the law "love your neighbor as yourself." Unlike Philo, however, he does not include the wealth of specific laws under the rubric of philosophical principles and leaves behind traditional Jewish life. No longer committed to justifying Jewish practices in broader moral terms, Paul gives priority to the ethical principles of the Decalogue and subsumes them under an even more universal command. In Paul's words, "love does no wrong to a neighbor; therefore, love is the fulfillment of the law." The general principles replace ritual laws, the faithful Christian no longer being bound by the Jewish tradition.[12] While Philo may well have provided Paul with a model for thinking about the relationship between philosophy and law, he would have been rather surprised about the use to which his idea was put had he lived long enough to see the letter to the Romans.

Nature and Jewish Law

Philo investigates the character of biblical law by comparing it with other legal codes. He rejects the approach of legislators, who draw up "without embellishment and nakedly the things held righteous among their people," because it is "unreflecting and careless and not philosophical." The mere listing of legal instructions does not do justice to the intrinsic connection between law and broader philosophical concepts. Laws cannot be reduced to a list of specific actions, singled out for either reward or punishment because they serve overall intellectual and educational purposes. Moses is praised for introducing his law code with a treatise on the creation of the world, thus "not stating at once what should be practiced or avoided, because it was necessary to mold beforehand the minds of those who will use the laws" (*Opif.* 2). This introduction immediately raises broader questions about the relationship between philosophical principles or advice, which is voluntarily adopted for the purpose of individual improvement, and commandments, which demand unanimous obedience from everybody.

Such issues are discussed in contemporary Rome, while there is no trace of a similar interest in Alexandria. Seneca rejects the approach of his predecessor Posidonius, who argued that "the law should be brief so that it can be easily grasped by the ignorant." In Posidonius's view, Plato made a mistake when adding introductions to his treatises on the laws because that procedure obscures the precise expectation of the commandments. Seneca, by contrast, defends Plato and insists that introductions are vital because they set the readers' minds in the right philosophical direction, enabling them to perform the precepts with full intention. Regarding philosophy as "a law of life," Seneca advocates the importance of specific admonitions. Precepts constantly remind the wavering mind of its moral duties and prevent lapses into sin. "Sometimes we know, but pay no attention," he observes with fine psychological insight, and therefore we need to be constantly reminded. In Seneca's view, the only difference between "philosophical principles and precepts" is that the former are "general precepts, while the latter are specific." Both, however, lead human beings in the direction of moral improvement, one providing universal insights, the other instructions for specific situations. Seneca's discussion illuminates Philo's remarks on the connection between the biblical creation account and Jewish law and shows how much his approach resonates with Roman concerns. Philo renders the Jewish tradition familiar and understandable in the broader context of the empire.[13]

Philo introduces the concept of nature at the beginning of his treatise *On the Creation,* signaling that it will serve him as a broader explanation of Jewish law. As he puts it: "The beginning is, as I said, most marvelous. It contains an account of the making of the world, implying that the world is in harmony with the law and the law with the world and that the man who observes the law is thus a citizen of the world, directing his actions in relation to the [rational] purpose of nature (πρὸς τὸ βούλημα τῆς φύσεως τὰς πράξεις ἀπευθύνοντος), in accordance with which the entire world also is administered" (*Opif.* 3). This passage has often been discussed in modern scholarship with a view to the question of whether Philo embraces

Stoic concepts or rather translates them into particularistic Jewish notions. Several scholars have argued that he has adopted the Stoic notion of "living in agreement with nature" for which this school was widely known in antiquity. The founder of the school, Zeno, had already defined the goal of life as "living in agreement with nature." Cicero furthermore had explained that "law is the highest reason implanted in nature, which commands what ought to be done and forbids the opposite," while Seneca recommended that "you should measure all things by the demands of nature." Such views have been adduced to show Philo's inspiration by Stoicism, which prompted him to offer a universalistic interpretation of Mosaic law. Other scholars, however, have warned that Philo engages Stoic thought only in a limited or rhetorical sense, while departing from its actual meaning. In this view, Philo remains particularistic and insists on Jewish ritual, while dressing his arguments in Stoic style.[14] In order to do justice to the complexity of Philo's position we have to go beyond the above quoted introduction to *On the Creation*, which is too brief and isolated to provide meaningful insight. It is time to examine Philo's views throughout the *Exposition* and ask what the law of nature precisely means to him.

The tenth commandment—"You shall not covet your neighbor's house, you shall not covet your neighbor's wife or his manservant or his maidservant or his ox or his ass or anything else that is your neighbor's" (Exod 20:17)—provides Philo with an opportunity to contemplate the role of desire in Jewish ethics. He reads the commandment as a prohibition of desire as such, irrespective of its particular objects mentioned in the Bible. A commandment concerned with social justice is thus transformed into an instruction about the care of the self. In Philo's view, Israelites are encouraged to train themselves to eliminate desire. "All the grievous passions of the soul," he explains, "move and shake it against nature and do not allow it to be healthy, the hardest of them being desire." Desire is identified as the worst of the passions, their archetype so to speak, and contrasted to nature, which represents the rational norm. Philo's definition of passion as a movement against nature verbally echoes Zeno, who first spoke about passion as "a movement of the soul contrary to nature."[15] Philo's commitment to Stoic ethics is profound and leads to a rigorous ethical position that demands eradication of the passions.

While Philo was already in his earlier Alexandrian days familiar with the Stoic notion of passion, it is only in the *Exposition* that he specifies the intellectual process that according to the Stoics' theory makes up a passion and renders it controllable: "The presentation of something present and considered good arouses and awakes the soul when at rest and lifts it to great elation, like a light flashing upon the eyes" (*Dec.* 143). The key to understanding desire is the perception of something that is available as good, while in reality it is not so. Philo's perspective seriously takes into account the concrete circumstances of one's individual life. In his view, the passions are not an inherent part of the soul, as Plato thought, but rather a mistaken conception of specific things that present themselves as attractive options. Eradicating desire means adopting the right rational attitude toward the impressions hitting the soul. This highly intellectual definition of passion is based on Chrysippus, the third head of the Stoic school, who defined the passions as wrong "judgments."[16] Passion is seen as contrary to nature because it is aroused by the mistaken assumption that certain superfluous things, such as money, are good and therefore desirable. Appropriate reasoning, however, exposes them as lacking any intrinsic value and automatically eliminates their attraction. Philo has clearly been inspired by such Stoic ideas and offers a radically new reading of the tenth commandment, which serves as one of the "heads" of Mosaic law. He thus identifies conformity to nature by uprooting the passions as one of the overall guidelines of Jewish ethics.

Philo interprets other commandments of the Decalogue in terms of conformity to nature. The first commandment to worship only one God is presented as a call to follow nature or lead a life "inscribed on the tables of nature." Monotheism emerges as a natural religion and can be deduced from the creation, as we saw in chapter 5. Moreover, the commandment "you shall not kill" is said to derive from the recognition that humans are created as sociable beings and by nature destined to preserve society. Murder is primarily a subversion of the laws of nature and only secondarily an offense against God. Shabbat observance is natural in two senses: it conforms to the rhythm of waking and resting instituted by nature, and it celebrates the number seven, which plays a special role in nature. Philo thus justifies the two central aspects of the Jewish ritual, namely, the idea of a day of rest and its particular timing on the seventh day. He extracts both from the special circumstances of the Jewish tradition and recommends them as a universal practice that would be beneficial to anyone. Philo moreover explains the prohibition of adultery in terms of conformity to nature, insisting that it protects the natural instinct for procreation by preventing an excess of passion. The commandment to honor one's parents reflects in his view a natural impulse to reciprocate parental care, which is generally observed in nature. Philo says that those who have received a good upbringing are "glad to give nurture to old age, having been trained by none but nature." He even suggests that this lesson can be learned from the animals, such as birds, which often nurse their elderly parents.[17]

The background of Philo's interpretation of the Ten Commandments is Stoic. This school, as Gisela Striker puts it, was "the first to introduce the idea of nature as a kind of personal lawgiver." Zeno is reported to have established this approach in his lost treatise *On the Nature of Man*, in which he defines the goal of life as "living in agreement with nature, namely, living in accordance with virtue." This approach identifies nature with virtue and opposes the Epicureans, who identify pleasure as humanity's natural goal. As far as the extant fragments can tell, Zeno may not have provided satisfactory explanations regarding the precise connection between nature and virtue. His students and followers wondered how life according to nature leads to virtue, which is intrinsically concerned with the welfare of others. Chrysippus suggests that individual nature determines one's orientation in the world from birth to death. Like animals, human beings are endowed with an impulse to self-preservation, which renders their own constitution dear to them (*oikeiosis*). The gap between our initial focus on self-preservation and ethical behavior at a more mature stage is bridged by the idea of humanity's natural development. "Acquaintance of the things that are in harmony in nature," Chrysippus explains, will make us aware of the fact that "our individual natures are part of the nature of the whole universe." As human beings become increasingly rational, they recognize the overall harmonious nature of the universe and direct their ways toward a larger whole. This process requires sublimation of one's personal desires and limitation of one's profit. Cleanthes, on the other hand, addresses the issue of a potential clash between the personal and the universal by giving priority to the notion of "common nature." In his view, the latter is the only path to be followed, leaving hardly any space for the nature of the individual person.[18] Philo adopts Cleanthes's approach on this matter, with which he was already familiar at the beginning of his career, and never discusses the potential tension between individual and universal nature. Chrysippus's approach is evidently of little concern to him, while Cleanthes's perspective enables him to identify Mosaic law with nature.

Philo's explanation of the Ten Commandments in terms of nature not only echoes classical Stoic ethics, but also resonates well with Roman discourses. Philosophers in Rome were occupied with the question of how their particular constitution related to the norms of nature. Cicero identifies the "highest reason implanted in nature" with Roman law, insisting that the latter reflects eternal justice, while the law of other nations lacks a rational foundation. Roman law is unchanging in his view, expressing the same universal values from its initial documents up until republican times. Seneca's epistle *On Nature as Our Best Provider* similarly reflects on the relationship between nature and Roman culture. Seneca assumes a personified notion of nature, speaking of "her" as "demanding," "caring," and "ordering" specific things, such as abstaining from luxurious kinds of bread or golden drinking cups. Nature is moreover identified with the "builder of the universe" (*mundi conditor*), who provides the particular laws of conduct in society. In another *Epistle* Seneca explains that nature teaches humans by examples from life, that is, by analogy. "Our school of philosophy," he writes with pride, teaches by observing the surroundings rather than indulging in bookish study. Roman society plays an important role in this context. Public figures, such as Fabricius, who rejected Pyhrrhus's gold, exemplify how nature's commandments are heeded and implemented.[19] Seneca has drawn a subtle connection between nature's universal commandments and Roman exempla. Philo advocates a strikingly similar course. The Jew coming of age learns to identify nature's commandments in Jewish law and history, taking the patriarchs as role models for individual conduct. The universal law of nature and a particular culture are thus connected for Philo in the same way as for Cicero and Seneca.

Specific Roman values are moreover associated with Mosaic law. Philo's interpretation of adultery, for example, shows Roman traces. He attributes central importance to this issue, repeatedly inscribing it into nature and offering an overall philosophy of sexuality. The argument is based on the assumption that the nuclear family provides a man with a perfect framework for procreation and enables him to have children with one woman. Ignoring many biblical examples of polygamy or extramarital sex, Philo identifies every sexual act not aimed at legitimate procreation as "contrary to nature." He vehemently rejects adultery, prostitution, homosexuality, and intercourse with menstruating or sterile women. This ideal of heterosexual and monogamous unions echoes Roman legislation and family ideals. In 2 BCE Augustus published the *Lex Julia de adulteriis* against adultery, following the public scandals of his daughter Julia, who was put on trial and exiled. The emperor set an authoritative example of enforcing family values.

From then on the notion of modesty in sexual matters was a central slogan in Roman politics, culture, and literature. As we saw in the previous chapter, Philo embraces the Roman ideal of the family in his interpretation of biblical women. He also applies it to his discussion of Jewish law and associates it with the Stoic notion of nature. This move is all the more remarkable in light of the *Allegorical Commentary*, in which Philo complains in a Platonic mode that "marriage and the raising of children" withers "the flower of wisdom before it blooms." After arriving in Rome, Philo identifies marriage as a central and natural pillar of Jewish ethics, distinguishing Judaism from the "barbarian" practices of the Egyptians and Persians. Marriages with siblings, customary in Egypt, or with mothers, as practiced in Persia, are dismissed as contrary to nature.[20] Philo's polemics against the Egyptians has immediate political implications, suggesting that the ambassadors of the rivaling embassy in Rome represent a culture opposed to the values on which the Roman Empire is based. Judaism, by contrast, emerges as a civil religion that is useful for the general benefit of Roman citizens.

Another prominent case of Roman influence is Philo's discussion of paternal authority in the context of the commandment to honor one's parents. In his view, parents are situated by nature halfway between God and humans because they have produced new life. This elevated status endows them, and especially the father, with unprecedented authority not mentioned in the Bible. When encountering continuous and stern disobedience in a son, a father is entitled to upbraid, admonish, and even chain him. Should these measures prove ineffective, both parents may apply the death penalty. While Deut 21:18–21 already had foreseen the possibility of executing a "rebellious son," the biblical legislator demands the involvement of both parents from the beginning of the disciplinary process as well as the approval of a committee of elders for the final decision. In Philo's scenario the father acts far more independently. This change of emphasis has to do with Roman practices, as Philo himself suggests. In the *Embassy* he mentions the Roman law of *patria potestas*, or paternal authority, which accords the father "absolute power over the son," including the death penalty. In the *Exposition* Philo applies this Roman law to the interpretation of the Decalogue, suggesting that Jews and Romans share the same perception of the father's role in the family, which is embedded in nature.[21]

Philo interprets the biblical prohibition of murder with special attention to contemporary Roman culture. After discussing numerous occasions for murder, such as banquets, he turns to two issues that look rather more marginal and even a bit surprising, namely, abortion and child exposure. Exodus 21:22, which deals with accidental abortion, is taken to deal with intentional abortion and exposure as cases of murder prohibited by the sixth commandment. Although abortion was legal in the ancient world, on condition of the father's consent, Philo prohibits it from the moment the embryo is formed. Aborting an embryo amounts to interfering "with the laboratory of nature." Philo moreover explains at length the severity of child exposure. Parents who are thus inclined are "breaking the laws of nature" and behave worse than animals, because they prevent their offspring from receiving the upbringing they deserve. They have made sex contrary to nature, namely, without serious intention to procreate. Mothers who expose their children cause the flow of their milk, "the fountain which nature rained into the breasts," to diminish. Philo recommends that parents learn from the animals, which do not deprive their offspring of maternal nourishment. He is so concerned to show Moses's abhorrence of child exposure that he mentions concrete examples, such as throttling and desertion in a remote place, stressing in each case how the child is brutally murdered.[22] These concrete details as well as Philo's personal engagement indicate that he relates to an acutely topical issue.

Roman discourses throw light on Philo's position. Child exposure is an important subject of Stoic philosophy in contemporary Rome, while no parallel sources are extant from Alexandria. The Stoics are distinguished already by Cicero on account of their attention to "the love of parents for their offspring," which is seen as a provision of nature shared by animals as well. Parents have a natural duty to nurture their offspring. As we have seen in the previous chapter, Seneca praises his mother, Helvia, for having raised all her children, and Musonius Rufus, a thinker highly congenial to Philo, stresses the natural duty to raise one's offspring and points to the social benefits of raising many children. Human beings, he stresses, should not be meaner than little birds, which "rear their young and find sustenance for all that are born to them."[23] Philo engages such Roman discussions in his interpretation of the Decalogue, using images from nature to enforce his argument. Under his pen Mosaic law speaks to contemporary issues and inscribes the Jews into Stoic discourses in Rome. The observant Jew becomes not only a citizen of the world, as Philo promises at the beginning of the *Exposition*, but also an exemplary citizen of the Roman Empire.

Jewish Holidays as Training Grounds for the Self

Philo prefaces his discussion of the Jewish holidays by a philosophical consideration of the nature of feasting. He argues that "the law calls every day a feast, thus accommodating itself to the blameless life of righteous men, who follow nature and her laws." This introduction places the Jewish holidays, which are rooted in national history and divine revelation, into a wider philosophical context. A feast is defined as a time consecrated to the ideal of living according to nature rather than to commemorating particular historical events. Jews are like "those who practice philosophy among the Greeks or barbarians and live a blameless and irreproachable life." They aspire to tranquility and are "the best observers of nature and everything contained in it." Philo concludes his introduction to the holidays by stressing that those "delighting in virtues, live their whole life as a feast." These general explanations of the Jewish holidays resonate with Seneca, who devotes an entire epistle to the subject of *Festivals and Fasting*. He criticizes the commonly held view of feasts as occasions for material pleasures and instead recommends true feasts, which are modest in terms of material goods but orient people toward nature. Roman holidays are also said to make humanity aware of its true purpose and produce ethereal joy.[24]

While perfect joy and feasting are available only to God, human beings can aspire to authentic joy by celebrating the holidays in a proper way. This is done by assimilating them to God's feast. Philo initially highlights the centrality of the Shabbat, which is next in importance to the eternal feast of virtue. It occurs every seventh day, he explains, corresponding to a number of special cosmological significance. Philo moreover asserts that the Shabbat rest is not intended to encourage "amusement" or "laziness." The purpose of the Shabbat is rather to give a necessary relaxation to the body and enable it to resume work with new vigor. These explanations respond to a typically Roman prejudice against the Shabbat as a day of idleness. Seneca is the first known author who complains about this day being "useless" (*inutiliter*), because by "introducing one day of rest in every seven they [Jews] lose in idleness almost a seventh of their life." Tacitus and Juvenal later express similar views, which are significantly lacking in the extant sources from Hellenistic Egypt. Philo addresses an audience familiar with these Roman criticisms and offers an alternative view of the Shabbat as a day that reinvigorates the Jews and enables them to work even harder during the rest of the week.[25]

In Philo's vision the Shabbat is moreover a day for higher intellectual activities. Moses bids the Jews "to pursue philosophy at that time and improve the soul and the dominant mind." The synagogues become on the Shabbat "schools of good sense." The contemporary Roman dimension of this interpretation is immediately visible. As we saw in chapter 3 in the context of the historical writings, Philo attributes the same attitude to Augustus, who praises the synagogues in Rome because they become on the Shabbat "schools of good sense, temperance, courage, and justice and the other virtues."[26] Appealing to a wider non-Jewish audience, Philo hopes that his readers will embrace Augustus's perspective and recognize the Jewish synagogues as congenial places of philosophical education.

Philo gives special emphasis to the biblical instruction that slaves are set free on the Shabbat (Exod 20:10). Assuming a distinctly urban setting, where housework rather than field labor is at stake, he provides new philosophical explanations for the servants' rest. While the biblical command is based on the idea of humans imitating God's rest on the seventh day, Philo argues for an intended inversion of social hierarchies. "The masters," he says, "must be accustomed to doing things by themselves, without waiting for the services and attentions of their servants," so that they will be able to face potential difficulties courageously. The Shabbat trains masters to return to a natural lifestyle, preserve their independence from material goods, and prepare themselves for potential reversals of fortune. The servants are also transformed on the Shabbat because they learn "not to give up their hopes, but experience relaxing after six days as an ember or spark of freedom and look forward to their complete liberation, if they continue to serve well and love their masters."[27] Philo touches here upon a sensitive issue, namely, the future liberation of the slaves, which should come about by peaceful means rather than by revolt. Yet here, too, he expresses the idea of a reversal of social roles, probably expecting that a temporary relaxation will release tension and thus actually reinforce existing hierarchies.

Philo's social interpretation of the Shabbat closely echoes discussions in Roman Stoicism. Seneca explains that a true feast is modest in the extreme so that masters "become intimate with poverty" and momentarily experience what slaves go through every day. This will prepare them for strokes of bad luck and render them more steadfast. Seneca also praises the Roman custom of celebrating a holiday by having masters and slaves dine together in full equality. He probably thinks of the Saturnalia in honor of the god Saturn, which was well known for its inversion of social structures.

The Roman Stoic Epictetus subsequently comments on this feast, arguing that its reversal of roles provides only limited freedom, which cannot replace full philosophical freedom in life.[28] These Roman discussions, which point to the social dimension of the Saturnalia, indicate a lively interest in holidays as an occasion for social reversal and philosophical invigoration. Philo's interpretation of the Shabbat engages such discourses and inscribes Jewish customs into contemporary Roman culture. This interpretation must have appeared all the more natural given the similarity of sound between the word "Saturnalia" and the Greek pronunciation of the Shabbat, that is, "Sabbata."

Similar values animate Philo's interpretation of other Jewish holidays. The Passover, he explains, prompts an inversion of regular hierarchies by allowing all male Israelites to offer a sacrifice rather than relegate this function to the priests. The festive meal on this occasion is of course modest, the unleavened bread indicating proximity to nature. Like the Shabbat and the Feast of Tabernacles, the Passover is anchored in a special date of the calendar, namely, the spring equinox. Philo introduces Yom Kippur as a quintessential feast precisely because it is a day of fasting. He responds to potential criticism by stressing once more the difference between material and spiritual feasts. In his view Yom Kippur provides true merriment at the time of harvest, when fresh fruits are likely to distract the human mind from the essential values of life. Devoting themselves to prayer and abstaining for one day from food and drink, observant Jews become aware of the blessings generally available to them. Yom Kippur renders human beings thankful to God and strengthens the most basic element of proper worship. These interpretations of the Jewish holidays correspond with Philo's position in the historical writings, in which he describes the Feast of Tabernacles as "the common feast of the Jews during the autumn equinox," thus inscribing it into nature and rendering it understandable in the eyes of a wider, non-Jewish audience.[29]

Philo's appeal to Roman values in his discussion of the Jewish holidays carries apologetic tones. He must have been aware of the fact that Apion mocks them in his writings. For example, Apion explains the Shabbat as a day of rest after the Israelites contracted a groin disease during the exodus. They "called the day 'sabbaton,' preserving Egyptian terminology, because the Egyptians call the disease of the groin 'sabbo'" (Josephus, *C.Ap.* 2.21). Josephus one generation later still faces this slander and expresses considerable irritation, probably prompted by the fact that he encounters it among contemporary Romans. Philo, who directly faces Apion as the head of the rivaling Egyptian embassy to Gaius, must have been familiar with his views and counters them by a philosophical exposition of the Jewish holidays that highlights their affinity to philosophy and Roman values.

One God and His Temple

The Jerusalem Temple was central to Judaism during the Second Temple period, when it served both as the main sanctuary for offering sacrifices to the God of Israel and as a religious symbol in a wide spectrum of Jewish literature. Many Jews, however, were unhappy with the way it was administered by the Hasmonean priests. The central issue of the debate was ritual purity, which led some to reject the Temple and found a separate community near the Dead Sea. The author of a famous scroll from Qumran, the so-called *Miqsat Maase ha-Torah,* explains to an unnamed leader in Jerusalem that "we retired from the majority of the people and all their impurities" because the proper ritual requirements were not observed in the Temple. Authors of other scrolls found at Qumran construct an ideal Temple that fulfills sectarian expectations and properly governs the religious life of the Jews.[30]

Philo offers a completely different perspective and interprets the Jerusalem Temple in a philosophical manner, stressing Jewish monotheism, individual ethics, and pilgrimage. For Philo the Temple is both a concrete site and a place in the soul. While ignoring the concrete Temple in his earlier writings from Alexandria, he pays special attention to it in his later works, as we saw in chapter 2 in connection with Gaius Caligula. In the *Exposition* Philo discusses the Temple under the category of the first commandment, which establishes monotheism or, in his words, God's "monarchy." Philo initially goes through the familiar proofs for the existence of one God and then discusses the way that Moses considered "necessary to give honors to him." The Temple is presented as the central venue of honoring God, even though Philo stresses that the universe as a whole is a more perfect and holier temple, rendering purely ethereal service to God. The Temple "wrought by hands" is nevertheless an important institution in his eyes because it acknowledges the "impulse of people who pay their tribute to piety and wish by sacrifices either to give thanks to the blessings that have come upon them or beg forgiveness and interceding on their behalf." Sacrificing is in Philo's view a religious act fraught with moral intention.

It is not a ritual aimed at the deity's satisfaction, but rather serves to effect a transformation in worshipers, who reflect on their deeds and judge them by divine standards.[31]

Philo's interpretation of sacrifice closely corresponds to Stoic notions popular in Rome. We saw in chapter 3 that Philo is familiar with Varro's idea that worship starts with a sense of gratitude toward benefactors. In the historical writings Philo applies this notion to his criticism of Gaius, arguing that the emperor had done nothing beneficial to deserve divine honors. In the present context he uses it to interpret the Jerusalem Temple as a space to express gratitude toward God. Philo thus renders Jewish worship congenial to Cicero's summary of Stoic theology, which is based on the idea that gratitude for benefactions is the beginning of each god's particular cult. More importantly, Cicero describes Stoic theology as an approach that respects the traditional cults while reinterpreting them in a philosophical vein. His Stoic spokesman Balbus is concerned, like Philo, to point to the proper way of "revering and worshiping" the gods in a customary way, while at the same time insisting on the following point: "But the best and also the purest, holiest, and fully pious form of worshiping the gods is ever to venerate them with purity, sincerity, and innocence of mind and speech." Philo uses the same vocabulary of spiritual purity when speaking about sacrifice in the Jerusalem Temple (θύειν εὐαγῶς). He fully agrees with Balbus, who accepts traditional cults, while stressing that the worship of the gods must lead to personal piety, virtue, and happiness.[32]

Philo further highlights the moral dimension of the Temple cult by pointing to pilgrimage as a journey that tests the worshiper's true intentions and commitment. Pilgrimage is necessary, he explains, because the one God has only one Temple, so everybody has to come to Jerusalem. Philo expands the approach of the book of Deuteronomy, which had established Jerusalem as the only place chosen by God to "put his name and make his habitation there." In Philo's view, monotheism justifies the exclusiveness of the Jerusalem Temple and requires every Israelite to leave behind family, friends, and homeland in order to "live abroad" and render service to God. Philo speaks of such journeys as tokens of insurance that the sacrifice will be offered in a "pure spirit," because only the person "drawn by the more powerful attraction of piety" can endure detachment from everything known and dear.[33]

Philo supports his argument by pointing to the reality of pilgrimage in his own day. "Countless multitudes from countless cities," he says, come at each feast from the ends of the earth to the Jerusalem Temple in the hope of finding a "safe shelter from meddlesome and turbulent life." According to Philo, the pilgrims "seek to find good weather and release from worries, which have joked and burdened them from their earliest youth, to spend some time taking respite in cheerful tranquility." He moreover speaks of their "leisure time" being devoted to "holiness and the honoring of God" and of the friendships that are formed between people who did not know each other beforehand (*Spec.* 1.67–70).

This description of pilgrimage has often been taken as historical evidence for the popularity of pilgrimage during the Second Temple period. For many scholars Philo's reference confirms the obvious, namely, that ancient Jews observed the Torah, which enjoins every male Jew to go three times a year on a pilgrimage to Jerusalem (Exod 23:17). Others have been more cautious, stressing that there is little evidence for massive Jewish pilgrimage during the First Temple period, while the phenomenon may subsequently have expanded. On such estimations, pilgrimage during the Roman period was not very developed. The *Letter of Aristeas* supports this cautious approach, because it never mentions pilgrimage, while enthusiastically speaking about Jerusalem and the Temple. Philo is indeed the first Jewish author in postbiblical times who describes the experience of pilgrimage to the Jerusalem Temple and makes it a central item of his theology. Yet even he does not really assume that every Jew goes to Jerusalem "at each feast" because he immediately explains that pilgrimage liberates pilgrims from burdens "carried from their earliest youth." This indicates that pilgrimage is considered a once-in-a-lifetime event.[34] Whatever the frequency of pilgrimage may have been, Philo plays an active role in shaping the discursive reality of the Temple.

A new reading of Philo's text suggests itself. His image of pilgrimage must be appreciated as a literary construct with important theological and cultural implications for contemporaneous Judaism. Philo's reference to "countless multitudes from countless cities" provides the first clue. This expression is a literary exaggeration reminiscent of similar expressions in the historical writings, where Philo constructs Jewish identity around the notion of Jerusalem as the mother-city of Jews throughout the world. Moreover, Philo depicts pilgrimage in nostalgic terms as a return to a pure form of Judaism. The individual person is supposedly no longer distracted by worldly concerns—as if pilgrimage itself did not require considerable practical management—and is completely devoted to holiness. Pilgrimage offers a welcome opportunity for socializing and reconstituting the Jewish people as a homogeneous nation oriented toward philosophy. Philo creates a religious focus for his people that is devoid of national and political connotations. The Temple, instead of worldly leadership, defines Jewish identity. In a world populated by many local temples, but only one emperor, Jewish culture neatly fits into the wider landscape of the empire without competing with contemporary structures of power.

The topical relevance of Philo's interpretation of pilgrimage becomes obvious when we look at the Gospel of Luke, which we have already encountered on several occasions as a text with strong Roman affinities. Pilgrimage is introduced here into Jesus's biography, while the other gospels lack this motive. Mark and Matthew know nothing of Jesus's pilgrimage, whereas Luke presents his parents as going up to the Jerusalem Temple "every year" at Passover. In Luke's story the Temple fulfills an important part in defining Jesus's religious role. While his parents start returning home, he stays behind to discuss theology with "teachers," even though he is only a child. Jesus shows both his exceptional wisdom and his true commitment to God. Going up to the Jerusalem Temple and rejoicing in its intellectual opportunities, he transforms himself from a talented boy into a religious leader. Jesus significantly confronts his anxious mother, who had been looking for him, asking her: "Why did you search for me? Did you not know that I have to be in my Father's house?"[35] Jesus's pilgrimage plays a constitutive role in Luke's biography. Its narrative function is rather similar to that of the pilgrimage Philo imagines in the *Exposition*, where the Jerusalem Temple is a central aspect of Jewish identity.

Philo also anticipates the Second Sophistic. Plutarch, himself a priest of Apollo at Delphi, constructs a similarly philosophical and culturally pregnant image of temple worship. The temple offers in his view a space for meeting and discussion, leading the person entering its gates to true knowledge. In his treatise *The E at Delphi* Plutarch locates Greek culture in the temple, where prominent teachers, such as Ammonius, discuss Greek philosophy, especially the Socratic imperative "know yourself." This Greek culture in a preeminent local temple is acknowledged by the Roman emperor Nero, who "stayed here some years ago." For Plutarch as for Philo, constructing one's culture around a local temple implies highlighting intellectual and nonpolitical aspects of the religious tradition, which complement rather than rival Roman power and thus can easily be acknowledged by Rome's representatives. The image of Nero's visit to the Greek shrine relies on the same policy as the one implemented by Claudius, who, as we saw earlier, confirmed the religious, but not the political rights of the Jews.[36]

Following his overall philosophical approach to the Temple, Philo explains the sacrifices in terms of the worshiper's moral and religious progress. Philo is highly aware of the fact that his interpretations resort to allegory and express his personal insights rather than accepted wisdom. The laying of hands on the sacrificial animal, for example, signifies in his view a confession of moral blamelessness before God, because the law "requires of the one who brings a sacrifice to sanctify primarily his mind by exercise in good and profitable thoughts." Philo expects worshipers to confess "out of a pure conscience" that they have committed no sin. The offering itself involves a full acknowledgment of God's beneficent and unique role. He has created the world and given numerous benefits to all of humankind, acts that require honor and thanksgiving of a rational sort. Philo's ideas on these issues are shared by other Greek authors in the Roman Empire. Philostratus, the third-century biographer, offers a similar interpretation of cult and sacrifice. In his *Life of Apollonius of Tyana* he introduces the temple of Aesclepius as a quiet space outside the city where real contemplation is possible. Apollonius clarifies the nature of true worship by insisting that it is mainly about caring for the self and adapting one's lifestyle to divine standards of virtue. Those who come only for worldly benefits and assume that the deity requires concrete sacrifices cannot be accepted.[37]

Philo constructs the Jerusalem Temple as an important site of Jewish identity and spirituality, which confirms ethical values cherished in the Roman Empire. His emphasis on the moral intention of the worshiper and the experience of pilgrimage are likely to have resonated well with his non-Jewish readers, suggesting to them that the Jews, too, possess an updated, philosophical cult that nurtures shared moral values. Philo also must have hoped that his readers would be persuaded about the false nature of Apion's slanders regarding the Jewish Temple. In a fragment preserved by Josephus, Apion says that the Jews were so hostile to the Greeks and their culture that they made a vow to sacrifice every year a Greek on their altar in the Temple (*C.Ap.* 2.92–96).

Conclusion

Philo's exposition of Mosaic law is motivated by the apologetic need to counter Apion's slanders and persuade a broader Roman audience of the value of Jewish customs. Confronted with harsh criticism of the Jewish religion, which has immediate political implications for his embassy to Gaius, Philo devotes several treatises to the Decalogue and the special laws, which hardly interested him in his early Alexandrian period. He engages typically Stoic notions, using them not only as general gestures, as he did at the beginning of his career, but accepting the fundamental ethical principles of the school most popular in Rome. Philo also appeals to the *realia* of Roman feasts and law to explain the Jewish tradition in an understandable way. While facing a political situation similar to the one Josephus will face a generation later, Philo has much stronger philosophical interests and has quickly familiarized himself with the intellectual climate in the capital of the empire. Stoicism has deeply changed the way he sees his ancestral tradition, alerting him to the philosophical role of the law, family values, the Jerusalem Temple in a worldwide community, and the ideal of freedom from the emotions and living according to nature.

Philo's philosophical interpretation of Mosaic law offers an enlightened form of ethnicity. While he has extracted Jewish ritual from the realm of obedience to God and grounded it in moral principles, he has also described his particular nation in the most positive terms. The Israelites emerge as a people committed to ethical values who live by the laws of nature, embark on pilgrimages, and celebrate authentic holidays. The Jews constitute a flesh-and-blood community acting in the world and benefiting the Roman Empire. This image complements other aspects of the *Exposition* that we have encountered in earlier chapters, namely, Philo's conception of God as the creator, who is actively involved in creation, and the patriarchs and matriarchs as historical figures with exemplary characters.

Philo's achievement can further be appreciated by looking at Justin Martyr, who follows in his footsteps a hundred years later. Arriving in Rome and distinguishing himself from the Gnostics, who also make a name for themselves in the city, Justin stresses the universal values of his interpretation of Christianity, which resonates well with Roman discourses. He stresses Christian commitment to family values and bemoans the practice of child exposure. Christian places of worship are advocated as schools of moral instruction, which function especially on the day of rest.[38] In comparison to Philo, however, Justin's philosophical interests are rather limited and hardly extend beyond some vague references to Stoic and Platonic ideas. His apologetic situation also differs. While heroically dying as a martyr, Justin does not have to defend himself against ethnic prejudices.

PART 3

Young Philo among Alexandrian Jews

9 Biblical Commentary

Having appreciated Philo in his later works, which he wrote in the context of his embassy to Rome, we are now in a position to address the riddle of his early years. Relying on the comparative method outlined in chapter 1, I turn now to the *Allegorical Commentary,* which radically differs from the later treatises in terms of genre, style, and philosophical orientation. These differences prompt us to investigate the context in Alexandria, where Philo began his career before embarking on his diplomatic mission in Rome. The *Allegorical Commentary* offers a glimpse into the intellectual world of Philo as a young man, when he addresses fellow Jews in Alexandria and engages in a verse-by-verse commentary on the Greek translation of Genesis.[1] In this part of the book we move from the mature statesman and advocate of Judaism in Rome to the budding philosopher and Bible scholar in Alexandria. Philo's early work is based on a close reading of Scripture and creates a quite complicated web of allegorical interpretations rather than providing a continuous narrative easily accessible to the uninitiated. Philo's commentary is the first of its kind extant in Judaism and naturally raises questions regarding the circumstances of its emergence. How, in other words, did he conceive of the idea of investigating the Bible in such a scholarly manner? Moreover, what role did the intellectual climate of Alexandria play in shaping Philo's approach?

The Alexandrian Context of the *Allegorical Commentary*

Alexandria, the Hellenistic center of scholarship, helps us understand the nature of Philo's Bible commentary and its hermeneutic assumptions.

Running commentaries were produced there in a great variety of areas, ranging from Homer's epics to tragedy and history, and also were institutionally supported at the Museum, which was an early form of a university. Alexandria produced the first systematic, literary commentaries on the Homeric epics, which set the standards for all subsequent scholarship in the Western tradition. Alexandrian scholars addressed a professional audience, starting their work with comments on minute details of the text, asking, for example, why Homer started the *Iliad* with a reference to Achilles's wrath.[2]

Aristarchus of Samothrace (second century BCE) was the most learned and influential scholar of Homer in Alexandria. He wrote two successive editions of the text, treatises on specific topics, and two running commentaries. The critical signs in Aristarchus's edition were linked to his commentaries, in which he discussed the literary problem at stake. Whether or not he ever pronounced the famous principle, preserved by Porphyry, that "Homer is to be elucidated by Homer," he paid special attention to the internal coherence of the entire corpus.[3] Assuming that Homer had authored both the *Iliad* and the *Odyssey,* Aristarchus inquired into his characteristic style and presentation of dramatic figures. Issues of verisimilitude and contradictions between lines became central concerns. Insisting that Homer could not have written anything "ridiculous," Aristarchus bracketed some epic lines, because "horses do not drink wine" and "it is implausible that horses speak."[4] He moreover addressed problems of contradictions, often solving them by suggesting a gap in the text. In this view, the poet remains silent about certain things, which the reader has to conjecture and fill in. Aristarchus dealt, for example, with a tension between two lines, one of which presents Achilles as laying down his weapon and the other assuming that he carried it. Asking where the weapon suddenly came from in the later line, Aristarchus suggests that Achilles picked it up in the space between the lines even though the poet does not explicitly say so (*Schol. Il.* 21.17A).

Alexandrian Jews were familiar with this type of scholarship, and some applied it to their Scriptures. The Jewish exegete Demetrius, active in Alexandria in the second century BCE, inquires into problems of contradiction and verisimilitude. He asks, for example, "how the Israelites had weapons, seeing that they departed from Egypt unarmed." This problem arises out of a tension between Exod 5:3, where Moses's departure without weapons is mentioned, and Exod 17:8–9, where the Israelites are involved in a military confrontation with Amalek. The problem is solved by Aristarchus's method of assuming a gap in the text that the author left for the reader to fill in.

Demetrius suggests that the Israelites used the weapons of the Egyptians, who had drowned in the Red Sea. He also discusses problems of verisimilitude, examining why "Joseph at the meal gave a five-fold portion to Benjamin even though he was incapable of taking in such quantities of meat," assuming that the Bible would not suggest an unrealistic portion of food. Demetrius solves the problem by showing that Joseph was concerned about the symbolic value of the food, wishing to create an equal standing between him and his maternal brother on one hand and the rest of the brothers on the other. His distribution of an exceptionally big portion to his younger brother thus becomes reasonable in psychological terms.[5]

In this Alexandrian environment Philo produces a minute and systematic commentary on the opening chapters of Genesis, beginning in the extant treatise with the summary of the creation in Gen 2:1.[6] He addresses fellow Jews in his hometown who are keenly engaged in Bible interpretation and have already formed their own, sometimes rather divergent, views. Philo expects his readers to honor the "ancestral constitution" and be so familiar with the Bible that he refers to specific motifs as being mentioned "somewhere" or "often." He implies Jewish readers who have grown up with the Scriptures and require no explanation about Moses, the Torah, and Judaism in general. Philo moreover assumes that his readers will be skeptical about his allegorical approach and occasionally urges them "not to be astonished by the rules of allegory." He also wonders "what sense this [verse] makes to those interpreting the literal sense." Philo frequently addresses such readers by personal appeals, sometimes mocking literal interpretations and once explaining that Moses had used a certain formulation "urging [you] to avoid the literal interpretation."[7]

Philo's orientation toward a Jewish audience committed to the literal meaning of Scripture is especially visible in his treatise *On the Confusion of Tongues,* which opens with an extensive quotation of a literary analysis of the biblical story offered by some "impious" colleagues. Philo is annoyed by their comparison of Gen 11:1–9 to a passage in Homer's *Odyssey,* which prompted them to conclude that the two canonical texts contain similar myths and are not true in a scientific sense. As I have shown elsewhere, these interpreters are Alexandrian Jews inspired by Homeric scholarship at the Museum.[8] Familiar with critical methods, they investigate the Scriptures from a literary point of view and compare them to the Greek epics. They even suggest that Moses was inspired by Homer and a fable, but improved some details of his *Vorlage.* While Philo rejects such a radically literary approach, insisting on the unique and homogeneous nature of Scripture, he still confronts the scholars' arguments, eager to persuade their potential followers.

In the *Allegorical Commentary* Philo anticipates readers aware of questions raised by critical scholarship but open to his allegorical approach. Sometimes he mentions other literal exegetes, whom he trusts to "refute on their own account" criticisms of Scripture. Their work, he explains, will rely on "ready explanations from the outward sense of Scripture for the questions as they arise" (*Conf.* 14). Philo thus distinguishes between literal readers, who are in his view impious, and others who share his basic concern to defend the unity of the biblical text. He respects some of the latter to the extent that he integrates their interpretation in his own commentary. In the context of the Tower of Babel he reports, for example, that "those attending only to the outward and ready things believe now that the origin of the Greek and barbarian languages has been sketched out [in the biblical story]" (*Conf.* 190). Philo stresses that he will not censure such colleagues, "for perhaps they, too, speak the truth," yet urges them "not to stop here, but to attend to allegorical explanations." Literal exegetes, whom he hopes to introduce to his allegorical approach, are his implied audience. Philo wishes to show that Moses himself "has provided starting points" for allegory, implying that the latter is not a whimsical reading of the text but expresses the author's intention. In Philo's view, "the sacred oracles most clearly provide clues" for the allegorical interpretation.[9]

Responding to critical interpretations of the story of the Tower of Babel, Philo offers his allegorical interpretation "neither in a contentious spirit nor in order somehow to meet sophistry with sophistry, but rather following the chain of natural sequence, which does not allow stumbling, but whenever there is a stumbling-block (κἄν εἴ τινα ἐμποδὼν εἴη) easily removes it, so that the course of the narratives may be unobstructed" (*Conf.* 14). Philo conceptualizes allegory as a solution to "stumbling-blocks" in the literal text. While some of his colleagues study textual problems as indications of different compositional layers, Philo insists that such problems can be solved and the integrity of Scripture be preserved. Recovering the smoothness of the biblical narratives by an allegorical interpretation, he aims at restoring their original logic.

Philo as a young man is immersed in typically Alexandrian commentary work. The numerous treatises of the *Allegorical Commentary* abound with scholarly expressions relating to the literal level. Typical formulations are "let us now examine the following [expression],"[10] "the question next in sequence,"[11] "why [was it written]," and "one must investigate."[12] The *Allegorical Commentary* moreover assumes Moses's authorship of the Bible and studies his particular style, taking into account the possibility of infelicities or even "barbarisms." It is only in this series of works that Philo offers numerous cross-references to other biblical verses, undoubtedly sharing the famous hermeneutic principle, attributed to Aristarchus, according to which a text needs to be explained by itself. These exegetical methods and the technical terms of academic inquiry are typical of Alexandrian scholarship.[13]

The Alexandrian context of Philo's Bible commentaries deserves to be fully appreciated in view of two alternative cultures. In the land of Israel the form of systematic commentary had not yet developed, as the genre of rewritten Bible still prevailed. The book of Jubilees and the *Genesis Apocryphon* are typical examples. At Qumran prophetically inspired interpretation was favored and presented in the form of *pesharim*. Scholarly approaches were introduced only later by the rabbis, who most probably were inspired by Alexandrian techniques.[14] Rome did not develop a commentary culture either. Reflecting Roman disdain for "hair-splitting" inquiries, as Seneca called them, Lucian addresses the issue with characteristic sarcasm. In an imagined encounter with Homer he asks him whether he had actually authored the lines bracketed by the Alexandrian scholars. Assured of their authenticity, Lucian concludes, "I held the grammarians Zenodotus and Aristarchus guilty of pedantry in the highest degree."[15] While the late Philo would have sympathized to some degree with Lucian's parody of Alexandrian scholarship, as a young man he delves precisely into this kind of laborious commentary activity, earnestly applying literary Homeric methods to the Jewish Scriptures. The choice of the commentary genre reflects Philo's original Alexandrian context, when he is still distant from Roman discourses and the characteristic irony of the Second Sophistic.

Allegorical Solutions to Textual Problems

Philo continues the Alexandrian tradition of textual scholarship and offers a verse-by-verse commentary on the Greek translation of Genesis. He regularly quotes the Septuagint (LXX), being unaware of its divergence from the Hebrew text, and sometimes also slightly adapts it to his own interpretation.[16] While sharing with his predecessors a concern for literary problems, such as contradictions between verses or issues of verisimilitude, Philo adds a new, allegorical dimension. The issues that occupied

Aristarchus and Demetrius are thus no longer treated exclusively on the literal level but taken as starting points for allegorical contemplations about the soul. Philo once programmatically says, "We should understand the statements in the books in which Moses acts as an interpreter more figuratively, as the impression at hand made by the words is greatly at variance with truth" (*Post.* 1). Unlike his predecessors, Philo accepts biblical verses even when they are not true in the conventional sense because he creates via allegory a creative space of contemplation that lies outside the field of rigorous investigation into historical truth.

The biblical story of Cain provides Philo with other occasions to define his position with regard to seemingly unreasonable verses. In his view, the motif of Cain's "going out from God's face" is utterly "impossible," seeing that God is omnipresent and does not leave any space to which one could flee. Philo investigates why Moses nevertheless mentions this motif and insists that "nothing of the propositions is meant literally." The reader is invited to choose "the way of allegory dear to philosophical men" and understand that Cain metaphorically fled by abandoning the proper notions of God and joining those "who have willingly departed from the Existent One" (*Post.* 1–9).

Philo subsequently raises another problem of verisimilitude regarding Cain and inquires "why he, even though alone, is presented as founding and building a city."[17] He emphasizes the problem beyond the necessities of the literal text, suggesting that Cain would have had to build a city with all the architectural equipment of a metropolis like Alexandria, including theaters and stadia. Seeing the unlikelihood of such an event, Philo concludes that the verse "is not only a paradox, but contrary to reason." His solution is allegory: "Perhaps then, as these things diverge from the truth, it is better to say allegorically (ἀλληγοροῦντας λέγειν) that Cain intended to set up his own creed as one builds a city" (*Post.* 51). Philo hesitantly introduces his allegorical interpretation of the biblical passage, suggesting that "perhaps then" it is better to take recourse to the underlying meaning. His argument for an allegorical reading of Cain as the founder of a wicked creed rests on the suggestion that the literal text "diverges from the truth." Philo makes special efforts to elaborate on the unrealistic nature of the verse, using Aristotelian notions of paradox and contrariness to reason.[18] Philo's detailed study of the problem of verisimilitude indicates how important it is for him to anchor allegory in the literal text, thus hoping to persuade his literalist readers of its plausibility.

Many other examples of problems of verisimilitude could be adduced, but I will mention just one more, which pertains to the description of paradise:

> It is worth inquiring why the two rivers Pheison and Geon encompass countries, the one Evilat, the other Ethiopia, while none of the others [does so]. Yet the Tigris is said to be over against the Assyrians, while the Euphrates is not said to be over against anything (Gen 2:11–14). And yet in reality the Euphrates flows round several countries and has many facing it. But the biblical story is not about a river, but about the improvement of character. (*All.* 1.85)

Following contemporary Alexandrian interest in geography, Philo notes that the biblical description of the Euphrates differs from that of the other rivers and inquires whether it corresponds to reality. He emphatically concludes that Scripture diverges from the truth and an allegorical solution is called for. Unlike previous Alexandrian scholars, however, he is not satisfied with a brief solution of the problem but takes it as a starting point for an extended allegory on the improvement of character. He instructs his readers how to develop prudence and courage, which will protect them from folly and cowardice. Justice, by contrast, symbolized by the river Euphrates, which is "not over against anything," does not provide this kind of protection against vice.[19]

Another central concern of the *Allegorical Commentary* is the question of contradictions between verses. Philo stresses that Moses "was in the habit of perfectly remembering the principles laid down from the beginning, deeming it right to bring [his statements] into harmony and render them consistent and agreeable with his previous statements."[20] Given this assumption of basic harmony, Philo pays attention to cases of apparent tension. He is challenged by the story of Abraham's migration from Chaldea to the land of Israel, which is told twice, once as Abraham's accompaniment of Terah, who dies in Haran (Gen 11:31–32), and another time as his personal response to God's command after his father's death (Gen 12:1–2). This crux in the biblical text, which modern scholarship solves by reference to different sources, deeply engages Philo. "Nobody familiar with the law book," he says, "will have remained oblivious to the fact that Abraham earlier rose from the land of Chaldea and settled in Haran, but after his father's death he moves from there again, so that he has now left two places. How can this be explained?" (*Migr.* 177).

Philo assumes that the problem is obvious to his readers. Committed to the unity of Scripture, however, he cannot disqualify one of the contradicting verses as a later addition or editorial mistake. His solution is allegory. Philo suggests that Gen 11:31 should be read not as if it is "a historical treatise" but rather as an allegory. In his view, Moses does not speak here about a physical journey but about "a teaching useful for life and suitable for men." Following these insights, Philo interprets Abraham's migration as a journey of the soul from the material to a higher spiritual realm and eventually to God.[21] The contradiction between verses thus has proved to be a fruitful springboard for inquiries into the deeper meaning of Scripture.

Two additional examples may illustrate Philo's attitude toward problems of contradiction in the Scriptures. The first pertains to the story of paradise: "And further [God] says: 'In the day you will eat thereof, you shall die the death' (Gen 2:17). Yet having eaten [from the tree of knowledge], they not only do not die, but even beget children and become the cause of life to others" (All. 1.105). While this problem of a contradiction easily could have been raised by Demetrius, Philo provides a novel answer beyond the literal level. He initially pauses to prepare his readers for the transition to the allegorical realm, asking, "What then should be said?" He then offers an extended allegory of the soul which relies on the Platonic notion that the pursuit of philosophy leads to an ethereal state where the body and its earthly desires are virtually dead.[22] Applied to Gen 2:17, this means that two kinds of death must be acknowledged, "one pertaining to man, the other in particular to the soul" (All. 1.105). The death of the soul is presented as a state of merely physical existence that results from a wicked and overly material lifestyle. While Adam and Eve lived in a physical sense after eating from the tree of knowledge, they were dead as far as their souls were concerned because they had disobeyed God and become wicked. Once more the allegorical reading has smoothed the biblical narrative.

Another example pertains to Abraham's epithet "elder," concerning which Philo raises the following question: "Does not everyone reading in the most holy books know that the wise man Abraham is introduced as more short-lived than almost all his own forefathers? But none of those, I think, even though they lived long lives, were described as elders, but only Abraham" (Sobr. 17). Philo appeals here to Jewish readers versed in Scripture who will appreciate the contradiction of passages. He must have meant the list of forefathers recorded in Gen 5:4–31, where the average age is close to 800, while Abraham reached the age of only 175 (Gen 25:7).

At the same time, however, his descendants reached the ages of only 137 and 110.[23] It is only in view of previous generations that Abraham's epithet appears problematic. Philo mentions this point in order to stress the contradiction between the biblical passages and prepare for his allegorical interpretation. Moses, he insists, "customarily called" biblical heroes either old or young as a reference to their respective maturity or foolishness. In this view Abraham is rightly called "elder" because he is exceedingly virtuous and wise (*Sobr.* 16).

Philo's combination of Alexandrian philology and extended allegory is innovative at the time. Using textual problems in order to question the hegemony of literal readings, Philo suggests that the author intended an allegorical meaning. This approach relies on a delicate balance between the literal and the allegorical dimension of Scripture. Philo stresses problems in the literal text in order to make room for allegory on the one hand while assuming authorial intention and anchoring allegory within the literal text on the other. The literal dimension of Scripture thus is not dismissed but shown to be problematic to a degree that renders the allegorical meaning plausible, if not necessary. This double-bound position creates the characteristic complexity and ambiguity of Philo's work.

Given the fame of Stoic allegory in the Hellenistic period, it bears emphasis that this school has not shaped Philo's allegorical method because it ignored authorial intention. Aiming to "accommodate fables" to their scientific notions, Stoics "converted [them] into physiological terms." They extrapolated "scientific theory" even from "impious fables" because they assumed that their authors were unaware of the deeper meanings of their own texts. A key role in justifying such allegories is played by etymologies, which point beyond an author's intention to a larger reservoir of unintended meanings. While Philo sometimes uses etymology as an additional justification for allegory, such instances have been overemphasized. He rather deserves to be acknowledged as an innovative exegete who combined for the first time the Alexandrian tradition of literary scholarship with allegorical readings based on Platonic philosophy.[24]

Mystical Intertextuality

From early on, Alexandrian scholars showed an intertextual orientation, reading particular verses in light of others. Aristarchus and Demetrius, for example, adduced other lines of their respective canonical text in

order to illuminate the meaning of a word or a hero's character.[25] Such
cross-references were short and usually supported by a shared key word.
Familiar with this Alexandrian approach, Philo reaches a new degree of
intertextuality. He no longer uses this technique only for scholarly purposes
but offers numerous intertexts and often dwells on them in their own right.
His engagement is rather creative, leading to a rich web of associations and
frequent expressions of religious ecstasy.

Most of Philo's intertexts derive from the Pentateuch, especially the
books of Genesis and Exodus. The treatise *On the Migration of Abraham*, for
example, opens with a rich web of exegetical associations. Philo supports
his allegorical interpretation of God's command to Abraham to "depart
from your father's house" (Gen 12:1) by a quotation from Gen 28:17, which
shares the key word "house." Without explaining the context of the secondary verse, he merely mentions the "ascetic" or self-trained man, namely
Jacob, who says, "It is not this, but (only) the house of God." Philo takes
this verse to mean that God is not contained in the visible realm and applies it to Gen 12:1 by suggesting that Abraham is ordered to leave the
material realm, represented by the house. Philo then throws further light
on God's command by quoting a verse with no linguistic connection, but
concrete philosophical relevance, namely, Moses's exhortation to "heed
to yourself."[26] In Philo's view, Moses inculcated self-examination in light
of the general dichotomy between the material and the spiritual realms.
People heeding themselves will discover spiritual sources and not cleave
to material things. Abraham, it is implied, embraced Moses's principle and
showed the way by embarking from his house and family. Philo draws the
conclusion that "whenever the mind begins to know itself and to engage
with mental objects, it will thrust away that part of the soul which inclines
toward the sense-perceptible image" (*Migr.* 13). Of special symbolic value
is the exodus of the Israelites as well as the departure of Joseph's bones,
the symbol of the body, from Egypt. Philo provides a rich cluster of verses,
reading several biblical stories in light of each other and creating an overall
tapestry that depicts the soul's ascent from the material realm.

Philo regularly introduces intertexts from Genesis by the simple for-
mula "for it is said" (λέγεται γάρ), "he [Moses] said" (φησί), or "[the ex-
pression] is introduced" (εἰσάγεται). Sometimes he integrates a biblical
key word in his own exposition without identifying it as a quotation or
uses a vague reference, such as "Moses somewhere says."[27] Quotations from
Leviticus are much rarer and tend to be introduced by precise and elaborate

references, such as "it is said in the book of Leviticus" or "it is said in the law regarding leprosy."[28] The scarcity of quotations from Leviticus, as well as their conscientious introduction, suggests that Philo expects his readers to be less familiar with this book. Genesis is assumed to be well known and constantly used, but Leviticus is apparently less familiar and perhaps also less attractive in Philo's eyes.

Most interesting and innovative are Philo's quotations from the Prophets and Psalms, which were known in Alexandria at least since the time of Ben Sira's grandson but had not yet been used in the interpretation of the Pentateuch. Under Philo's pen these somewhat more esoteric writings reveal a mystical experience, which is often described by sexual imagery. Philo confesses that he has become a "disciple" of the prophet Jeremiah, who was not only "initiated, but also a worthy hierophant." The key text from Jeremiah is, "Have you not called me house and father and husband of your virginity?" (Jer 3:4). Intriguingly, the word "husband" is neither attested in the Hebrew text nor in the Septuagint and may well be Philo's creative paraphrase of the word "prince."[29] He thus may have enhanced Jeremiah's sexual imagery in order to prepare his allegory of the soul, which is impregnated by God:

> He [Jeremiah] has thus most clearly introduced the idea that God is a house, the incorporeal place of the incorporeal ideas, that he is the father of all things, as he begat them, and the husband of wisdom, dropping his seed of happiness for the mortal race into good and virgin soil. It is appropriate for God to hold converse with undefiled and untouched and pure nature, namely, with a true virgin, but it is the opposite with us. The intercourse of men for the purpose of procreation turns virgins into women. Yet whenever God consorts with the soul, he turns her who was previously a woman into a virgin, because he takes away the ignoble and emasculate desires, through which she became a woman, and introduces in their stead genuine and unmixed virtues. Therefore he does not consort with Sarah before "she has left behind all womanish things" (Gen 18:11) and has once more become a virgin, who has not known men (*Cher.* 49–50).

The prophetic text provides the key to understanding the mystery of God's intercourse with the human soul, which Philo identifies in the story of Sarah's pregnancy. In the case of Sarah, too, he has creatively paraphrased the biblical text, rendering a verse about her "ceasing to be in the way of women," namely, becoming menopausal, into a verse that describes how she actively leaves behind feminine things. On the basis of Jeremiah, Philo suggests that Sarah became a virgin again by intercourse with God, who impregnated her with virtues.

Hosea, a prophet favoring sexual images, plays a special role in Philo's *Allegorical Commentary*. The end of his prophecy is significant because he mentions God's "fruit," likening God to a productive tree and recommending in a mystical fashion that "whoever is wise, let him understand these things" (Hos 14:8–9). Philo quotes these verses twice in order to illuminate the secret of God's intercourse with the human soul. When discussing the meaning of Isaac's name, that is, "he will laugh" (Gen 21:6), Philo adduces Hosea's words as "spoken by fire," thus alluding to the burning issue at stake. He fears that his readers may understand Sarah's statement that God "has made laughter for me" as an admission of her actual intercourse with him. Such a reading amounts in his eyes to pure mythology and must be rejected.[30] Philo stresses that God formed Isaac, but not in a physical sense. Inspired by Hosea he offers the following reading: "I grasped the invisible organ of speech, which invisibly prompts and strikes the instrument [of human speech], and was struck with admiration and amazement at this saying . . . for the whole of heaven and earth, to tell the truth, is the fruit of God, of the tree of his eternal and evergreen nature. And to know and confess such things is for wise and understanding, not for insignificant men" (*Mut.* 140). Following Hosea's reference to secret knowledge among the wise, Philo interprets Sarah's birth of Isaac as the birth of virtues in the soul. Only God can impregnate the human soul with such ethereal fruits, which Sarah acknowledges as pure joy or laughter.

A similarly mystical role is played by the book of Psalms. Philo introduces the psalmist as "a divinely inspired man [who] testifies to my explanation" (*Plant.* 29). A little later he writes even more enthusiastically: "One of the Bacchic company of Moses (ὁ τοῦ Μωυσέως δή θιασώτης), who has tasted of this unadulterated light and is not found among the indifferent ones, addresses himself in the *Hymns* to his own mind, speaking thus: 'delight in the Lord'" (LXX Ps 36:4). Moved by the voice to a heavenly and divine love . . . , he is snatched away in his whole mind by a sting of divine possession and finds true joy only in God" (*Plant.* 39). The psalmist is described here in terms of ecstatic revelry, which his readers easily would have associated with Dionysius or Bacchus.[31] Philo appreciates the psalmist because he expresses his religious fervor in an intensive and personal manner. This inward and mystical orientation is highlighted by interpreting the psalmist's imperative "delight in the Lord," which originally appeals to readers as an address to himself (the psalmist). In Philo's view, there is an ongoing dialogue in the ecstatic mind, which is drawn toward heaven by "divine love." Reading Genesis in light of Psalms, Philo is able to suggest that Moses has written the Torah with a similar awareness of the soul's ascent to God.

Commenting on the book of Genesis, Philo thus relies on two different techniques, one scholarly, the other mystical. On one hand, he carefully studies the literal text and identifies textual problems as "stumbling-blocks," which Moses planted in his stories in order to alert the reader to deeper meanings. On the other hand, Philo adduces other verses from the Pentateuch, the Prophets, and the Psalms in order to convey a more spiritual and mystical meaning to the concrete stories about the patriarchs. Regarding both techniques Philo relies on features of Alexandrian scholarship, which he transfers to new realms of allegory and spirituality.

Philo's *Questions and Answers*

Apart from the *Allegorical Commentary* Philo wrote another series of treatises on large parts of the books of Genesis and Exodus, *Questions and Answers on Genesis and Exodus* (*Q&A*), which share the same format of quoting verses and offering an allegorical interpretation.[32] At the same time, however, the *Q&A* is informed by a different exegetical purpose, which has drawn considerable attention in recent scholarship. Most conspicuously, the *Q&A* lacks the intertextual, esoteric dimension characteristic of the *Allegorical Commentary*. The interpretations are rather short and highly accessible, providing a kind of handbook of exegesis. No appeal is made to secret knowledge for the initiate. No elaborate literary interpretations by other interpreters are discussed. The *Q&A* most probably addresses a community of students that Philo was able to attract following the publication of his *Allegorical Commentary*. The lack of detailed scholarly queries and the pedagogic nature of the answers would suit students, who could easily find instruction in Philo's work.[33]

The first indication of Philo's implied audience in the *Q&A* is the rarity of references to critical interpreters. While the *Allegorical Commentary* was written with a view to such colleagues, frequently referring to the details of their work, the *Q&A* primarily addresses readers for whom allegory is an accepted method of interpretation that requires no explanation. In this series Philo refers mainly to other, congenial allegorists. Critical scholarship is no longer presented in a way that allows the reader to form an independent opinion, but rather as an abbreviated symbol of the negative Other. In the *Allegorical Commentary*, for example, he explains that some of his colleagues engage in "a detailed enquiry" about the changes of Abraham's and Sarah's names. He even refers to one particular scholar who sarcastically said, "Great and surpassing indeed are the gifts which Moses says the Leader of all provided." In the *Q&A*, by contrast, such scholarly concerns are no longer mentioned. Philo instead mocks such interpreters in a general way so that the reader can only be astonished by the foolishness of such exegetes.[34]

In the *Q&A* Philo even locates critical interpreters outside "the company of God," thus stressing the illegitimacy of their positions. He assumes a kind of orthodox position, in Walter Bauer's sense of an attempt to impose uniform structures on an earlier variety of views. In Judaism the emergence of orthodox structures is usually associated with the rabbinic movement, but Philo in some sense anticipates the sages of the land of Israel.[35] The fact that the rabbis were increasingly able to define "correct" ideas, because they had assumed sufficient political authority to do so, throws light on Philo. His decision to "excommunicate" and silence other interpreters indicates his growing self-confidence and probably also an increase of real power within the Jewish community of Alexandria. While in the *Allegorical Commentary* he still sought dialogue with Jews holding opposite views, in the *Q&A* he is in a position to dismiss them altogether. Philo's considerably greater self-confidence in the *Q&A* is also reflected in the fact that he now presents allegorical interpretations as "natural." Instead of introducing them hesitantly and with a view to persuading critical scholars, he can simply appeal to his readers as "us, who naturally allegorize." On another occasion Philo goes even further, speaking of us, "the students of Moses, manifestly knowing the intention of our teacher . . . , [who] allegorically indicates."[36] In this skillful rhetorical move Philo associates allegorical exegesis with a natural understanding of Moses's original message. He and his allegorical followers emerge as the authentic "students of Moses."

Philo's move from a more dialogical and scholarly approach to an authoritative teaching position is conspicuous throughout the *Q&A*. It is striking that views that were still presented in a polite fashion in the *Allegorical Commentary* are harshly dismissed in the *Q&A*. Philo speaks, for example, about a wrong opinion offered by "unrestrained and gluttonous people with a belly," while in the *Allegorical Commentary* he discusses the same interpretation as a plausible, yet ultimately unsatisfactory explanation. He similarly reacts to those offering a literal interpretation of Cain's statement "Am I my brother's keeper?" (Gen 4:9). In the *Q&A* he altogether rejects their interpretation because it leads to anthropomorphic notions of God and thus to "atheistic opinion." In the *Allegorical Commentary*, by contrast, he argues gradually and by comparison to Abraham that Cain's words should not be taken literally.[37]

Congenial allegorical readers, by contrast, receive renewed attention in the *Q&A*. There is no parallel in the *Allegorical Commentary* to the extended list of allegorical interpretations on the tree of life in paradise. While Philo earlier focused on one allegory, barely mentioning another, in the *Q&A* he provides a detailed account of five different allegorical interpretations. Philo addresses an audience used to allegories, which no longer need to be justified, and expects his readers to take a keen interest in the variety of allegorical readings, which may appear rather similar to the outsider. Philo also evaluates his allegorical colleagues and identifies the last ones on the list as "distinguished and excellent men."[38]

The hermeneutic style of the *Q&A* is characterized by brevity and simplicity. Short questions and clear answers are presented in a user-friendly fashion. Another prominent feature is Philo's general insistence on the veracity and clarity of Scripture. He no longer stresses textual problems, as he had done in the *Allegorical Commentary*, where he sometimes even dwelt on difficulties beyond the necessities of the literal text in order to prepare his readers for his move to allegory. In the *Q&A*, by contrast, he deemphasizes textual "stumbling-blocks." Philo often comments on the literal text with emphasis on its clarity. Such comments have a rather apologetic connotation, seeing that in the *Allegorical Commentary* he still recognized significant problems.

Some examples will illustrate Philo's tendency. A verse previously identified as "mythological" now becomes "clear" in the literal sense. Moreover, Philo admitted in the *Allegorical Commentary* that the serpent of paradise is a mythical image, while he now makes considerable efforts to show the plausibility of the literal image. Taking recourse to the notion of a miracle and historical conjecture, Philo no longer introduces his own allegorical interpretation as a solution to a problem of verisimilitude, but rather as an additional meaning next to the acceptable literal sense. Furthermore, Philo acknowledged in the *Allegorical Commentary* that there is a problem of verisimilitude in the story of Sarah's barrenness, because a woman said to be sterile cannot suddenly bear children. This problem is no longer addressed in the *Q&A*, where Philo simply says that the biblical note about Sarah's barrenness points to divine providence.[39] In this case, too, the *Q&A* emerges as having been written in a more pious spirit. Rather than highlighting problems of verisimilitude in the style of the *Allegorical Commentary*, Philo insists on the truth value of the biblical text.

Assuming the veracity of Scripture in the *Q&A*, Philo offers a surprisingly uniform version of questions and answers that considerably differs from his style in the *Allegorical Commentary*. In the *Q&A* the literal and allegorical meanings are conceived as straightforward and complementary messages, leading the reader to a proper religious attitude. Paradoxically, the literal text is considered to be of much higher truth value, while receiving far less attention than in the *Allegorical Commentary*. In the *Q&A* Philo puts the traditional question-and-answer format to a new, educational use. It serves here for the first time as a framework for organizing and transmitting a corpus of coherent teaching. Philo's didactic purpose is immediately visible in the very general nature of his questions. He often simply asks, "Why is it written?" These questions create a framework for discussing major portions of the Torah in a verse-by-verse fashion and are intended to raise the reader's curiosity, focusing the attention on a particular verse. Philo thus creates a platform to expound his own views, praising congenial verses as "most exemplary" or of "most universal application."[40]

Philo often formulates his questions in such a way that they imply the answer, thus firmly guiding the reader toward the correct solution. In the context of anthropomorphic images he regularly raises questions that stress the very thing they are supposed to query, namely, that God has no share in human qualities. He can ask, for example, "Why does [Moses] say, 'He led the animals to man to see what he would call them,' seeing that God does not doubt?" (*QG* 1.21). The question determines the answer, and Philo's "solution" is nothing but an emphatic restatement of its implied message, namely, that "doubting is truly foreign to the divine power."[41] The question-and-answer format is no longer an instrument for probing into the intricacies of the biblical text, but rather a springboard for plain religious teaching.

In the *Q&A* Philo presents his answers in a highly didactic form. Several congenial answers are often listed in stenographic style, providing an easily accessible overview or a kind of handbook. Appealing to readers who are obviously less scholarly than those addressed in the *Allegorical Commentary*, Philo writes in short sentences and often summarizes his thoughts in one key sentence. He wants to make sure that readers of all levels can grasp his message, even if they don't have much time for study. This didactic style differs remarkably from Philo's procedure in the *Allegorical Commentary*, in which he expresses himself in complicated sentences, often referring to a perplexing variety of secondary and tertiary verses. The *Q&A* is not only simple and straightforward, but also consistent, offering complementary rather than contrary answers. Philo's answers build on each other, relying on the same allegorical code, which needs to be only briefly recalled when used on other occasions.[42]

Philo's Achievement

Philo's commentary activity on the Jewish Scriptures must be appreciated in the context of Alexandria, where he became familiar with critical methods of scholarship and engaged in a lively dialogue with colleagues in the Jewish community, some of whom had adopted the methods of Homeric scholarship practiced at the Museum. He developed an innovative approach, stressing the textual difficulties or "stumbling-blocks" in the Bible and using them as stepping stones for allegorical interpretation. Philo argued that the imperfection of the biblical text was intentional, as Moses thus wished to alert his readers to a higher spiritual meaning. Philo is moreover the first known interpreter who made extensive use of secondary and tertiary texts, innovatively adducing verses from the Prophets and Psalms in order to interpret Genesis. This intertextual approach enabled him to uncover a mystical meaning in the Pentateuch that hinted at the soul's ascent to God, often described in overtly sexual imagery.

Philo's biblical commentaries had a significant impact on the work of the Christian church father Origen, who started his career in Alexandria and moved in the early third century CE to Caesarea. While other Alexandrian authors, such as Valentine and Basilides, may have used his hermeneutic methods in their textual scholarship, Origen's work is much better preserved and shows that he deeply appreciated Philo's *Allegorical Commentary*, from which he explicitly quotes in his *Commentary on Matthew* (15.3, 17.7).[43] Origen was the first Christian author who wrote systematic commentaries on the Old Testament, which had thus far been only sporadically integrated in Christian theology.[44] Already from the beginning of his exegetical work, Origen stresses that "the divine Scripture . . . is full of riddles and parables and dark words and other manifold images of obscurity, which are hard to decipher by human nature."[45] Origen explains the hermeneutical potential of such obscurities in *On First Principles*, where he says, "The Logos of God has arranged that certain snares as it were and stumbling-blocks and impossibilities (τίνα οἰονεὶ σκάνδαλα καὶ προσκόμματα καὶ ἀδύνατα) are introduced in the midst of the law and the history, in order that we may not be drawn in all directions by the style, which has undiluted charm, thus either falling altogether away from the right doctrines by not learning anything worthy of God or being unable to move away from the letter, thus learning nothing more divine" (*PArch* 4.15).

Origen argues in the spirit of Philo that a perfectly beautiful style would distract the reader from the theological truths of the biblical text. There is a danger of becoming ensnared by the charm of words and reading smoothly on the surface rather than diving into the depth of the text. Origen's approach to the Scriptures is paradoxical, suggesting that precisely those passages which lack stylistic beauty or general plausibility hold the key to deeper insights. The rough surface of the text prompts the reader to search for the truth beyond. Origen speaks of the "interweaving" of historically true and impossible stories (*PArch* 4.15). The literal sense is thus accepted as long as it agrees with reason, while the overall intention of Scripture is to elevate the reader to more hidden messages pertaining to the soul. Textual "stumbling-blocks" provide the necessary springboard. The illustrations Origen uses look as if they have been directly taken from Philo's *Allegorical Commentary*. Origen asks, for example, "Who is so foolish as to think that God, in the manner of a human husbandman, planted paradise?!,"[46] while Philo condemns such a literal reading as mythological and warns his readers, "May no such impiety possess human reason so as to assume that God tills the soil and plants paradise!" (*All.* 1.43). Like Philo, Origen problematizes the biblical notice about Cain "going forth from the presence of God" and insists that it must not be taken literally. Readers "who are not altogether blind" are instead invited to reflect upon the meaning of God's presence and compare this story to similar ones that cannot be taken literally (*PArch* 4.16). As we saw above, Philo also insists that a literal reading of Cain's hiding is impious and recommends "the way of allegory dear to philosophical men" (*Post.* 1–12). Philo thus serves Origen as a major source of inspiration, guiding him both in his overall hermeneutic principles and in specific questions of exegesis. Philo encouraged him to interpret Scripture in an allegorical manner and uncover Platonic motifs of the soul's ascent. He also provided a model for an enlightened defense of Scripture. While Philo objected to the radically literal and scholarly reading of Scripture proposed by some of his colleagues in the Jewish community of Alexandria, Origen opposed "Gnostic" approaches to the Old Testament, which criticized its mythological images of God.

Philo's Bible interpretation goes through a significant development following his success as a teacher. Beginning his career as one of numerous Jewish exegetes, Philo hesitantly offers a new combination of literary scholarship and allegorical interpretation, initially addressing an expert audience and gradually introducing its members to a more mystical reading of the Bible. After drawing larger crowds to his teaching, Philo offers a summary of his ideas in the user-friendly format of the *Q&A*. This move toward a more general audience, still within the Jewish community of Alexandria, is significant in view of Philo's subsequent journey to Rome, where he encounters even broader audiences. His pedagogic experience in Alexandria would have prepared him for his later diplomatic role among gentiles.

10 A Platonic Self

Throughout the *Allegorical Commentary* Philo is concerned with the human self, introducing to Judaism a new language of introspection and spirituality. Interpreting the book of Genesis allegorically, he leads the reader from the concrete figures of the Bible to the intricacies of the human soul. Abraham's journey from Chaldea to the land of Israel, for example, is interpreted as an intellectual journey. God's command to leave "your land and your family" refers in Philo's view to the soul's departure from the bodily realm. The aim is to know oneself and the ethereal realities that cannot be grasped by the senses. Philo even shares his personal experience. When coming to write on philosophical topics, he says, "Sometimes I have come empty and suddenly became full . . . so that under divine possession, I behaved like a corybantic ecstatic, becoming unaware of everything: place, persons around me, myself, words spoken, and things written."[1] With this reference to divine possession and corybantic ecstasy Philo inscribes himself into the Platonic tradition, where such images had been used to describe inspiration and insight.

In this chapter we examine the contours of the self in Philo's *Allegorical Commentary* and appreciate them not only in light of Plato's works, but also in view of their interpretation in Alexandria. As Platonism took different forms in different centers of learning, authors must be appreciated in their local contexts.[2] We moreover saw in the previous chapter that Philo as a young man is thoroughly immersed in the discourses of his hometown and adopts the dominant literary genre of commentary. We must now ask how he relates to the philosophical discourses that were prominent in Alexandria, especially the expositions of Platonic philosophy. Which philosophical assumptions does Philo adopt from his environment, and where does he make his own contribution?

The Soul's Flight from the Material Realm to God

Philo devotes a whole treatise of the *Allegorical Commentary* to the subject of flight, starting with Hagar's flight from Sarah (Gen 16:6–12) and then turning to other cases of flight, all of which he interprets philosophically. The overall message of the treatise is that matter and earth belong to the lower realm, which is associated with evil and must be avoided, while heaven is the abode of perfect virtue. Fleeing evil involves an upward move. The most striking turn of the treatise comes in paragraph 63, where Philo deals with the biblical cities of refuge and associates them with Plato:

> An excellent man, one of those admired for their wisdom, expressed this splendidly in the *Theaetetus:* "It is impossible for evils to pass away—for necessarily something contrary to the good always remains—and yet they cannot dwell among the gods and thus go around in mortal nature and this earthly place. Therefore it is necessary to try to escape from here to there as quickly as possible. And flight is becoming like god as far as possible (φυγὴ δὲ ὁμοίωσις θεῷ κατὰ τὸ δυνατόν). And godlikeness is to be righteous and holy, with wisdom." (*Fug.* 63, quoting Plato, *Theaet.* 176a–b)

Addressing an audience familiar with Plato, Philo refers to a known passage in the *Theaetetus,* the so-called digression. The Platonic dialogue generally deals with questions of epistemology and ends by negating all forms of empirical knowledge. The *Theaetetus* is somewhat exceptional among Plato's dialogues because it questions conclusions reached in the *Republic* and the *Phaedo* regarding the ideal Forms as a stable and objective kind of knowledge. While the *Theaetetus* eclipses these categories, they subsequently resurface in the *Sophist.* The digression, however, offers another kind of stable category, namely, god. David Sedley interprets this passage as Plato's reflection on the emergence of his own philosophy. In Sedley's view the idea of godlikeness echoes Socrates's search for stable truth in the realm of religion and points to an epistemological lacuna to be filled in by Plato's own paradigm of absolute knowledge, namely, the Forms. Felix Bartels has recently taken up this direction of research and stresses the philosophical connections between the digression and Plato's metaphysics in other dialogues.[3] For Philo, the digression is so central that he refers to it in isolation from the rest of the dialogue, using it as the basis of his ethics in the *Allegorical Commentary.*

Philo's emphasis on Plato's *Theaetetus,* and especially on the digression, is significant in the Alexandrian context, where the dialogue was popular. Two Alexandrian interpretations of this text are extant and illuminate the tendency of Platonism in Philo's hometown. An anonymous, running commentary on the dialogue, the first of its kind extant from antiquity, has been dated by Harold Tarrant to the first century BCE. The author opposes the prevailing Skeptic tendency of the Platonic school and shows that even Plato's most Skeptical dialogue, the *Theaetetus,* can be interpreted in dogmatic fashion. The commentator criticizes those who "consider Plato as an Academic [i.e., a Skeptic], who expounds nothing by way of dogma." In response to this approach he offers a close reading of the *Theaetetus* and argues that Plato did not disavow knowledge as such, but only refrained from teaching it in a manner of dogmatic instruction, preferring instead a dialogical style.[4] The digression, which orients the reader to search for secure knowledge in god, naturally assumes new significance.

Another Alexandrian interpreter of the *Theaetetus* is known to us, namely, Eudorus, active in the first century BCE.[5] This Platonist also highlights the digression and explores its precise meaning in the following way: "Plato describes this [the ideal of godlikeness] most clearly by adding 'as far as possible,' wisely referring only to what was possible, namely, [becoming like god] through virtue. The creation and government of the world belong to god, while the organization of life and the management of one's existence belong to the wise man."[6] Eudorus negotiates the tension between the philosopher's similarity to god and his essential difference. The tension between the two is alleviated by pointing to humanity's limited role in the universe, which leaves room for god's special qualities and functions. The ideal of assimilation to god refers in Eudorus's view to an imitation of divine virtue and constitutes the basis of human ethics. A person should strive to become good by fleeing from this world to heaven.

Eudorus's keen interest in the topic of godlikeness is shared by the anonymous commentator on the *Theaetetus.* While the latter's explanations on the relevant lines are lost, we still posses his statement that "godlikeness," rather than the Stoic ideal of *oikeiosis,* or familiarity with oneself, is the basis of justice. The commentator distinguishes between Plato's transcendental approach, which points to higher spiritual realms, and the Stoic demand that humans should derive the pattern of right action from their own nature. This sharp distinction warns us that modern assumptions about a pervasive syncretism may be exaggerated in the Alexandrian context. John Glucker criticizes scholars who attribute too much importance to Antiochus's brief visit in Alexandria, when he supposedly founded an influential school of Stoicizing Platonism.[7] The interpretations of Plato's *Theaetetus* suggest that Alexandrian intellectuals enthusiastically focused on transcendental ethics, self-consciously distancing themselves from the Stoic approach and its emphasis on the immanence of values.

In this distinctly Alexandrian milieu Philo introduces the *Theaetetus* in his commentary on the Jewish Scriptures. Addressing the apparent redundancy of the biblical expression "dying a death" (Exod 21:14), Philo suggests that Moses implied two types of death, one physical and one spiritual. Living a life without virtue is in Philo's view tantamount to spiritual death. This insight is further supported by two verses from the book of Deuteronomy that speak about "cleaving to the Lord" as a condition of life and "loving the Lord" as "your life and length of days."[8] Philo stresses that Moses recognizes only those as living who take refuge with God and become his suppliants, while others are in his view dead (*Fug.* 56). This "deathless life" of friendship with God is celebrated by adducing Plato's famous passage from the *Theaetetus.* Through this association of texts Philo offers a radically new framework for Jewish ethics. While biblical authors affirmed this world and knew nothing of a fundamental contrast between spiritual and material realms, Philo argues that Moses expresses the same ideas as Plato. He, too, assumes that evil is associated with the material realm and justice with heaven. Philo translates the biblical God, who often behaves in an emotional and human fashion, into an utterly transcendent, abstract, and perfectly good deity.[9] He highlights and elaborates verses relevant to the Alexandrian discourse about the soul's ascent to God and locates the human self in the soul, which is capable of extracting itself from the material world and striving upward.

Philo further appreciates the flight of the soul in light of the biblical places of refuge for unintentional slayers (Exod 21:12–14). He dwells on the term "place," stressing that it "seems to me excellently said." The word "place," or *topos,* must have caught his attention because it is also mentioned in the *Theaetetus* just after the passage quoted above. Socrates speaks there about the penalty of the wicked, who will be condemned to an evil life on earth, while "the blessed place that is pure of all evil will not receive them after death." God, the object of humanity's imitation, is associated with the blessed place and immortality. Philo weaves these themes together, insisting that the term "place" in the biblical text does not refer to a physical space, but "allegorically to God himself."[10] The reader is invited to contemplate the soul's flight to the divine refuge. The biblical image of concrete cities of refuge for murderers thus has been translated into a typically Alexandrian story about the soul's flight from the material realm to God, who punishes the wicked and rewards the righteous.

Philo further quotes from the *Theaetetus* the lines following the previously cited passage:

> Beautifully spoke one of the wise men of old, who shares the very same path as I (εἰς ταὐτὸ τοῦτο συνδραμὼν) and dared to say: "God is in no wise and in no manner unjust, but utterly and perfectly righteous and there is nothing more like him than the one among us who in his turn would become as righteous as possible. The true excellence of a man depends on him, as does his failure and unmanliness. For insight into him equals wisdom and virtue, while ignorance of him leads to sin and patent wickedness. All the other apparent forms of excellence and wisdom, if pertaining to political power, are vulgar, and if to handicraft, merely mechanical." (*Fug.* 82, quoting Plato, *Theaet.* 176c)

Philo speaks of Plato as a fellow traveler who "shares the very same path as I." This self-positioning is striking and indicates the degree to which Philo as a Jew felt congenial with Plato. This serene image, however, is based on an intriguing emendation of Plato's text, which subjects the pagan philosopher to Judaism. While Plato says that the "true excellence of a man depends on this (περὶ τοῦτο)," namely, this process of self-elevation, Philo makes him sound like a monotheist, stressing that the "true excellence of a man depends on him (περὶ τοῦτον)," namely, God. Plato's image as a fellow traveler thus depends, at least to some degree, on a reinterpretation or usurpation of his thought.

At the same time, however, the above passage shows how Philo adopts Plato as a role model, using him to express things that he considered to be beyond common boundaries. He admits that Plato "dared to say" (ἐθάρρησεν εἰπεῖν) certain things about the deity, perhaps hinting at suppressed thoughts that Philo recognizes as missing in the Jewish Scriptures. Indeed, Plato rather than the Bible is Philo's source of inspiration for the idea that the human soul may ascend and assimilate to an utterly transcendent and perfect God. He interprets Moses as a thinker congenial to Plato who shares his ideas, even though Moses does not explicitly say so. Philo requires the *Theaetetus* to set up human spirituality for Jewish ethics. While Plato has been made to speak about the exclusive God of Judaism, Moses

has adopted Plato's theory of the soul. Accepting Plato's approach and relying on his reputation in order to legitimize it within Judaism, Philo even
concludes his discussion with a typically Platonic appeal to his readers as
"initiates and hierophants of holy mysteries" (*Fug.* 85).

Man Is Not the Measure of Things

Philo dwells on another theme of the *Theaetetus,* namely, Protagoras's
maxim that "man is the measure of all things."[11] Plato discusses this maxim
at length because it relates to a central concern of his philosophy, namely,
the question of whether knowledge is subjective or objective. Socrates in
the *Theaetetus* explains Protagoras to mean that the truth is private and relative, being dependent on the beholder's look. The same wind, he says, may
feel either cold or hot to different people. Following Protagoras, the perception of a thing would be treated as if it were its essence, while in reality it
amounts to accepting mere appearances. Socrates challenges this approach
and insists that perceiving things, which are in permanent motion, cannot
produce accurate knowledge of them. He then offers an alternative view,
which serves as a starting point for Philo: "Knowledge is not in the sensa-
tions, but in the process of reasoning about them, for it is possible, apparently, to apprehend being and truth by reasoning, but not by sensation."[12]
This statement comes closest to asserting objective knowledge, based on
real being, given of course the fact that the *Theaetetus* does not refer to the
ideal Forms, which provide criteria for judging sense-perceptible objects.
Philo appreciates Plato's statement because it denies the value of sense perception and empirical knowledge without assuming that human reason is
capable of independently attaining the truth. Philo is happy to suggest that
true knowledge comes from God and mystical insight. He ignores the apo-
retic or skeptical stance of the *Theaetetus,* especially the final admission that
no positive theory of knowledge has been offered (*Theaet.* 210a–c). Philo
also ignores the message of the subsequent dialogue, *The Sophist,* in which
Plato affirms the possibility of gaining objective knowledge of things that
have "real existence," namely, "certain ideas which are only conceived by the
mind and have no body" (*Soph.* 246b).

In the *Allegorical Commentary* Philo pays considerable attention to Protagoras's anthropocentric maxim, using it as the ultimate Other in his construction of Jewish ethics. In his view, it is no longer a mistaken, but serious
approach to the problem of knowledge, as it was in Plato's dialogue, but

rather a self-willed denial of God and his beneficence. Under Philo's pen the villain Cain symbolizes Protagoras's approach. Interpreting Gen 4:17, where it is said that "Cain knew his wife and she conceived and bore Enoch," Philo explains the following:

> Of what sort then is the impious man's opinion? That the human mind "is the measure of all things," an opinion, they tell us, held by an ancient sophist by the name Protagoras, and an offspring of Cain's madness. I base myself on this, namely, that the woman, having been known by him, gives birth to Enoch. Interpreted Enoch means "your gift." If then "man is the measure of all things," all things are a gift and present of the mind, so that seeing has been given to the eye, hearing to the ears, and perceiving to each of the other senses, and indeed speaking to the thought meant to be pronounced. If all these are gifts then surely also thinking with its myriads of thoughts, decisions, wishes, plans, notions, insights, skills, and dispositions and an indefinite number of other powers. How are you then willing to speak solemnly and give honor to the holiness of God and hear about it, if you cherish in you the mind opposite to God, which forcefully appropriates all the goods and evils of men, mixing both for some, while sending to others one of the two unmixed? (*Post.* 35–37)

Philo engages here the epistemological themes of the *Theaetetus* and embraces Socrates's criticism of Protagoras. In his view, too, sense perception is unreliable and even dangerous. In contrast to Plato, however, Philo does not go through the motions of exposing the weaknesses of Protagoras's argument but simply opposes the human-centered approach to a proper acceptance of God, the ultimate source of all stable knowledge. Philo seems to have read Protagoras's maxim in light of the digression, which affirms God as the objective standard of justice. Appeal to the divine, which remains marginal in the *Theaetetus,* thus has assumed central significance for Philo. Keen to outline the right religious attitude, he even identifies the human-centered position as "madness" and suggests a kind of excommunication of its adherents. Cain and his friends won't be tolerated in Philo's community, and "eternal death" will await them (*Post.* 39). While Plato envisioned divine punishment on a personal basis, Philo thinks of a constitution of the Jewish community, whose members police each other in the name of God.[13]

Philo is highly aware of the fact that the issue of man as the measure of things is a central point of dispute among philosophers. He positions himself in light of the following options: "Those who argue at length that man is the measure of everything are in conflict with those who deny the criterion of both sense and mind; and, more generally, those who maintain that everything is beyond our apprehension oppose those who say that the vast majority of things can be known" (*Her.* 246). Empiricists and Skeptics are contrasted to each other, the former surely implying the Stoics. Antiochus of Ascalon, the second-century BCE philosopher known for his combination of Stoic and Platonic elements, embraces Protagoras's maxim and asserts that the human mind is indeed the "criterion of truth" and the judge of sense perception. Philo shows his awareness of the Stoic position, referring to those "who are reputed to be the best philosophers" and claim that the First Cause is apprehended through a perception of the world. This approach relies on the human senses and, as we saw in chapter 5, characterizes Stoicism throughout its long and diverse tradition. While Philo largely embraces Stoicism at the mature stage of his career, he is far more Platonic as a young man and rejects Stoic epistemology. Throughout the *Allegorical Commentary* he stresses God's transcendence and makes humanity's knowledge dependent on God. Philo thus locates himself as a reader of Plato's *Theaetetus* between the Skeptics and the Stoics. He advocates a dogmatic approach to Plato's dialogue, which strongly resembles that of the anonymous commentator but stresses God to a new degree not known from other extant authors in Alexandria. Philo may well have been inspired by Plato's statement in a later dialogue, where he seems to reflect from a distinctly religious perspective on Protagoras's maxim, saying, "For us God will be the measure of all things in the highest degree—a degree much higher than any man, as they say."[14]

In contrast to the *Exposition*, the *Allegorical Commentary* gives much attention to epistemological questions, breathing the spirit of Alexandrian discussions of the *Theaetetus*. Philo often asks, "How does our mind apprehend the fact that an object is white or black?" or "Is sense perception the origin of the perceiving by the senses?" He emphatically states that God "is the cause and source of the sciences and types of knowledge." Moreover, "seeing the light of God is identical to knowledge, which opens the soul's eye and provides more far-shining and distinct perceptions than those of the ears."[15] Philo's keen interest in these matters, which vanishes in his later writings from his Roman period, has to do with the lively Alexandrian discussions as well as his own theological interests.

In order to complete our analysis of the impact on Philo of Plato's epistemology in the *Theaetetus*, we have to ask how he relates to the ideal

Forms, which are not mentioned in this dialogue but loom large in others. Does Philo also eclipse them? In a certain sense Philo is loyal to the *Theaetetus* because he de-emphasizes the Ideas. However, he has entirely different reasons for doing so than Plato, who engages in this dialogue in an exercise of thinking through epistemological issues, tentatively assuming that objective knowledge cannot be defined by the Forms. Philo, on the other hand, regards the Forms as a challenge to God's exclusive authority. He generally speaks about "paradigms" and often reduces their meaning to the concrete sense of a "sort" or "kind" of things, such as kinds of languages, studies, or plants.[16] Philo nevertheless is aware of the original Platonic meaning of the Ideas and solves the problem of a potential clash with religion by suggesting that God himself created the ideal Forms and paradigms. Long before writing the famous passage in the *Exposition,* which we have seen in chapter 5, Philo asserts that God "made both the patterns and the copy." Philo's discussion in the *Allegorical Commentary* shows that he understands his position in the context of Alexandrian Platonism, casting himself into the role of Plato's fellow traveler. His views have not sprung from a supposed opposition between Judaism and Hellenism, as some modern commentators have assumed, but rather emerged as part of a broader Alexandrian discourse that focused on the *Theaetetus* and paid less attention to the ideal Forms.[17]

The Pregnant Soul

The *Theaetetus* provides Philo with the metaphor of a pregnant soul, which he uses pervasively in discussions of Jewish spirituality. He even formulates his own experience as a student in such terms: "When I was first excited by the goads of philosophy to desire her, being still young, I consorted with one of her maids, grammar, and dedicated to the mistress all the things I begot from her, namely, writing, reading, and the study of the writings of the poets" (*Congr.* 74). Philo self-evidently speaks about learning as a process, which implies intercourse with different ladies. He reviews three preliminary disciplines, emphasizing that each of these has its "subtlety and charming powers" but should not become a goal in itself. The "lawful wife" is philosophy, defined as "the cultivation of wisdom," which in turn is the "knowledge of things divine and human and their causes." While the idea of encyclical studies and the metaphor of studying as intercourse with the muses were widespread in the Hellenistic age, Philo shows signs of direct inspiration from Plato, especially the *Theaetetus.*[18]

Philo's indebtedness to Plato clearly emerges when he distinguishes right insight from preliminary school quarrels, saying: "Those who make the enquiry into the greatness and movement of the things in heaven no trivial concern, reach different opinions and disagree with each other until the man versed in midwifery, who is also a judge (ὁ μαιευτικὸς ὁμοῦ καὶ δικαστικὸς ἀνὴρ), will take a seat with them and inspect the offspring of the soul of each and will cast away the products not worth rearing. The useful ones, by contrast, he will preserve and consider worthy of appropriate cultivation" (*Her.* 247). Philo quotes here Socrates's self-definition in the *Theaetetus*, where he introduces himself as the "son of a midwife and myself practiced in the art of midwifery."[19] Plato applies the image of everyday midwifery to philosophy and speaks about "inspecting" and "testing" the offspring of mental pregnancies and then either "rearing" or "throwing them away." Plato's Socrates sees himself as intellectually "sterile of wisdom," questioning others while not providing any answers by himself (*Theaet.* 150b–51c). The dialectical discussion between him and his young friends is productive because he helps them give birth to ideas with which they are pregnant without yet being able to deliver them. The philosophical idea thus has been conceived by the human soul itself but requires a midwife to come forth. Socrates concludes that his midwifery is essential to the process of apprehending the truth as much as is god, who compels him to assume this role.

Not surprisingly, Philo shifts the focus to God. After introducing the "man versed in midwifery," he moves on to the subject of ecstasy, quoting various biblical verses in support of a distinction between prophetic and other kinds of ecstasy. Adam, for example, experiences ecstasy as a "silence and rest of the mind," while Isaac is seized by ecstasy and serves as a "tester" of his son's mental offspring. Abraham, however, illustrates the highest form of ecstasy, which replaces the Socratic model. Philo interprets the biblical reference to the sunset at the time of Abraham's ecstasy as a sign that his own mind was put to rest before receiving prophetic inspiration. He stresses that "the prophet announces nothing of his own, but all his words belong to another, someone else prompting him."[20] Philo moreover insists in direct response to Plato that "whenever the soul by herself gives birth, [the ideas] are abortive and premature, but those which God waters with heavenly snow are perfect and complete in all their parts." God, not the human mind, is "the sole guardian" of thoughts, while the human soul is not credited with the conception of philosophical ideas. The biblical reference to Sarah's sterility draws Philo's attention because of the apparent paradox of her sterility and fertility. This image must be understood in light of God's role in both physical and spiritual pregnancies, as he "opens the womb."[21] Philo considerably limits human agency. In his view, the soul cannot independently become pregnant with proper ideas, and the dialogue between philosophical friends does not produce significant insight. The Platonic motif of Socrates's sterility, which prompts his friends to be productive, instead seems to have been associated with the description of the human soul as such. In the *Allegorical Commentary* God plays the dual role of impregnator and midwife of worthy ideas and knowledge. The soul of the righteous consequently becomes a vessel for the divine seed, which is passively filled with ideas.

The biblical matriarchs exemplify the process of barren souls receiving divine seed and giving birth to ethereal offspring. Philo stresses that divine impregnation can occur only when the senses are "barren." Sarah, whose menopause is interpreted as a departure from the feminine senses, represents such a virtuous soul, which receives God's sperm and gives birth to true wisdom. Rachel, by contrast, who demands children from her husband—"if not, I will die" (Gen 30:1)—fails to understand that the "mind is the cause of nothing, but God who is antecedent to the mind, the only cause."[22] Gender plays a role in Philo's discussion of the pregnant soul. While the matriarchs symbolize the human soul, and are thus highly positive, it is understood that they have intercourse with God only after they have cleansed themselves of the feminine senses. Sarah could unite with God after "leaving behind everything feminine." Moreover, the passivity that is identified as typical of women seems to have rendered the biblical matriarchs welcome figures to imagine the reception of divine seed. Philo says in connection with Eve, the paradigmatic first woman: "The most proper and exact name for sense perception is 'woman.' For just as the man reveals himself in action and the woman in passivity, so the mind proves itself in activity and perception in passivity, namely, in the way of women" (*All.* 2.38).

Philo's interpretation of spiritual pregnancies resonates with his Alexandrian environment. The anonymous commentator on the *Theaetetus* explains that Socrates "gives priority to his own art of midwifery over that of women for in their case it is not difficult to diagnose what is born, whether a phantasm or truth. In the case of young minds, however, it is not easy to distinguish whether they hold false or true opinions."[23] According to the anonymous commentator, Socrates's midwifery guarantees reliable knowledge and affirms that Plato taught positive dogmas rather than a skeptical attitude. While sharing the Alexandrian commentator's intellectual sensibilities, Philo limits Socrates's role. For him, he is an intermediary figure on the way to ultimate knowledge granted by God. This bold erotic language and the overriding emphasis on divine impregnation distinguish Philo among Alexandrian Platonists. Integrating mythological language into philosophical discourse, he offers a new version of the idea that human women have intercourse with divine figures.

The Divided Soul

In the *Allegorical Commentary* Philo uses strong language to depict the inner conflicts of the soul. "Reason," he says, "is at war with passion and cannot dwell in the same place." A "war," he continues, goes on in the soul, because the "body fails to cooperate" with the *logismos* and prevents its beneficial activities. On yet another occasion Philo speaks of the war between the mind and the passions as a confrontation in which only one party can be victorious. If passion "wins an evil victory, mind gives in." Once he warns that if the mind relaxes and "lowers itself to the passions," it will be "dragged by bodily necessity."[24] Philo encourages his readers to let "reason be strong enough to cleanse the passions." He even shares a personal experience in order to illustrate the characteristic warfare in the human soul:

> Reason will curb and bridle the rush and force of passion. I myself have often known passion. Whenever I have attended extravagant parties and costly dinners and did not arrive with reason in my company, I became a slave of the things provided there and was driven by untamed masters: entertainments for the eye and ear and all that brings pleasure by way of taste or smell. Yet whenever I arrived with reprimanding reason, I was a master rather than a slave and, putting forth all my strength, won a noble victory of endurance and self-control, fighting vigorously against all the things that arouse immoderate desires. (*All.* 3.156–57)

Philo vividly depicts his experience of an ongoing conflict between reason and the passions or desires. While the latter respond to external stimuli, reason enforces discipline and opposes the unruly passions. This dynamic between the different parts of the soul reflects a universal principle that is highlighted throughout the *Allegorical Commentary*. God is said to have created the human mind and the sense perceptions as well as their ideal archetypes. The mind bears fruits connected to "things done in thinking," while sense perception and its results are connected to the realm of the tangible. According to Philo, these two elements operate with regard to different objects of knowledge. Reason perceives of the Ideas, while the senses passively receive impressions of the material world. Philo moreover states that the "sense-perceptible has been assigned to the irrational part of the soul." Once he summarily says, "One must understand that our soul is threefold and has one reasonable part, one high-spirited, and one that is the seat of the desires." Harmony is achieved when the two lower parts are ruled by reason, as "horses by a driver." "The mind," Philo concludes, "is so to speak God to the irrational part."[25]

The division of the soul is assumed in a strikingly self-evident manner, even though it has not been introduced before in biblical or postbiblical Judaism. Philo mentions it without offering any explanation, obviously expecting his readers to be familiar with it. This procedure raises questions about the origin of the idea. Where has Philo taken his inspiration from? A first clue is provided by the following statement: "Some of the philosophers have distinguished the three parts [of the soul] from each other only with respect to their function, while others also with regard to their place" (*All.* 3.115). These philosophers must be students of Plato, who famously divided the soul into three parts. Plato introduces the notion in the *Republic* and the *Phaedrus* in order to account for the everyday experience that human beings are torn between different options, both wishing something and detesting it. Such contrasting impulses, Plato explains, have their origin in different parts of the soul. The inhibitive and controlling function is seated in reason, and the unruly instincts come from the passions. The notion of a divided soul explains why inner conflicts are an intrinsic aspect of human life. Different parts of the soul permanently pull in different directions irrespective of a person's environment or stage of life.[26] Philo's reference to different views on the division of the soul reflects an ongoing discussion among Platonists, who focused either on the *Republic* and the *Phaedrus*, where the different functions are presented, or on the *Timaeus*, where their locations are stressed, the appetitive part being associated with the body and reason with the heart. In Alexandria, Eudorus seems to have given preference to the former approach, as he says that the soul's peculiar function is "to form judgments of the intelligible and the perceptible objects."[27]

Philo is so versed in Plato's work that he regularly uses his images of the soul in the *Allegorical Commentary*. His distinction between a "reasonable," an "appetitive," and a "high-spirited" part are directly borrowed from Plato. The *Phaedrus* introduces the image of the charioteer, namely reason, who drives a pair of winged horses, which represent the spirited and the covetous parts of the soul. While one of the animals is noble, the other is of low quality and impedes the soul's upward move. The wings rise up and strive to return to the realm of the Ideas, which the soul has seen before its incarnation. The horses, on the other hand, especially the lower one, pull it down to earthly things. A mighty struggle ensues, and only those souls that give the reins to the charioteer win a place in the ethereal realm. Others, which give free rein to the horses, sink down and are unable to grasp the truth.[28]

Philo keenly appreciates these Platonic images and uses them when he interprets Jewish Scriptures. When he speaks about the spirited element "being driven as a chariot by purified reason" or the "strong yearning to perceive the Existent One," which gives "wings" to the eyes, he relies on the myth of the soul in the *Phaedrus*. His comparison of the passions to a horse and the mind to a horseman, "mounted on the passions," similarly echoes Plato.[29] Platonic ideas and terms are also tangible in the following passage, which depicts the relationship between the mind and sense perception: "When the charioteer is in command and guides the horses with reins, the chariot goes the way he wishes, but when the horses rebel and take over, the charioteer is often pulled down and the animals are dragged into a pit by the violence of their motion—leading everything into a disaster" (*All.* 3.223). Philo uses the image of the soul from the *Phaedrus,* giving an especially dramatic twist to the fall of the unsuccessful charioteer. Unlike Plato, he does not distinguish between two types of horses, but rather treats them as one highly negative symbol of sense perception. Plato's distinction between the two horses nevertheless resurfaces in another passage, where Philo briefly states that the two animals symbolize desire and high spirit. Philo also shares Plato's conviction that the mind originally dwelled in an ethereal realm before entering the body and experiencing the trauma of material limitations.[30]

Philo further inscribes the biblical tradition into Platonic discourses by creatively reading the biblical account of humanity's creation in light of a similar passage in Plato's *Timaeus*. Aware of the fact that he introduces an entirely new idea to ancient Judaism, he hesitantly says, "Therefore I think."

Philo interprets God's plural expression "let us make man" (Gen 1:26) as an indication that he created only the rational part of the human soul, while relegating the creation of its emotional and material parts to his subordinate powers. God deemed it right, Philo explains, that the "sovereign part of the soul was created by the Sovereign and the subject parts by the subjects." Moreover, the biblical summary of humanity's creation, with emphasis on a single actor ("God created man"), is interpreted as a statement about the ideal human, who is "most pure mind" and "invisible and unmixed *logismos*, without any addition." The archetype of the human emerges to be purely spiritual and kindred to God, while concrete human beings are mixed creatures, living at a considerable distance from God and hoping to regain their original proximity to him. The opposition between the spiritual and the material realms, which characterizes the cosmos, is thus also reflected in the human constitution and emerges as the basis of Philo's anthropology. In the *Allegorical Commentary* he consistently adopts Plato's theory of the soul and highlights inner conflicts between rational and material elements.[31]

However, Philo ignores certain elements of Plato's theory of the soul. All of them are connected to questions of boundaries with the eternal or divine realm, touching upon the status of humanity in the universe. Philo does not accept the notion of the soul's immortality, which places it on the same level as the gods and prompts it to enter ever new bodies. Philo avoids this idea because it challenges the exclusive status of the Jewish God, the only eternal being, as he insists. Philo moreover ignores the Platonic idea of learning as a process of recollection, where the soul recovers Ideas grasped before entering a particular body. We have already seen that Philo is highly ambivalent about the prospect of an independent human mind with direct access to absolute truth. He rather envisions the soul as dependent on God for insight, not seeing by itself the ideal Forms and recollecting their contours in the lives of individuals. God provides humans with "secure knowledge" and draws them up to him, "as far as possible," stamping the mind "with the impress of the powers that are within the scope of its understanding."[32]

Despite these differences Philo's *Allegorical Commentary* is filled with Platonic motifs of a divided soul, to the extent that key passages from the *Phaedrus* and other works often seem like a close intertext of the Jewish Scriptures. Philo insists with Plato that humanity is given to a permanent inner struggle between the rational and the material elements. The aim of ethics is to "estrange ourselves from the body and its desires." While Plato demands that the wise should "not cooperate with the body as far as possible" and "live as nearly as possible in a state of death," Philo recommends "dying to the life of the body."[33]

Conclusion

Philo as a young man has emerged as a keen Platonist who is well integrated into the philosophical discussions of his hometown Alexandria. He reads the biblical stories in light of the *Theaetetus* and other Platonic works, which provide the notion of the soul's flight from the material to the heavenly realm, with direct implications for epistemology and ethics. Among other Alexandrian Platonists Philo is conspicuous. While sharing their commitment to a dogmatic form of Platonism and a keen interest in the *Theaetetus,* he is not concerned with a systematic interpretation and the overall consistency of Plato's oeuvre. Philo instead selects certain ideas that he finds congenial in the context of Judaism and uses Plato's texts as starting points for his own creativity. For instance, he enthusiastically adopts the notion of godlikeness, while he subordinates the ideal Forms to God. He dramatically develops the notion of a pregnant soul to suggest that God is its ultimate impregnator of truth.

In the *Allegorical Commentary* Philo is deeply immersed in spiritual questions, not yet paying attention to historical and political realities around him. The human self is constructed as universal, detached from specific lives and circumstances. Philo himself is turned inward, observing the struggle of his soul between material and rational elements. He neither reflects yet upon himself as an author in the text nor shares experiences from life in the world. The center of his ethics is God, whom humanity is called to imitate. This upward view to real values transcends the world and disconnects the individual from society.

Philo's achievement can be appreciated with a view to a pagan and a Christian Platonist who were both active closely after him. Plutarch's teacher Ammonius is a Greek philosopher who advocates Plato's theory of the soul. He speaks about the soul's ascent to higher realities and humanity's yearning for the ideal world perceived in an earlier existence. Unlike Philo, Ammonius thus assumes the immortality of the soul and its transmigration into different bodies. The Christian apologist Justin Martyr, by contrast, follows in Philo's footsteps and rejects the notion of the soul's immortality. While appreciating the Platonic approach more than any other philosophical school, because it is more transcendent and spiritual, Justin insists on God's exclusive authority. Without his consent and initiative, the human soul cannot act.[34] Philo thus has prepared the ground for Christian spirituality, which is based on the Jewish Scriptures and Plato's oeuvre, and in the case of Justin probably also on at least some of Philo's works.

11 An Utterly Transcendent God and His Logos

Philo's theology in the *Allegorical Commentary* differs significantly from that of the *Exposition,* where the creation of the world and God's immanent providence are central. At the beginning of his career, when he engages in scholarly and partly mystical exegesis and advocates a transcendent approach to ethics, Philo develops a theology that stresses God's complete otherness. The divine is beyond the world and requires an intermediary, the Logos, to establish some contact with the material realm, including humanity. Philo is eager to distance God from anything concrete and mostly speaks of him in negative terms, thus introducing to Judaism a new religious language.

In this chapter we investigate Philo's notions of divine transcendence and the Logos, which are intricately connected. Thus far it has been overlooked that the Logos is virtually absent from the *Exposition,* while playing a central role in the *Allegorical Commentary.* The latter is natural, because a mediating figure becomes necessary to the extent that the deity is conceived in abstract terms. Inasmuch as the gap between God and the world increases, there is a demand for an intermediary to turn to. We focus here on the nature and intellectual background of Philo's transcendent theology and ask how he creates a vibrant religion in the face of an unfathomable God. How, in other words, can human beings relate to a wholly Other being as a source of spirituality and ethics? We investigate this question in the context of discourses in Alexandria, where such issues provoked a lively interest.

God Has No Human Shape and No Quality

Alexandrian philosophy sheds light on Philo's sensitivity to issues of anthropomorphism in the Jewish Scriptures. We saw in chapter 10 that the Platonist philosopher Eudorus stresses divine transcendence in his discussion of humanity's godlikeness. In his view, such imitation must necessarily remain partial, as the deity is essentially above humanity. "The God beyond" (ὁ ὑπεράνω θεός) is a characteristic term of Eudorus's theology.[1] Moreover, the Jewish philosopher and Bible interpreter Aristobulus, active in the second century BCE, raises questions about biblical anthropomorphisms. Seeing that God is described as having arms and a face, he urges his readers "to receive the interpretations in their natural sense (πρὸς τὸ φυσικῶς) and to get hold of suitable notions about God, and not lapse into a mythical and human way of thinking (εἰς τὸ μυθῶδες καὶ ἀνθρώπινον κατάστημα)." Aristobulus's work is extant only in small fragments, so we cannot grasp the full implications of his approach. It is clear, however, that he offers metaphorical interpretations of biblical anthropomorphisms and is sensitive to issues of divine transcendence. The motif of God's hand, for example, is compared to the expression "the king has a mighty hand" and is said to signify power.[2]

Philo engages this Alexandrian discussion when identifying in the Bible a "worthy principle," namely, that God "is not like man." Quoting LXX Num 23:19, Philo urges his readers to "transcend all human speech" about God.[3] Throughout the *Allegorical Commentary* Philo quotes and explains this verse six times, obviously taking a keen interest in it, while mentioning it only once in the *Exposition*. Philo is acutely aware of the fact that the principle of God's transcendence is counterintuitive. "We cannot think in terms outside of ourselves," he admits, "and are unable to overcome our specific weaknesses," namely, attaching ourselves to material and concrete patterns. To conceive of God in human terms amounts to creating him in our own image and gravely misunderstanding his nature.

Philo is so concerned about God's transcendence that he dedicates two full treatises to this subject: *On the Giants*, which deals with the story about the giants in Gen 6:4–12, and *The Unchangeableness of God*. As David Winston and John Dillon observe, these two treatises are closely connected and insist that biblical anthropomorphisms must not be taken literally.[4] A special challenge is the biblical story about the giants, born of human women and "sons" or "angels of God."[5] This story collapses conventional boundaries between God and humanity. Philo immediately alerts his readers that it belongs to the realm of "the poets' myths," perhaps those mentioned by Homer and Hesiod. Philo rejects such images and insists that "mythmaking" is alien to Moses, who does not introduce "any kind of myth," but rather wishes to "show that some men are earth-born, some heaven-born, and some God-born." In Philo's allegorical interpretation the earth-born men hunt material pleasures, the heaven-born use their mind and acquire an encyclical education, and the "men of God" are priests and prophets who "raised their heads above the sense-perceptible realm and were translated into the world of the intelligible." This interpretation is inspired by Plato's discussion of the mythological giants as a type of human who clings to the material realm and accepts as true only that which can be touched and seen (*Soph.* 246a–c). Plato uses the ancient myth to distinguish between two approaches to knowledge, namely, sense perception in relation to material things and intellection with regard to the Ideas.[6] Philo adopts this paradigm and applies it to the biblical story, suggesting that there are three types of human representing three stages of perception, the lowest and the highest closely corresponding to Plato's categories. Philo thus distinguishes between correct and wrong ways of thinking about God, criticizing materially inclined minds that see him in mythological terms.[7]

Another difficulty Philo addresses is the biblical image of God regretting humanity's creation (Gen 6:6–8). The Greek translators already may have been puzzled by this anthropomorphism and softened it by suggesting that God was "deliberating" and "contemplating" rather than "feeling sorry in his heart." However, God's summary statement, "I have become angry that I made them," highlights his emotions and is translated into Greek literally.[8] For Philo the idea of God's remorse is unacceptable so he calls his readers to avoid the straightforward meaning of the verse, namely, "because I made them, I have become angry." He even admits that read literally the verse "would imply that God changes his mind, the very thing that the all-providential nature of God does not bear." Instead, he offers an allegorical interpretation: "Perhaps Moses wants to show that the wicked are made by the wrath of God, while the righteous are made by his grace." Despite this exegetical tour de force Philo remains alert to the mythological impression the biblical story makes on his readers, suspecting that they will think of God as a passionate figure who changes his mind.

A more fundamental investigation into biblical anthropomorphisms is thus called for. Philo appeals to two apparently contradictory verses concerning the similarity between humans and God. One verse says that "God is not like man" (Num 23:19), while another says that God teaches a man "as a father instructs his son" (Deut 8:5). Philo brings these two verses into dialogue with each other and distinguishes between different approaches to thinking about God's nature:

> Among the laws dealing with instructions and prohibitions—laws in the literal sense—two principles about the Cause stand out above others. In one of them it says "God is not like man" (Num 23:19), while according to the other he is like man. However, while the first is attested by the surest truth, the latter is introduced for the instruction of the many. Therefore it says about him, "Like a man he shall teach his son" (Deut 8:5). For the sake of instruction and admonition it is thus said and not because his nature is such.[9]

Philo admits here a positive, pedagogical role of biblical anthropomorphism, which does not reflect God's nature but is helpful for the "friends of the body," who are unable to abide by ethical standards without concrete images and threats. This accommodation of myth departs from Plato's model, which envisioned only the elite and banned Homer's stories from the ideal city. In Plato's view, the gods themselves never wished to be perceived in concrete terms and will not tolerate that humans imagine them in ways that falsify their nature and operate in the realm of seeming rather than being.[10] Philo responds to such criticism and interprets the anthropomorphic images in the *Odyssey,* which Plato identified as prime examples of poetic lies. Quoting the same line as Plato, Philo insists that the story "may not be true, but it is at all events good and profitable that it should be current."[11] While Philo's commitment to the education of the broad masses prevents him from altogether dismissing the literal level of ancient stories, either biblical or Homeric, he gives clear priority to the "friends of the soul," who are able to perceive intelligible natures. They should approach the deity in the following way:

> They do not compare the Existent to any form of created things, but rather extract him from all quality (πάσης ποιότητος). For to conceive of his existence as bare and without any characteristics is one of the ways contributing to his blessedness and supreme felicity; and thus they do not give him form, but receive in their minds the conception of being. But those who have made an agreement and a truce with the body are incapable of taking off the garment of flesh and perceiving the unique and self-sufficient and simple nature, which is unmixed and unparalleled (μόνην καὶ καθ' ἑαυτὴν ἀπροσδεᾶ καὶ ἁπλῆν φύσιν ἰδεῖν ἀμιγῆ καὶ ἀσύγκριτον). (*Deus* 55–56)

Stressing the contrast between the two epistemological approaches, Philo dwells on God's transcendence in thoroughly Platonic terms. Plato already has proposed philosophical "patterns of right speech about the gods." Foremost among such patterns is acknowledging the unchangeableness of god, who does not "wish to alter himself" but "abides forever simply in his own form."[12] Rejecting anthropomorphic conceptions of the gods, Plato develops an alternative philosophical approach to theology, which presents the gods as proper role models for humankind. He stresses that the gods are "fairest and best possible" in character, "truly good and always to be spoken of as such," enjoying an eternal, unchanging, and noncomposed existence. They resemble, in other words, the ideal Forms. Philo similarly stresses the simple and noncomposed nature of God as well as his true being. Exodus 3:14 (LXX), where God says of himself "I am he that is," is the basis of Philo's theology. While not quoting this verse in the *Exposition*, he mentions it three times in the *Allegorical Commentary*, adding that "God alone has veritable being;[13] therefore, Moses will necessarily say of him 'I am he who is,' implying that others next to him do not have being, according to the nature of being, but are only by opinion considered to exist" (*Det.* 160). Philo applies here the Platonic distinction between true being and appearance to the description of the Jewish God, conferring on him the characteristic of the ideal Forms. This image of God is supported by the Greek translation of Exod 3:14, which renders the Hebrew expression "I am" as a masculine participle, thus encouraging more general philosophical speculation.[14] While Plato regularly speaks about the divine in the neuter, Philo is happy with the masculine connotation of the Septuagint expression.

Philo departs from Plato in one important respect, namely, his avoidance of speaking about God as "good." He suggests instead that he is beyond "all quality" and that he "is not only nonanthropomorphic, but also lacks any quality."[15] Even Moses was allowed to perceive of only his mere existence, while a more detailed inquiry into his "essence and quality" would have been misguided and childish. Philo in the *Allegorical Commentary* is thus much less certain than Plato about God's benevolent nature. Whereas Plato asserted that god is good and can be "found," but not declared to all, Philo concludes that God is altogether beyond human knowledge.[16]

John Whittaker argues in a pioneering article that Philo's theology must be understood in the context of Alexandrian Platonism with its characteristic Pythagorean tendency. He points to the fragment of Eudorus, quoted above, that speaks about "the god beyond." Whittaker moreover stresses that Philo quotes the Pythagorean Philolaus, concerning god as "a supreme ruler of all things, ever One abiding, stable and without motion, Himself alone like unto Himself, different from all others."[17] Philo is also familiar with circles of Pythagorean Platonists, whom he mentions as holding the following view: "The Unoriginate resembles nothing among created things, but so completely transcends them (ὑπερβάλλον), that even the swiftest understanding falls far short of apprehending him and acknowledges its failure" (*Somn.* 1.184). Whittaker's argument is highly convincing and confirms the Alexandrian context of Philo's transcendent theology. His analysis leads us to notice many further statements in this spirit throughout the *Allegorical Commentary*. Philo's assertions that God is "himself one and whole," "unoriginate and incorruptible," "incorporeal," and "above his potencies" indeed make sense in the context of Alexandria.[18]

It is time to move beyond these insights and realize that Philo played a pioneering role in developing negative theology in Alexandria. In the most extreme passage of his work he offers a view that is more radically negative than any of those expressed in the fragments of his Platonist and Pythagorean predecessors. In that passage he insists that literally nothing can be known about God: "Nothing that can give assurance can give firm assurance concerning God, because he has not shown his own nature to anyone (οὐδενὶ γὰρ ἔδειξεν αὐτοῦ τὴν φύσιν), but has rendered it invisible to the whole race. Who can say of the First Cause either that it is without body or that it is a body, either that it is of such a quality or that it is of no quality? Generally, who can declare anything with certainty concerning his essence or quality or state or movement?" (*All.* 3.206). The degree of Philo's negative theology is best appreciated by looking at his assertion that we cannot even know whether God is with or without a body. This remark collapses the most basic distinction of Platonic ontology, namely, the distinction between an inferior material and a superior spiritual realm. Philo explores the full implications of the principle that God is unknown and draws a conclusion of total negation. He thus anticipates the anonymous commentator of Plato's *Parmenides*, who gives much attention to the problem of god's transcendence, asking whether such a notion does not imply a claim about the nothingness of the deity.[19]

Philo, however, questions neither God's existence nor his centrality for humans. Given that God cannot be perceived by the regular tools of rationality, Philo resorts to the idea of God actively approaching humans and graciously providing them with insights. In chapters 9 and 10 we saw that Philo adduces verses from the Prophets and Psalms to suggest ecstatic insights. He also develops the Platonic motif of spiritual pregnancies, suggesting that God impregnates the human soul and gives birth to virtuous notions. In both cases God initiates the contact with humans and lavishes on them goods that are beyond their intellectual abilities and achievements. Mystery covers these divine approaches with the result that the human mind is remarkably passive.

Similar notions resurface in Philo's theology. Moses is the ideal figure who receives insight into God because he rejects conventional ways of knowing him. Rejecting Stoic proofs of God from the creation, Moses's mind is said to have been "initiated into the great mysteries." Philo moreover explains that "having lifted his eyes above the creation, he receives a clear impression of the Uncreated, so as to apprehend him from himself as well as his shadow." Philo dismisses the creation, which serves in the *Exposition* as the main path to know God, as a mere shadow that obstructs insight. Instead he suggests that God may approach someone and permit that person to see his existence without recourse to the material world. Philo suggests that preparing for the approach of God is best done by turning inward and knowing oneself. Readers understand that they should leave behind sense perception and the sights of the world. Departure from the body frees the human mind to hold converse with itself and ultimately be blessed with a "divine frenzy."[20] Prayer becomes a central gesture. Philo points to Moses as someone who shows the way by praying that God "may open his treasure before us." Intriguingly, God's treasure contains both good and evil. Insisting that his readers grasp the full implications of this statement, Philo says, "You see that there are treasuries of evil things." God, however, "opens the treasure of good things, while shutting up those of the evil things."[21] Philo touches here once more on the tantalizing question of God's nature. Leaving open whether God is identified with all of his treasures, including evil, he stresses that God regulates himself, showing the world only his good aspects.

Philo's notion of God's absolute transcendence is revolutionary in ancient Judaism. No prior Jewish author imagined God as radically beyond the material realm and even beyond the good. Among subsequent "Gnostics" and Platonists, however, his interpretation of Plato, with its characteristic emphasis on divine grace, became rather more common. The notion of God's absolute transcendence, to the extent that he can literally not be known, has often been identified as a significant characteristic of different

Gnostic systems.[22] Whether or not a consistent theology can be reconstructed for the various authors, whom early Christian writers grouped together as appealing to secret knowledge (*gnosis*), some of them express views remarkably similar to those of Philo. Valentinus, for example, who probably grew up in second-century Egypt, envisions God as transcendental and "invisible." It is after a fierce internal fight of the human soul and through the grace of Jesus that humans may receive a vision of God. Basilides, who taught in Alexandria in the second century CE, also stresses the utterly transcendental nature of God, who creates an evolving world and a select race of initiates. Similarly, the Gnostic Eugnotus devotes a separate hymn to the indescribability and ineffability of God.[23]

Second-century Platonists moved in similar theological directions. Numenius, the philosopher known for his sympathy to Eastern traditions, including Judaism, speaks about two gods—the Self-Existent and the demiurge. The evidence is too fragmentary to allow a full appreciation of his thought, but Numenius clearly conceives of a higher God beyond the material world and may to some extent even have been inspired by Philo's work.[24] More evidence is available from the Alexandrian Platonist Ammonius, who inspired Plutarch and Plotinus, thus giving a significant impetus to the emergence of Neoplatonism. In a speech preserved by Plutarch, he stresses the oneness and simple and pure nature of the deity. The absolutely transcendent god is distinguished from the demiurge, who is concerned with the lower realm of nature. In a strikingly parallel move to that of Philo, Ammonius further says that the transcendent deity approaches a person with the words "know yourself." This address is reciprocated by that person's response "you are."[25] Ammonius thus describes a process of mutual recognition and existential affirmation in which both the person and the deity are involved. It is through knowing oneself that one perceives of god, both aspects being facilitated by divine grace.

To be sure, Philo does not go so far as to sever the transcendent God from the demiurge. Yet he makes a pioneering contribution, preparing the way for Gnosticism and subsequent Platonism in the Greco-Roman period, which continued to develop in this direction, perhaps partly thanks to his work. In the *Allegorical Commentary* Philo perceives of a superior yet unknown aspect of God that is beyond the creation and beyond ethical judgment. This utterly transcendent God requires the Logos to bridge the gap between God and his creation.

The Logos as Intermediary

Most readers of Philo take the opening passage of his treatise *On the Creation* as their starting point for investigating the notion of the Logos. Philo introduces the Logos in the context of his creation account, according to which God acknowledges that a "beautiful copy could never be produced apart from a beautiful pattern" (*Opif.* 16). Therefore, God first created "the intelligible world" in the image of which he formed the material world. The intelligible world is contained by the divine Logos, or in Philo's words: "The universe that consisted of ideas would have no other location than the divine Logos, which was the author of this ordered frame. For what other place could there be for his powers sufficient to receive and contain, I say not all but any of them whatever uncompounded and untempered?" (*Opif.* 20).

Scholars have not been at ease to explain the sudden appearance of the Logos in this passage. There is a broad consensus that the Logos functions as a mediator between God and the material realm and, moreover, that some mixing of ideas is involved. Émile Bréhier even speaks of "un bizarre syncrétisme."[26] Most scholars identify a strong Stoic influence on Philo's concept of the Logos, even though the Logos plays no role as a separate entity in the cosmogony of that school.[27] Moreover, Stoic authors of the first century CE generally do not use this concept but instead speak about nature as rational. Nevertheless, many scholars interpret the above passage from the *Exposition* in a Stoic vein and take it as a key text that throws light on the overall nature and emergence of Philo's concept. The rest of Philo's diverse work is then read in light of this passage or, to put it in stronger terms, harmonized with the insights scholars have derived from it. Such an approach is encouraged by the English translation of Philo's works, which mistakenly puts this treatise at the very beginning, thus suggesting that it is a gate to Philo's thought.[28]

This approach, however, is highly problematic, as it fails to do justice to the historical development of Philo's thought. Taking a passage from the later *Exposition* as a key to texts written much earlier inevitably obscures the facts and results in confusion. David Runia opens up new possibilities of interpretation when paying attention to one aspect of the above text from the *Exposition*. Commenting on the sudden appearance of the Logos in Philo's creation account, he cautiously suggests that Philo "appears to assume a certain familiarity of his reader with the main lines of his theology."²⁹ Runia seeks to explain such familiarity on the reader's part by reference to a shared philosophical background but admits that it is "not easy to locate." I build on this preliminary observation and argue that Philo indeed assumes familiarity with the concept of the Logos because he already had introduced and thoroughly discussed it in the *Allegorical Commentary.*

The term "Logos" appears for the first time in Philo's oeuvre in a thoroughly Pythagorean passage in which he discusses the significance of numbers. He speaks of the power of the number seven, which is visible in the sevenfold structure of cosmological, grammatical, medical, and musical phenomena as well as in its special mathematical qualities. Philo refers to the Pythagoreans, who explain the power of seven by "comparing it to the motherless and ever-virgin [goddess], because neither was she born nor shall she ever bear" (*All.* 1.8–15). Philo is thus familiar with a Pythagorean interpretation of the goddess Athena that takes her well-known qualities in Greek myth as a sign of the world's mathematical structure. Her origin from Zeus's head, without a mother, points to the primal quality of the number seven, which is not derived by multiplication. The goddess's virginity moreover confirms that the number seven cannot be multiplied within the first decade of numbers. While criticizing the Pythagorean approach as "indulging in myth," Philo relies on it as evidence for the power of the seven. He accepts the Pythagorean notion that a mathematical structure infuses the universe with order and power, which are rooted in the divine.

In this context Philo mentions for the first time the term "Logos." Explaining LXX Gen 2:3, where God is said to rest on the seventh day "from all his works, which God began to create," he once more highlights the significance of the number seven.³⁰ He stresses that God's resting refers to his ceasing to shape mortal things "whenever he begins to create things divine and things belonging to the nature of seven" (*All.* 1.16). Philo reads the biblical verse in light of his characteristic distinction between a material and a spiritual realm that are identified with different notions of creation. He also invests the number seven with spiritual and even divine qualities, suggesting its close proximity to God. The spiritual creation is exclusively associated with the latter and therefore can take place only when the material creation comes to an end. This cosmic dichotomy is also reflected in the human soul, where the Logos plays an important function of mediation: "But the explanation pertaining to character is this: whenever the Holy Logos, which corresponds to the number seven (ὁ κατὰ ἑβδομάδα ἅγιος λόγος), comes upon the soul, the number six and all mortal things that the soul seems to make therewith come to a stop" (*All.* 1.16). The Logos is identified as "holy" and belonging to God, while also corresponding to the number seven and infusing the world with a special, ethereal power. Whereas God ceased to deal with mortal things after he created the world, his Logos plays a concrete role in the human soul, preventing it from producing inferior mortal things, symbolized by the composite number six.

Philo moreover adduces the biblical motif of God blessing the seventh day and hallowing it (Gen 2:3). The Logos assumes the role of a hallowed presence that pervades the lower, material realms with which God cannot come into direct contact. It fulfills a role similar to that of the numbers in the Pythagorean scheme. Philo further expands his interpretation of Gen 2:3 and suggests that God blesses "the dispositions set in motion in accordance with the number seven and the truly divine light" (*All.* 1.17). This motion seems to be prompted by the Logos, which intervenes in the created world and encourages humans to devote themselves to immortal values. The Nazirite, who vows to abstain from drinking wine for seven days as an expression of devotion to God, serves as a paradigmatic example. This strict abstinence is interpreted in terms of the Nazirite's orientation toward "the seven and the perfect light" and is rewarded by divine blessings and hallowing.

Genesis 2:4 (LXX) provides Philo with further motifs to discuss the role of the Logos:

> "This is the book of the creation of heaven and earth, when it came into being" (LXX Gen 2:4).[31] This refers to the perfect Logos, which moves according to the number seven and is the beginning of the creation both of the mind ordering itself according to the Ideas and of mental sense perception, if it is possible to say so, which also orders itself according to the Ideas. [Moses] calls "book" the divine Logos, in which are inscribed and engraved the structures of other things. In order that you may not suppose that the deity creates something according to definite periods of time, but may understand that the creation is beyond human perception, definition, and comprehension, he adds "when it came into being," not defining time by a concrete figure. (*All.* 1.19–20)

Philo explores here the multiple meanings of the word "Logos," which range from "word" and "book" to "rationality." He identifies the biblical motif of a book as a reference to a superior Logos, which provides a rational structure to the world and is connected to the Platonic Ideas. While the latter are taken for granted, Philo self-consciously offers new ideas about the Logos. He is highly aware of the fact that his readers may be surprised, wondering himself whether "it is possible to say so." The Logos is described in terms of the Pythagorean theory of numbers and then credited with a special role in the creation. Philo regards it as "the beginning" or source of the creation, suggesting an ideal creation that is not governed by such material qualities as time. Relying on Platonic and Pythagorean notions, Philo introduces radically new conceptions. Within the Platonic tradition he argues for the first time that the Ideas are not eternal but have been created by God. Within the Jewish tradition he is the first to suggest that the creation of the world has been anticipated by an ideal creation brought about by the Logos.

Philo's innovative approach may well have been inspired by the particular wording of LXX Gen 2:4–5, which differs significantly from the Hebrew original. The Hebrew text is introduced by two loosely connected clauses: "On the day when the Lord God made the earth and the heaven, and no plant of the field was yet on the earth and no herb of the field had yet sprung up." The Greek translators, however, connected the two subclauses and translated the nominative cases of "plant" and "herb" as accusatives, thus making them dependent on God's creative act. More importantly, they added the temporal preposition "before" and suggested the following sequence of events: "God made the heaven and the earth and every green thing of the field before it appeared on the earth (πρὸ τοῦ γενέσθαι ἐπὶ τῆς γῆς) and all grass of the field before it sprang up (πρὸ τοῦ ἀνατεῖλαι)" (LXX Gen 2:4–5). As Martin Rösel observes, the Greek translators assume here the Platonic notion of an ideal creation that precedes the material world.[32] The Alexandrian translators seem to have read the biblical creation account in light of Plato's *Timaeus*, in which a given ideal cosmos provides the paradigm for the creation of the material world (*Tim.* 28a–29d). Philo is acutely aware of this Alexandrian tradition and seems to ask how such an ideal creation can be imagined in the context of Jewish theology. For him it is clear that God must have initiated the creation of the Ideas via the Logos. "By his own supremely manifest and far-shining Logos," he explains, "God creates both the Idea of the mind, which he [Moses] symbolically calls 'heaven,' and the Idea of sense perception, which he figuratively calls 'earth'" (*All.* 1.21).

Philo's Logos theology thus emerges in a thoroughly Alexandrian context with its characteristic orientation toward Platonic and Pythagorean ideas. It provides an answer to the question of how the utterly transcendent God can have been involved in the creation. Sensitive to the diverse meanings of the word "Logos," which range from concrete items such as a book to abstract rationality, Philo attributes central importance to this concept and constructs it as an ideal mediator between the material and the ethereal realms. Inspired by his intellectual environment, Philo makes a significant contribution of his own.

Our conclusion is further supported by the evidence of other Platonists. Most interesting for our purposes are Thrasyllus, Philo's contemporary, who also had grown up in Alexandria and later moved under Tiberius's tutelage to Rome, and Moderatus, a Platonist living just one generation after him, as well as Plutarch, the latter of whom we have already encountered in numerous contexts of Philo's biography. Thrasyllus speaks of a "Logos of Forms," which he explains in Stoic terms of a seminal force active in the *physis* of each thing, while Moderatus attributes to the Logos a prominent role in the process of the creation. Interestingly, he thinks that according to Plato the creation comes about by a withdrawal of the unified Logos.[33] Most importantly, Plutarch offers a Platonic interpretation of the Egyptian myth of Isis and Osiris, stressing the role of the Logos in the creation. Isis is identified as the female principle of nature, called by Plato the "all receptive," which is transformed by reason into all kinds of shapes and forms. Plutarch counters suspicions that the creation may reflect illegitimate contamination by stressing that Hermes, namely, Logos, testifies to the propriety of the process. Plutarch adds that "before this cosmos was made visible and its rough material was completely formed by the Logos, it was tested by nature" (*Is. and Os.* 54). Here, too, the Logos is involved in the preexistent stage of the creation, shaping materials with which god does not come into contact. Philo thus emerges as the first Platonist who envisages a role for the Logos in the early stages of the creation and perhaps encourages others to follow him.

It now remains for us to see how Philo uses and develops his concept of the Logos throughout the *Allegorical Commentary*. In particular we ask how he shapes it as a mediator in the ongoing relationship between God and humanity. Initially, the Logos plays an important role in epistemology. While God himself is unknowable, his Logos can be perceived by human beings. Philo even says that apprehending God means apprehending his Word. Abraham did not perceive God—"for what human mind could contain the vastness of that vision?"—but instead encountered "a manifestation

222 Young Philo among Alexandrian Jews

of one of the Potencies that attend him." Philosophers, Philo moreover explains, will see "his image, the most holy Logos."[34]

God actively approaches humans via his Logos, showering on them virtues and opening his "treasure." He moreover offers spiritual food in the form of manna. Creatively associating two verses from Exodus, Philo suggests that the manna is identical with the divine Logos, which "resembles dew." The Logos is "delicate to conceive and to be conceived, surpassingly clear and transparent to behold." More importantly, the Logos enables "participation" (μετουσία). The human soul dispels gloom and inferior vision when it has communion with the divine Logos. When souls "have experienced the Logos," they will have access to new insights.[35] While Philo conspicuously refrains from providing any details about these states of communion with God's Logos, it is clear that the very idea of a rapprochement between the human and the divine realms is important for his theology.

Philo moves toward the notion of divine emanation, in which the Logos plays a prominent role. According to his allegorical interpretation, the six biblical cities of refuge represent six manifestations of God, the highest of which is the Logos, while the other five are different divine powers. Philo praises the Logos as the best mother city to which humans are encouraged to take refuge, while he credits the "creative power" with the production of the cosmos and the "royal power" with the government of the world. It is through the "gracious power" that God takes pity on and feels compassion for his creatures, and two aspects of his "legislative power" prescribe duties and prohibitions.[36] Philo seems to envision these different powers as emanations of God, which can be arranged in descending order of distance to him. The Logos is closest, and the legislative powers are farthest removed. He speaks about the "rich abundance of these beneficial powers," which are adapted to peoples' varied needs. Different paths are thus envisioned for different types of people: "[Moses] bids the swift runner to exert himself and run without taking a breath toward the supreme divine Logos, which is the source of wisdom, in order that he may draw from the stream and gain as a prize eternal life rather than death" (*Fug.* 97). Philo's image of humans taking refuge in the divine Logos and thereby achieving spiritual immortality is a daring expression of a vibrant religiosity, which culminates in humanity's proximity to, if not union with, God's emanation. The Logos enables the swiftest, namely, the most philosophical people, to come into direct contact with the deity. Less qualified people will turn to his lower powers, some recognizing him in the creation, others in his legislation. In

Philo's view, the lower powers have a concrete representation in the tables of the law, the lid of the arch, and the winged cherubim. Only the divine Logos, he insists, "which is high above these (ὑπεράνω τούτων) does not accept a visible form, as it resembles none of the objects of sense." Philo thus describes the Logos in terms of absolute transcendence, which we encountered at the beginning of this chapter in connection with God. It takes the place of God vis-à-vis the visible world but allows humans to perceive him, participate in him, and even take refuge in him. Philo summarily says that the Logos "dwells and walks among those who honor the life of the soul." This divine presence among humans is considerable, given that Philo calls the Logos "second" to God himself, who is the "most generic being."[37]

The significance of Philo's Logos theology is evident in light of subsequent "Gnostics" and Platonists, who also assume intermediary figures on the way to God. Valentinus, like Philo, was inspired by Plato's works and imagined a "living aion," which functions as an image of God visible to humans. While the evidence about Valentinus is too fragmentary to allow a proper appreciation of the aion and its role in his theology, Basilides seems to have imagined a detailed set of emanations. According to Irenaeus's account, he spoke of God as giving birth to different emanations, initially the Nous and the Logos, then judgment and wisdom, the latter of which gives birth to the "powers." Moreover, the second-century Platonist Albinus stresses that the notion of assimilation to god cannot refer to the "god beyond," but rather to an intermediary.[38]

Conclusion

In the *Allegorical Commentary* Philo develops a theology that significantly differs from his position in the *Exposition,* where he elevates the creation to a Jewish dogma and confidently states that "following nature they might win the best of goals, knowledge of him that truly is" (*Dec.* 81). The *Exposition* no longer reflects the profound doubts Philo entertained as a young man concerning the creation and the knowability of God. At the beginning of his career he intensively engaged the discourses of his hometown Alexandria and adopted a typical orientation toward Platonism and Pythagoreanism with their characteristic emphasis on transcendence. He developed these ideas further than his predecessors and formulated for the first time a negative theology that posits an unknowable God beyond good and evil. Philo also interprets the Jewish Scriptures creatively and develops a theory of the Logos as an intermediary figure that permits human beings to approach the divine realm without compromising God. Many of Philo's ideas subsequently resurface in Gnostic and Platonic authors, who may have been inspired by him, as many of them hailed from Alexandria.[39]

Philo as a young man expresses theological ideas that later become popular in the Greek East but remain marginal in Rome. His later creation theology in the *Exposition,* by contrast, engages Roman discourses and resonates with authors who become canonical in the Christian church. We thus can draw the conclusion that the creation became a crucial watershed. Allocating the creation a central place in one's philosophy or theology expresses a commitment to this world and by implication a readiness to be involved in politics, namely, Roman structures of power. Doubts about the value of the creation, by contrast, indicate a withdrawal from the world, including politics. Philo has moved from one mode to the other, developing from an inward author in Alexandria, with radically transcendent ideas about God, humanity, and the world, to an ambassador and writer in Rome who is confident about God's presence in the world and acutely sensitive to current discourses in the capital of the empire. No other author whose work has survived underwent such a dramatic and impressive development, being creative and fruitful in both areas and visibly affecting wider discussions initially in the East and then also in the West.

12 Stoicism: Rejected, Subverted, and Advocated

The question of Philo's attitude toward Stoicism in the *Allegorical Commentary* is a complex matter. In comparison to the *Exposition* and the philosophical writings, he is considerably more reserved about the main tenets of this school. He does not yet, for example, praise certain Stoics, such as Panaetius, for abandoning the idea of recurrent conflagrations of the world, but generally dismisses "the marvelmongers' fable of the conflagration." In comparison to other Alexandrian philosophers, however, Philo shows already in the early phase of his career an interest in Stoicism and even admits that this school enjoys the "best reputation."[1] His *Allegorical Commentary* is the clearest evidence of Stoic thought in first-century Alexandria, where Platonism generally prevailed and carefully distinguished itself from Stoicism, as we have seen.

Our task is to investigate the precise nature of Philo's attitude toward Stoicism at the beginning of his career. We have to ask not only which Stoic ideas are known to him as a young man, but also how he interprets and uses them, heeding Carlos Lévy's warning about "just how mistaken the thesis is that Philo unconditionally adheres to Stoicism."[2] Having already seen the full use he makes of Stoic ideas in his later works, we may now appreciate the beginnings of Philo's engagement with this school, when he is still far more general and ambivalent. A central aspect of this inquiry has to do with the relative priority of Stoicism in Philo's early works. Given that at the beginning of his career he is an enthusiastic Platonist who stresses God's utter transcendence and the soul's flight from the material world, how much space does he make for Stoic ideas? Does he take the Stoics' philosophical assumptions seriously, or does he rather use some of their terms as rhetorical decorations or general gestures? Moreover, what role do the exigencies of Bible interpretation play in selecting relevant motifs from Stoicism?[3]

One of the main factors hampering the discussion is the eclecticism of modern scholars, who use passages from Philo's later and earlier works interchangeably, without awareness of their respective historical and philosophical contexts. Scholars thus have overlooked the considerable differences between Philo's works and offered harmonizing readings. Assuming a rigorous historical approach, we differentiate between his later works, where we have already identified many Stoic ideas, and the *Allegorical Commentary*, which may produce other results. We appreciate the early treatises on their own terms as evidence of Philo's attitude as a young man. Scholars also tend to lack historical awareness regarding the Stoic school and rarely differentiate among its different phases. As much as Philo is mistakenly seen as one supposedly homogeneous author, so also Stoicism is often treated as if it were one coherent system, irrespective of developments over time and space. Such a holistic approach, however, is challenged by the Stoics themselves, who were already in antiquity aware of differences within their school. Antipater wrote a no longer extant treatise on "the difference between Cleanthes and Chrysippus," the two heads of the school following the founder, Zeno. Plutarch examines differences between the Stoics, suggesting that they contradict each other to the extent that no overall school philosophy can be identified. While Plutarch polemically exaggerates the variety of Stoic thought, he provides sufficient evidence to suggest a highly complex picture. Diogenes Laertius, a more neutral summarizer of Greek philosophy, confirms this impression by pointing to intellectual diversity among the Stoics. Panaetius is regularly mentioned as advocating divergent views.[4] A rigorous historical approach, to both Philo and Stoic philosophy, thus provides more nuanced and precise answers to the question of Philo's attitude toward this school. Applying historical methods, we investigate which Stoic views Philo singles out for criticism in the *Allegorical Commentary*, which notions he reinterprets, and finally, which views he is happy to advocate.

Stoic Materialism Rejected

In the *Allegorical Commentary* Philo positions himself in contrast to Stoic materialism, rejecting especially the idea of recurrent conflagrations of the world, which challenges the idea of God's transcendence and omnipotence. According to Stoic thought, the highest god is part of the world's revolutions and thus included in the material realm, which is subject to destruction and regeneration. Diogenes Laertius explains this process in some detail. God or Zeus is generally held to be identical with the "seminal reason of the universe" responsible for every growth, while Zeno and some of his followers directly identify the cosmos with the substance of god. "At certain periods of time," Diogenes further explains, the demiurge "absorbs into himself the whole of substance and again creates it from within himself." The cosmos "is doomed to perish," because its parts deteriorate and perish. The cyclical generation and destruction of the world are possible because the world is composed of divinely penetrated substance, and the infinite void surrounding it provides space for seasonal expansion (D.L. 7.135–48).

Such theories are anathema to Philo. He dismissively mentions the myth of the conflagrations and the mistaken assumption of a void, stressing that these are proved wrong by God, who sets boundaries to the one existing cosmos and providentially steers it. Philo moreover points out that God is incomprehensible and cannot be measured or contained by something measurable. As a Platonist, he vehemently rejects the Stoic notion of god as immersed in the material realm. Stoic cosmology lacks in his eyes the necessary awareness of God's transcendence and overarching power. Philo's criticism is especially significant in view of the fact that Plutarch expresses similar views a generation later. As a Platonist Plutarch complains that the Stoics violate universal assumptions about the divine by insinuating that the demiurge is involved in the conflagrations. By periodically absorbing perishable matter and mortal gods, the demiurge acquires "the attribute of destruction." Plutarch opposes this approach and argues that it implies a substantial attack on traditional piety.[5]

In *The Migration of Abraham*, which is devoted to the soul's departure from the material realm, Philo addresses further aspects of Stoic materialism. Discussing Abraham's departure from Chaldea (Gen 11:31), he attributes to its inhabitants Stoic tenets, which the patriarch appropriately leaves behind. "These men," he complains, "assumed that this visible cosmos was the only thing in existence, either considering it to be a god or containing god in itself as the soul of the whole. Having divinized fate and necessity, they filled the life of man with much impiety, teaching that nothing except the phenomena exists as the cause of everything, and that the circuits of the sun and the moon and the other heavenly bodies portion out good things and their opposite to each of the existing things." Philo has outlined here a central Stoic doctrine embraced by Zeno, Chrysippus, and Posidonius, according to which the cosmos is penetrated by the divine rather than subordinated to it. Rejecting this approach, Philo stresses that Moses "differs from [this] opinion about God and holds neither the cosmos nor the soul of the cosmos to be the primal God." The visible world is instead held together by the invisible bonds of God, who takes "forethought that what was well bound should not be loosened." The notion of divine bonds providentially holding together the cosmos and thus negating the laws of nature, according to which every creation implies destruction, echoes Plato's *Timaeus*.[6] In this dialogue the demiurge keeps the created cosmos bound together and protects it from destruction. Philo relies on this Platonic image when opposing Stoic cosmology and insisting on God's transcendence.

Given Philo's strong objections to Stoic cosmology, it is not surprising that he dismisses the Stoics' proof of the demiurge from the observance of nature. He personally appeals to his readers to stop looking at heaven and earth, turning inward instead to an exploration of their own nature. It is in their souls that they will perceive God, as if through a mirror. Here, too, Philo uses Platonic terms and recommends divine frenzy as a state of higher perception. He is still far removed from the later stages of his career, when he praises the Stoic Panaetius for rejecting the idea of the world's conflagration, raises the creation to the level of a Jewish dogma, and uses it as the main proof of God, deducing divine providence from the observation of nature.[7]

Stoic Ethics Subverted

Most of Philo's engagements with Stoic philosophy belong in the category of subversion. He is clearly familiar with Stoic ethics and ostensibly approves of them, but then refrains from using the ideas in a Stoic sense. Philo rather interprets them for his own purposes, sometimes turning them upside down, so that we have to examine the precise mechanism of this process as well as the reasons for his unusual approach. Our inquiry focuses on three prominent Stoic notions, namely, passion, *oikeiosis,* and individual choice.

Throughout the *Allegorical Commentary* Philo never identifies a Stoic treatise or philosopher by name, giving this school less attention than Plato, whose work he explicitly cites and discusses, as we saw in chapter 10. Once, however, Philo refers to an anonymous work on the four passions, which arouses our curiosity. He says, "Four are the passions in the category of pleasure, as some treatise on this particular topic reminds us." The English translator of Philo's works renders this clause in a strikingly free manner and interprets it as a reference to a book Philo planned to write, which was either "never written or is lost."[8] Yet the expression "some treatise reminds us" refers to an extant text that Philo found rather than composed. Moreover, he never formulates references to his own work in such a way, instead using first-person language, such as "we will show" or "we have treated elsewhere."[9] With the above reference to a treatise on the passions, Philo alerts his readers to a separate treatise on the topic that he does not care to identify more specifically.

This anonymous treatise must have derived from the Stoic school, which was famous in antiquity for dividing the passions into four categories. Diogenes Laertius traces this doctrine back to Zeno, who is said to have written a treatise *On the Passions*. According to the Stoics, the four central types of passion are grief, fear, desire, and pleasure. Diogenes further explains that the Stoics also recognized "good emotional states," which are the counterpart of the passions. Joy, for example, is inversely analogous to pleasure, caution to fear.[10] Philo's reference to a treatise dealing with the "four passions in the category of pleasure" echoes these Stoic discussions, while lacking precise formulation. He presents one type of passion, namely pleasure, as the overall term for bad emotional states. Philo nevertheless has the Stoic distinction in mind, having read a treatise on the passions that either focuses on the bad emotional states or, more likely, treats both states but has attracted his attention especially in the field of pleasure.

Stoic concepts of passion, however, have little impact on Philo's thought. Immediately after mentioning the treatise on the topic he speaks about a "war on the passions," which requires a "charioteer" to control them and deal with the "stiff-necked or restive horses." Philo moreover says, "The soul is saved whenever the high spirit accepts the reins of the rational part" (*All.* 3.137). The assumption of a divided soul, with a passionate or material side dragging down the loftier element, is distinctly Platonic, as we saw in chapter 10. The image of a charioteer steering horses is taken directly from the *Phaedrus*. The term "high spirit" and the transcendent orientation of Philo's discussion of the soul echo numerous passages in the Platonic oeuvre. Philo thus has referred to a Stoic treatise on the passions, seemingly using its ideas, but in reality translating them into the well-established notions of Platonic ethics. He continues to locate the passions in the material realm of the soul, implicitly rejecting the Stoic notion of the *hegemonikon*, or directive faculty, which is seen as one central function affecting in a unitary fashion all parts of human sensation, feeling, and judgment.[11] Having interpreted the Stoic treatise from a strongly Platonic perspective, Philo also subordinates the notion of the four passions to his hermeneutic needs. Discussing the creeping animals mentioned in Lev 11:42, he suggests that Moses refers allegorically to the lover of pleasure, who also moves on his belly. This reading is supported by reference to the treatise on the passions, which shows that the number four plays a special role in ethics and is adumbrated by the four legs of the creeping animals. Relying on "some treatise," Philo is able to inscribe himself into broader discourses and appeal to philosophical authority for his allegorical approach. Little, if anything, has transpired of the Stoic concept of the four passions.

Philo does not mention the most basic aspect of the Stoic theory of the passions, which any treatise, even a more popular one, would have conveyed. The Stoics uniquely interpreted passion as a result of wrong judgment rather than as an intrinsic part of the soul. Diogenes Laertius traces this idea to Zeno, who speaks of an "irrational and counter-natural movement of the soul," while Chrysippus explicitly identifies the passions with "[wrong] judgments." Diogenes also mentions the latter's treatise on the passions, where avarice, for example, is said to derive from the mistaken judgment that money is good. The fifth-century anthologist Stobaeus moreover says that the Stoics locate the passions in the *hegemonikon*, arguing that they constitute an "impulse which is excessive and disobedient to the dictates of reason or a movement of the soul, which is contrary to nature." Rational people confront the presence of something seemingly bad or pleasurable with proper judgment. Rather than automatically acting on the stimulation, they preserve intellectual independence and act only after a thorough examination of the real value involved. Irrational people, by contrast, accept appearances at face value and behave contrary to nature. Reflecting on these values in the first century BCE, Cicero locates the Stoic passions "in judgment" and explains that they are a movement of the soul contrary to reason. Philo's younger contemporary Seneca insists that anger, the archetypical passion, does not derive from an innate impulse, but rather from a conscious assent to external impressions. He recommends that his readers recognize passion as a "surrendering to these [the impressions] and following up such a chance prompting." "An impulse," Seneca concludes, "never exists without the mind's assent (*sine adsensu mentis*)."[12]

Given the prominence of the Stoic concept of the passions as wrong judgments, it is striking that Philo in the *Allegorical Commentary* never mentions it in its characteristic details. While once speaking about a "movement to irrational passion," using an expression that closely echoes Zeno's definition, Philo does not define the passions as wrong processes of reasoning. He is not concerned with the issue of assent, focusing instead on the welcome result of suppressing the passions, namely, "freedom of emotion," or *apatheia*. Philo praises the perfect man, "who completely cuts out the high spirit," and compares him to the "wrangling soul and the man of progress, who is unable to cut off passion, . . . schooling it instead by carefully judged speech." According to Philo, Moses exemplifies "the perfect wise man, who thoroughly cleanses and shakes off the passions." Aaron, on the other hand, "accepts the necessary and simple pleasure, but declines the excessive and superfluous kind in the category of dainties." The Stoic ideal of freedom from the emotions is thus identified with the highest form of ethics, suitable to the perfect righteous, such as Moses, while the middle path of restraining the passions, symbolized by Aaron, is also accepted as a positive path. It is questionable whether the ideal of *apatheia* applies to regular human beings, who will not be able to measure up to Moses. Philo possibly raised the Stoic ideal to an unattainable level. Aaron, by contrast, who symbolizes moderation in an Aristotelian sense, represents a realistic approach that readers can embrace. Philo further explains that Moses entirely cuts out the high spirit, appreciating only "complete freedom from emotion," and that "God dispenses to the wise man the best portion, namely, the ability to cut out the passions; you observe how the perfect man always pursues perfect freedom from the passions (τελείαν ἀπάθειαν)."[13] This freedom is interpreted in terms that echo Plato's ethics, namely, as a removal of the "warlike part" of the soul, which provides peace for the rest.

Philo uses the notion of *apatheia* in a highly idiosyncratic manner. Most conspicuously, he applies it in the context of a divided soul, assuming that the material part, or the *thumos*, is metaphorically cut out rather than subdued. The Platonic idea of a divided soul is thus once more affirmed. The Stoics, by contrast, argued that freedom from the emotions can be achieved because all passions result from rational assent and are therefore completely under human control. Cicero often mentions this ideal as a key aspect of

Stoic ethics, focusing on its positive outcome, namely, peace of mind and a life according to nature.[14] While the Stoics appealed to individuals to take personal responsibility for their emotions and liberate themselves from material constraints, Philo impresses on his readers God's strict demands. Whereas the Stoics warned of a departure from reason and nature, Philo identifies the "disobedient" part as an element rebelling against God. *Apatheia* becomes a goal in itself rather than a way to achieve personal tranquility. In Philo's interpretation the person conforming to God's will enjoys freedom from the emotions, and *apatheia* is connected to the "waiting for salvation by God." The discussion culminates in a prayer that the soul "having waited for God's salvation may attain happiness." Philo adds a biblical verse from the book of Exodus, where God is depicted as casting horse and rider into the sea. According to Philo's allegorical interpretation God throws away the four passions. Philo thus has translated Stoic ethics into Jewish theology with a Platonic flavor.[15]

Philo's subversive reading of Stoic notions of passion and *apatheia* implies significant criticism. He is obviously unable to accept the idea of a unified soul that operates on rational grounds, sometimes judging things wrongly and thus producing passion. He instead holds onto Platonic ethics and systematically assumes the division of the soul, with its characteristic tension between the different parts. Despite these reservations Philo uses Stoic terms, enriching his Platonic approach and Bible interpretation by popular images with strong emotional appeal. Philo's ambivalent encounter with Stoic notions of passion is highly significant in the first century CE and anticipates Plutarch, who devotes a special treatise to moral virtue in which he attacks the Stoic doctrine. Plutarch initially reports that, according to the Stoics, "passion in fact is knavish and intemperate reason, formed from an evil and perverse judgment." He shows that this notion is contrary to our experience as human beings and annuls Plato's division of the soul into material and rational parts, as expressed especially in the image of the charioteer steering restive horses. Plutarch moreover insists that it is impossible for reason to altogether eradicate passion and instead calls for moderation. The treatise *On Moral Virtue* is followed by two works addressing topics that Seneca made central in Stoic philosophy, namely, *On the Control of Anger* and *On Tranquility of Mind*. Mentioning Seneca once by name and relying on some "notes," perhaps from his readings, Plutarch is likely to have used his fluency in Latin to study the Roman philosopher's works and interpreted them in a Platonic mode. Anger, he asserts, can be cured by rigorously training the "irrational and obstinate element of the soul" and by strengthening reason to hold back the passions. Criticism of Stoic tenets is expressed indirectly, by questioning, for example, a saying of Democritus quoted by Seneca. On the whole Plutarch is attracted to the Stoic idea of interpreting adverse circumstances in a positive manner, which does not disturb one's tranquility of mind. He is keen to incorporate such insights into his ethics, without, however, accepting their theoretical underpinning in Stoicism or compromising his Platonic commitment.[16]

While Philo as a young man does not explicitly criticize the Stoic concept of passion, he is as reluctant as Plutarch to accept its theoretical assumptions. He uses some Stoic terms for educational purposes, keenly aware of their practical and rhetorical effectiveness. Like Plutarch, he also retains the notion of moderation, which he associates with Aaron. Upon arrival in Rome, however, Philo embraces the Stoic approach more wholeheartedly and develops an ethical theory oriented toward the immanent world. As we saw in chapter 8, he then speaks about passion as a "movement contrary to nature" and describes in thoroughly Stoic terms the intellectual process that goes into the experience of desire, namely, wrongly assuming something to be good that is actually indifferent. In his mature and more Roman period Philo more rarely refers to the division of the soul, avoiding such Platonic terminology even in the context of the creation of human beings in God's image, where he stresses that only humanity's good aspects can be ascribed to the deity. Regarding the passions, he thus moves from a superficially Stoic yet basically Platonic approach to a more Stoic position.[17]

A similarly complex picture emerges with regard to the Stoic concept of *oikeiosis*. Deriving from the verb *oikeiousthai*—to make familiar, to make one's own—this term is not easy to translate. Brad Inwood and Pierluigi Donini have suggested rendering it as "affiliation," namely, a natural affiliation that a person feels toward his or her own constitution and preservation. Both Cicero and Diogenes Laertius start their explanation of Stoic ethics with an exposition of this principle. Both explain *oikeiosis* by reference to the newborn baby and argue that the "primary impulse" of an animal, including a human being, is to "preserve itself, because nature from the beginning renders it dear to itself." Diogenes quotes Chrysippus's treatise *On Goals,* in which he says that "the first affiliation of each animal is to its own constitution and the awareness of it." Diogenes and Cicero moreover indicate that the Stoics developed their notion in response to the Epicureans, who insisted that humanity's primary impulse is to seek pleasure. Diogenes distinguishes the Stoic approach by its emphasis on nature, which initially directs people toward their self-preservation and then increasingly also toward rational behavior in society. Zeno is introduced as defining humans by an innate orientation to a "life in agreement with nature, namely, a life according to virtue, for nature leads us toward her." According to Diogenes, several other Stoics also held this view, while leaving it open how virtue is precisely connected to nature. We may indeed ask how the Stoics envisioned the move from self-preservation, with its focus on one's own constitution, to rational and moral behavior in society, which is based on concern for the welfare of others. This shift appears to be a natural development, as everybody matures and becomes increasingly aware of being part of a larger whole. Diogenes once more refers to Chrysippus, who says in his book *On Goals* that "our individual natures are part of the nature of the universe." Consideration for the whole requires a sublimation of one's own primary needs and orients toward society at large.[18]

Cicero's Stoic spokesman Cato dwells in detail on the development from infancy to maturity. He distinguishes between the "first appropriate act" concerned with self-preservation and a conscious choice of things in accordance with nature. Only the latter is identified with the morally good. In Cicero's forceful words, "It is at this final stage that the good properly so called first emerges and comes to be understood in its true nature." The Stoics considered human development to be so significant that they expected an adult to look down on "all the things for which he originally felt affection." The difference between the two stages even demands two separate ethical terms, *kathekonta*, describing the first appropriate acts in childhood, and *katorthomata*, referring to consciously chosen and rightly performed acts in adulthood.[19] According to Stoic ethics, primary objects are not sought for their own sake but are merely the object of an inborn impulse. Rightly performed acts, by contrast, involve choice and imply a self-aware following of nature. Despite these differences the two stages of life are assumed to be meaningfully connected. In a sense there is a persistent orientation throughout life toward one's natural constitution while that constitution matures to a more rational form and enables one to choose the good for its own sake.

Philo uses the term *oikeiosis* eleven times in the *Allegorical Commentary*, *kathekonta* sixteen times, and *katorthomata* seventeen times. He is obviously interested in engaging Stoic discourses and once explicitly refers to the distinction made "by philosophers" between righteous actions and first appropriate acts. Such philosophers were undoubtedly Stoics, as Philo echoes their definition of these terms. He associates the appropriate acts with the first stage of life, when a person automatically acts with a view to self-preservation, while righteous acts belong to the mature stage of life and are consciously chosen for their own sake. Reason, he moreover stresses with the Stoics, is the source of right acts.[20]

Philo, however, does not fully embrace these Stoic concepts. Unlike Chrysippus, he never presents the primary stage of human life as a positive starting point that reveals a person's true nature and provides a guideline for ethics. He equally ignores the classical Stoic position that "notions of justice and goodness come naturally." Philo instead offers a highly idiosyncratic interpretation of the terms *katorthomata* and *kathekonta*. In his scheme they are diagonally opposed approaches, signifying secularism and religious devotion, respectively. Primary acts amount to inferior human opinions, while righteous acts are "sacred and holy and purified notions." God, Philo explains, nourishes the human soul with sacred ideas.[21] Stoic terms, which emphasize the individual human mind, have been translated into religious concepts, which deprecate human autonomy and celebrate divine beneficence. Philo's implied criticism of the primary acts corresponds to his outspoken rejection of Protagoras's principle that "man is the measure of all things." As we saw in chapter 10, Philo opposes the idea of human beings as the ultimate reference point of ethics and instead stresses divine authority. In the same religious spirit he translates the Stoic *katorthomata* into acts of piety and contrasts them to human selfishness.

The notion of *oikeiosis* undergoes a similar transformation. Under Philo's pen it becomes something like fellowship or even union with God. Taking as his starting point the biblical command to "love God and listen and cleave to him" (Deut 30:20), he offers the following explanations: "His [Moses's] way of calling them [the Israelites] to give honor to him [God], who is the worthy object of strong longing and love, is most expressive, showing the constant and continuous and unbroken nature of the harmony and union that comes through making God our own (*oikeiosis*)." Philo does not explain what exactly he means by "making God our own." It is clear, however, from the context that his idea fundamentally differs from the Stoic notion of a person's affinity with his or her own nature as part of the universe. Philo speaks about yearning to see God and receive a revelation, which will liberate one from falsehood and unreliable knowledge.[22] While

God is ultimately beyond human reach, everybody is encouraged to approach and love him. The vision of God as the goal of life is in Philo's view the true meaning of *oikeiosis*.

Philo uses additional theological and Platonic notions to develop his highly idiosyncratic understanding of the term *oikeiosis*. He once equates it with fellowship with God, as opposed to indulgence in sense perception. The righteous person, who is symbolized by Leah, Jacob's hated wife, will distance himself or herself from everything created and material in order to make God his or her own. Philo translates the Stoic concept, which relies on the immanence of virtue, into a strongly transcendent theology in Platonic style. Instead of implementing one's own, natural constitution, one is asked to alienate oneself from the world and strive for the utterly Other. Human insights come from divine impregnation rather than an observation of nature. Not surprisingly, Philo identifies Abraham's "standing before the Lord" (Gen 18:22) as a case of *oikeiosis* and fellowship with God, which leads to an indwelling of the divine spirit. By contrast, fellowship with the flesh results in ignorance and alienation from God. Philo moreover speaks of a "special fellowship with God" in the context of accepting his absolute sovereignty. In Philo's view, "never-ending slavery" under God is better than freedom and highest sovereignty in the mundane world.[23]

Having identified a person's affiliation with his or her own constitution as a yearning for God, Philo reinterprets also the Stoic notion of individual choice. The Stoics were intensely concerned with the right choice of moral agents. Acknowledging human beings as autonomous moderators of their own actions, the Stoics provided criteria of identifying good and evil in order to orient oneself in life. They are famous in antiquity for arguing that virtue is the only condition for happiness and thus the only goal of life, while rejecting anything else as "indifferent." Diogenes Laertius notes that "they say that only the morally beautiful is good" (D.L. 7.101). Neither material assets, such as health, nor reputation in society counts toward virtue and happiness. Identifying the truly good is consequently of central importance.

The Stoics distinguished between things that are good and always desirable for their own sake, and evil things, which are always to be avoided, while also acknowledging certain things "that are neither." The neutral category includes assets that are considered valuable in society, such as life, health, and freedom. Diogenes mentions several Stoics who argue that the latter "are not good in themselves, but are indifferent, yet in the category of the things preferred." The distinction between morally good and indifferent things is based on an assessment of the use to which they can be put. Good things can be put to good use only and therefore are good under all circumstances, while indifferent things may be put to different uses and potentially even do harm. Insisting that indifferent things cannot contribute to happiness, the Stoics nevertheless conceded that some of them are "preferred" while others are "rejected." Choosing a preferred indifferent is not equal to living "a life in agreement with nature" but has some value in conducing to it. Wealth and health, for example, are not good in themselves and do not constitute happiness but "assist toward living a life in agreement with nature." Disease and poverty, on the other hand, even though indifferent, are to be rejected because they easily divert one from leading a natural life.[24]

The Stoics encouraged a high degree of self-awareness and self-examination. A person going through the above-mentioned process of evaluating the various options and choosing a particular action must be sophisticated and self-disciplined. To accept health as preferable yet ultimately indifferent demands a subtle balance between attachment and detachment. Such a position can be maintained only by constant self-observation and monitoring. The Stoics even added a further distinction that prompts additional awareness. They said that some of the preferred indifferent things are preferable for their own sake, while others for the sake of something else. Natural ability, for example, is in the first category, and wealth in the second.

Philo is clearly aware of these Stoic discussions. He speaks of the mind distinguishing between "the good and the indifferent and the bad." He moreover mentions that Jacob, who eliminates the passions, possesses self-mastery and "a sense of utter indifference to the things that are indifferent." Philo takes these categories for granted to the extent that he never explains them. He does not even discuss the most complicated of them, namely, indifferent things. At the same time, however, he also does not mention nature or processes of self-evaluation, so central to the Stoic argument. This arouses questions about Philo's intentions. While familiar with these Stoic notions, he evidently has no interest in their precise meanings and theoretical underpinnings. Once he even uses the term "indifferent" as a synonym to counterfeit good and evil, thus collapsing Stoic categories.[25] Why, then, does Philo use these Stoic terms at all? Would it not have been easier for him to present his own ideas in his own words? The attraction of Stoic terms appears to lie in their educational value and emotional appeal. Philo thus can apply familiar notions and inscribe his own theology into popular philosophical debates that he expects to be appealing to his readers.

Philo's ambivalent attitude toward Stoic notions of individual choice is significant in light of his later intellectual development. As we saw in Parts I and II, his arrival in Rome brought about a profound exposure to new discourses and especially to Roman Stoicism. In the case of ethics, too, Philo shows a more Stoic orientation in his later writings, as can be seen in his detailed discussion of individual choice in the treatise *Every Good Man Is Free*. He repeats here the distinction between good, bad, and indifferent things but now supplies some explanations missing in his earlier works. The reader learns that good things derive from virtue and are consciously chosen. The righteous person, Philo adds, always acts thus, while not even contemplating bad acts. Concerning indifferent things, "the mind as on a balance preserves equipoise, having been trained neither to yield to them, as if they have compelling power, nor to feel annoyed by them, as if they are worthy of escape" (*Prob.* 61). The righteous preserve their inner freedom, not being compelled to do anything contrary to virtue. In his later career Philo fully embraces the Stoic terms, which he briefly mentions in the *Allegorical Commentary* without yet exploring their full meaning. It is clear that in his youth Philo has just begun to recognize Stoic ethics, making some gestures toward it within an otherwise Platonic and decidedly theological system.

Cleanthes's Religious Concept of Nature Advocated

Cleanthes, the second head of the Stoic school, consistently stressed the religious dimension of Stoic doctrines. He interpreted nature as a universal and religious norm, insisting that "only the common nature should be followed" (D.L. 7.89). His successor Chrysippus instead highlighted the nature of the individual human being, an approach that Philo found unacceptable, as we have seen. Although Cleanthes's works are lost, a large fragment of his *Hymn to Zeus* is fortunately preserved. In this prayer he emerges as a devout monotheist who praises Zeus as the creator and ruler of the universe. He moreover speaks about Zeus's "universal law" and promises that those embracing it will live a good life, while those ignoring it will be unhappy. Cleanthes dislikes variety of choice and dismisses the various materialistic options that are often preferred to the one right path of ethics.[26]

Philo never mentions Cleanthes but may well have been familiar with his approach, which is highly congenial to his own. He could easily interpret Cleanthes's prayer to Zeus as an appeal to the Jewish creator God and associate his vision of a life according to the universal laws of nature in terms of Jewish law. We already saw in chapter 8 that some of the notions of Jewish law that Philo develops in his later writings are strikingly close to those of Cleanthes. When Philo in the *Allegorical Commentary* discusses the ideal of living in agreement with nature, he also expresses views similar to those of Cleanthes. Once he says that "the first men said the goal of happiness is to be able to live in accordance with nature."[27] These "first men" are undoubtedly Stoics, as they are uniquely known in antiquity for this definition of life's goal. Diogenes Laertius stresses that Zeno in his treatise *On the Nature of Man* was the first to define the goal as "living in agreement with nature, namely, living according to virtue." Cleanthes is also said to have embraced this ideal in his treatise *On Pleasure* (D.L. 7.87). Philo explains the Stoic ideal by reference to the God of Israel, thus not only consistently implementing his own approach, but also following in the footsteps of Cleanthes. He quotes two verses from the song of Moses in Exodus, treating God's supreme and eternal sovereignty as well as his sanctuary and inheritance. According to Philo's philosophical reading of these verses, humans are encouraged to accept God's inheritance by becoming rational and orderly. As he formulates it, "Follow the ordering of the All-perfect and by faithfully imitating his constant and undeviating path, embrace a self-restrained and unobstructed way of life" (*Plant.* 49). By indicating that the right path is "unobstructed," Philo alludes to divine rewards. The righteous, who follow God, are expected to lead a smooth life.[28]

On another occasion in the *Allegorical Commentary* Philo explicitly refers to the Stoic ideal: "This is the goal celebrated by the best philosophers, namely, to live consistently with nature" (*Migr.* 128). This time he identifies the Stoics not as the first, but as the best philosophers. In his view, Abraham, "traveling as the Lord has told him" (Gen 12:4), implements the known ideal: "This happens [i.e., living consistently with nature] whenever the mind enters in the path of virtue and walks in the track of right reason and follows God, carefully remembering his instructions and always and everywhere confirming them by deeds and words" (*Migr.* 128). Philo assumes here the typically Stoic identification of nature with virtue, which is ultimately rooted in God. While his notion of "following God" echoes the Platonic ideal of *homoiosis,* or becoming like God, it also resonates with

Cleanthes's approach. Highlighting that the law serves as a bridge between the divine and the human realms, Philo in fact offers the same religious approach to ethics as the Stoic philosopher.

Philo thus wholeheartedly embraces the more theological interpretation of Stoic philosophy, such as the one formulated by Cleanthes in his *Hymn to Zeus*, retaining both its vocabulary and its spirit. Regarding nature he adopts a Stoic position already at the beginning of his career when he is still wholly immersed in Alexandrian Platonism and has not yet encountered Roman Stoicism during his embassy to Gaius. In his later work Philo further develops this direction and grounds the details of Jewish law in nature as a universal norm. In the *Allegorical Commentary*, he is not yet interested in this avenue but rather focuses on the individual's personal relationship with God. The righteous, he explains, "have God as a guide of their ascent," in contrast to Cain, the self-lover. Even though the righteous are unlikely to ever see God, their orientation toward him already grants happiness. On the other hand, those "who have set before them many goals of life" lack the spirit of God. Human beings in Philo's view should not seek to define their own goals of life. There is no need to consider a variety of options, as only one preestablished and divinely revealed end exists. Philo criticizes those who credit themselves with their moral progress because they fail to acknowledge God as its author. He also stresses that God vouchsafes a person's course of life and prevents him or her from slipping into transgression. For this purpose the biblical image of Miriam, who is said to have "spied out from a distance" to her baby brother Moses, is interpreted in a new light. In Philo's reading she anticipated the "goal of life, namely, that it may meet us with good auspices, sent down from high heaven by the Consummator." Philo identifies the biblical ideal of "living before God" with the "goal of happiness," which he defines as "the mind being worthy of the survey and careful watch of the most excellent of all beings."[29] The goal of life turns out to be a personal voyage with God, who surveys and protects the righteous following his instructions.

Conclusion

In the *Allegorical Commentary* Philo expresses a highly complex attitude toward Stoicism that involves an explicit rejection of the materialism of this school, creative subversion of Stoics' ethical theories, and a whole-hearted appreciation of its more religious tenets. While expecting his readers to know some Stoic terms, such as *oikeiosis,* he does not assume that they will care much about their precise meanings. Instead of discussing such terms in detail, Philo refers to them in a general manner, using them in idiosyncratic and often Platonic ways. Given his ambivalence toward basic Stoic tenets, it is remarkable that Philo realized the attraction and emotional appeal of Stoicism as a young man in the predominantly Platonic environment of Alexandria.

Philo's trajectory from deep ambivalence to adoption of central Stoic tenets popular in Rome has significant implications for our understanding of broader intellectual processes in the first century CE. Philo ushers in a turn to Stoicism among Eastern Platonists and anticipates Plutarch in his selection of emotionally appealing tenets. Both thinkers vehemently rejected the interpretation of Stoicism associated with Chrysippus. Both opposed the theoretical assumptions of Stoic ethics, while using emotionally and religiously appealing tenets. As much as Philo in the *Allegorical Commentary* dismisses the idea of a conflagration of the world as a "myth," Plutarch asks impatiently, "Why then again in every book of physics, by Zeus, and of morals, too, does he [Chrysippus] write ad nauseam that from the moment of birth we have an affinity with ourselves, our members, and our offspring?"[30] This emphasis on practical ethics, which eclipses the controversial theories of the school's middle phase, is also characteristic of contemporary Rome.

Epilogue: Philo at the Crossroads of Judaism, Hellenism, and Christianity

Looking back at Philo's life and achievements, we realize how rich, complex, and versatile his personality was. He grew up in the greatest cultural center of the Greek East, Alexandria, then went as a diplomat to Rome and acculturated with impressive speed to the intellectual and cultural climate there. Philo addressed all the burning issues of the first century CE, engaging in a wealth of literary genres and negotiating Jewish, Greek, and Roman traditions. No other author of that period accomplished as diverse tasks as writing systematic commentary, historiography, biography, and philosophical treatises. No other author is known to have undergone such a significant intellectual development as Philo, who moved from biblical exegesis and introverted, transcendent, sometimes mystical positions to historiography and more worldly, Stoic views, sometimes using irony. This movement is visible on all planes: Philo's assumption of political responsibilities, his choice of more accessible literary genres, his becoming present as an author in his texts, his growing emphasis on the creation and God's presence in the world, his turn to conceptualizing Judaism in distinctly Roman terms, his increasing focus on people's involvement in society, his growing appreciation of women as mothers and wives, and finally his turn to more immanent ethics.

These dramatic developments were prompted by the political situation and especially Philo's visit to Rome, the center of the empire with its particular intellectual life. His audience changed, and he no longer addressed fellow Jews in Alexandria but enlightened intellectuals in Rome. He moved from the periphery to the center, from internally to outwardly oriented and apologetic discussions, refashioning himself on the way and reinterpreting

242

his tradition as well as the Greco-Roman heritage. A significant expression of these changes is the fact that Philo began to position himself and the Jewish tradition in Rome, drawing sharp distinctions to "the Greeks." This move from East to West was prepared by Philo's personality and intellectual profile. Already during his early years in Alexandria he took a keen interest in the Stoic school, realizing its emotional appeal and using its language despite rather strong Platonist reservations. Upon arriving in Rome he easily could build on his knowledge and expand his familiarity with Stoicism, applying it in many details to his discussion of Judaism. Moreover, as a relatively young man Philo already turned from the highly specialized circles of biblical scholars to wider Jewish audiences. Setting up some kind of a school in Alexandria, he prepared himself for his later role as an author addressing even broader, non-Jewish audiences. At the same time we see a prominent continuity in his thought and personality, namely, his religious devotion. Whether he is interpreting Plato's texts or Stoic ideas or commenting on current political events, Philo consistently stresses God's role.

Philo's biography illuminates crucial developments in the first centuries of the Common Era. The effect of Rome on his personality and thought illuminates similar phenomena in Greek culture and early Christianity. In both of these subcultures we see a clear division between authors who were oriented toward Rome and those who turned their backs on Roman fashions. On the Greek side the Second Sophists distinguished themselves as authors deeply involved with Rome, often looking with an ironic smile on the compromises this entailed. They regularly adopted views and literary genres Philo had chosen beforehand during his Roman period. Neoplatonists, by contrast, continued the inward and transcendent tendencies of the young Philo, composing commentaries on Plato's masterpieces and ignoring the creation as well as Rome's role in it. On the Christian side, Paul, Luke, and Justin Martyr most forcefully embraced Roman discourses and expressed views Philo discussed in his late works. They succeeded in shaping Christianity and establishing what would become orthodoxy. The Gnostics, on the other hand, continued the overall line of Philo's early work, writing commentaries on the Scriptures and aspiring toward complete transcendence. Their works were marginalized to the extent that most of them have survived only fragmentarily in the polemics against them. Origen occupies a special place in this scenario. Working mainly in the Greek East, initially in Alexandria and then in Caesarea, he posthumously aroused sharp criticism from more orthodox quarters but finally achieved canonical status within the church. He adopted Philo's style of commentary from the Alexandrian period, while at the same time highlighting the creation, as Philo did in his later years. Origen neglected Philo's historical and more general writings, which were favored by other Christian authors with a prominent Roman orientation.

Philo's biography moreover helps us understand the development of Judaism from the Second Temple period to the rabbinic movement. He illustrates a form of Judaism that positioned itself within the general culture, embracing new historical and cultural developments in the world rather than opposing them. The rabbis who assumed leadership after the destruction of the Second Temple and the demise of numerous apocalyptic movements also worked largely in cooperation with Rome and engaged both Roman and Greek discourses (Rabbi Akiva and some other opponents notwithstanding). Philo's work was probably known to Rabbi Hoshaya, colleague of Origen in Caesarea, who opens the Midrash Genesis Rabbah with an interpretation that relies on Philo's image of God as an architect. Hoshaya opposes the Christian appropriation of the creation, suggesting that Philo's image should rather be interpreted in a distinctly Jewish context, namely, as an indication that God looked into the Torah when creating the world.[1] Philo's specific interpretations as well as his overall paradigm of combining Jewish with Greek learning thus remained meaningful also in rabbinic Judaism.

Appendix 1
Philo's Dates and Works

ca. 20 BCE, Philo is born in Alexandria.

ca. 10–35 CE, Philo works in Alexandria in the context of the Jewish community.

THE ALLEGORICAL COMMENTARY

Allegorical Interpretation (*All.*) 1–3—*Legum allegoriae*

On the Cherubim (*Cher.*)—*De cherubim*

On the Sacrifices of Cain and Abel (*Sacr.*)—*De sacrificiis Abelis et Caini*

The Worse Attacks the Better (*Det.*)—*Quod deterius potiori insidari soleat*

On the Posterity and Exile of Cain (*Post.*)—*De posteritate Caini*

On the Giants (*Gig.*)—*De gigantibus*

On the Unchangeableness of God (*Deus*)—*Quod Deus sit immutabilis*

On Agriculture (*Agr.*)—*De agricultura*

On Planting (*Plant.*)—*De plantatione*

On Drunkenness (*Ebr.*)—*De ebrietate*

On Sobriety (*Sobr.*)—*De sobrietate*

On the Confusion of Tongues (*Conf.*)—*De confusione linguarum*

On the Migration of Abraham (*Migr.*)—*De migratione Abrahami*

Who Is the Heir? (*Her.*)—*Quis rerum divinarum heres sit*

On the Preliminary Studies (*Congr.*)—*De congressueru eruditionis gratia*

On Flight and Finding (*Fug.*)—*De fuga et inventione*

On the Change of Names (*Mut.*)—*De mutatione nominum*

On Dreams (*Somn.*)[1] 1–2—*De somniis*

QUESTIONS AND ANSWERS

Questions and Answers on Genesis (*QG*) 1–4—*Quaestiones et solutiones in Genesin*

Questions and Answers on Exodus (*QE*) 1–2—*Quaestiones et solutiones in Exodum*

38 CE (summer), Pogrom in Alexandria.

38 CE (autumn), Philo travels to Rome as the head of the Jewish embassy to Gaius.

38–41 CE, Philo is active in Rome as an ambassador and author, probably leading also the negotiations with Claudius after Gaius's assassination in early
41 CE. In early 39 Gaius receives Philo's embassy.

40 CE (summer), Gaius announces his plan to set up a statue in the Jerusalem
Temple.

ca. 40–49 CE, Philo writes a new series of works, addressing a wider Greco-
Roman audience.

THE HISTORICAL WRITINGS
On the Embassy to Gaius (Legat.)—*Legatio ad Gaium*
Against Flaccus (Flacc.)—*In Flaccum*

THE PHILOSOPHICAL WRITINGS
On the Rationality of Animals (Alex.)—*De animalibus* (ed. Terian)
An Apology on Behalf of the Jews (Hypoth.)—*Hypothetica*
Every Good Man Is Free (Prob.)—*Quod omnis probus liber sit*
On Providence (Prov.) 1–2—*De providentia*
On the Eternity of the World (Aet.)—*De aeternitate mundi*
On the Contemplative Life (Cont.)—*De vita contemplativa*

THE EXPOSITION OF THE LAW
On the Creation (Opif.)—*De opificio mundi*
On the Life of Abraham (Abr.)—*De Abrahamo*
On the Life of Joseph (Jos.)—*De Iosepho*
On the Life of Moses (Mos.) 1–2—*De vita Mosis*
On the Decalogue (Dec.)—*De decalogo*
On the Special Laws (Spec.) 1–4—*De specialibus legibus*
On the Virtues (Virt.)—*De virtutibus*
On Rewards and Punishments (Praem.)—*De praemiis et poenis*

ca. 49 CE, Philo dies.

Appendix 2

Did Philo Write an *Allegorical Commentary* on Genesis Chapter 1?

We have seen in chapters 5 and 9 that Philo's *Allegorical Commentary* starts with the interpretation of Gen 2:1 and that his treatise *On the Creation of the World* does not belong to this series, but rather introduces the *Exposition of the Law*. The question thus arises whether he originally wrote an allegorical commentary on Genesis chapter 1. If he did, his commentary must have been lost at a very early stage, because there is no evidence of it in the manuscript tradition or Eusebius's list of Philo's works (HE 2.18.1–8). Indeed, the text of the *Allegorical Commentary*, which was edited in Caesarea and provides the source of all the extant manuscripts of Philo's works, does not seem to have contained the interpretation of Genesis chapter 1.[1] Modern scholars are divided over this question and debate where the *Allegorical Commentary* originally started. Leopold Cohn, Isaak Heinemann, and Jenny Morris cautiously argued on grounds of general plausibility that Philo probably did not compose an allegorical commentary on the first chapter of Genesis, while Thomas Tobin and Gregory Sterling affirmed its existence, mainly on the basis of Philo's own references. Let's examine the arguments and add some of our own.

Following Cohn, Heinemann argued that it is "highly unlikely" that Philo wrote an allegorical commentary on Genesis chapter 1, because he would not have wanted to question the literal sense of the creation account, which served important theological purposes.[2] According to Heinemann, Philo has such a strong allegorical orientation in this commentary series that he preferred to leave the first chapter of Genesis uncommented in order to avoid the danger of allegorizing the creation out of existence. Heinemann's perspective is supported by the insights from chapters 10–11 of this book, where we saw that Philo at the beginning of his career was highly ambivalent about God's contact with the material world and warned his readers not to deduce God's character from the creation. At the same time, however, he never went as far as the "Gnostics" and questioned the validity of the biblical creation account. Philo's ambivalence could indeed have resulted in a decision to refrain from treating the creation within the *Allegorical Commentary*. This conclusion, however, is not mandatory. We can equally speculate that Philo would have preferred to write a commentary and address all the theological issues involved in the creation. If he did, his allegorical commentary on the first chapter of Genesis must have reflected the highly transcendental orientation of his youth.

Morris argued that "it is perfectly plausible that he did not [comment on Genesis 1] . . . ; the *Allegorical Commentary* deals principally with the history of mankind, which only begins in Gen. 2.1 The abrupt beginning . . . does not need to surprise, since this method of starting directly with the text to be expounded is found in the later books of Philo's commentaries and appears also in Rabbinic Midrash."[3] These arguments against the assumption of an allegorical commentary on Genesis chapter 1 are less convincing, because Philo's extant commentary indicates that he interpreted the creation of heaven and earth as allegories of the soul (*All.* 1.1.). It thus would have been easy for him to turn the whole first chapter into a story about humankind. Moreover, Philo himself usually introduces his various treatises of the *Allegorical Commentary* with brief reference to what he previously established. The fact that he slowed down as he progressed is less surprising than assuming a complete lack of an introduction to the very first treatise of the series. Finally, it is not clear how the evidence of rabbinic literature can help us understand Philo, because rabbinic works are not treatises written by individual writers, but rather compilations of interpretations offered by generations of rabbis. Such cooperative efforts are less likely to have a proper introduction than the work of a highly individualized author opening a series of commentaries on Genesis.

Tobin and Sterling, on the other hand, stressed that it would have been highly unusual for Philo to start his commentary series without a proper introduction and identified phrases in his extant texts that may point to a lost treatise.[4] In my view their most compelling example of a reference to lost material is *All.* 1.1, where Philo quotes Gen 2:1 and says "while he [Moses] has previously presented the creation of mind and sense perception, he now fully explains the consummation of both." To be sure, this clause cannot be a direct reference to Philo's own commentary, because he would otherwise have used first-person language, as he did on numerous other occasions when recalling his own interpretations. Tobin and Sterling nevertheless suggest that Philo's formulation, while overtly referring to Moses, implies an allegorical interpretation that can only be Philo's. Tobin relies in this context on the assumption that the *Exposition* was written before the *Allegorical Commentary* and seeks to show that *All.* 1.1 refers to ideas not expressed in Philo's treatise *On the Creation*. However, we have seen throughout this book that the sequence of these two series is the reverse and Philo started his writing career with the *Allegorical Commentary*. The above quoted reference to what Moses "previously" said in an allegedly allegorical mode is thus of even greater significance than Tobin assumes, as there was no prior treatise to which Philo could have referred. Philo, in other words, can hardly have started his very first book with such a reference to previous insights. The assumption of lost commentary material thus becomes likely.

Moreover, Tobin's and especially Sterling's stylistic argument that Philo can hardly have started his exegetical corpus without a proper introduction is supported by Origen, who followed Philo in many respects, as we saw in chapter 9, and introduced his commentaries on Scripture. Ronald Heine recently investigated Origen's extant introductions to his exegetical works, highlighting that he revised his introductions as he expanded his commentaries.[5] This procedure throws light on Philo, who regularly introduces his various treatises, helping the reader to appreciate the specific book within the larger context of his oeuvre. Philo is thus likely to have provided some explanation at the outset of the *Allegorical Commentary*, identifying the purpose of his exegetical project, his methods, and perhaps alternative strategies.

However, if Philo indeed wrote an allegorical commentary on Genesis chapter 1, more than one treatise must have been lost. This is so because he covers an average of fifteen verses in each of his treatises of the *Allegorical Commentary*. He usually starts commenting on the verse following the one interpreted in the previous treatise. Therefore, the assumption of scholars that one treatise, which covered all of Genesis chapter 1, got lost is highly unlikely, as Philo either would have skipped large amounts of biblical material or would have written a treatise twice as long as the others. Given the physical limitations of scrolls in antiquity as well as Philo's thorough and systematic approach, both avenues are unlikely.

What are the chances of two allegorical treatises on the first chapter of Genesis falling into oblivion before Eusebius's time? Origen can shed light on this question as well. While his detailed commentary on the book of Genesis is no longer extant, the fragments of this commentary as well as other related works indicate that he made special efforts to reappropriate this text from the hands of "Gnostic" exegetes, who were keen to disconnect the superior God from the material creation.[6] Origen emphatically argues for a providential and beneficent demiurge, who created the best possible world ex nihilo. For this purpose he explicitly relies on Philo and the image of God as the architect, which he probably drew from Philo's later treatise *On the Creation*, in which he celebrates God as the beneficent and providential creator.[7] If indeed Philo previously wrote two allegorical treatises on the first chapter of Genesis, they would have reflected his reservations about God as the demiurge and thus would have played into the hands of the "Gnostics." Origen must have given absolute priority to the treatise from Philo's later years, which reflects a Roman-Stoic orientation and was perfectly suited to counter heterodox approaches. Origen's predilection is likely to have resulted in a reading curriculum in his school at Caesarea that gave exclusive attention to Philo's *On the Creation*, marginalizing the treatises of the *Allegorical Commentary* on the first chapter of Genesis. It is even possible that Origen began the tradition of reading *On the Creation* before the now extant *Allegorical Commentary*, which starts with the interpretation of Gen 2:1. This arrangement would have caused the original commentary on Genesis chapter 1 to quickly fall into oblivion.

Notes

All translations are my own unless otherwise stated.

Chapter 1. An Intellectual Biography of Philo?

1. Jos., *J.A.* 18.259–60; see also Sterling, "Man of Highest Repute"; Runia, "Philo in Early Christian Literature"; Runia, "Philo of Alexandria"; Runia, "Philo in Byzantium"; Sterling, "'School of Sacred Laws'"; Inowlocki, "Relectures apologétiques"; Niehoff, "Eusebius"; regarding Philo's lost treatises, see Sterling, "Prolific in Expression"; Runia, "Confronting the Augean Stables."

2. See Niehoff, *Philo of Alexandria;* Weiman-Kelman and Mazor, *HaSimha SheBalev;* Kaiser, *Philo;* Oertelt, *Herrscherideal;* Seland, *Reading Philo;* Geljon and Runia, *On Cultivation;* Calabi, *Filone;* Inowlocki and Decharneux, *Philon d'Alexandrie;* Lisi, *Études Platoniciennes;* Kamesar, *Cambridge Companion;* Hadas-Lebel, *Philo;* see also Runia, "Why Philo"; Sterling, "Philo Has Not Been Used."

3. For previous efforts to appreciate Philo's different series of works, see Massebieau, *Classement* (based on historical references in the various treatises); Cohn, "Einleitung und Chronologie" (based on a literary analysis, which offers a relative chronology); Goodenough, *Introduction* (with emphasis on the difference between the historical writings and the *Exposition,* which address a Roman audience, and the *Allegorical Commentary,* which speaks to Alexandrian Jews); Birnbaum, *Place of Judaism* (stressing the general audiences of the *Exposition* and the Jewish audience of the *Allegorical Commentary*); Royse, "Works of Philo."

4. See also Goodman, "Philo as Philosopher," 41–42.

5. *Congr.* 74–80, 6–7; regarding Philo's knowledge of Hebrew, for which Rajak, *Translation and Survival,* has recently argued again on the basis of his Hebrew etymologies, consider the following: Philo never solves a textual problem in the Bible by recourse to the Hebrew, and he often offers "Hebrew" etymologies for the Greek rather than the Hebrew form of biblical names, apparently unaware of the Hebrew text (see, e.g., *Migr.* 165). Philo's exclusive access to the Bible in Greek has been

confirmed by Sterling, "Philo"; Sterling, "Interpreter of Moses"; Katz, *Philo's Bible;* for further details, see chap. 9.

6. *Prov.* 2.64; regarding Josephus's autobiography, see esp. Mason, "Josephus' Autobiography"; for details on the diversity of Alexandria, see Fraser, *Ptolemaic Alexandria;* Clauss, *Alexandria;* Georges, Albrecht, and Feldmeier, *Alexandria.*

7. *Legat.* 172, 181–83, 190, 206, 349–67; see also Royse, "Works of Philo," 53–55. Regarding the dates of the embassy, see Harker, *Loyalty and Dissidence,* 10–24, who convincingly argues that Philo's reference to his sea journey to Rome during the autumn, when it was already dangerous to travel (*Legat.* 190), indicates his precipitation immediately following the violence in Alexandria and provides strong evidence for the early dating of 38 CE; for different views, see Smallwood, *Philonis Alexandrini Legatio,* 24–27. Another historical treatise originally existed but is no longer extant, namely the "palinode" or reversal of the *Embassy,* which Philo announces in *Legat.* 373. Eusebius, moreover, speaks about "what happened to the Jews in the time of Gaius" (*H.E.* 2.5.1) in a way that prompted conjectures about lost books on Sejanus and Pilate (Morris, "Jewish Philosopher," 859–64). Eusebius's words, however, are ambiguous, referring more likely to a list of subject matters than to separate books.

8. *Flacc.* 41–85, 146–91; see also van der Horst, *Flaccus,* 34–37.

9. See Terian, *De Animalibus,* 28–34; Terian, "Critical Introduction," 289–94; Royse, "Works of Philo," 55–58, 61–62; Morris, "Jewish Philosopher," 864–65; Sterling, "Logic of Apologetics."

10. *Alex.* 54, 7; Jos., *J.A.* 1.8, *C.Ap.* 2.296; on the role of Josephus's patron, see Hollander, *Josephus,* 279–93; see also Salles, *Lire à Rome,* 93–122; Fantham, *Roman Literary Culture,* 2–11.

11. Cohn, "Einleitung und Chronologie," 432–34; Morris, "Jewish Philosopher," 840–44; Royse, "Works of Philo," 60–62; Bloch, "Alexandria"; Sterling, "Prolific in Expression," 64–75.

12. Philo's commentary on Gen 18:1–2 is not printed in the standard editions of his work but is preserved in an Armenian fragment published by Siegert, "Philonian Fragment."

13. For different views see Terian, "Priority of the *Quaestiones*"; Sterling, "Philo's *Quaestiones.*"

14. I continue to use the term "Gnostic" even though it has been questioned by Williams, *Rethinking "Gnosticism";* King, *What Is Gnosticism?;* and Markschies, *Valentinus,* because it allows me to refer to certain Christian authors who were not canonized by the Romanized church.

15. Bowersock, *Greek Sophists;* Bowie, "Greeks and Their Past"; Bowie, "Hellenes and Hellenism"; Gleason, *Making Men;* Swain, *Hellenism and Empire;* Jones, *Culture and Society in Lucian,* 6–23, 78–89; Goldhill, *Who Needs Greek?,* 60–107; Goldhill, *Being Greek;* Whitmarsh, *Greek Literature;* Anderson, *Pepaideumenos.*

16. See Sterling, *Historiography;* Hägg, *Art of Biography,* 148–86; Harrill, *Paul the Apostle;* D'Angelo, "Roman Imperial Family"; Cancik, "Mittelmeer."

17. See Watson, *Paul;* Harrill, "Paul and Empire"; Lampe, *Die stadtrömischen Christen;* Thorsteinsson, *Roman Christianity;* Becker, "Paulus"; Becker, "Die Tränen."
18. See Nasrallah, "Rhetoric of Conversion"; Nasrallah, *Christian Responses.*
19. See Perkins, *Roman Imperial Identities;* Moss, *Myth of Persecution;* Morgan, *Roman Faith;* Markschies, *Antikes Chistentum;* Nasrallah, "Mapping the World"; for different views, see Clark, *Christianity.*
20. Goodman, "Josephus as Roman Citizen"; Goodman, "Roman Identity"; Mason, "Josephus as a Roman Historian"; Mason, "Flavius Josephus"; Mason, *A History;* Hollander, *Josephus;* see also Barclay, *Flavius Josephus,* 362–69; Haaland, "Jewish Laws"; S. Cohen, "Josephus;" Sievers and Lembi, *Josephus and Jewish History;* for different views, see Rajak, *Josephus.*
21. On the history of such dichotomies, see Niehoff, "Alexandrian Judaism"; for criticism of this approach, see S. Cohen, *From the Maccabees,* 37–45; Gruen, *Heritage and Hellenism;* Gruen, *Diaspora.*
22. Plut., *Cat. M.* 22, *Dem.* 1.2, *Mor.* 612d–e; see also Stadter, *Plutarch and His Roman Readers,* 70–81, 130–48; Stadter, "Plutarch and Rome"; De Rosalia, "Il latino."
23. Jos., *C.Ap.* 1.288–302, 2.2–7; while Apion certainly served as the head of the Egyptian embassy, Chaeremon's membership is highly likely; see Tcherikover and Fuks, *Corpus Papyrorum Judaicarum* (hereafter *CPJ*), 2.39, 44; van der Horst, *Chaeremon,* IX.
24. See Grimal, *Sénèque,* 66–78; Scarpat, *Il pensiero religioso,* 70–76; cf. Griffin, *Seneca,* 42–43; Griffin, "Imago," who attributes little importance to Seneca's stay in Egypt.
25. See D.L. 3.61–62; on the Alexandrian Museum and the library, see Fraser, *Ptolemaic Alexandria,* 1.305–35; Nesselrath, "Das Museion"; on Alexandrian Platonism, see Schironi, "Plato at Alexandria"; Tarrant, "Date of the Anon."; Sedley, "Three Platonist Interpretations"; Bonazzi, "Eudorus"; Dörrie, "Platoniker Eudorus"; Boyancé, "Études Philoniennes"; Theiler, "Philo"; Tobin, *Timaios of Locri;* Baltes, *Timaios Lokros,* 22–24; for different views, see Dillon, *Middle Platonists,* 114–35; and Dillon, "Philo and Hellenistic Platonism." On Homeric scholarship in Alexandria, see Fraser, *Ptolematic Alexandria,* 1.447–79; Schmidt, "Homer of the Scholia"; Montanari, "L'Erudizione"; Montanari, "Zenodotus"; Nünlist, *Ancient Critic;* Dickey, *Ancient Greek Scholarship.*
26. See Wright, *The Letter of Aristeas;* Walter, *Der Toraausleger;* Holladay, *Fragments,* 1.51–92; Collins, *Between Athens and Jerusalem;* Barclay, *Jews;* Niehoff, *Jewish Exegesis,* 19–74.
27. On Philo's conception of Roman synagogues and his networks in Roman circles, see chap. 2; see also Rutgers, *Jews.*
28. For an updated discussion of the term "apology," see Collins, "Apologetic Literature."
29. Long, "Roman Philosophy"; see also Cic., *Off.* 1.1–10, 1.152, 2.1–8, 3.7–15; for Cicero's reflections on his role as statesman and philosopher in Rome, see esp. *Fin.* 1.1–12; Lévy, *Cicéron.*

30. Plut.,*Ant.* 80; Arius, *apud* Stobaeus, *Eccl.* 2.6.1; Cic., *Fin.* 1.13; Sen., *Ep.* 108.3–4, 13–15; Long, *Stoic Studies*, 107–33; Inwood, *Reading Seneca*, 7–22; Morford, *Roman Philosophers*, 131–66; Laurand, *Stoïcisme.*

31. Sen., *Brev. Vit.* 13.1–9; *Ira* 1.9.1–4, 1.17.1–7, 3.3.1–6, 3.14–17; *Ep.* 108.24–25; Plut., *Cato Mai.* 22.4–5; Lucian, *Salaried Posts* 17. On Roman Stoicism, see esp. Inwood, *Reading Seneca;* Reydams-Schils, *Roman Stoics;* on Roman constructions of Others, see esp. Isaac, *Invention of Racism;* Petrocheilos, *Roman Attitudes.*

32. Cic., *Ac.* 2.11–12; Jos., *C.Ap.* 2.141–44, 2.28–30, 2.80–88; Bowersock, "Foreign Elites"; Barnes, "Antiochus of Ascalon," 70–76; Barclay, *Flavius Josephus*, 167–68, 240–42.

33. For the chronology of Seneca's works, see Griffin, *Seneca*, 396–97; on Philo's family, see chap. 2.

34. Note that Eusebius imagined Philo reading his treatise on the embassy "in the reign of Claudius before the whole Senate of Rome" (*E.H.* 2.18.8).

35. Plut., *Ira* 13, 2, 6, 10 (= *Mor.* 461f, 453d, 456a, 458c); Philostr., *Apol.* 1.3, 4.35, 4.46, 5.19, 7.16.

36. See Whitmarsh, *Greek Literature*, 1–38, 75–76; Bowie, "Greeks and Their Past"; Swain, *Hellenism and Empire*, 289–329. Kovelman, *Between Alexandria and Jerusalem;* Boyarin, *Socrates;* and Furstenberg, "Agon with Moses," have pointed to interesting similarities between the humor of the rabbis and the irony of the Second Sophistic.

37. Philostr., *Apol.* 2.4; for background on Philostratus, see Bowie, "Philostratus"; Elsner, "Protean Corpus"; for analysis of Lucian's references to the Greek heritage, see Branham, *Unruly Eloquence*, 65–124 (with emphasis on Plato); Mheallaigh, *Reading Fiction with Lucian*, 1–38 (with emphasis on parallels in postmodern literature).

38. Wahlgren, "Sprachwandel"; Kim, "Literary Heritage"; see also Swain, *Hellenism and Empire*, 17–42.

39. Winter, *Philo*, 59–108.

40. On Philostratus's canonization of the Second Sophists, see Eshleman, *Social World*, 125–48.

41. See Philo, *Prob.* 13; Plut., *De Cap. Ex inim.* 8 (*Mor.* 90C); see also Schmitz, "Plutarch and the Second Sophistic"; Ziegler, *Plutarchos*, 19–26; Russell, *Plutarch*, 2–17, 63–83; Bonazzi, "Theoria and Praxis"; Niehoff, "Philo and Plutarch."

42. *Contra* Wolfson, *Philo*, esp. 107–15, who argues for Philo's broad influence on Western thought.

Chapter 2. Philo's Self-Fashioning in the Historical Writings

1. Jos., *J.W.* 1.1–8, 3.354; *Life* 1–19, 336–67; S. Cohen, *Josephus*, 101–60; Mason, *Josephus Flavius*, 11–21; Hadas-Lebel, *Flavius Josephus*, 43–58; Hollander, *Josephus*, 46–67, 252–93.

2. *Flacc.* 131; the term "accuser" (κατήγορος), describing Lampo, relies on the same root as "to place a charge" (κατηγορέω), which Philo uses to describe his own literary activity.

3. Greenblatt, *Renaissance Self-Fashioning.*

4. Luc., *Ver. Hist.* 1.4; see also Bompaire, *Lucien écrivain,* 587–613.

5. *Legat.* 150; Suet., *Claud.* 19.3; Sen., *Tranq.* 9.4–5; on the Alexandrian library and Museum, see chap. 1.

6. *Legat.* 250–51; *Flacc.* 26, 110; see also Sen., *Ep.* 77.1–5, describing the excitement of people waiting in the harbor of Puteoli for the arrival of the Alexandrian ships. On traveling in the Roman Empire, see Adkins and Adkins, *Handbook,* 167–200; André and Baslez, *Voyager,* 224–29; Casson, *Travel,* 149–62; Harland, *Travel and Religion;* Niehoff, *Journeys;* Meeks, *First Urban Christians,* 16–23; Hezser, *Jewish Travel,* 161–70; Levinson, "Language of Stones." On the use of the name Dicaercheia as part of the archaizing style of the Second Sophistic, see Bowie, "Greeks and Their Past," 33. Josephus uses both the Greek and the Latin name of the city (*Life* 16), while Philostratus refers only to Dicaearchea (*Apol.* 7.16.1).

7. *Alex.* 3, 54; Terian, *De Animalibus,* 25–28; see also Burr, *Tiberius;* Schimanowski, "Die jüdische Integration"; Jördens, "Judentum und Karriere"; for details on the philosophical dispute, see chap. 3.

8. *J.A.* 18.259, 19.276–77, 18.147–67, 20.100; on Marcus's marriage and business career, see Fuks, "Marcus"; on the importance of Greek names among the Second Sophistic, see Bowie, "Greeks and Their Past," 31–33.

9. Regarding Agrippa's connections, see Jos., *J.A.* 18.143, 18.167–68, 18.188, 18.202–3, 18.236–37, 19.236–45; regarding his political achievements, see *J.A.* 18.298–304, 19.279–85; Josephus received historical materials after writing the *War* (*Life* 366) and following this assigned Agrippa a greater role in Claudius's accession to the throne than he had done before.

10. See esp. Kushnir-Stein, "On the Visit of Agrippa"; Barrett, *Caligula,* 80.

11. *Flacc.* 103 (tr. van der Horst); see also van der Horst, *Philo's Flaccus,* 190, who shows that the visit mentioned here must be the one in 38 CE, because Gaius was not yet emperor during Agrippa's previous visit to Alexandria in 36 CE, when he came in the company of Tiberius (*Flacc.* 28).

12. Smallwood, *Philonis Alexandrini Legatio,* 252–53.

13. *Legat.* 172, 370; Jos., *J.A.* 18.257–59, mentions three ambassadors and identifies the grammarian Apion as their head.

14. On the dates, see Smallwood, *Philonis Alexandrini Legatio,* 256–61; Harker, *Loyalty and Dissidence,* 11–12.

15. Sen., *Ira* 2.1.1–4.1, *Ep.* 113; see also Sorabji, *Emotion,* 17–75; Griffin, *Seneca on Society,* 125–48.

16. Sen., *Ira* 2.1.1–5; *Ep.* 78.2–4, 78.13; Philo, *Legat.* 180; see also Edwards, "Self-Scrutiny"; Stowers, *Letter Writing,* 36–40, 91–101; Griffin, *Seneca,* 7, 43–59, 396.

17. *Legat.* 200–203; see also Smallwood, *Philonis Alexandrini Legatio,* 260–65.

18. Ez., *Exagoge* fragm. 15 (ed. Holladay, *Fragments*); see also Lanfranchi, *L'exagoge,* 250–51; Whitmarsh, *Beyond,* 218–20.

19. Philo mentions Aeschylus in *Prob.* 143 and used scenes from *The Persians* to interpret the biblical battle at the Red Sea (for details, see Niehoff, *Philo on Jewish Identity,* 52–58).

20. *Legat.* 186–88; Aesch., *Pers.* 247–55.

21. *Pers.* 290–336; on Aeschylus's sympathetic portrayal of the queen mother, see Gruen, *Rethinking,* 16–18.

22. On the term "Alexandrian," see *CPJ* 1.41, n. 102; Smallwood, *Philonis Alexandrini Legatio,* 27–31, 255; Collins, *Between Athens and Jerusalem,* 113–22.

23. *Legat.* 367; see also Bilde, "Gaius's Attempt," 72–74; Gruen, "Caligula."

24. *Legat.* 353–63; Jos., *C.Ap.* 2.66–67, 2.137.

25. For Greek strategies of constructing identity in a Roman context, see Whitmarsh, "Thinking Local"; Goldhill, "What Is Local Identity?"

26. *Legat.* 359, 45–46, 79. Suetonius and Dio also mention Gaius's performing in the theater (Suet., *Cal.* 11, 54.1–2; Dio 59.5.4–5); see also Calabi, "Theatrical Language," 111–13; Edwards, "Beware of Imitations."

27. Jos., *Life* 16; see also Mason, *Josephus Flavius,* 24–27; Niehoff, "Parodies of Educational Journeys."

28. Luc., *Nigr.* 15–20; see also Goldhill, *Who Needs Greek?,* 60–107; Whitmarsh, *Greek Literature,* 265–79.

29. Sen., *Ep.* 67.5–10, 13.14–5; Luke 22:43–44, 23:46 (cf. Mark 14:32–42, 15:34); Just., *2 Apol.* 12.1, 3.1, 9.1, 14.1–15.5; see also Ehrman, *New Testament,* 109–11; Harrill, *Paul the Apostle,* 1–12, 97–101; Moss, *Myth,* 58–61, 83–125; Perkins, *Suffering Self;* King, "Willing to Die"; Coleman, "Fatal Charades"; Edwards, *Death;* Nasrallah, "Rhetoric of Conversion."

30. Claud., *Letter to the Alexandrians, CPJ* no. 153, 2.39–40; Jos., *J.A.* 19.227–46; Suet., *Claud.* 11.1–12.1; Dio 60.1.1–4, 60.4.2, 60.5.1–5; see also Levick, *Claudius,* 32–39, 184–85; for more details, see chap. 3.

31. *Cons. Pol.* 13.1, 17.3; see also Griffin, *Seneca,* 208–10; for more details, see chap. 3.

32. Claud., *Letter to the Alexandrians, CPJ* no. 153, 2.41; see also Levick, *Government,* 134–37.

33. *J.A.* 19.281–85; Feldman, ad loc.; *CPJ* 2.44, n. 16; *CPJ* no. 156 a, c, d; see also Pucci Ben Zeev, *Jewish Rights,* 304–13; Levick, *Claudius,* 183–85; for different views, see *CPJ* 1.70–71, n. 45; Smallwood, *Philonis Alexandrini Legatio,* 10–11. Josephus may have received his version of the edict from Agrippa's son. The edict on papyrus responds to the petition of the Egyptian embassy and closes with Claudius's special thanks to Claudius Balbillus, a member of the Egyptian embassy. Claudius's change of opinion also may have been prompted by the trial of Agrippa in the summer of 41 CE in Rome, when Isidorus, an infamous Alexandrian gymnasiarch, leveled charges against him on behalf of the Alex-

andrians. While the nature of these accusations cannot be reconstructed, we can still make out that a certain Balbillus is on the Alexandrian side. According to the editors of the papyrus he is probably the same man as the one Claudius thanks at the end of his *Letter to the Alexandrians.*

34. Zeitlin, "Did Agrippa Write?"; Schwartz, *Agrippa,* 200–202; Doering, *Ancient Jewish Letters,* 265–66.

35. *Legat.* 199–203, 207, 248–53, 259–60.

36. On the tensions between Agrippa and Tiberius, see Jos., *J.A.* 18.186–204; for Philo's position, see *Legat.* 141–42 (on which see also Niehoff, *Philo on Jewish Identity,* 119–28); for Claudius's position, see Suet., *Claud.* 11.3; Dio 60.6.8.

37. *Legat.* 268, 333–35; cf. Jos., *J.A.* 18.301–9; on the letters between Seneca and Paul, see Nasrallah, "'Out of Love for Paul.'"

38. *mBik.* 3.4, *mSot.* 7.8.

Chapter 3. Power, Exile, and Religion in the Roman Empire

1. "Ioudaeos impulsore Chresto assidue tumultuantis Roma expulit" (Suet., *Claud.* 25.4); see also Stern, *Greek and Latin Authors,* 2.113–17; Hengel, *Acts,* 107–8; Watson, *Paul,* 167–71; Leon, *Jews of Ancient Rome,* 23–27. Only some Jews can have been expelled, because Josephus, Dio Cassius, and Tacitus otherwise would have mentioned this expulsion.

2. See also Eden, *Apocolocyntosis,* 4–12; on the circumstances of Seneca's exile, see Griffin, *Seneca,* 60–62; Griffin, "Philosophy, Politics."

3. Sen., *Cons. Pol.* 12.3–13.4; Jos., *J.A.* 19.227–46; Suet., *Claud.* 11.1–12; Dio, 60.1.1–4, 60.5.1–5; see also Levick, *Claudius,* 88–90; Momigliano, *Claudius,* 22–29; Scramuzza, *Emperor Claudius,* 60–63; Jacobson, "Attitude of Roman Emperors."

4. *Cons. Helv.* 4.1–2, 11.7, 8.6; D.L. 6.49; see also Meinel, *Seneca über seine Verbannung;* Doblhofer, *Exil,* 248–51; Claassen, *Displaced Persons,* 92–96.

5. *Cons. Helv.* 9.5–6, 10.4.

6. *Clem.* 2.2.2; see also Griffin, *Seneca,* 67–128, 133–44; Braund, *Seneca,* 2–4, 16–17.

7. Sen., *Apoc.* 1.1, 2.1, 6.2, 7.3, 10.1–4, 11.2, 12.2, 13.4–5 (ed. P. T. Eden); see also Nussbaum, "Stoic Laughter."

8. Suet., *Claud.* 41.1–42.2; see also Levick, *Claudius,* 17–20; Claudius's literary ambitions are ridiculed by Seneca in *Apoc.* 5.4.

9. *Legat.* 41, 60, 63, 66, 73.

10. Suet., *Gaius* 23.3; see also Wallace-Hadrill, *Suetonius,* 50–72, 110–12.

11. Dio 59.8.4, 59.10.6; see also Millar, *Study of Cassius,* 78–102, 174–92; Swain, *Hellenism,* 402–8.

12. Baldwin, *Suetonius,* 281; and Millar, *Study of Cassius,* 78, suggest that they may have used Seneca's satire on Claudius.

13. Dio 60.13.4; Suet., *Claud.* 37.1–2.

14. Dio 60.14.1, 60.16.7, 60.16.4

15. Dio 58.28.4, 59.10.6.
16. Goodenough, *Politics*, 104–5; Goodenough, *Introduction*, 75–76.
17. *Legat.* 43–51, 74.
18. See also Smallwood, *Philonis Alexandrini Legatio*, 181–82; Barraclough, "Philo's Politics," 449–52; Griffin, *Seneca*, 182–94, 202–21; Swain, *Hellenism*, 157–61, 312–23, 402–4; Millar, *Study of Cassius*, 83–102.
19. βίον καρπουμένους φιλόσοφον (*Flacc.* 184).
20. *Flacc.* 109, 158–59, 163–64; Suet., *Gaius* 28.
21. *Flacc.* 116, 128–46, 170; see also Alexandre, "Monarchie divine."
22. ξένους καὶ ἐπήλυδας (*Flacc.* 54).
23. Isa 5:12–25; Ezek 20:23–24; Jer 23:1–4; Amos 5:26–27.
24. ἀπόλιδες καὶ ἀνέστιοι (*Flacc.* 123); *Flacc.* 121–22.
25. *Legat.* 155; see also Smallwood, *Philonis Alexandrini Legatio*, 234–39; Levick, *Augustus*.
26. Jub 1:12–18; T.Mos. 3:1–4:9; Syb. Or. 3:265–380; P.Hab. 4:6–12, 6:1–15, 11:2–15; see also Bloch, "Leaving Home"; Najman, *Losing the Temple*.
27. *Migr.* 1–25, *Agr.* 65, *Cher.* 120, *Conf.* 77–82, *Her.* 267; see also Runia, "Flight and Exile"; on Platonic motifs in the *Allegorical Commentary*, see chap. 10.
28. Plut., *Mor.* 604B–C, 600A–601F; see also Froidefond, "Plutarque"; Ziegler, *Plutarchos*, 4–60; Jones, *Plutarch and Rome*; Swain, *Hellenism*, 135–86; Pelling, *Plutarch and History*, 1–10; van Hoof, *Plutarch's Practical Ethics*, 116–50; Feldmeier, "Der Mensch."
29. Acts 18:2 (τὸ διατεταχέναι Κλαύδιον χωρίζεσθαι πάντας τοὺς Ἰουδαίους ἀπὸ τῆς Ῥώμης), Luke 19:41–44, 20:20–24; Mason and Robinson, *Early Christian Reader*, 494; see also Pervo, *Acts*, 446–47; Sanders, *Jews in Luke-Acts*, 24–50; Ehrman, *New Testament*, 115–32.
30. Acts 16:20–37; see also Levick, *Government*, 65–66; Harrill, *Paul the Apostle*, 97–101; Wills, "Depiction of the Jews."
31. Claud., *Letter to the Alexandrians*, CPJ 2.39–40; Suet., *Claud.* chap. 22, 25.5; see also Hurley, *Suetonius*, 176–78.
32. Varro, fragm. in Aug., *Civ. Dei* 6.2–6, 4.22–24, 4.27, 4.31–32; see also Rüpke, *Religion*, 59–66, 121–28; van Nuffelen, "Varro's"; Cancik, "Historisierung"; Boys-Stones, *Post-Hellenistic Philosophy*.
33. *Legat.* 86, 143–51.
34. Cic., *N.D.* 1.41; Cornutus, *Gr. Theol.*; Varro, fragm. in Aug., *Civ. Dei* 6.5; see also Brisson, *How Philosophers*, 41–49; Boys-Stones, *Post-Hellenistic Philosophy*; Nesselrath et al., *Cornutus*.
35. Hom., *Il.* 5.388, 5.842, 5.889; Plut., *Amat.* 757B; Heracl., *Hom. Prob.* 31.1; see also Purves, "Ares."
36. Aug., *RG* 4.21–22; Ovid, *Fasti* 5.545ff; see also "Ares," in Pauly et al., *Paulys Realencyclopädie*, 1.666–67; Rives, *Religion*, 142; Liebeschuetz, *Continuity*, 86–87; Lipka, *Roman Gods*, 177.

37. *Legat.* 156, 161; *Flacc.* 46; see also S. Cohen, *Beginnings.*
38. Luke 20:45–21:4; cf. Mark 1:22, 2:66, 3:22, 8:31, 10:33, 11:18, 14:43, 15:1.
39. *Legat.* 155–56; Leon, *Jews of Ancient Rome,* 142.
40. Plut., *Numa* 3.6, 7.2–3, 11.1–13.7, 15.6, 28.4; see also Levick, *Augustus,* 150–54; van Nuffelen, "Varro's," 182–85; van Nuffelen, *Rethinking the Gods,* 200–216.
41. Jos., *C.Ap.* 2.10–11, 2.80, 2.89–96.
42. *Legat.* 245, 316–20; see also Mitchell, "Further Thoughts."
43. See also Meeks, *First Urban Christians,* 9–50; Harrill, *Paul the Apostle,* 83–84; Cancik, "Mittelmeer."
44. *Flacc.* 116; see also Leonhardt, *Jewish Worship,* 45–47.

Chapter 4. Roman Philosophy and the Jews

1. Cic., *Ac.* 2.11–12; see also Barnes, "Antiochus," 70–76.
2. *Cont.* 58 (γέλως), 63; Jos., *C.Ap.* 2.223 (see also Barclay, *Flavius Josephus,* 300); Luc., *Symp.* 39–42 (see also König, *Saints and Symposiasts,* 248–51); for details on Philo's predominantly Platonic orientation in the *Allegorical Commentary,* see chap. 10.
3. *Prob.* 81, 125; *Alex.* 4, 7, 13, 22, 27–34, 75; *Cont.* 1–21; *Prov.* 2.1.
4. *Alex.* 9; see also Pl., *Theaet.* 143b–d, where a slave similarly reads aloud a philosophical treatise.
5. *Alex.* 11–13, 17, 19–20, 22, 42 (trans. Terian and comments ad loc.).
6. *Alex.* 24–25, 27, 16, 47–49, 71 (trans. Terian).
7. *Alex.* 75, 77–80, 82–85, 100 (trans. Terian).
8. *Deus* 45–46; *Det.* 82.
9. Cic., *N.D.* 2.140–47, 3.70–79; see also Cicero in his own voice in *Leg.* 1.25–27.
10. Cic., *Off.* 1.11–14, 1.50, 1.105–7; Sen., *Ep.* 121.
11. Just., *Dial.* 4.2–5; Plut., "That Animals Are Rational" and "On the Cleverness of Animals"; Philostr., *Apol.* 2.14.1–2.16; Porph., "On Abstinence"; Plot., *En.* 4.7.14; see also Sorabji, *Animal Minds;* for different views, see Berthelot, "Philo and the Kindness towards Animals."
12. For source-critical analyses of Philo's treatise, see Terian, "Critical Introduction," 278–79; Wendland, *Philos Schrift;* on Stoic notions of providence, see D. Frede, "Theodicy."
13. *Prov.* 2.1; Cic., *N.D.* 3.79; Sen., *Prov.* 1.1.
14. *Prov.* 2.2, 2.10 (παρὰ Θεῷ τῶν εἰρημένων πρότερον οὐδὲν καθ' ἑαυτὸ τῆς ἀγαθοῦ μοίρας ἠξίωται), 2.16, 2.18–28; Marc. Aur., *Med.* 2.15.
15. *Prov.* 2.35–47; Philo's comparison of God to a gymnasiarch is rooted in a long Stoic tradition that can be traced to Chrysippus (Plut., *Mor.* 1050E).
16. Cic., *N.D.* 2.133–59, 2.164.
17. Sen., *Prov.* 2.1 ("nihil accidere bono viro mali potest"), 2.2–4, 3.1 ("non sint quae videntur mala"), 4.1–3, 4.11–12, 5.1, 6.1–2; *N.Q.* bk. 3, 6; see also Prost, *Théories hellénistiques,* 227–56; Inwood, *Reading Seneca,* 157–200.

18. *Prov.* 1.6–14, 1.20–21, 1.26, 1.31; on the Philonic authorship of *On the Eternity of the World,* which has sometimes been doubted, see Leisegang, "Philons Schrift"; Runia, "Philo's *De Aeternitate Mundi*"; Niehoff, "Philo's Contribution," 53–55.

19. Arist., *Caelo* 280a2 (on the importance of Aristotle for Philo's interpretation, see Bechtle, "La problématique," 378–81); Eus., *P.E.* 7.12.14 (ἵνα δὲ μὴ σοφίζεσθαι με ταῦτα νομίσῃς). In this context Eusebius manipulates Gen 19:24 by amalgamating two separate references to God, implying that "the Lord [who emerged] from the Lord" refers to Christ. The literal meaning of the *Timaeus* is in my view the original sense—see also Vlastos, "Creation"; Hackforth, "Plato's Cosmogony"; Sedley, *Creationism,* 98–107; *contra* Cornford, *Plato's Cosmology,* 24–27; Taylor, *Commentary,* 59–63.

20. Taur., *apud* Philop., *Aet.* 6.21 (ed. Rabe, 186, εἰ γέγονεν εἰ καὶ ἀγενές ἐστιν); Dillon, "Tampering," 59; Arnaldez, *De Aeternitate Mundi,* 58–62.

21. See also Tarrant, *Thrasyllan Platonism,* 178–213, 108–47.

22. "in Timaeo mundum aedificavit Platonis deus" (*Disp. Tusc.* 1.63); "si semper fuerunt, ut Aristoteli placet" (ibid., 1.70); see also Dörrie, "Erneuerung"; Lévy, "Cicero and the *Timaeus*"; Sedley, "Cicero and the *Timaeus.*"

23. *Aet.* 15–16, referring to Arist., *Caelo* 280a. Plutarch mentions the Alexandrian philosopher Eudorus as a metaphorical interpreter of the *Timaeus,* who assumed with the earlier Platonists that the speech about the creation of the world is a mere figure (*An. Procr.* 1013A–B). The date of the anonymous treatise *On the Nature of the World and the Soul,* which is a creative reading of the *Timaeus,* is uncertain but probably belongs to the middle or later first century CE (see also Baltes, *Timaios Lokros,* 21–24; Tobin, *Timaios of Locri,* 3–7).

24. *Aet.* 8, 40–51, 90–99; Plut., *Mor.* 1052D.

25. On the Stoics mentioned in *Aet.* 76–77, see also Karshon, "Philo," ad loc.

26. *Prob.* 6–10, 15, 53–54, 58 (see also Furstenberg, "Every Good Man," ad loc.).

27. *Prob.* 22–26 (the key terms are ἑκουσίως, γενναίως, ὑπομένων).

28. *Prob.* 60; Epict., *Disc.* 4.1.68, 4.1.81; see also Bobzien, *Determinism and Freedom.* 330–57, with emphasis on Epictetus's innovation in comparison to earlier Stoics.

29. Cic., *Par. Stoic.* 5.34 ("Quid enim est libertas? Potestas vivendi ut velis, . . . ipsius voluntas atque iudicium"), *Off.* 1.66–69, 1.81, 1.90, 2.23–24; see also Graver, *Stoicism and Emotion,* 15–83.

30. Sen., *Prov.* 2.10; *Ira* 3.14.1–15.3; *Ep.* 26.10; *Vit. Beat.* 15.5–6 ("deum sequere!"); see also Inwood, *Reading Seneca,* 302–21; Edwards, "Free Yourself!"

31. Philo, *Prob.* 19; Epict., *Disc.* 4.1.1, 4.1.29–32, 4.1.47–50, 4.1.68–75, 4.1.89–106, 4.1.131 (ἄγου δὲ μ᾽ ὦ Ζεῦ); see also Forschner, "Theorie der Freiheit."

32. *Prob.* 118–20, 93–96.

33. *Prob.* 119, 95–96; Plut., *Cat. Mai.* 12.5, 22.1–23.1; Strabo, *Geogr.* 3.4.19; see also Fears, "Stoic View"; Bowersock, *Augustus,* 108–10; Isaac, *Invention of Racism,* 381–405; Petrocheilos, *Roman Attitudes.*

34. *Prob.* 57; Gen 27:40.

35. Philo, *Prob.* 75; Pliny, *N.H.* 5.73.
36. *Hypoth.* 11.3–17; Eus., *P.E.* 8.5.11 (ὑπὲρ Ἰουδαίων ὡς πρὸς κατηγόρους); for the historical context of the *Hypothetica,* see also Sterling, "Logic of Apologetics"; Cover, "Colonial Narratives"; Chaer., fragm. 6–7, 10–11 (ed. and trans. van der Horst, *Chaeremon*).
37. *Cont.* 43, 64; on Philo's Therapeutae, see also Taylor, *Jewish Women Philosophers.*
38. See *Cont.* 2, 34–35, 73–74; Sen., *Ira* 3.14–17; *Ep.* 83.9–10, 83.23–25, 108.15–16; on the Roman ideal of frugality at the symposium, see König, *Saints and Symposiasts,* 26–29; see also Goldhill, *End of Dialogue.*
39. *Cont.* 31, 75.
40. *Cont.* 32–33, 68; Plut., *Quest. Conv.* 1.1.1–5 (*Mor.* 614a, d); Max., *Memorable Sayings* 1.2, 1.8–9, 10 (trans. Shackleton Bailey); see also Juv., *Sat.* 14.189; Quint., *Inst.* 1.2.7–8; see also Stein-Hölkeskamp, *Das römische Gastmahl;* D'Arms, "Roman Convivium." Cicero still recommends in a traditional Greek manner that table talk should be "easy and not in the least dogmatic, it should have the spice of wit" and even warns the host "not to debar others from participating in it, as if he were entering on a private monologue" (*Off.* 1.134; see also Egelhaaf-Gaiser, "Täglich").
41. Jos., *C.Ap.* 1.1–27, 2.292, 2.190–92; *J.A.* 1.1–10; *Avot* 1.3–5, 3.16–17 (see also Goldin, *Studies in Midrash,* 57–76; Niehoff, "Not Study Is the Main Objective"); *mPes.* 10.1–9 (cf. Stein, "Influence of Symposia").
42. Just., I *Apol.* 1.1, 68.3, 14.5, 59.1–6, 26.6–8, 20.1–5, 67.3–5, 43.1–8, 58.1; II *Apol.* 2.15–20, 7.1–9 ; see also Goodenough, *Theology,* 206–11; Lieu, *Marcion,* 15–25; Niehoff, "Justin's *Timaeus.*"

Chapter 5. Creation Theology and Monotheism

1. The order of Philo's works in the English translation is based on the critical edition by Cohn and Wendland, who, however, amended the order in their German translation.
2. *Opif.* 171, 3; *Abr.* 2–6; *Spec.* 2.40, 2.223; see also Sterling, "Prolific in Expression," 64–75.
3. *Opif.* 3, 170–2; *Mos.* 2.46–58; *Praem.* 1. Philo's emphasis on monotheism must be appreciated in light of the fact that the Pentateuch does not explicitly formulate a monotheistic creed (Stroumsa, *Abrahamic Religions;* Smith, *God in Translation;* Knohl, *Biblical Beliefs;* Liebes, *Ars Poetica,* 76–93; Schäfer, *Zwei Götter;* Markschies, "Price of Monotheism"); for different approaches, see Assmann, "Monotheism and Polytheism"; Hirsch-Luipold, "Der eine Gott."
4. Septuagint (hereafter LXX) Exod 3:14 (ἐγώ εἰμι ὁ ὤν).
5. *All.* 1.43–44; *Somn.* 1.67; Pl., *Rep.* 2.379–82; see also Guthrie, *History of Greek Philosophy,* 4.487–93; Männlein-Robert, "Umrisse des Göttlichen"; on Philo's Platonism in the *Allegorical Commentary,* see chaps. 10–11.

6. *Fug.* 63 (quoting Pl., *Theaet.* 176B); *All.* 3.97–99; for Philo's references to God as beneficent creator, see e.g. *Cher.* 127; *Deus* 108; *Plant.* 2–10; *Her.* 246–48; *All.* 2.1–13, 1.31–38; *Fug.* 68–72; *Mut.* 30–33; *Ebr.* 199; *Somn.* 1.75; see also Runia, *On the Creation*, 144.

7. Arius *apud* Stob., *Ecl.* 51, 6a (ed. Pomeroy 36–39); Sen., *Ep.* 65.19, 95.51–53, 45.9, 90.34; *Ira* 1.5–6; Cic., *N.D.* 2.81–90, *Leg.* 1.15–19; see also Horsley, "Law of Nature"; Bréhier, *Idées philosophiques*, 23–32; Schwabe, "Introduction," XXV–XXVIII; Calabi, *Filone*, 51–66; Vogt, *Law, Reason;* Inwood, *Reading Seneca*, 224–48; Schofield, "Stoic Ethics," 233–56; on Philo's earlier notion of nature, see chap. 11.

8. D.L. 7.134; Cic., *Ac.* 1.6; see also Reydams-Schils, *Demiurge and Providence;* Kaiser, *Studien*, 33–44.

9. *Opif.* 12, 16, 21; Pl., *Tim.* 29E–30B; Runia, *Philo of Alexandria and the "Timaeus"* and *On the Creation.*

10. D.L. 7.134–37; Plut., *Comm. not.* 1075B; *Stoic. rep.* 1052A; see also M. Frede, "Case for Pagan Monotheism," 70–75; Stroumsa, *Abrahamic Religions*, 9–20; Most, "Philosophy and Religion," 311–16.

11. Cic., *N.D.* 2.64; D.L. 7.142; Philo, *Aet.* 76; Cic., *N.D.* 2.3, 2.13–15, 3.8–10, 3.16, 3.25; Plut., *Comm. not.* 1074E–75F.

12. *Opif.* 16, 20, 24; Pl., *Tim.* 27A–29E.

13. Philo, *Opif.* 69–77 (on which see also Runia, *On the Creation*, 222–35); D.L. 7.138–39; Marc. Aur., *Med.* 2.11; many Stoic philosophers composed books *On Divine Providence* (see Cic., *N.D.* 1.3, 2.58, 2.154–63, 3.26); see also D. Frede, "Theodicy," 95–108.

14. *Opif.* 16, 20; see also Cornford, *Plato's Cosmology*, 34–39, who stresses the polytheistic nature of Plato's approach; on Philo's Logos theology, see chap. 11.

15. See esp. Wolfson, *Philo*, 1.204–17, 1.240–48; Radice, "Philo's Theology," 131–35; for more nuanced views, see Collins, "Natural Theology."

16. Sen., *Prov.* 1.1–2, 6.1; *Ep.* 65.16–20, 117.19, 41.5, 65.2.

17. *Abr.* 60, 69; see also Liebes, *Ars Poetica*, 76–93.

18. *All.* 1.51; *Migr.* 150, 170, 183–85; *Congr.* 133–34.

19. LXX Exod 20:2–3; Philo, *Dec.* 51–61 (note especially the expression τὸν δ' ἀνωτάτω καὶ πρεσβύτατον, τὸν γεννητήν, τὸν ἄρχοντα τῆς μεγαλοπόλεως), 154–55 (see also Calabi, *Filone: De Decalogo*, 69–75, 124–25).

20. *Spec.* 1.14, 1.18, 1.20, 1.32–35.

21. Jub 2:1–16; cf. VanderKam, "Made to Order," who argues for a more substantial interpretation of the creation in Jubilees; Sir 43:1–33 (see esp. Sir 43:11 and 43:28, which has survived in the original Hebrew ראה קשת וברך עושיה, and והוא גדול מכל מעשיו; ed. of the Academy of the Hebrew Language and the Shrine of the Book); Sir 1:1–10, 24:1–17; for general background, see Lance and Gribetz, *Jewish and Christian Cosmogony.*

22. Aristob., fragm. 4 *apud* Eusebius, *P.E.* 13.12.3 = Holladay, *Fragments*, 3.162; Wis 6–9; on the dates and philosophical orientation of the Wisdom of Solomon,

see Winston, *Wisdom of Solomon,* 20–25; Niebuhr, "Die Sapientia Salomonis"; Niehoff, "Sapientia."

23. *C.Ap.* 2.190–214; for details on Roman family values and their effect on Philo and Josephus, see chap. 8.

24. Cf. Feldman, *Josephus's Interpretation,* 229, who argues that Josephus twists the Stoic argument by stressing the changes to which land and sea were subject. Josephus, however, seems to have in mind the regular changes of nature, such as low tide and high tide.

25. Just., 1 *Apol.* 13.1, 20.3, 58.1; see also Lieu, *Marcion,* 332–66; Stroumsa, *Another Seed;* Niehoff, "Justin's *Timaeus.*"

26. Orig., *C.C.* 1.27, 3.44, 3.55, 3.69, 3.75, 4.73, 6.1, 6.7–8, 6.15, 7.42–45, 7.61, 4.14–18, 4.79 (ed. Marcovich), 4.61, 6.49; regarding Philo's influence on Origen, see Daniélou, *Origène,* 179–90; Runia, *Philo in Early Christian Literature,* 157–73; van den Hoek, "Philo and Origen"; on Celsus and his sources, see Lona, *Die "Wahre Lehre,"* 27–50; Niehoff, "Jewish Critique"; Baumgarten, "Rule of the Martian."

27. Orig., *P.A.,* preface par. 4; *C.C.* 4.79, 7.42–44; see also Crouzel, *Origen,* 181–85.

28. Baltes, *Weltentstehung* 1.163; Porph., in Procl., *Com. Plat. Tim.* 1.382; Jul., *C. Gal.* 49A–B, 96C; Sal., *About the Gods and the World* chap. 7 (trans. Murray, *Five Stages,* 197–98); see also Meredith, "Porphyry and Julian"; Murray, *Five Stages,* 171.

Chapter 6. Character and History in the *Lives* of the Biblical Forefathers

1. *Legat.* 12, 14–17, 22–25, 42, 162–65; *Flacc.* 2–11, 78.

2. A fragment of Apion's writings on Moses is preserved by Jos., *C.Ap.* 2.10–11; on the role of ancestral examples in Rome, see Arendt, *Between Past and Future,* 91–143.

3. *Virt.* 52, *Praem.* 53, *Abr.* 2–4, *Jos.* 1; for modern reconstructions of the place of the *Life of Moses* in relation to the *Exposition,* see Cohn, "Einleitung und Chronologie," 434; Goodenough, "Philo's Exposition"; Morris, "Jewish Philosopher," 854–55; Feldman, *Philo's Portrayal,* 19–27; Pearce, "King Moses," 42–43; Royse, "Works of Philo," 50–51; Bloch, "Alexandria in Pharaonic Egypt," 75–77; Wilson, *Philo,* 3–4; Sterling, "Prolific in Expression," 64–75.

4. *Mos.* 1.2–4, 1.212, 1.74; on Apion and Chaeremon, see Barclay, *Flavius Josephus,* 170–71, 153; van der Horst, *Chaeremon.*

5. *Mos.* 1.2 (note the Greek expression ὅστις ἦν ἐπ' ἀληθείας), 1.12, 1.62, 1.146, 1.211; *Legat.* 349; Jos., *C.Ap.* 2.10; throughout the *Life* Philo blurs the difference between Scriptural and oral sources, referring to the former as something "they say" (see e.g. *Mos.* 1.9, 1.165).

6. ἀναγκαῖον ἄρξασθαι (*Mos.* 1.5).

7. Mason, *Josephus Flavius*, 116–19; see also Hägg, *Art of Biography*, 187–238; Swain, "Biography"; for an overview of earlier forms of biography, which apparently did not influence Philo, if he was at all familiar with them, see Momigliano, *Development of Greek Biography;* Hägg, *Art of Biography*, 10–147.

8. Cic., *Brut.* 36.137, 3.14, 10.42, 11.44, 15.57–61, 16.63–17.66, 37.139–38.145; Cic., *De or.* 2.59; see also Woodman, *Rhetoric*, 70–159.

9. Nepos, *Preface, Milt.* 1, *Them.* 1–2, *Cim.* 1, *Dion* 1, *Tim.* 1, *Them.* 1, *Alcib.* 1; see also Geiger, *Cornelius Nepos*, 66, 93–8.

10. For interpretations of Plutarch's achievement as unprecedented, see esp. Ziegler, *Plutarchos*, 272–73; Wilamowitz-Moellendorff, "Plutarch"; Sorabji, *Self*, 172–80; Uxkull-Gyllenband, *Plutarch*, 110–12, argued for Stoic influences on Plutarch's *Lives; contra* Leo, *Griechisch-römische Biographie*, who suggests a peripatetic background for the Hellenistic biography.

11. See esp. Sen., *Ep.* 22–24; *Ot.* 1.4–3.5; *Constant.* 1.1–2.3, 7.1; *Ep.* 64; Sen., *Brev. Vit.* 13.1–9, 14.1–5; Epict., *Disc.* 1.4; see also Reydams-Schils, "Authority and Agency."

12. Cic., *Off.* 1.107–12; see also Prost, "Psychologie de Panétius;" note that Cicero speaks of Panaetius's treatise *On Moral Duties* as "unquestionably the most thorough discussion of moral duties that we have and I have followed him in the main—but with slight modifications" (*Off.* 3.7). Philo mentions Panaetius in *Aet.* 76. On Stoic notions of the self, see Sorabji, *Self*, 115–36, 157–71; Reydams-Schils, *Roman Stoics*, 20–25; cf. Gill, "Personhood and Personality"; Gill, *Structured Self*, who stresses the typical over the individual.

13. Sen., *Brev. Vit.* 15.4–5, 15.2, 17.6; *Ep.* 24, 64; *Tranq.* 1.12.

14. *Mos.* 1.9, 1.15–24, 1.59; cf. Exod 2:6; Cic., *Off.* 1.122–23.

15. εἰ καὶ μικρὸν ὅσα γε τῷ δοκεῖν, ἀλλ᾽ οὐκ ἀπὸ φρονήματος μικροῦ (*Mos.* 1.51).

16. *Flacc.* 78, *Legat.* 41–43; Sen., *Ep.* 77.10.

17. *Mos.* 1.12, 18–21; Ez., *Exag.* 36 (Holladay, *Fragments*, 2.355).

18. *Mos.* 1.22; Pl., *Phaedo* 72E, *Theaet.* 183D; see also Feldman, *Philo's Portrayal*, 47–55.

19. *Mos.* 1.43–44, cf. Exod 2:11–12.

20. *Mos.* 1.25–28, 1.47–50; note also Panaetius's concern to appreciate a person throughout life (Cic., *Off.* 1.111–19).

21. *Mos.* 1.63–86, 1.86, 1.147, 1.150–59, 1.163 (ἀποικίαν ἔστελλεν), 1.170 (εἰς ἀποικίαν), 1.220, 1.222, 1.237, 1.328; on Macro, see chap. 3.

22. *Mos.* 1.334, 2.1–2, 2.292.

23. *Mos.* 2.37; 2.71–76; 2.81–84, 97–98, 102.

24. *Jos.* 157, 166, 204.

25. *Jos.* 5, 37, 40, 42, 207–31, 246, 262; *Prov.* 2.16; see also Sen., *Ira* 3.36.1–3, *Ep.* 83.1, *Ep.* 3.2.

26. *Jos.* 15, 21, 173; Sen., *Ira* 1.7.1–1.9.4, 2.2.2, 2.3.1–2; see also Sorabji, *Emotion*, 55–75; Inwood, *Reading Seneca*, 23–64; on Philo as a rational ambassador, see chap. 2.

27. *Jos.* 42, 67, 71; on Macro, *Every Good Man Is Free* and the *Hypothetica*, see chaps. 2 and 4.

28. *All.* 3.26, 3.236–39; *Migr.* 160; *Somn.* 2.105–8.

29. *Jos.* 42, 157, 204, 135–36.

30. *Abr.* 63–67; on the notion of colonization in the historical treatises, see chap. 3.

31. On Plutarch's Platonism, see Dillon, *Middle Platonists*, 184–230; Duff, *Plutarch's Lives*, 34–45.

32. In other contexts Plutarch sometimes blurs the distinction between biography and history; see also Duff, *Plutarch's Lives*, 18–19; Wardman, *Plutarch's Lives*, 2–10.

33. Plut., *Per.* 1.2–4; *Aem.* 1.1–2; see also Russell, "On Reading Plutarch's Lives"; Pelling, "Moralism"; Pelling, "Plutarch"; Duff, *Plutarch's Lives*, 52–72; Swain, "Plutarch's Lives"; Ziegler, *Plutarchos*, 266–68.

34. Plut., *Alex.* 1.3, 6.1–5; *Alcib.* 1.1–3, 2.2–4, 4.1–4.

35. Phil., *Vit. Apol.* 1.2.1–1.3.1, 1.7.1–1.8.2; see also Bowie, "Philostratus," 25–29; Whitmarsh, "Philostratus"; Eshleman, "Eastern Travel in Apollonius"; Hägg, *Art of Biography*, 318–41.

36. Luke 1:1–2:52, 24:36–53; see also Hägg, *Art of Biography*, 148–86; Burridge, *What Are the Gospels?*; Burridge, "Reading Gospels."

37. For further details on Roman attitudes toward ancestors, see Baroin, "Remembering One's Ancestors."

Chapter 7. Biblical Ladies in Roman Garb

1. On Eve see *All.* 2.23, 2.44–51, 2.72–73, 2.79–99, 3.49; cf. Pl., *Phaedr.* 246b–47c; for details on Philo's Platonic background, see chaps. 10 and 11; on Sarah see *Cher.* 50, *Fug.* 128, *Ebr.* 60, *QG* 4.15, *Congr.* 71–79, *QG* 3.2; on Philo's gender categories, see Baer, *Philo's Use;* Sly, *Philo's Perception*, 91–110; Romney Wegner, "Philo's Portrayal"; Boyarin, *Carnal Israel*, 77–106; Mattila, "Wisdom."

2. On women in Hellenistic Egypt, see Taylor, *Jewish Women*, 227–64; Pomeroy, *Women;* Rowlandson, *Women.*

3. *Legat.* 319–20; Suet., *Claud.* 11.1–2.

4. Suet., *Tib.* 50.2–3; Tac., *An.* 5.1.1–5; Sen., *Cons. Marc.* 1.1–5, 4.1, 16.1–5; see also Mauch, *Senecas Frauenbild;* Balsdon, *Roman Women*, 90–95; Barrett, *Livia*, 155–58; Bauman, *Women and Politics*, 124–28, 131–33, 166–67; Burns, *Great Women*, 5–23; on the date of Seneca's *Cons. Marc.*, see Griffin, *Seneca*, 366.

5. Sen., *Ep.* 63.5; see also Morford, *Roman Philosophers*, 165–66; Lattimore, *Themes*, 275–80; Weisser, "Why Does Philo Criticize?"

6. ἡ γυνὴ θυμηρεστάτη καὶ τὰ πάντα ἀρίστη (*Abr.* 245).

7. Dio 56.3.3; Mus., 13A.1–4 (trans. Lutz), who uses the same key word as Philo, namely, κοινωνία (companionship); Sen., *Ep.* 104, 1–5; Tac., *An.* 15.63, *Agric.* 6.1; Jos., *J.A.* 1.288, 1.298, 1.302, 1.306, 1.318 (see also Feldman, *Josephus's Interpretation*, 328–32); on the Roman ideal of harmonious marriages, see Veyne, "Roman Empire," 33–42; Grimal, *Love in Ancient Rome*, 48–69; Treggiari, *Roman Marriage*, 214–61, 249–51; Dixon, *Roman Family*, 67–71; Dixon, "Sentimental Ideal."

8. Sen., *Cons. Helv.* 19.4–5; Sen., *Ep.* 57; Tac., *An.* 3.34, "uxor carissima et tot communium liberorum parens" (quoted in Blank-Sangmeister, *Römische Frauen*, 56).

9. Suet., *Gaius* 8.3–9.1, *Claud.* 17.3; Dio 22.22; see also Hurley, *Suetonius*, 181.

10. *J.A.* 1.186–87; the text of the Roman funerary inscription is available in Lefkowitz and Fant, *Women's Life*, 208–11; Blank-Sangmeister, *Römische Frauen*, 92–97; see also Morgan, *Roman Faith*, 128–37.

11. See Reydams-Schils, *Roman Stoics*, 53–82; Treggiari, *Roman Marriage*, 183–228; Dixon, *Roman Mother*, 71–104.

12. On Arius, see Ar., *Epitome of Stoic Ethics* 91 (trans. Arthur J. Pomeroy = von Arnim, *Stoicorum* 3.686), who uses the same key terms as Philo: κοινωνικός, φύσις; on Augustus's legislation, see Suet., *Aug.* 34.1–2; Dixon, *Roman Mother*, 21–30; on Claudius's policy, see Suet., *Claud.* 16.3; on Musonius, see Mus., 14.4–5, 14.9, 12.2–3. The Stoic philosopher Hierocles continued this line of argumentation in the early second century CE; see Stobaeus, *Anth.* 4.67.22; Ramelli, *Hierocles*, 73, 108–12; see also Heinemann, *Philons griechische*, 261–77; Biale, *Eros and the Jews*, 37–39. Rabbinic legislation shared this general ideal, without emphasizing the element of marital love (Schremer, *Male and Female*, 299–308).

13. Gen 12:10–20; on the rabbinic interpretation of Sarah, see Zohar, "Figure of Abraham"; Niehoff, "Associative Thinking."

14. For a list and brief discussion of Roman women in Plutarch's *Lives*, see Catellani, "Plutarch's 'Roman' Women"; see also Foucault, *Care of the Self*, 193–210.

15. *Mor.* 770c, 750c–52a, 139f–41b, 143a, 146a, 242e–f; see also Pomeroy, *Plutarch's Advice*; Feichtinger, "Soziologisches."

16. *Mos.* 1.7, cf. Exod 2:1.

17. Acts 18:2–3, 24:24, 25:13; Luke 1:26–38; see also D'Angelo, "(Re)Presentations"; D'Angelo, "Women in Luke-Acts"; Schüssler Fiorenza, "Feminist Critical Interpretation"; Spencer, *Salty Wives*; Osiek and Balch, *Families*; Kraemer and D'Angelo, *Women*. Regarding Luke's dependence on Mark, see Ehrman, *New Testament*, 72–78, 96–99; Koester, *Ancient Christian Gospels*, 332–48; Sanders and Davies, *Studying*, 51–66, 276–98.

18. On Roman law, see Treggiari, *Roman Marriage*, 15–16, 407–8, 467–68; Riddle, *Contraception*; Evans Grubbs, "Hidden in Plain Sight."

19. See also Bradley, "Wet-Nursing."

20. *Mos.* 1.12, 1.16; Jos., *J.A.* 2.221, 2.226. In rabbinic literature Miriam is praised as a prophetess who received the divine announcement concerning Moses's birth and persuaded her parents to have sex in order to fulfill the prophecy. Her "seeing" Moses floating on the river is interpreted as a prophetic vision (*Mekh. De Rabbi Ishmael*, Shir. 10, ed. Lauterbach, 2.81–82).

21. Mus. 14.19; see also Reydams-Schils, *Roman Stoics*, 153–55. Already Cleanthes, the second head of the Stoic school, wrote a no longer extant treatise *On the Thesis That Virtue Is the Same in Men and Women* (D.L. 7.175).

22. *Abr.* 112–13 (cf. Gen 18:1–10); *Jos.* 4, *Mos.* 1.18–24; Sen., *Cons. Helv.* 17.3, 3.2–6.

23. Suet., *Aug.* 34.1–2, 65.1–4. Not satisfied with such stringent punishment, Augustus wished Julia dead and ruled that her corpse could not be buried in his mausoleum (Suet., *Aug.* 65.1–4, 101.3; *Tib.* 50.1). On Philo's discussion of adultery in the *Special Laws,* see chap. 8.

24. Regarding Potiphar's wife in the *Allegorical Commentary,* see *All.* 3.237, *Migr.* 19, *Somn.* 2.106.

25. Sen., *Ira* 2.28.7; Mus. 12.2–4.

26. On Josephus, see Feldman, "Hellenizations"; Feldman, *Josephus's Interpretations;* Niehoff, "Desires Crossing Boundaries."

Chapter 8. Stoic Ethics in the Service of Jewish Law

1. *Migr.* 90; *contra* Belkin, *Philo and the Oral Law;* N. Cohen, *Philo Judaeus,* who both argue on methodologically questionable grounds that Philo adopted rabbinic traditions, which are attested only much later; see more cautiously, Doering, *Schabbat,* 315–77; see also Goodenough, *Jurisprudence,* who argues on methodologically questionable grounds that Philo reflects decisions of Alexandrian law courts.

2. *Spec.* 3.3–5, 1.3; Tac., *Hist.* 5.5.2; Hor., *Serm.* 1.9, 70; Petr., *Satyr.* 102.13–14; Jos., *C.Ap.* 2.137–44; see also Stern, *Greek and Latin Authors,* 2.41, 1.324–26; 1.443–44; Schäfer, *Judeophobia,* 98–100; Isaac, *Invention of Racism,* 472–74.

3. Jos., *C.Ap.* 2.145–47, 2.7; on Josephus's integration in Rome, see chap. 1.

4. *Dec.* 19, 175; *Spec.* 1.1; *Dec.* 82, 162–65, 168–71; *Spec.* 4.132. Philo's innovation has been appreciated by Amir, "Decalogue"; Termini, "Taxonomy"; Pearce, "Decalogue"; *contra* Wolfson, *Philo,* 200–202; N. Cohen, *Philo Judaeus,* 78–80, who mistakenly identify some later rabbinic passages as sources of Philo; on the liturgical use of the Decalogue, see Urbach, "Ten Commandments."

5. On the unique features of the Decalogue, see Weinfeld, "Uniqueness"; Najman, "Decalogue"; Pearce, "Philo of Alexandria."

6. Jub 1:1–29, 2:25–33, 50:6–7; *Dam. D.* 1.1–9, 2.1–8, 3.1–12; *Com. R.* 2.4–26, 8.15–26; see also Segal, *Jubilees;* Werman and Shemesh, "Halakha"; cf. Hayes, *What's Divine about Divine Law?,* 92–139, who stresses the continuum between Philo and other Second Temple authors.

7. Aristob., fragm. 4, 8 (ed. Holladay, *Fragments,* 3.174–75); Ar. 127, 143; Wright, *Letter of Aristeas,* 246–313; Hayes, *What's Divine about Divine Law?,* 105–10.

8. *Dec.* 37–39, 50, 154, 177, 17, 13–14; *Spec.* 1.86–87, 3.104–7; see also Exod 20:5–6, 12, where punishments for the transgression of the Decalogue are mentioned. The philosophical dimension of Philo's explanations is also visible in his emphasis on the revelation of the Decalogue in the desert (on which see Calabi, "Il Deserto"; Calabi, *Filone: De Decalogo,* 41–43, n. 25; Pearce, "Decalogue," 992–96).

9. Cic., *Fin.* 3.11–12, 26, 31–32; *Leg.* 1.16–17, 1.32–35, 1.58.

10. Sen., *Ep.* 94.4, 19–27, 31, 37, 42; *Ep.* 81.19–21; *Ben.* 1.6.1.

11. *Congr.* 120; on Philo's views in the *Allegorical Commentary*, which resemble Cleanthes's, see chap. 12.

12. Rom 13:8–10; more generally on Paul's attitude toward Mosaic law, see esp. Deming, "Paul, Gaius"; Watson, *Paul, Judaism;* Barclay, "Paul and Philo"; Boyarin, *Paul;* Hayes, *What's Divine about Divine Law?*, 151–62. The Decalogue serves in additional early Christian contexts as a marker of Christian identity; see esp. the discussion about the "royal law" and the "whole law" in *Jam.* 2.7–11; on which see Avemarie, "Die Werke"; Niehoff, "Implied Audience"; for different views, see Flusser, "Ten Commandments"; Kloppenborg, "Diaspora Discourse."

13. Sen., *Ep.* 94.1–21, 25, 31, 38; Cic., *Rep.* 2.1–3; see also Kidd, "Moral Actions."

14. D.L. 7.87; Cic., *N.D.* 2.81–90; *Leg.* 1.13–19; Sen., *Ep.* 118.12, 65.19, 95.51–53; Arius *apud* Stob., *Ecl.* 51, 6a (ed. Pomeroy 36–39); see also Bréhier, *Idées philosophiques,* 23–32; Schwabe, "Introduction," XXV–XXVIII; Calabi, *Filone,* 51–56; Martens, *One God, One Law;* Najman, "Written Copy"; Hayes, *What's Divine about Divine Law?*, 112–15; for discussions of the Stoic ideals, see Striker, *Essays,* 221–80; Inwood, *Reading Seneca,* 224–48; Schofield, "Stoic Ethics," 233–56.

15. *Dec.* 142 (πάντα μὲν γὰρ τὰ ψυχῆς πάθη χαλεπὰ κινοῦντα καὶ σείοντα αὐτὴν παρὰ φύσιν καὶ ὑγιαίειν οὐκ ἐῶντα χαλεπώτατον δ᾿ ἐπιθυμία); D.L. 7.110 (παρὰ φύσιν ψυχῆς κίνησις); see also *Dec.* 150 and *Spec.* 4.78–81; for a different interpretation, see Svebakken, *Tenth Commandment,* 122–24.

16. D.L. 7.111 (τὰ πάθη κρίσεις εἶναι); see also Inwood and Donini, "Stoic Ethics," 699–705; Graver, *Stoicism and Emotion,* 35–48.

17. On monotheism, see *Dec.* 81, *Spec.* 1.31; on murder, see *Dec.* 132–34; on the Shabbat, see *Spec.* 2.56–59, 2.97–103; on adultery, see *Spec.* 3.7–11; on honoring parents, see *Dec.* 110–17.

18. Striker, *Essays,* 249; D.L. 7.85–89; see esp. Chrysippus's formulation κατ᾿ ἐμπειρίαν τῶν φύσει συμβαινόντων (D.L. 7.87).

19. Cic., *Leg.* 1.13–19, 2.10–35; Sen., *Ep.* 119.2–4, 119.15, 120.4–5, 118.13–15.

20. *Spec.* 3.9, 3.22–28, 3.32–33, 3.37–48, 3.51; *Gig.* 29; Suet., *Aug.* 34.1–2, 65.1–4, 65.1–4, 101.3; *Tib.* 50.1; Sen., *Ep.* 94.26. See also D'Angelo, "Eusebeia"; D'Angelo, "Gender"; for literature on Roman legislation and family ideals, see chap. 7.

21. *Legat.* 28, *Spec.* 2.225–35; see also Mus., *Lect.* 16, who reacts to Roman practices by limiting the father's authority; see also Heinemann, *Philons griechische,* 250–51; Nicholas, *Roman Law,* 76–80; on rabbinic law, which renders the execution of the rebellious son virtually impossible, see Halbertal, *Interpretative Revolutions.*

22. *Spec.* 3.108–16; *Virt.* 128–33.

23. Cic., *Fin.* 4.17–23; Sen., *Cons. Helv.* 16.3–4; Mus., *Lect.* 15; see also Evans Grubbs, "Hidden in Plain Sight"; Harris, "Child Exposure."

24. *Spec.* 2.42, 2.45–46, 2.52–54; Sen., *Ep.* 18.1–15, 65.19, 95.51–53, 45.9, 60.2, 90.34, 108.15, 110.11–12, 95.19; see also Philo's discussion of the true feast in the *Allegorical Commentary,* where he stresses theological issues, especially God's tran-

scendence, rather than human practice (*Cher.* 84–93); Stein-Hölkeskamp, *Das Römische Gastmahl,* 211–19.

25. *Spec.* 2.60; Sen. *apud* Aug., *C.D.* 6.11 (= Stern, *Greek and Latin Authors,* 1.431); see also Schäfer, *Judeophobia,* 86–89.

26. *Spec.* 2.61–62, *Legat.* 312.

27. *Spec.* 2.66–69, 3.137–43.

28. Sen., *Ep.* 18.8, 47.14–16; Epict., *Disc.* 4.1.

29. *Spec.* 2.145–63, 2.193–203; *Flacc.* 116.

30. *Miqsat Maase ha-Torah* (ed. Quimron and Strugnell, *Discoveries in the Judean Dessert* 10.58 [פרשנו מרוב העם ומכול טמאתם]; *The Temple Scroll* (ed. Yadin); *Florilegium;* see also Sir 24:8–12, 50:1–26; *Ar.* 83–120.

31. *Spec.* 1.12, 1.65–67, 1.195.

32. *Spec.* 1.68; Cic., *N.D.* 2.60–62, 2.71, 2.153.

33. *Spec.* 1.67–68; Deut 12:5–18.

34. Philo's reference has been taken as historical evidence by Jeremias, *Jerusalem,* 76–77; Levine, *Jerusalem,* 248–53; J. Schwartz, "Pilgrimage," 1089. Goodman, "Pilgrimage Economy," suggests far more cautiously that Herod rebuilt the Second Temple in the hope of increasing pilgrimage as a means of income, but may well not have seen the fruits of his investment; Rutherford, "Concord and Communitas," assumes a middle position.

35. Luke 2:49; for an attempt to reconstruct Jesus's historical pilgrimage, see Haber, "Going Up to Jerusalem."

36. Plut., *Mor.* 385B, 351D–52A; see also Elsner and Rutherford, "Introduction," 24–27; Galli, "Educated Pilgrims"; Leonhardt, *Jewish Worship,* 22, who briefly alludes to the similarity between Philo's notion of pilgrimage and Greek practices but has in mind Classical Greek rather than contemporary sources.

37. Philost., *Vit. Apol.* chaps. 7–12; see also Petsalis-Diomidis, *Truly beyond Wonders;* Downie, *At the Limits.*

38. I *Apol.* 27.1–5, 29.1–2, 67.1–8.

Chapter 9. Biblical Commentary

1. On the chronology of Philo's works, see chap. 1; regarding his reliance on the LXX rather than the Hebrew text, see Katz, *Philo's Bible;* Amir, "Authority and Interpretation"; Sterling, "Interpreter of Moses"; Royse, "Some Observations"; Royse, "The Text"; Tov, "Septuagint between Judaism and Christianity"; see also Tov, "Septuagint Translation," for special translation features of LXX Genesis. Note that Philo preserves earlier names of biblical books, such as "Exagoge" for Exodus, and refers to subdivisions not known to us (e.g., *Her.* 252, *Migr.* 14). Philo's commentary on Gen 18:1–2 is preserved in an Armenian fragment, published by Siegert, "Philonian Fragment." Regarding the volume of the *Allegorical Commentary,* especially the question of whether he commented on Genesis chapter 1, see Appendix 2.

2. See scholia on *Il.* 1.1. (ed. Erbse, *Scholia Graeca*, 1.3) (hereafter *Schol. Il.*); for background on Alexandrian scholarship and the Museum, see Schironi, "Alexandrian Scholarship"; Fraser, *Ptolemaic Alexandria*, 1.305–35, 447–79.

3. *All.* 3.188; on Aristarchus's maxim, see Fraser, *Ptolemaic Alexandria*, 1.464; Porter, "Hermeneutic Lines and Circles," 70–80; Pfeiffer, *History of Classical Scholarship*, 1.225–27.

4. *Schol. Il.* 1.100A, 19.416–17A, 1.129A, 2.55A, 2.76A, 2.319A, 2.667A, 3.74A, 16.666A. On the method of bracketing, or "athetizing," see Schironi, "Alexandrian Scholarship."

5. Eus., *P.E.* 9.29.16, 9.21.14; for another investigation into a problem of contradiction, discussed by Demetrius, see Eus., *P.E.* 9.29.1–3; see also the Jewish exegete and philosopher Aristobulus (second century BCE), who examines why the burning bush "burns irresistibly, [but] does not consume anything entirely" (Eus., *P.E.* 8.10.16).

6. See Appendix 2 regarding the question of whether Philo wrote an allegorical commentary on Genesis chapter 1.

7. *Conf.* 2; *Migr.* 8, 48; *Plant.* 90; *Det.* 15, 167; *Somn.* 1.93.

8. *Conf.* 2–6; for details, see Niehoff, *Jewish Exegesis*, 77–94; on the literary quality of the Bible in Philo's eyes, see also Kamesar, "Philo and the Literary Quality"; Kamesar, "Philo, Grammatike."

9. *Conf.* 190–91, *Plant.* 36; see also *Det.* 167, where Philo stresses that Moses "wishes to convey" the allegorical meaning.

10. τὸ ἑπόμενον . . . συνεπισκεψώμεθα (*Post.* 32); διαπορητέον δὲ ἑξῆς (*Det.* 32); see also *All.* 1.101, *Det.* 57, *Gig.* 67, *Sobr.* 1.

11. ἑξῆς κἀκεῖνο διαπορητέον (*All.* 1.101); see also *Post.* 32, 49; *Deus* 51; *Det.* 57.

12. Διὰ τί; (e.g., *All.* 1.2, 1.33, 1.48, 1.85; *Gig.* 1; *Fug.* 60; *Spec.* 1.213); σκεπτέον (e.g., *All.* 2.80, 3.252; *Post.* 40; *Sobr.* 31, 62; *Fug.* 157); see similar expressions in *All.* 1.91, 2.42, 3.4, 3.28; *Post.* 1, 22; *Conf.* 169; *Gig.* 1; *Fug.* 87.

13. See esp. Aristarchus in *Schol. Il.* 1.13–16A, 7.334–35A, 8.43A, 8.328A, 11.659A; on the Aristotelian background, see Arist., *Apor. Hom.* fragm. 142, 145–48, 150–53, 155–59; Arist., *Poet.* 1461a5; Schironi, "Theory into Practice."

14. See esp. Paz, "From Scribes to Scholars"; Niehoff, "Commentary Culture"; see also Fraade, "Rewritten Bible"; Fraade, "Rabbinic Midrash," for the distinction between rabbinic and Second Temple Midrash.

15. Sen., *Brev. Vit.* 13.1; Luc., *Ver. Hist.* 2.20; see also Kim, *Homer*, 140–74.

16. For examples of Philo quoting only the LXX in cases of divergence from the Hebrew text, see *All.* 1.18, where he quotes LXX Gen 2:3 and relies on the notion of God ceasing from all the works, which he "began" to make rather than "made," as in the Masoretic Text; *All.* 1.19, where he quotes LXX Gen 2:4, which refers to the "book of the creation" rather than the "generations"; *Migr.* 215, where he quotes LXX Exod 1:21, assuming that the midwives built houses for themselves, while according to the Hebrew text God did so; *Migr.*

58, where he relies on the LXX for the notion of God "approaching" (ἐγγίζων) rather than "being near" (קרבים); for examples of Philo adapting the LXX to his own interpretations, see *Cher.* 49–50, *Mut.* 140, and below. Rajak, *Translation and Survival,* suggests, mainly on the basis of the Hebrew etymologies, that Philo knew Hebrew. Amir, "Authority and Interpretation," however, has already shown that the etymologies are likely to have derived from separate lists.

17. *Post.* 49 (referring to Gen 4:17).

18. Arist., *Poet.* 1460b33; *Apor. Hom.* fragm. 147, 167.

19. *All.* 1.86–87; see also *Somn.* 1.166–70, 2.246; *Det.* 13–16, *Plant.* 112–13. Note two geographers active in Alexandria, namely, Eratosthenes, who dismissed Homer's epics as a source of geographical knowledge, and Strabo, who appreciated him as such (Strabo 1.2.7–8, 1.2.7–14, 1.2.24, 1.2.30, 1.2.35; see also Schenkeveld, "Strabo on Homer," 52–64; Biraschi, "Strabo and Homer").

20. *Det.* 81, καὶ μὴν τῶν ἐξ ἀρχῆς ὑποθέσεων ἄκρως εἴωθε διαμεμνῆσθαι τὰ ἀκόλουθα καὶ ὁμολογούμενα τοῖς προτέροις δικαιῶν ἐφαρμόττειν.

21. *Somn.* 1.52; *Migr.* 178–86.

22. Pl., *Phaed.* 80–81a; see also Wis 7:13, 8:17, 15:3; Winston, *Wisdom,* 59–63; Niebuhr, "Sapientia."

23. Gen 25:25, 50:22. Isaac lived roughly the same number of years as his father (Gen 35:28).

24. On Stoic allegory, see Cic., *N.D.* 1.41, 2.64; Boys-Stones, *Metaphor, Allegory;* Brisson, *How Philosophers Saved Myths,* 41–49; Buffière, *Les mythes;* Steinmetz, "Allegorische Deutung." Although I disagree with Long, "Stoic Readings of Homer," who argues that the Stoics practiced only etymology, and not allegory, I am convinced by his distinction between Philo's allegory and Stoic hermeneutics (Long, "Allegory in Philo"). For different views, see Pépin, *La tradition;* Amir, "Philo's Allegory"; Kamesar, "Logos Endiathetos"; Stein, *Philo,* 162–85.

25. Aristar. in *Schol. Il.* 21.538–39, 7.130A, 1.180A, 6.71A, 6.479–80A, 5.734–36A, 5.299A, 5.684A, 8.441A, 11.636; Dem., fragm. 2.14–15 (ed. Holladay, *Fragments*); the Alexandrian approach differs from Aristotle, who regularly studied Homeric lines without drawing comparisons to other lines (Arist., *Apor. Hom.* fragm. 148, 151); see also Runia, "Structure"; Runia, "Further Observations"; Cover, *Lifting the Veil,* 115–24, 134–44.

26. *Migr.* 5, 8 (referring to Moses's exhortation mentioned in Gen 24:6, 34:12; Deut 12:13, 12:19, 12:30, 15:9); see also *Migr.* 13 (referring to Gen 13:9).

27. See *Plant.* 108, 19 (Gen 2:7, 1:27); 32 (Gen 2:8); 44 (Gen 2:9, 25:27); 73 (Gen 21:33); 78 (Gen 32–33); 85 (Gen 28:21); 110 (Gen 30:37); 132 (Gen 29:35); 134 (Gen 30:18); 140 (Gen 9:21–22).

28. *Plant.* 26 (Lev 1:1), 111 (Lev 13:12).

29. *Cher.* 49; the German translator Leopold Cohn, ad loc., suggests that Philo's use of "husband" comes from his own pen; on the importance of prophets for

Philo's mystical exegesis, see also Hay, "Philo's View"; Goodenough, *By Light, Light,* 75–80; see also Liebes, "Work of the Chariot," for possible connections between Philo and later Jewish mysticism. The prophetic writings are mentioned for the first time as part of a tripartite canon by the grandson of Ben Sira, who began around 132 BCE to translate his grandfather's wisdom book for an Alexandrian audience (Prologue, *Wisdom of Ben Sira*).

30. *Plant.* 138, *Mut.* 137–40; see also *Gig.* 6, where Philo rejects the literal meaning of the story of the giants who were born from the "angels of God" and human women.

31. For details on Bacchic revelry, see Burkert, *Greek Religion,* 110–11. See also Kaiser, *Studien,* 63–82, who draws attention to the spiritual role of the Psalms in Philo's work, assuming that they were used in Jewish liturgy as prayers.

32. The question of the original scope of the *Q&A* is still debated. A more limited scope with roots in the reading cycle of the synagogue has been assumed by Royse, "Works of Philo," 37–38. By contrast, Cohn, "Einleitung und Chronologie," 403–4, argued that the *Q&A* originally extended beyond the books of Genesis and Exodus, seeing that John of Damascus refers to Φίλωνος ἐκ τῶν ἐν τῷ Λευιτικῷ ζητημάτων.

33. See also Wan, "Philo's *Quaestiones et Solutiones,* 10–33, 59–65; Cohn, "Einleitung und Chronologie"; Royse, "Works of Philo"; *contra* Terian, "Priority of the *Quaestiones*"; and Sterling, "Philo's *Quaestiones,*" who both suggest that the *Q&A* was a kind of notebook preceding the *Allegorical Commentary;* for the school setting of Philo's teaching, see Sterling, "School of Moses," Sterling, "Philo's School."

34. *Mut.* 60–61; *QG* 3.43, 3.53; for an overview of Philo's references to other interpreters, see Hay, "References to Other Exegetes."

35. Bauer, *Orthodoxy and Heresy;* for a useful survey of the history of Bauer's reception in modern scholarship, see Harrington, "Reception"; see also the more recent account by Ehrman, *Lost Christianities,* 163–80; on the emergence of orthodox structures in rabbinic literature, see esp. Boyarin, "Tale of Two Synods"; Schremer, *Brothers Estranged.*

36. *QG* 4.243, 3.8.

37. *QG* 1.18, cf. *All.* 2.9–10, *QG* 1.69, *QG* 1.93; see also *QG* 4.2; *QE* 2.45; *QG* 4.60–61, 4.233.

38. *QG* 1.10, cf. *All.* 1.56–59.

39. *QG* 1.25, cf. *All.* 2.19; *Agr.* 96–97, cf. *QG* 1.32, *Mut.* 143, cf. *QG* 3.18; see also *QG* 1.12, cf. *All.* 1.85; *QG* 1.6, cf. *All.* 1.43 and *Plant.* 33–35; *QG* 1.3, cf. *Fug.* 179–80.

40. *QG* 1.70, 4.90; cf. *All.* 3.42.

41. *QG* 1.21, 1.55; see also *QG* 1.42, 1.47, 1.60–61, 1.65–66, 1.68, 1.73.

42. *QG* 1.27–30 (cf. *All.* 2.49–52), *QG* 1.1 (cf. *All.* 1.19–20), *QG* 1.17 (cf. *All.* 2.1–8), *QG* 1.20 (cf. *All.* 90–91, *Mut.* 63), *QG* 1.32, 1.35, 1.41–42, 1.51–57, 1.64, 1.76; see *QG* 1.31, where Philo introduces the symbolic meaning of the serpent and then applies it

in *QG* 1.48. See also Papadoyannakis, "Instruction," for details on later didactic uses of the *Q&A* format.

43. On Gnostic exegesis, see Löhr, "Editors and Commentators"; on Origen and his Bible commentary, see Heine, *Origen;* Fürst, "Origenes"; Fürst, "Bibel"; Neuschäfer, *Origenes,* 1.86–102; on Philo's influence on Origen, see Daniélou, *Origène,* 179–98; van den Hoek, "Philo and Origen"; Runia, *Philo in Early Christian Literature,* 157–83.

44. See, e.g., *Letter of Barnabas* and Justin, 1 *Apol.* 36–42; for the overall development of commentary culture in Early Christianity, see Stroumsa, *Scriptural Universe.*

45. Prologue to the Commentary on Psalms (PG 12.1077); see also Heine, "Restringing Origen's Broken Harp," who identified the extant parts of the original Alexandrian prologue, which was later replaced by a prologue to the expanded Caesarean commentary.

46. Orig., *PArch* 4.16 (τίς δ' οὕτως ἠλίθιος ὡς οἰηθῆναι τρόπον ἀνθρώπου γεωργοῦ τὸν θεὸν πεφυτευκέναι παράδεισον, PG 11.377).

Chapter 10. A Platonic Self

1. *Migr.* 34, 1–13 (interpreting LXX Gen 12:1); cf. Pl., *Ion* 536a–d, 533e; *Symp.* 215e; *Crit.* 54d; see also Calabi, "Le Migrazioni."

2. The development of the Platonic tradition is increasingly considered in Philonic research, see esp. Runia, "Was Philo a Middle Platonist?"; Sterling, "Platonizing Moses," 99–103; Dillon, *Middle Platonists,* 114–39; Bonazzi, "Towards Transcendence."

3. *Theaet.* 172c–77c (note that Plato himself calls this passage a "digression" [πάρεργον]); Sedley, *Midwife,* 74–86; Sedley, "Ideal of Godlikeness"; Bartels, "Zur Deutung"; for other views, see Guthrie, *A History,* 5.89–92; Kahn, *Plato,* 47–52, 88–89. Plato develops the notion of ideal Forms in *Phaedo* 65d–68e, *Rep.* 5.473c–7.519b; *Rep.* 597b (on which see also Guthrie, *A History,* 5.487–521).

4. *Comm. Theaet.* col. 54, 39–43, 55.9–10 (ed. Diels and Schubart, *Anonymer Kommentar,* 36; Bastianini and Sedley, "Commentarium," 246–50); see also Tarrant, "Date of the Anon.," 170–72, 187, whose historical arguments are not compromised by his untenable suggestion that the anonymous commentator may have been Eudorus; Sedley, "Three Platonist Interpretations," 83–84, 93–103, and "Plato's *Auctoritas,*" accepts the early dating, while rejecting the identification with Eudorus; for a later dating of the commentary, see Bonazzi, "Le commentateur anonyme," 310–12; on the Skeptic phase in Platonism, see Tarrant, *Scepticism or Platonism?*; Schofield, "Academic Epistemology"; Bonazzi, "Continuité."

5. On Eudorus see Stob., *Ecl.* 2.48; Bonazzi, "Eudorus"; Dillon, *Middle Platonists,* 114–39.

6. Eud. in Stob., *Ecl.* 2.66 (ed. Meineke 21).

7. *Comm. Theaet.* col. 54.43–55.13, 7.14–20 (see comments by Bastianini and Sedley, "Commentarium," 494–95); Stob., *Ecl.* 2.68 (ed. Meineke 21); Cic., *Ac.* 2.11–12; see also Bonazzi, "Commentary as Polemical Tool," 598–99; Tarrant, "Date of the Anon.," 180–84; on Antiochus, see Glucker, *Antiochus,* 90–97; Karamanolis, *Plato and Aristotle in Agreement?*, 44–84. For details on the Stoic notion of *oikeiosis,* see chap. 12.

8. *Fug.* 56–57, quoting Deut 4:4, 30:20; on Philo's interpretation of these verses, see also Helleman, "Philo of Alexandria," 53–55; Liebes, *Ars Poetica,* 73–110; Schäfer, *Origins,* 154–74; Afterman, "From Philo to Plotinus."

9. On biblical ethics and theology, see Barton, *Ethics in Ancient Israel;* Knohl, *Divine Symphony;* Liebes, *God's Story.*

10. *Fug.* 75, 69–71; Pl., *Theaet.* 177E; *contra* Dillon, *Middle Platonists,* 145, who reads Philo's discussion in light of the *Exposition* and mistakenly argues that he combined the idea of godlikeness with the Stoic emphasis on nature.

11. Pl., *Theaet.* 152A (πάντων χρημάτων μέτρον ἄνθρωπον εἶναι); for ancient discussions of this maxim, see Ryu, *Knowledge of God,* 162–64.

12. *Theaet.* 186d, trans. Fowler.

13. For similar echoes of Protagoras's maxim, see *Somn.* 2.193, *All.* 3.32–35; *Plant.* 20–25 (on which see also Geljon and Runia, *On Cultivation,* 112–19).

14. *All.* 3.97–103; *Plant.* 80 (referring to Pl., *Apol.* 21D); D.L. 9.78–80; Cic., *Ac.* 30–31; *Comm. Theaet.* col. 63; Pl., *Laws* 716c; see also Sedley, *Midwife,* 38–117; see also M. Frede, "Stoic Epistemology"; Bréhier, *Les idées philosophiques;* 209–17; Lévy, "Sceptical Academy"; Lévy, "Deux problèmes doxographiques," 85–102; Lévy, "La conversion du scepticisme."

15. *All.* 2.7–8, 2.69; *Migr.* 39–42; see also *All.* 1.1, 1.21–24, 2.23–25, 2.35–48, 2.69–73, 3.56–68, 3.108–12.

16. *Conf.* 9; *Plant.* 15; *Deus* 55; *Det.* 75–76, 78.

17. *Ebr.* 99, 133; *Mut.* 135; *Somn.* 2.45; *Opif.* 23; Radice, "Philo's Theology"; Radice, "Observations"; Wolfson, *Philo,* 1.229–30; Runia, *On the Creation,* 151–52.

18. *Congr.* 74–79; see also Mendelson, *Secular Education,* 1–33.

19. μαίας υἱὸν καὶ αὐτὸν μαιευτικόν (*Theaet.* 151c).

20. προφήτης γὰρ ἴδιον μὲν οὐδὲν ἀποφθέγγεται ἀλλότρια δὲ πάντα ὑπηχοῦντος ἑτέρου (*Her.* 259).

21. *Migr.* 33, 81; *Congr.* 3–7 (referring to Gen 16:1, 29:31).

22. *Migr.* 142; *Her.* 249–66, 51; *Cher.* 43–50; *All.* 2.46–48; *Fug.* 128; see also Sly, *Philo's Perception of Women,* 145–54; Niehoff, "Mother and Maiden."

23. *Comm. Theaet.* 52.30–39, 53.37–54.2; see also Bastianini and Sedley, "Commentarium," 406, 408, 410, 537–40.

24. *All.* 3.116–17 (note esp. the clause μάχεται ὁ λόγος τῷ πάθει καὶ ἐν ταὐτῷ μένειν οὐ δύναται); *All.* 1.103, 3.186, 2.28–29, 2.90–93; see also Whittaker, "How to Define the Rational Soul."

25. *All.* 1.21–44, 1.40, 1.70–72.

26. Pl., *Rep.* 439c–41b, *Tim.* 69b–70e, *Phaedr.* 246a–51b; Sorabji, *Emotion*, 305–10; Sorabji, *Self*, 115–36; see also Runia, "God and Man," 68–71; Dillon, *Middle Platonists*, 174–75, who also discusses Stoic motifs.

27. Eud. in Plut., *An. Procr.* 1012f–13b.

28. Pl., *Phaedr.* 246a–48a; note esp. the following terms: λογιστικόν, ἀλόγιστον καὶ ἐπιθύμητικόν, and θύμοειδής.

29. *All.* 3.127; *Plant.* 22; *All.* 2.99–104, 3.132–37.

30. *Agr.* 73, *All.* 2.22.

31. *Fug.* 69–72; *Tim.* 41a–d; see also Runia, *On the Creation*, 236–37, dealing with *Opif.* 69–71, where the idea is repeated.

32. *All.* 2.1–3, 1.89, 1.38; note also *All.* 3.93, where Philo uses the verb "to recollect" in the everyday sense of remembering, i.e., not forgetting; *contra* Yli-Karjanmaa, *Reincarnation*, who argues that Philo fully embraced Plato's theory of the soul's transmigration.

33. *All.* 1.103 (cf. Pl., *Phaedo* 65c), *Gig.* 14 (cf. Pl., *Phaedo* 67e, 64a); see also *All.* 2.76–77, where Philo speaks about fatal pleasures, "not the death that severs soul from body but the death that ruins the soul by vice."

34. Ammon. in Plut., *Table Talk* 9.14.6; Justin, *Dial.* chaps. 4–8.

Chapter 11. An Utterly Transcendent God and His Logos

1. Eud. in Stob., *Ecl.* 2.66 (ed. Meineke 21); see also Bonazzi, "Eudorus"; Bonazzi, "Towards Transcendence," 236–41; Kaiser, *Philo*, 167–69.

2. Aristob., fragm. 2, in Eus., *P.E.* 8.10.2–3 (ed. Holladay, *Fragments* 3.136); Walter, *Der Toraausleger*, 135–36; Gutman, *Beginnings*, 1.213–16; Bloch, *Moses und der Mythos.* I have argued elsewhere that Aristobulus's approach is not Stoic, but Aristotelian (Niehoff, *Jewish Exegesis*, 58–74).

3. *Sacr.* 94–95, see esp. the expression τὸ οὐχ ὡς ἄνθρωπος ὁ θεὸς ἵνα πάντα τὰ ἀνθρωπολογούμενα ὑπερκύψωμεν.

4. Winston and Dillon, *Two Treatises*; cf. Dillon, "Nature of God," whose analysis is hampered by his overarching polemic against Wolfson and his undifferentiated approach to Philo's earlier and later writings.

5. *Gig.* 58–60, cf. Hom., *Od.* 7.59; Hes., *Theog.* 185ff. While Philo quotes the marginal LXX version of Gen 6:4, which reads "angels of God," his interpretation mentions "men of God" and shows his familiarity with the original LXX version, which reflects the Hebrew *Vorlage* בני האלהים. On LXX Gen 6:4 see also Rösel, *Übersetzung*, 146–58; *contra* Harl, *La Génèse*, 125; Katz, *Philo's Bible*, 20–21.

6. Pl., *Rep.* 5.473c–7.519b, 597b; see also Guthrie, *History of Greek Philosophy*, 5.487–521.

7. Philo's emphasis on God's transcendence distinguishes him from Stoic approaches, which also stress the nonanthropomorphic nature of god but interpret it in the sense of a divine immersion in the world (D.L. 7.134–37, 7.148).

8. The expression וינחם is rendered by ἐνεθυμήθη, the expression ויתעצב אל לבו by διενοήθη, and the expression נחמתי by ἐθυμώθην; see also Rösel, *Übersetzung*, 161–63.

9. *Deus* 53–54; similarly also in *Sacr.* 94, *Conf.* 135.

10. Pl., *Rep.* 379c–82e; see also Clay, "Plato and Homer"; on the canonicity of Homer, see Finkelberg, "Canonising and Decanonising Homer"; for Plato's distinction between knowledge and opinion, see Pl., *Rep.* 478b–e, *Phaedr.* 246a–48e; *Tim.* 28A, 69c–70e.

11. *Somn.* 1.233, referring to *Od.* 17.485; for other instances where Philo juggles his demand for absolute transcendence and pedagogical needs, see Calabi, "Conoscibilità e inconoscibilità."

12. ἀεὶ ἁπλῶς ἐν τῇ αὐτοῦ μορφῇ (Pl., *Rep.* 381c); see also *Rep.* 377b–79b; see also Tobin, *Creation of Man*, 36–56.

13. ὁ θεὸς μόνος ἐν τῷ εἶναι ὑφέστηκεν.

14. See also Starobinski-Safran, "Ex. 3.24 dans l'œuvre de Philon."

15. ἄποιος γὰρ ὁ θεός οὐ μόνον οὐκ ἀνθρωπόμορφος (*All.* 1.36); see also *Husb.* 129.

16. *Post.* 169, *Det.* 89; Pl., *Tim.* 28c.

17. *Opif.* 100; Eud., in Simpl., *In Phys.* 181.17, quoted in Whittaker, "Neopythagoreanism," 78.

18. *All.* 1.44, 1.51; *Deus* 55; *Conf.* 137; see also Bonazzi, "Towards Transcendence," 236–39; Kaiser, *Philo*, 183–84; Calabi, *God's Acting*.

19. See references and discussion in Lernould, "Negative Theology."

20. *All.* 3.100–103; *Migr.* 185–90; see also Feldmeier, "Gotteserkenntnis durch Selbsterkenntnis."

21. *All.* 3.104–6, referring to Deut 28:12, 32:34–35.

22. Brakke, *Gnostics*, 52–70; Leisegang, *Die Gnosis*, 1–59; Wilson, *Gnostic Problem*, 183–201; recent scholarship has shown how problematic it is to approach Gnosticism as a heresy and has stressed the diversity of Gnostic approaches to the extent of questioning whether it still makes sense to speak about "Gnosticism"; see esp. King, *What Is Gnosticism?*, 191–236; Brakke, *Gnostics*, 1–28; Markschies, *Gnosis;* Lieu, *Marcion and the Making of a Heretic;* regarding the connections between Philo and Gnosticism, see Pearson, "Philo and Gnosticism"; Anderson, *Philo of Alexandria's Views*. The effect of Gnosticism on later forms of Judaism has been subject to lively debates, with Scholem (*Jewish Gnosticism* and *Major Trends*) arguing for its decisive influence on Jewish mysticism, while Idel (*Kabbalah*, 114–27) and Liebes ("De Natura Dei") have stressed internal Jewish developments that may have been inspired more directly by Philo.

23. Val., fragm. in Clem, *Strom.* 4.89.6, 2.114.3–6, quoted and discussed by Markschies, *Valentinus Gnosticus?*, 153–85, 54–86, 247–51; see also Leisegang, *Die Gnosis*, 281–97; Brakke, *Gnostics*, 99–102, who stresses immanent elements in Valentinus's theology; Bas., fragm. in Hipp., *Elench.* 7.20ff, quoted and discussed by

Leisegang, *Die Gnosis*, 213–22; Eugn. fragm. in *Nag Hamadi Codex* 3.71.13–73.3, quoted and discussed by van der Broek, *Gnostic Religion*, 151.

24. See Sterling, "Theft of Philosophy"; Köckert, *Christliche Kosmologie*, 84–126.

25. Plut., *The E at Delphi* 191e–394c; see also Dillon, *Middle Platonists*, 189–92.

26. Bréhier, *Les idées*, 89.

27. For Stoic notions of immanent rationality ("Nous") in the creation, see D.L. 7.135–37; for useful overviews of the term "Logos" in Greek literature, see Tobin, "Logos"; Löhr, "Logos." Among scholars who have suggested Stoic influence, see esp. Dillon, *Middle Platonists*, 158–61; Winston, *Logos and Mystical Theology*, 15–20; Wolfson, *Philo*, 1.226–31 (who also identifies Aristotelian echoes); see also Morris, "Jewish Philosopher," 994–95, who points to significant differences between Stoic notions and Philo's concept of the Logos, esp. regarding the question of transcendence.

28. On the right order of Philo's works, see also chaps. 1 and 5 and Appendix 1.

29. Runia, *On the Creation*, 143.

30. The Greek translators added an important dimension to the Hebrew verse, according to which God "rested from all his work which God created to do."

31. The LXX translates the expression "the generations of heaven and earth" (תולדות השמים והארץ) as "the book of the creation of heaven and earth" (ἡ βίβλος γενέσεως οὐρανοῦ καὶ γῆς).

32. Rösel, *Übersetzung*, 59.

33. Thras., fragm. in *Harm.* 12 (quoted by Tarrant, "Logos" 201); Mod., fragm. in Simpl., *In Phys.* 9.230.34–231.21 (quoted by Hubler, "Moderatus" 120).

34. *All.* 3.100, *Mut.* 15, *Conf.* 97, *Migr.* 174, *All.* 1.38.

35. *All.* 1.165, 3.104, 3.169–73.

36. *Fug.* 94; because of a lacuna in the text, the precise role of the legislative powers is not clear; see also Idel, *Absorbing Perfections*, on the interaction between the different powers of God in Philo's theology; Idel, *Enchanted Chains*, on Neoplatonic models of emanation and their significance for Jewish mysticism; Ben Sasson and Halbertal, "Divine Name," on Philo's names for the divine attributes in comparison to those of the rabbis.

37. *Fug.* 101, *Post.* 122, *All.* 2.86.

38. Val., fragm., in Clem., *Strom.* 4.89.6, quoted and discussed by Markschies, *Valentinus Gnosticus?*, 153–57; Bas., fragm. in Ir., *Her.* 1.24.3–7, quoted and discussed by Leisegang, *Die Gnosis*, 245–49; Alb., *Didasc.* 28; see also Tarrant, "Date of the Anon.," 186.

39. See also Runia, "Witness or Participant?," who forcefully argues that one must take into account that Platonic thinkers read Philo, a possibility that is often rejected on the grounds that Philo is not explicitly mentioned and would not have been read in pagan circles because he is Jewish and addresses biblical stories.

Chapter 12. Stoicism: Rejected, Subverted, and Advocated

1. *Aet. 76, Her.* 228, *All.* 3.97.
2. Lévy, "Philo's Ethics," 157; cf. scholars who stress Stoic influence on Philo: Pohlenz, *Die Stoa*, 369–79; Bréhier, *Les idées*, 252–59; Reydams-Schils, "Socratic Higher Ground."
3. See Nikiprowetzky, *Le commentaire*, who has stressed the overarching importance of exegesis in Philo's work, to which all philosophical ideas are in his view subordinated.
4. Plut., *Stoic. rep.* 1034a–e; D.L. 7.92, 7.142, 7.149; on Plutarch's reliability as a critic of Stoicism, see Babut, "Polémique et philosophie."
5. *Her.* 228–29; Plut., *Comm. not.* 31 (= *Mor.* 1074e–75d).
6. *Migr.* 179–82; D.L. 7.148; Pl., *Tim.* 41a; see also Runia, *Philo of Alexandria and the "Timaeus,"* 204, 458–61.
7. *Migr.* 185–90; Pl., *Ion* 536a–d, 533e; *Symp.* 215e; *Crit.* 54d; for Philo's later views, see chap. 5.
8. *All.* 3.139, τις κατ' ἐξαίρετον λόγος μέμνηται, which Colson has translated as "for the passions that come under the head of those in the realm of pleasure are four in number, as has been mentioned in a treatise specially devoted to that subject." While the Hebrew translator Yehoshua Amir rightly understood the reference to an external treatise, he mistakenly identified it with the Torah, which Philo never calls "some treatise." The German and the French translators, Isaac Heinemann and Claude Mondésert, respectively, offer literal yet somewhat general renderings.
9. *Sacr.* 163, *Sobr.* 9, *Dec.* 101, *Spec.* 1.204.
10. D.L. 7.110–16; see also Graver, *Stoicism and Emotion*, 51–55 (with emphasis on Chrysippus's ideas); Lévy, "Philo d'Alexandrie et les passions," 29–32.
11. On the *hegemonikon*, see Graver, *Stoicism and Emotion*, 21–24.
12. D.L. 7.110–11; Stob. 2.88, 8 (= Long and Sedley, *Hellenistic Philosophers*, 2.404, 1.410); Cic., *Tusc.* 3.24–25; Sen., *Ira* 2.1.1–2.3.2; see also Inwood and Donini, "Stoic Ethics," 699–705; Sorabji, *Emotion and Peace of Mind*, 29–54; Krentz, "Πάθη and Ἀπάθεια"; Graver, *Stoicism and Emotion*, 1–51; Weisser, *Éradication ou modération*, 23–34, 319–29.
13. *All.* 2.100, 3.140–4, 3.129–34; see also Weisser, *Éradication or modération?*, 284–97, 319–30.
14. D.L. 7.117; Cic., *Tusc.* 4.37–43, 3.74, 4.57–62; see also Graver, *Cicero on the Emotions*, 160–71; Inwood and Donini, "Stoic Ethics," 684–87; Weisser, *Éradication ou modération*, 41–44; Striker, *Essays*, 183–88.
15. *All.* 3.131; see also Lévy, "Philo's Ethics," 154–61; for different views, see Bréhier, *Les idées*, 252–55; Winston, "Philo of Alexandria," 202–4; Dillon, *Middle Platonists*, 151–53; Dillon, "Pleasures and Perils."
16. Plut., *Virt. mor.* 3, 4, 6, 7, 8, 12 (= *Mor.* 441c–42a, 443c, 445b–c, 447a–c, 448d, 451c); *Coh. Ira* 11, 13 (= *Mor.* 459b–d, 461f); *Tranquil.* 1, 2 (= *Mor.* 465b–c); Sen., *Tranq.* 13.1; on Plutarch's fluency in Latin, see chap. 1; on his ambivalence concerning

the Stoic notion of *apatheia*, see also Babut, "Plutarque et le Stoïcisme," 319–33; Opsomer, "Plutarch and the Stoics," 94–98. Note also Galen, another Platonist of the imperial age, who accuses especially Chrysippus of ignoring the irrational parts of the soul, which are self-evident from a Platonic point of view. According to Galen, Chrysippus's position leads to a self-contradiction because he "does not believe that the soul's passionate part is different from the rational" (Gal., *Plac.* 4.2.1–6, 5.6.34–37 = Long and Sedley, *Hellenistic Philosophers*, 2.406, 2.408–9, 1.411–13).

17. *Dec.* 143, *Opif.* 72–74.

18. D.L. 7.85–87; see also Inwood and Donini, "Stoic Ethics," 678–82; Striker, *Essays*, 281–97 (with a useful comparison to Aristotelian, Platonic, and Epicurean approaches); Pohlenz, *Die Stoa*, 111–18.

19. Cic., *Fin.* 3.16–25; see also Striker, *Essays*, 286–91; cf. Diogenes's definition of the *kathekonta*, according to which reason prompts humans to do their primary duties (D.L. 7.108–10).

20. *All.* 1.56, 3.18, 3.210; *Cher.* 14; *Plant.* 94, 100; *Sacr.* 43, 73; *Post.* 11; *Deus* 72, 100.

21. *All.* 3.126, 2.32, 1.97; *Deus* 135; D.L. 7.53; see also Lévy, "Philo's Ethics," 146–49; Lévy, "Philo et les passions," 32–33.

22. *Post.* 12–20.

23. *Post.* 12, *Cher.* 18, *Gig.* 29, *Plant.* 55; see also *Post.* 140, 157, where Philo uses the terms *oikeiosis* in the context of an affinity between teacher and student; see also Lévy, "Ethique de l'immanence."

24. D.L. 7.101–7; see also Inwood and Donini, "Stoic Ethics," 690–99; Graver, *Stoicism and Emotion*, 48–53; see also Morgan, *Popular Morality*, on the widespread attraction of certain values.

25. *All.* 2.17, *Her.* 253, *Fug.* 152.

26. Cl., *Hymn to Zeus*, ll. 24–29 (ed. Thom, *Cleanthes*, with comments); see also Mohnike, *Kleanthes der Stoiker* (with detailed notes on Cleanthes's life); Liebes, *Mnemosyne*, 105–8; Pohlenz, *Die Stoa*, 117.

27. τὸ γὰρ ἀκολουθίᾳ φύσεως ἰσχῦσαι ζῆν εὐδαιμονίας τέλος εἶπον οἱ πρῶτοι (*Plant.* 49); see also *All.* 3.97, where Philo refers to the "first men," who conceived of God by studying the creation. This, too, is a reference to Stoic philosophy.

28. See also *Sacr.* 42, where Philo explicitly speaks about the divine rewards for virtuous action.

29. *All.* 3.37, 3.47; *Det.* 114; *Post.* 21; *Gig.* 53; *Agr.* 169–73, 180; *Plant.* 93; *Her.* 121; *Cher.* 86; *Conf.* 144–45; *Somn.* 2.142; *Mut.* 216.

30. Plut., *Stoic. Rep* 12 (= *Mor.* 1038b).

Epilogue

1. For details, see Bacher, "Church Father"; and Barthélemy, "Est-ce Hoshaya?," who suggested that Hoshaya may have edited Philo's *Allegorical Commentary* in Caesarea; on Greek and Greek learning in Genesis Rabbah, see Hirshman, "Greek Words," and Hirshman, "Reflections."

Appendix 1

1. There is uncertainty whether this and *On the Life of Moses* belong to the series to which they are customarily assigned.

Appendix 2

1. On the Caesarean edition of Philo's works in Caesarea, see Barthélemy, "Est-ce Hoshaya?"; Royse, "The Text."
2. Cohn, "Einleitung," 392–93; Heinemann, "Allegorische Erklärung," 9.
3. Morris, "Jewish Philosopher," 832.
4. Tobin, "Beginning"; Tobin, "Philo and the Allegorical Reinterpretation"; Sterling, "Prolific in Expression."
5. Heine, "Introduction."
6. Heine, *Origen*, 83–126; Heine, "Origen's Alexandrian *Commentary*."
7. Orig., testimonium C II1, fragm. D 2 (ed. Metzler 50, 62).

Bibliography

Abbreviations

ANRW	*Aufstieg und Niedergang der Römischen Welt*
CQ	*Classical Quarterly*
GRBS	*Greek, Roman, and Byzantine Studies*
HTR	*Harvard Theological Review*
JBL	*Journal of Biblical Literature*
JJS	*Journal for the Study of Judaism*
JRS	*Journal of Roman Studies*
NTS	*New Testament Studies*
SBL	Society of Biblical Literature
SPhA	*Studia Philonica Annual*
VC	*Vigiliae Christianae*

Philo's Works

Cohn, Leopold, and Paul Wendland. *Philonis Alexandrini Opera Quae Supersunt.* Berlin: Typis et Impensis Georgii Reimeri, 1886–1930.

Colson, F. H. *Philo.* Cambridge, MA: Harvard University Press, 1981.

Daniel-Nataf, Suzanne, Yehoshua Amir, and Maren R. Niehoff, eds. *Philo of Alexandria: Writings* [in Hebrew]. Jerusalem: Bialik Institute and Israel Academy of Sciences and Humanities, 1986–.

Terian, Abraham. *Philon d'Alexandrie: Alexander vel de ratione quam habere etiam bruta animalia (e versione armeniaca). Introduction, traduction et notes.* Paris: Cerf, 1988.

———. *Philonis Alexandrini De Animalibus: The Armenian Text with an Introduction, Translation, and Commentary.* Chico, CA: Scholars, 1981.

Cited Literature

Adkins, Lesley, and Roy Adkins. *Handbook to Life in Ancient Rome.* New York: Oxford University Press, 1994.

Afterman, Adam. "From Philo to Plotinus: The Emergence of Mystical Union." *Journal of Religion* 93 (2013): 177–96.

Alesse, Francesca, ed. *Philo of Alexandria and Post-Aristotelian Philosophy*. Leiden: Brill, 2008.

Alexandre, Monique. "Monarchie divine et Dieux des nations chez Philon d'Alexandrie." In Inowlocki and Decharneux, eds., *Philon d'Alexandrie*, 117–47.

Algra, Keimpe, ed. *The Cambridge History of Hellenistic Philosophy*. New York: Cambridge University Press, 1999.

Amir, Yehoshua. "Authority and Interpretation of Scripture in the Writings of Philo." In *Mikra*, ed. M. J. Mulder, 421–54. Minneapolis: Fortress, 1988.

———. "The Decalogue According to the Teachings of Philo of Alexandria" [in Hebrew]. In Segal, ed., *The Ten Commandments*, 95–125.

———. "Philo's Allegory in Relation to Homeric Allegory" [in Hebrew]. *Eshkolot* 6 (1971): 35–45.

Anderson, Charles A. *Philo of Alexandria's Views of the Physical World*. Tübingen: Mohr Siebeck, 2011.

Anderson, Graham. "The Pepaideumenos in Action: Sophists and Their Outlook in the Early Empire." *ANRW* II 36, 1 (1989): 72–208.

André, Jean-Marie, and Marie-Françoise Baslez. *Voyager dans l'antiquité*. Paris: Fayard, 1993.

Annas, Julia, ed. *Oxford Studies in Ancient Philosophy*. Vol. 6. Oxford: Clarendon, 1988.

Arendt, Hannah. *Between Past and Future*. Middlesex: Penguin, 1961.

Arnaldez, Roger. *De Aeternitate Mundi. Introductions et notes*. Paris: Cerf, 1969.

Assmann, Jan. "Monotheism and Polytheism." In *Religions of the Ancient World: A Guide*, ed. S. I. Johnston, 17–31. Cambridge, MA: Harvard University Press, 2004.

Avemarie, Friedrich. "Die Werke des Gesetzes im Spiegel des Jakobusbriefs." *Zeitschrift für Theologie und Kirche* 98 (2001): 282–309.

Babut, Daniel. "Plutarque et le Stoïcisme." PhD diss., Université de Paris, 1969.

———. "Polémique et philosophie dans les deux écrits anti-stoïciens de Plutarque." *Revue des Études Anciennes* 100 (1998): 11–42.

Bacher, Wilhelm. "The Church Father Origen and Rabbi Hoshaya." *Jewish Quarterly Review* 3 (1891): 357–60.

Baer, Richard Arthur. *Philo's Use of the Categories Male and Female*. Leiden: Brill, 1970.

Baldwin, Barry. *Suetonius*. Amsterdam: A. M. Hakkert, 1983.

Balsdon, J. P. V. D. *Roman Women*. London: Bodley Head, 1962.

Baltes, Matthias. *Die Weltentstehung des Platonischen Timaios nach den antiken Interpreten*. Leiden: Brill, 1976.

———. *Timaios Lokros*. Leiden: Brill, 1972.

Barclay, John M. G. *Flavius Josephus: Against Apion, Translation and Commentary*. Leiden: Brill, 2007.

———. *Jews in the Mediterranean Diaspora*. Edinburgh: T&T Clark, 1996.

———. "Paul and Philo on Circumcision: Romans 2:25–9 in the Social and Cultural Context." *NTS* 44 (1998): 536–56.

Barnes, Jonathan. "Antiochus of Ascalon." In Griffin and Barnes, eds., *Philosophia Togata I*, 51–97.

Baroin, Catherine. "Remembering One's Ancestors, Following in Their Footsteps, Being Like Them: The Role and Forms of Family Memory in the Building of Identity." In Dasen and Späth, *Children, Memory*, 19–48.

Barraclough, Ray. "Philo's Politics: Roman Rule and Hellenistic Judaism." *ANRW* XXI 1, 2 (1984): 417–553.

Barrett, Anthony. *Caligula*. New Haven, CT: Yale University Press, 1989.

———. *Livia*. New Haven, CT: Yale University Press, 2002.

Bartels, Felix. "Zur Deutung der Digression des Theaitet (172c–177c)." *Philologus* 159 (2015): 29–72.

Barthélemy, Dominique. "Est-ce Hoshaya Rabba qui censura le Commentaire Allégorique?" In *Philon d'Alexandrie. Lyon 11–15 Septembre 1966: Colloques Nationaux du Centre National de la Recherche Scientifique*. Paris: 1967, 45–78.

Barton, John. *Ethics in Ancient Israel*. Oxford: Oxford University Press, 2014.

Bartsch, Shadi, and David Wray, eds. *Seneca and the Self*. Cambridge: Cambridge University Press, 2009.

Bastianini, Guido, and David N. Sedley. "Commentarium in Platonis 'Theatetum.'" In *Corpus dei Papiri Filosofici Greci e Latini*, 3.227–562. Florence: Olschki, 1995.

Bauer, Walter. *Orthodoxy and Heresy in Earliest Christianity*. Translated by Robert A. Kraft. Philadelphia: Fortress, 1971.

Bauman, Richard A. *Women and Politics in Ancient Rome*. London: Routledge, 1992.

Baumgarten, Albert I. "The Rule of the Martian in the Ancient Diaspora: Celsus and His Jew." In *Jews and Christians in the First and Second Centuries*, ed. Peter J. Tomson and Joshua Schwartz, 398–430. Leiden: Brill, 2014.

Bechtle, Gerard. "La Problématique de l'âme et du cosmos chez Philon et les médio-platoniciens." In Lévy, ed., *Philon d'Alexandrie*, 377–92.

Beck, Mark, ed. *A Companion to Plutarch*. Oxford: Wiley-Blackwell, 2014.

Becker, Eve-Marie. "Die Tränen des Paulus (2 Kor. 2,4; Phil. 3,18)—Emotion oder Topos?" In *Emotions from Ben Sira to Paul*, ed. Renate Egger-Wenzel and Jeremy Corley, 361–77. Berlin: de Gruyter, 2011.

———. "Paulus als Weinender Briefeschreiber (2 Kor. 2,4)." In *Der Zweite Korintherbrief*, ed. Dieter Sänger, 11–26. Göttingen: Vandenhoeck & Ruprecht, 2012.

Belkin, Samuel. *Philo and the Oral Law*. Cambridge, MA: Harvard University Press, 1940.

Ben Sasson, Hillel, and Moshe Halbertal. "The Divine Name YHWH and the Measure of Mercy" [in Hebrew]. In *And This Is for Yehuda*, ed. Maren R. Niehoff, Ronit Meroz, and Jonathan Garb, 53–69. Jerusalem: Mandel Institute for Jewish Studies and Bialik Institute, 2012.

Berthelot, Katell. "Philo and the Kindness towards Animals (*De Virtutibus* 125–147)." *SPhA* 14 (2002): 48–65.

Biale, David. *Eros and the Jews.* New York: HarperCollins, 1992.

Bilde, Per. "The Roman Emperor Gaius's Attempt to Erect His Statue in the Temple of Jerusalem." *Studia Theologica* 32 (1978): 67–93.

Biraschi, Anna Maria. "Strabo and Homer: A Chapter in Cultural History." In *Strabo's Cultural Geography,* ed. Daniela Dueck, Hugh Lindsay, and Sarah Pothecary, 73–85. Cambridge: Cambridge University Press, 2005.

Birnbaum, Ellen. *The Place of Judaism in Philo's Thought.* Atlanta: Scholars Press, 1996.

Blank-Sangmeister, Ursula. *Römische Frauen: Ausgewählte Texte.* Stuttgart: Reclam, 2001.

Bloch, René. "Alexandria in Pharaonic Egypt: Projections in De Vita Mosis." *SPhA* 24 (2012): 69–84.

———. "Leaving Home: Philo of Alexandria on the Exodus." In *Israel's Exodus in Transdisciplinary Perspective,* ed. Thomas Evan Levy, Thomas Schneider, and William H. C. Propp, 357–64. Cham: Springer, 2015.

———. *Moses und der Mythos: die Auseinandersetzung mit der griechischen Mythologie bei den jüdisch-hellenistischen Autoren.* Leiden: Boston, 2011.

Bobzien, Susanne. *Determinism and Freedom in Stoic Philosophy.* Oxford: Oxford University Press, 1998.

Bompaire, Jacques. *Lucien écrivain, imitation et création.* Paris: E. de Boccard, 1958.

Bonazzi, Mauro. "The Commentary as Polemical Tool: The Anonymous Commentator on the Theaetetus against the Stoics." *Laval Théologique et Philosophique* 64 (2008): 597–605.

———. "Continuité et rupture entre l'académie et le Platonisme Études." *Études Platoniciennes* 3 (2006): 231–44.

———. "Eudorus of Alexandria and Early Imperial Platonism." In *Greek and Roman Philosophy 100BC–200AD,* ed. Robert W. Sharples and Richard Sorabji, 365–77. London: Institute of Classical Studies, 2007.

———. "Le commentaire anonyme du *Théétète* et l'invention du Platonisme." In *La mesure du savoir,* ed. Dimitri El Murr, 309–33. Paris: J. Vrin, 2013.

———. "Theoria and Praxis." In *Theoria, Praxis and the Contemplative Life after Plato and Aristotle,* ed. T. Bénatouil and Mauro Bonazzi, 139–61. Leiden: Brill, 2012.

———. "Towards Transcendence: Philo and the Revival of Platonism in the Early Imperial Age." In Alesse, ed., *Philo,* 233–51.

Bowersock, Glen. *Augustus and the Greek World.* Oxford: Clarendon, 1965.

———. "Foreign Elites." In *Flavius Josephus and Flavian Rome,* ed. Jonathan Edmondson, Steve Mason, and James Rives, 53–62. Oxford: Oxford University Press, 2005.

———. *Greek Sophists in the Roman Empire.* Oxford: Oxford University Press, 1969.

Bowie, Ewen L. "Greeks and Their Past in the Second Sophistic." *Past and Present* 46 (1970): 3–41.

———. "Hellenes and Hellenism in Writers of the Early Second Sophistic." In *Hellēnismos,* ed. Suzanne Saïd, 183–204. Leiden: Brill, 1991.

———. "Philostratus: The Life of a Sophist." In Bowie and Elsner, eds., *Philostratus,* 19–32.

Bowie, Ewen L., and Jaś Elsner, eds. *Philostratus.* Cambridge: Cambridge University Press, 2009.

Boyancé, Pierre. "Études Philoniennes." *Revue des Études Grecques* 76 (1963): 64–110.

Boyarin, Daniel. *Carnal Israel: Reading Sex in Talmudic Culture.* Berkeley: University of California Press, 1993.

———. *Paul: A Radical Jew.* Berkeley: University of California Press, 1997.

———. *Socrates and the Fat Rabbis.* Chicago: University of Chicago Press, 2009.

———. "A Tale of Two Synods: Nicaea, Yavneh and the Making of Orthodox Judaism." *Exemplaria* 12 (2000): 21–62.

Boys-Stones, G. R., ed. *Metaphor, Allegory and the Classical Tradition: Ancient Thought and Modern Revisions.* Oxford: Oxford University Press, 2009.

———. *Post-Hellenistic Philosophy: A Study of Its Development from the Stoics to Origen.* Oxford: Oxford University Press, 2001.

Bradley, Keith R. "Wet-Nursing at Rome: A Study in Social Relations." In *The Family in Ancient Rome: New Perspectives,* ed. Beryl Rawson, 201–29. New York: Cornell University Press, 1992.

Brakke, David. *The Gnostics: Myth, Ritual, and Diversity in Early Christianity.* Cambridge, MA: Harvard University Press, 2010.

Branham, Bracht R. *Unruly Eloquence: Lucian and the Comedy of Traditions.* Cambridge, MA: Harvard University Press, 1989.

Braund, Susanna Morton. *Seneca, De Clementia: Edited with Translation and Commentary.* Oxford: Oxford University Press, 2009.

Bréhier, Émile. *Les idées philosophiques et religieuses de Philon d'Alexandrie.* Paris: J. Vrin, 1950.

Brisson, Luic. *How Philosophers Saved Myths.* Chicago: University of Chicago Press, 2004.

Buffière, Félix. *Les mythes d'Homère et la pensée Grecque.* Paris: Belles Lettres, 1956.

Burkert, Walter. *Greek Religion.* Cambridge, MA: Harvard University Press, 1985.

Burns, Jasper. *Great Women of Imperial Rome: Mothers and Wives of the Caesars.* London: Routledge, 2007.

Burr, Viktor. *Tiberius Iulius Alexander.* Bonn: R. Habelt, 1955.

Burridge, A. "Reading Gospels as Biographies." In *The Limits of Ancient Biography,* ed. Brian McGing and Judith Mossman, 31–50. Swansea: Classical Press of Wales, 2006.

———. *What Are the Gospels? A Comparison with Graeco-Roman Biography.* Cambridge: Cambridge University Press, 1992.

Calabi, Francesca. "Conoscibilità e inconoscibilità di Dio in Filone di Alessandria." In *Arrhetos Theos*, ed. Francesca Calabi, 35–54. Pisa: Edizione ETS, 2003.

———. *Filone di Alessandria*. Rome: Carocci Editore, 2013.

———. *Filone di Alessandria: De Decalogo*. Pisa: ETS, 2005.

———. *God's Acting, Man's Acting*. Leiden: Brill, 2008.

———. "Il Deserto in Filone di Allessandria." *Adamantius* 14 (2008): 6–23.

———. "Le Migrazioni di Abramo in Filone di Alessandria." *Ricerche Storico Bibliche* 11 (2014): 251–67.

———. "Theatrical Language in Philo's *In Flaccum*." In *Italian Studies on Philo of Alexandria*, ed. Francesca Calabi, 91–116. Boston: Brill, 2003.

Cancik, Hubert. "Das Mittelmeer im lukanischen Geschichtswerk." In Faber and Lichtenberger, eds., *Ein pluriverses Universum*, 131–52.

———. "Historisierung von Religion—Religionsgeschichtsschreibung in der Antike." In *Historicization—Historisierung*, ed. Glenn W. Most, 1–13. Göttingen: Vandenhoeck & Ruprecht, 2001.

Casson, Lionel. *Travel in the Ancient World*. London: Allen and Unwin, 1974.

Catellani, Victor. "Plutarch's 'Roman' Women." In *Greek Romans and Roman Greeks*, ed. Erik N. Ostenfeld, 142–55. Aarhus: Aarhus University Press, 2002.

Chapman, Honora Howell, and Zuleika Rodgers, eds. *A Companion to Josephus in His World*. Oxford: Wiley-Blackwell, 2016.

Claassen, Jo-Marie. *Displaced Persons*. London: Duckworth, 1999.

Clark, Gillian. *Christianity and Roman Society*. Cambridge: Cambridge University Press, 2004.

Clauss, Manfred. *Alexandria*. Stuttgart: Klett-Cotta, 2003.

Clay, Diskin. "Plato and Homer." In Finkelberg, ed., *Homer Encyclopedia*, 2:672–75.

Cohen, Naomi. *Philo Judaeus*. Frankfurt: Peter Lang, 1995.

Cohen, Shaye J. D. *The Beginnings of Jewishness*. Berkeley: University of California Press, 1999.

———. *From the Maccabees to the Mishnah*. Philadelphia: Westminster, 1987.

———. "Josephus." In *The Jewish Annotated New Testament*, ed. Amy-Jill Levine and Marc Zvi Brettler, 575–77. Oxford: Oxford University Press, 2011.

———. *Josephus in Galilee and Rome*. Leiden: Brill, 1979.

Cohn, Leopold. "Einleitung und Chronologie der Schriften Philos." *Philologus Supplementband* 7 (1899): 385–436.

Coleman, K. M. "Fatal Charades: Roman Executions as Mythological Enactments." *JRS* 80 (1990): 44–73.

Collins, John J. "Apologetic Literature." In Collins and Harlow, eds., *Eerdmans Dictionary*, 352–54.

———. *Between Athens and Jerusalem: Jewish Identity in the Hellenistic Diaspora*. 2nd ed. Grand Rapids, MI: Eerdmans, 2000.

———. "Natural Theology and Biblical Tradition: The Case of Hellenistic Judaism." *Catholic Biblical Quarterly* 60 (1998): 1–15.

Collins, John J., and Daniel C. Harlow, eds. *The Eerdmans Dictionary of Early Judaism*. Grand Rapids, MI: Eerdmans, 2010.

Cornford, Francis Macdonald. *Plato's Cosmology*. London: K. Paul, Trench, Trubner, 1937.

Cover, Michael. "Colonial Narratives and Philo's Roman Accuser in the Hypothetica." *SPhA* 22 (2010): 183–207.

———. *Lifting the Veil*. Berlin: de Gruyter, 2015.

Crouzel, Henri. *Origen*. Edinburgh: T&T Clark, 1989.

D'Angelo, Mary Rose. "Eusebeia: Roman Imperial Family Values and the Sexual Politics of 4 Maccabees and the Pastorals." *Biblical Interpretation* 11 (2003): 139–65.

———. "Gender and Geopolitics in the Work of Philo of Alexandria: Jewish Piety and Imperial Family Values." In *Mapping Gender in Ancient Religious Discourse*, ed. Todd Penner and Caroline Von Stichele, 63–88. Leiden: Brill, 2006.

———. "(Re)Presentations of Women in the Gospels of Matthew and Luke-Acts." In *Women and Christian Origins*, ed. Ross Shepard Kraemer and Mary Rose D'Angelo, 171–98. New York: Oxford University Press, 1999.

———. "Roman Imperial Family Values and the Gospel of Mark: The Divorce Sayings (Mark 10:2–12)." In *Women and Gender in Ancient Religions*, ed. Stephen P. Ahearne-Kroll, Paul A. Holloway, and James A. Kelhoffer, 57–81. Tübingen: Mohr Siebeck, 2010.

———. "Women in Luke-Acts: A Redactional View." *JBL* 109 (1990): 441–61.

Daniélou, Jean. *Origène*. Paris: La Table Ronde, 1948.

D'Arms, John. "The Roman Convivium and the Idea of Equality." In *Sympotica*, ed. Oswyn Murray, 308–20. Oxford: Oxford University Press, 1990.

Dasen, Véronique, and Thomas Späth, eds. *Children, Memory, and Family Identity in Roman Culture*. Oxford: Oxford University Press, 2010.

Deming, Will. "Paul, Gaius, and the 'Law of Persons': The Conceptualization of Roman Law in the Early Classical Period." *CQ* 51 (2001): 218–30.

De Rosalia, A. "Il latino de Plutarco." In *Strutture formali dei "Moralia" di Plutarco*, ed. Gennaro D'Ippolito and Italo Gallo, 445–59. Naples: M. d'Auria Editore, 1991.

Dickey, Eleanor. *Ancient Greek Scholarship*. Oxford: Oxford University Press, 2007.

Diels, Hermann, and Wilhelm Schubart. *Anonymer Kommentar zu Platons Theaetet*. Berlin: Weidmann, 1905.

Dillon, John M. *The Middle Platonists: A Study of Platonism, 80 B.C. to A.D. 220*. London: Duckworth, 1977.

———. "The Nature of God in the 'Quod Deus.'" In Winston and Dillon, eds., *Two Treatises*, 217–27.

———. "Philo and Hellenistic Platonism." In Alesse, ed., *Philo*, 223–32.

———. "The Pleasures and Perils of Soul-Gardening." *SPhA* 9 (1997): 190–97.

———. "Tampering with the *Timaeus*: Ideological Emendations in Plato with Special Reference to the *Timaeus*." *American Journal of Philology* 110 (1989): 50–70.

Dixon, Suzanne. *The Roman Family*. Baltimore: Johns Hopkins University Press, 1992.

———. *The Roman Mother*. London: Routledge, 1988.

———. "The Sentimental Ideal of the Roman Family." In Rawson, ed., *Marriage*, 99–113.

Doblhofer, Ernst. *Exil und Emigration*. Darmstadt: Wissenschaftliche Buchgesellschaft, 1987.

Doering, Lutz. *Ancient Jewish Letters and the Beginnings of Christian Epistolography*. Tübingen: Mohr Siebeck, 2012.

———. *Schabbat: Sabbathalacha und -praxis im antiken Judentum und Urchristentum*. Tübingen: Mohr Siebeck, 1999.

Dörrie, Heinrich. "Der Platoniker Eudorus von Alexandria." *Hermes* 79 (1944): 25–39.

———. "Die Erneuerung des Platonismus im 1. Jahrh. vor Christus." In Heinrich Dörrie, *Platonica Minora*, 137–53. Munich: W. Fink, 1976.

Downie, Janet. *At the Limits of Art: A Literary Analysis of Aelius Aristideas' Hieroi Logoi*. Oxford: Oxford University Press, 2013.

Duff, Tim. *Plutarch's Lives: Exploring Virtue and Vice*. Oxford: Clarendon, 1999.

Eden, P. T., ed. *Apocolocyntosis*. Cambridge: Cambridge University Press, 1984.

Edwards, Catherine. "Beware of Imitations: Theatre and the Subversion of Imperial Identity." In Elsner and Masters, eds., *Reflections of Nero*, 83–97.

———. *Death in Ancient Rome*. New Haven, CT: Yale University Press, 2007.

———. "Free Yourself! Slavery, Freedom and the Self in Seneca's Letters." In Bartsch and Wray, eds., *Seneca and the Self*, 139–59.

———. "Self-Scrutiny and Self-Transformation in Seneca's Letters." *Greece and Rome* 44 (1997): 23–38.

Egelhaaf-Gaiser, Ulrike. "Täglich lade ich alle meine Nachbarn zu einem Mahl: Cicero und das convivium im spätrepublikanischen Rom." In *Der eine Gott und das gemeinschaftliche Mahl*, 76–97, ed. Wolfgang Weiss. Neukirchen-Vluyn: Neukirchener Verlag, 2011.

Ehrman, Bart D. *Lost Christianities*. New York: Oxford University Press, 2003.

———. *The New Testament: A Historical Introduction to the Early Christian Writings*. New York: Oxford University Press, 2000.

Elsner, Jaś. "A Protean Corpus." In Bowie and Elsner, eds., *Philostratus*, 3–18.

Elsner, Jaś, and Jamie Masters, eds., *Reflections of Nero: Culture, History, and Representation*. Chapel Hill: University of North Carolina Press, 1994.

Elsner, Jaś, and Ian Rutherford. "Introduction." In Elsner and Rutherford, eds., *Pilgrimage*, 1–37.

———, eds. *Pilgrimage in Greco-Roman and Early Christian Antiquity: Seeing the God*. Oxford: Oxford University Press, 2005.

Erbse, Hartmut. *Scholia Graeca in Homeri Iliadem (Scholia Vetera)*. Berlin: de Gruyter, 1969.

Eshleman, Kendra. "Eastern Travel in Apollonius and the Apocryphal Acts of Thomas." In Niehoff, ed., *Journeys in the Roman East*.

————. *The Social World of Intellectuals in the Roman Empire: Sophists, Philosophers, and Christians.* Cambridge: Cambridge University Press, 2012.

Evans Grubbs, Judith. "Hidden in Plain Sight: Expositi in the Community." In Dasen and Späth, eds., *Children, Memory,* 293–310.

Faber, Richard, and Achim Lichtenberger, eds. *Ein pluriverses Universum: Zivilisationen und Religionen im antiken Mittelmeerraum.* Paderborn: Ferdinand Schöningh, 2015.

Fantham, Elaine. *Roman Literary Culture: From Cicero to Apuleius.* Baltimore: Johns Hopkins University Press, 1996.

Fears, J. R. "The Stoic View of the Career and Character of Alexander the Great." *Philologus* 118 (1974): 113–30.

Feichtinger, Barbara. "Soziologisches und Sozialgeschichtliches zu Erotik, Liebe und Geschlechterverkehr." In *Plutarch: Dialog über die Liebe,* ed. Herwig Görgemanns, 261–66. Tübingen: Mohr Siebeck, 2006.

Feldman, Louis H. "Hellenizations in Josephus' Version of Esther." *Transactions of the American Philological Association* 101 (1970): 143–70.

————. *Josephus's Interpretation of the Bible.* Berkeley: University of California Press, 1998.

————. *Philo's Portrayal of Moses in the Context of Ancient Judaism.* Notre Dame, IN: University of Notre Dame Press, 2007.

Feldmeier, Reinhard. "Der Mensch als Wesen der Öffentlichkeit." In Berner et al., eds., *Plutarch,* 79–95.

————. "Gotteserkenntnis durch Selbsterkenntnis. Philos *Migratio* in ihrem religionsgeschichtlichen Kontext." In Maren R. Niehoff and Reinhard Feldmeier, eds., *Abrahams Aufbruch. Philo: De Migratio Abrahami.* Tübingen: Mohr Siebeck, 2017.

Finkelberg, Margalit. "Canonising and Decanonising Homer: Reception of the Homeric Poems in Antiquity and Modernity." In Niehoff, ed., *Homer and the Bible,* 15–28.

————. *Homer* [in Hebrew]. Tel Aviv: Tel Aviv University Press, 2014.

————, ed. *The Homer Encyclopedia.* 3 vols. Oxford: Wiley-Blackwell, 2011.

Fitzgerald, John T., ed. *Passions and Moral Progress in Greco-Roman Thought.* London: Routledge, 2008.

Flusser, David. "The Ten Commandments and the New Testament." In Segal, ed., *The Ten Commandments,* 165–86.

Forschner, Maximilian. "Theorie der Freiheit im Verhältnis zur klassischen stoischen Lehre." In *Epiktet: Was ist wahre Freiheit?: Diatribe IV 1,* ed. Samuel Vollenweider, Manuel Baumbach, Eva Ebel, Maximilian Forschner, and Thomas Schmeller, 97–118. Tübingen: Mohr Siebeck, 2013.

Foucault, Michel. *The Care of the Self.* Vol. 3, *The History of Sexuality.* Translated by R. Hurley. New York: Random House, 2004.

Fraade, Steven. "Rabbinic Midrash and Ancient Jewish Biblical Interpretation." In *The Cambridge Companion to the Talmud and Rabbinic Literature,* ed. Charlotte E.

Fonrobert and Martin S. Jaffee, 99–120. Cambridge: Cambridge University Press, 2007.

———. "Rewritten Bible and Rabbinic Midrash as Commentary." In *Current Trends in the Study of Midrash*, ed. Carol Bakhos, 59–78. Leiden: Brill, 2006.

Fraser, Peter. *Ptolemaic Alexandria.* Oxford: Clarendon, 1972.

Frede, Dorothea. "Theodicy and Providential Care in Stoicism." In *Traditions of Theology*, ed. Dorothea Frede and André Laks. Leiden: Brill, 2002.

Frede, Michael. "The Case for Pagan Monotheism in Greek and Greco-Roman Antiquity." In Mitchell and Van Nuffelen, eds., *One God,* 53–81.

———. "Stoic Epistemology." In Algra, ed., *Cambridge History,* 296–312.

Froidefond, Christian. "Plutarque et le Platonisme." *ANRW* II 36, 1 (1987): 184–233.

Fuks, Alexander. "Marcus Julius Alexander [in Hebrew]." *Zion* 13–14 (1948): 10–17.

Fürst, Alfons. "Bibel und Kosmos in der Psalmenüberlieferung des Origines." *Adamantius* 20 (2014): 130–46

———. "Origenes." In *Reallexikon für Antike und Christentum*, ed. Theodor Klauser et al., vol. 26, 460–567. Stuttgart: Hiersemann, 2014.

Furstenberg, Yair. "The Agon with Moses and Homer: Rabbinic Midrash and the Second Sophistic." In Niehoff, ed., *Homer and the Bible,* 299–328.

———. "Every Good Man Is Free: Hebrew Translation with Introduction and Notes." In Niehoff, ed., *Philo of Alexandria* [in Hebrew]. 5:319–404.

Galli, Marco. "Educated Pilgrims during the Second Sophistic." In Elsner and Rutherford, eds., *Pilgrimage,* 253–90.

Geiger, Joseph. *Cornelius Nepos and Ancient Political Biography.* Wiesbaden: Steiner, 1985.

Geljon, Albert C., and David T. Runia. *Philo of Alexandria. On Cultivation: Introduction, Translation, and Commentary.* Leiden: Brill, 2013.

Georges, Tobias, Felix Albrecht, and Reinhard Feldmeier, eds. *Alexandria.* Tübingen: Mohr Siebeck, 2013.

Gill, Christopher. "Personhood and Personality: The Four-Personae Theory in Cicero, 'de Officiis I.'" In *Oxford Studies in Ancient Philosophy*, ed. Julia Annas, 6:169–99. Oxford: Clarendon, 1988.

———. *The Structured Self in Hellenistic and Roman Thought.* Oxford: Oxford University Press, 2006.

Gleason, Maud W. *Making Men: Sophists and Self-Representation in Ancient Rome.* Princeton, NJ: Princeton University Press, 1995.

Glucker, John. *Antiochus and the Late Academy.* Göttingen: Vandenhoeck & Ruprecht, 1978.

Goldhill, Simon, ed. *Being Greek under Rome: Cultural Identity, the Second Sophistic and the Development of Empire.* Cambridge: Cambridge University Press, 2001.

———, ed. *The End of Dialogue in Antiquity.* Cambridge: Cambridge University Press, 2008.

———. "What Is Local Identity?" In Whitmarsh, ed., *Local Knowledge,* 46–68.

———. *Who Needs Greek?* New York: Cambridge University Press, 2002.

Goldin, Judah. *Studies in Midrash and Related Literature.* Philadelphia: Jewish Publication Society, 1988.

Goodenough, Erwin R. *By Light, Light.* New Haven, CT: Yale University Press, 1935.

———. *An Introduction to Philo Judaeus.* New Haven, CT: Yale University Press, 1940.

———. *The Jurisprudence of the Jewish Courts in Egypt.* New Haven, CT: Yale University Press, 1929.

———. "Philo's Exposition of the Law and His De Vita Mosis." *HTR* 26 (1933): 109–25.

———. *The Politics of Philo Judaeus.* New Haven, CT: Yale University Press, 1938.

———. *The Theology of Justin Martyr.* Jena: Frommansche Buchhandlung, 1923.

Goodman, Martin. "Josephus as Roman Citizen." In *Josephus and the History of the Greco-Roman Period,* ed. Fausto Parente and Joseph Sievers, 329–38. Leiden: Brill, 1994.

———. "Philo as Philosopher in Rome." In Inowlocki and Decharneux, eds., *Philon d'Alexandrie,* 37–45.

———. "The Pilgrimage Economy of Jerusalem in the Second Temple Period." In *Jerusalem: Its Sanctity and Centrality to Judaism, Christianity, and Islam,* ed. Lee I. Levine, 69–76. New York: Continuum, 1999.

———. "The Roman Identity of Roman Jews." In *The Jews in the Hellenistic-Roman World,* ed. Isaiah Gafni, A. Oppenheimer, and D. Schwartz, 85–99. Jerusalem: Zalman Shazar Center, 1996.

———. *Rome and Jerusalem.* New York: Alfred A. Knopf, 2007.

Graver, Margaret. *Cicero on the Emotions: Tusculan Disputations 3 and 4.* Chicago: University of Chicago Press, 2002.

———. *Stoicism and Emotion.* Chicago: University of Chicago Press, 2007.

Greenblatt, Stephen. *Renaissance Self-Fashioning.* Chicago: University of Chicago Press, 1980.

Griffin, Miriam T. "Imago Vitae Suae." In *Seneca,* ed. John G. Fitch, 41–61. Oxford: Oxford University Press, 2008.

———. "Philosophy, Politics, and Politicians in Rome." In Griffin and Barnes, eds., *Philosophia Togata,* 1–37.

———. *Seneca: A Philosopher in Politics.* Oxford: Clarendon, 1976.

———. *Seneca on Society: A Guide to De Beneficiis.* Oxford: Oxford University Press, 2013.

Griffin, Miriam T., and Jonathan Barnes, eds. *Philosophia Togata I: Essays on Philosophy and Roman Society.* Oxford: Clarendon, 1989.

Grimal, Pierre. *Love in Ancient Rome.* Norman: University of Oklahoma Press, 1980.

———. *Sénèque ou la conscience de l'empire.* Paris: Fayard, 1991.

Gruen, Erich S. "Caligula, the Imperial Cult, and Philo's *Legatio*." *SPhA* 24 (2012): 135–47.

———. *Diaspora*. Cambridge, MA: Harvard University Press, 2002.

———. *Heritage and Hellenism*. Berkeley: University of California Press, 1998.

———. *Rethinking the Other in Antiquity*. Princeton, NJ: Princeton University Press, 2011.

Guthrie, W. K. C. *A History of Greek Philosophy*. 5 vols. Cambridge: Cambridge University Press, 1962.

Gutman, Yehoshua. *The Beginnings of Jewish-Hellenistic Literature* [in Hebrew]. 2 vols. Jerusalem: Bialik Institute, 1963.

Haaland, Gunnar. "Jewish Laws for a Roman Audience: Toward an Understanding of Contra Apionem." In *Internationales Josephus-Kolloquium, Brussel*, ed. Folker Siegert and Jürgen U. Kalms, 282–304. Münster: Lit Verlag, 1999.

Haber, Susan. "Going Up to Jerusalem: Pilgrimage, Purity and the Historical Jesus." In Harland, ed., *Travel and Religion*, 49–67.

Hackforth, Reginald. "Plato's Cosmogony (Timaeus 27dff)." *CQ* 9 (1959): 17–22.

Hadas-Lebel, Mireille. *Flavius Josephus*. New York: Macmillan, 1993.

———. *Philo of Alexandria: A Thinker in the Jewish Diaspora*. Translated by Robyn Fréchet. Boston: Brill, 2012.

Hägg, Tomas. *The Art of Biography in Antiquity*. New York: Cambridge University Press, 2012.

Halbertal, Moshe. *Interpretative Revolutions in the Making* [in Hebrew]. Jerusalem: Magnes, 1997.

Harker, Andrew. *Loyalty and Dissidence in Roman Egypt*. New York: Cambridge University Press, 2008.

Harl, Marguerite. *La Génèse: la Bible d'Alexandrie*. Paris: Cerf, 1986.

Harland, Philip A., ed. *Travel and Religion in Antiquity*. Waterloo, Canada: Wilfrid Laurier University Press, 2011.

Harrill, Albert J. "Paul and Empire: Studying Roman Identity after the Cultural Turn." *Early Christianity* 2 (2011): 281–311.

———. *Paul the Apostle*. Cambridge: Cambridge University Press, 2012.

Harrington, D. J. "The Reception of Walter Bauer's Orthodoxy and Heresy in Earliest Christianity during the Last Decade." *HTR* 73 (1980): 289–98.

Harris, W. V. "Child Exposure in the Roman Empire." *JRS* 84 (1994): 1–22.

Hay, David M., ed. *Both Literal and Allegorical*. Atlanta: Scholars Press, 1991.

———. "Philo's View of Himself as an Exegete: Inspired But Not Authoritative." *SPhA* 3 (1991): 40–52.

———. "References to Other Exegetes." In Hay, ed., *Both Literal and Allegorical*, 81–97.

Hayes, Christine. *What's Divine about Divine Law?* Princeton, NJ: Princeton University Press, 2015.

Heine, Ronald E. "The Introduction to Origen's *Commentary on John* Compared with the Introductions to the Ancient Philosophical Commentaries on Aristotle." In *Origeniana Sexta: Origen and the Bible*, ed. Gil Dorival and Allan Le Boulluec, 3–12. Leuven: Peeters, 1995.

————-. "Origen's Alexandrian *Commentary on Genesis*." In *Origeniana Octava: Origen and the Alexandrian Tradition*, ed. Lorrenzo Perrone, 63–73. Leuven: Peeters, 2003.

————-. *Origen: Scholarship in the Service of the Church*. Oxford: Oxford University Press, 2010.

————-. "Restringing Origen's Broken Harp: Some Suggestions concerning the Prologue to the Caesarean Commentary on Psalms." In *Harp of the Spirit*, ed. B. E. Daley. Notre Dame: Notre Dame University Press, forthcoming.

Heinemann, Isaak. "Allegorische Erklärung des heilligen Gesetzbuches, Buch I–III." In *Die Werke Philos von Alexandria. In Deutscher Übersetzung*, vol. 3, ed. Leopold Cohn. Breslau: M&H Marcus, 1919.

————-. *Philons griechische und jüdische Bildung*. Breslau: M&H Marcus, 1932.

Helleman, W. E. "Philo of Alexandria on Deification and Assimilation to God." *SPhA* 2 (1990): 51–71.

Hengel, Martin. *Acts and the History of Earliest Christianity*. London: SCM, 1979.

Hezser, Catherine. *Jewish Travel in Antiquity*. Tübingen: Mohr Siebeck, 2011.

Hirsch-Luipold, Rainer. "Der eine Gott bei Philon von Alexandrien und Plutarch." In *Gott und die Götter bei Plutarch*, ed. Rainer Hirsch-Luipold, 141–68. Berlin: de Gruyter, 2005.

Hirshman, Marc. "The Greek Words in the Midrash Genesis Rabbah [in Hebrew]." In *Tiferet leYisrael. Festschrift for Israel Francus*, ed. Joel Roth, Menahem Schmelzer, and Yaacob Francus, 21–34. New York: Jewish Theological Seminary, 2010.

————. "Reflections on the Aggada of Caesarea." In *Caesarea Maritima: A Retrospective after Two Millennia*, ed. Avner Raban and Kenneth G. Holum, 469–75. Leiden: Brill, 1996.

Holladay, Carl R., ed. *Fragments from Hellenistic Jewish Authors*. 4 vols. Chico, CA: Scholars Press, 1983.

Hollander, William den. *Josephus, the Emperors, and the City of Rome*. Leiden: Brill, 2014.

Horsley, Richard A. "The Law of Nature in Philo and Cicero." *HTR* 71 (1978): 35–59.

Hubler, Noel J. "Moderatus, E. R. Dodds, and the Development of Neoplatonist Emanation." In Turner and Corrigan, eds., *Plato's Parmenides*, 115–30.

Hurley, Donna W. *Suetonius: Divus Clavdius*. New York: Cambridge University Press, 2001.

Idel, Moshe. *Absorbing Perfections: Kabbalah and Interpretation.* New Haven, CT: Yale University Press, 2002.

———. *Enchanted Chains.* Los Angeles: Cherub, 2005.

———. *Kabbalah: New Perspectives.* New Haven, CT: Yale University Press, 1988.

Inowlocki, Sabrina. "Relectures apologétiques de Philon par Eusèbe de Césarée: les exemples d'Enoch et des Thérapeutes." In Inowlocki and Decharneux, eds., *Philon d'Alexandrie,* 373–91.

Inowlocki, Sabrina, and Baudouin Decharneux, eds. *Philon d'Alexandrie.* Turnhout: Brepols, 2011.

Inwood, Brad. *Reading Seneca: Stoic Philosophy at Rome.* Oxford: Clarendon, 2005.

Inwood, Brad, and Perluigi Donini. "Stoic Ethics." In Algra, ed., *Cambridge History,* 675–738.

Isaac, Benjamin. *The Invention of Racism in Classical Antiquity.* Princeton, NJ: Princeton University Press, 2004.

Jacobson, Alex. "The Attitude of Roman Emperors to Their Predecessors" [in Hebrew]. Master's thesis, Hebrew University, 1989.

Jenott, Lance, and Sarit Kattan Gribetz, eds. *Jewish and Christian Cosmogony in Late Antiquity.* Tübingen: Mohr Siebeck, 2013.

Jeremias, Joachim. *Jerusalem in the Time of Jesus: An Investigation into Economic and Social Conditions during the New Testament Period.* Philadelphia: Fortress, 1969.

Jones, Christopher P. *Culture and Society in Lucian.* Cambridge, MA: Harvard University Press, 1986.

———. *Plutarch and Rome.* Oxford: Clarendon, 1971.

Jördens, Andrea. "Judentum und Karriere im antiken Judentum." In *Quaerite faciem eius semper. Dankesgabe für Albrecht Dihle zum 85. Geburtstag aus dem Heidelberger Kirchenväterkolloquium,* ed. Hans A. Gärtner, Herwig Görgemanns, and Adolf Martin Ritter, 116–33. Hamburg: Kovač, 2008.

Kahn, Charles H. *Plato and the Post-Socratic Dialogue.* Cambridge: Cambridge University Press, 2013.

Kaiser, Otto. *Philo von Alexandrien: Denkender Glaube, eine Einführung.* Göttingen: Vandenhoeck & Ruprecht, 2015.

———. *Studien zu Philon von Alexandrien.* Berlin: de Gruyter, 2017.

Kamesar, Adam, ed. *The Cambridge Companion to Philo.* Cambridge: Cambridge University Press, 2009.

———. "The Logos Endiathetos and the Logos Prophorikos in Allegorical Interpretation: Philo and the D-Scholia to the Iliad." *GRBS* 44 (2004): 163–81.

———. "Philo and the Literary Quality of the Bible: A Theoretical Aspect of the Problem." *JJS* 46 (1995): 55–68.

———. "Philo, Grammatike, and the Narrative Aggada." In *Pursuing the Text,* ed. John C. Reeves and John Kampen, 216–42. Sheffield: Sheffield Academic Press, 1994.

Karamanolis, George E. *Plato and Aristotle in Agreement?* Oxford: Clarendon, 2006.

Karshon, Nurit. "Philo: On the Eternity of World." In Niehoff, ed., *Philo of Alexandria* [in Hebrew], 405–63.

Katz, Peter. *Philo's Bible.* Cambridge: Cambridge University Press, 1950.

Kidd, Ian G. "Moral Actions and Rules in Stoic Ethics." In *The Stoics,* ed. John M. Rist, 247–58. Berkeley: University of California Press, 1978.

Kim, Lawrence. *Homer between History and Fiction in Imperial Greek Literature.* Cambridge: Cambridge University Press, 2010.

———. "The Literary Heritage as Language: Atticism and the Second Sophistic." In *Homer between History and Fiction in Imperial Greek Literature,* ed. Egbert J. Bakker, 458–82. Chichester: Wiley-Blackwell, 2010.

King, Karen L. *What Is Gnosticism?* Cambridge, MA: Belknap, 2003.

———. "Willing to Die for God: Individualization and Instrumental Agency in Ancient Christian Martyr Literature." In Rüpke, ed., *The Individual,* 342–84.

Kloppenborg, John. "Diaspora Discourse: The Construction of Ethos in James." *NTS* 53 (2007): 242–70.

Knohl, Israel. *Biblical Beliefs* [in Hebrew]. Jerusalem: Hebrew University Magnes Press, 2007.

———. *The Divine Symphony.* Philadelphia: Jewish Publication Society, 2003.

Köckert, Charlotte. *Christliche Kosmologie und kaiserzeitliche Philosophie.* Tübingen: Mohr Siebeck, 2009.

Koester, Helmut. *Ancient Christian Gospels.* London: SCM, 1990.

König, Jason. *Saints and Symposiasts.* Cambridge: Cambridge University Press, 2012.

Kovelman, Arkady. *Between Alexandria and Jerusalem.* Leiden: Brill, 2005.

Kraemer, Ross Shepard, and Mary Rose D'Angelo, eds. *Women and Christian Origins.* New York: Oxford University Press, 1999.

Krentz, Edgar M. "Πάθη and Ἀπάθεια in Early Roman Empire Stoicism." In Fitzgerald, ed., *Passions,* 122–35.

Kushnir-Stein, Alla. "On the Visit of Agrippa I to Alexandria in AD 38." *JJS* 51 (2000): 227–42.

Lamberton, Robert, and John J. Keaney, eds. *Homer's Ancient Readers.* Princeton, NJ: Princeton University Press, 1992.

Lampe, Peter. *Die stadtrömischen Christen der ersten beiden Jahrhunderte.* Tübingen: Mohr Siebeck, 1989. Translated by Michael Steinhauser as *From Paul to Valentinus: Christians at Rome in the First Two Centuries* (Minneapolis: Fortress, 2003).

Lanfranchi, Perluigi. *L'exagoge d'Ezéchiel le tragique.* Leiden: Brill, 2006.

Lattimore, Richmond. *Themes in Greek and Latin Epitaphs.* Urbana: University of Illinois Press, 1942.

Laurand, Valéry. *Stoïcisme et lien social: enquête autour de Musonius Rufus.* Paris: Classiques Garnier, 2014.

Lefkowitz, Mary R., and Maureen B. Fant. *Women's Life in Greece and Rome: A Source Book in Translation.* Baltimore: Johns Hopkins University Press, 1992.

Leisegang, Hans. *Die Gnosis.* Stuttgart: Alfred Kröner Verlag, 1985.

———. "Philons Schrift über die Ewigkeit der Welt." *Philologus* 92 (1937): 156–76.

Leo, Friedrich. *Die griechisch-römische Biographie.* Leipzig: B. G. Teubner, 1901.

Leon, Harry J. *The Jews of Ancient Rome.* 2nd ed. Peabody, MA: Hendrickson, 1995.

Leonhardt, Jutta. *Jewish Worship in Philo of Alexandria.* Tübingen: Mohr Siebeck, 2001.

Lernould, Alain. "Negative Theology and Radical Conceptual Purification in the Anonymous Commentary on Plato's Parmenides." In Turner and Corrigan, eds., *Plato's Parmenides,* 257–74.

Levick, Barbara. *Augustus: Image and Substance.* Harlow: Longman, 2010.

———. *Claudius.* London: Routledge, 1990.

———. *The Government of the Roman Empire: A Sourcebook.* 2nd ed. London: Routledge, 2000.

Levine, Amy-Jill, and Marc Zvi Brettler, eds. *The Jewish Annotated New Testament.* Oxford: Oxford University Press, 2011.

Levine, Lee I. *Jerusalem: Portrait of the City in the Second Temple Period (538 B.C.E.–70 C.E.).* Philadelphia: Jewish Publication Society, 2002.

Levinson, Joshua. "The Language of Stones: Roman Milestones on Rabbinic Roads." *Journal for the Study of Judaism* 47 (2016): 257–76.

Lévy, Carlos. *Cicero Academicus.* Rome: École française de Rome, 1992.

———. "Cicero and the *Timaeus.*" In *Plato's "Timaeus" as Cultural Icon,* ed. Gretchen J. Reydams-Schils, 95–10. Notre Dame, IN: University of Notre Dame Press, 2003.

———. "Cicéron, le moyen Platonisme et la philosophie Romaine: à propos de la naissance du concept Latin de qualitas." *Revue de Métaphysique et de Morale* 1 (2008): 5–20.

———. "Deux problèmes doxographiques chez Philon d'Alexandrie: Posidonius et Enésidème." In *Philosophy and Doxography in the Imperial Age,* ed. Aldo Brancacci, 79–102. Florence: L. S. Olschki, 2005.

———. "Ethique de l'immanence, éthique de la transcendance: le problème de l'Oikeiosis chez Philon." In Lévy, ed., *Philon d'Alexandrie,* 152–64.

———. "La conversion du scepticisme chez Philon d'Alexandrie." In Alesse, ed., *Philo,* 103–20.

———. "Philo d'Alexandrie et les passions." In *Réceptions antiques: Lecture, transmission, appropriation intellectuelle,* ed. Laetitia Ciccolini, Charles Guérin, Stéphane Iti, and Sébastien Morlet, 27–41. Paris: Rue d'Ulm, 2006.

———, ed. *Philon d'Alexandrie et le langage de la philosophie.* Turnhout: Brepols, 1998.

———. "Philo's Ethics." In Kamesar, ed., *Cambridge Companion,* 146–71.

———. "The Sceptical Academy: Decline and Afterlife." In *The Cambridge Companion to Ancient Scepticism,* ed. Richard Bett, 81–104. Cambridge: Cambridge University Press, 2010.

Liebes, Yehuda. *Ars Poetica in Sefer Yetsira* [in Hebrew]. Tel Aviv: Schocken, 2000.

———. "De Natura Dei: On the Jewish Myth and Its Metamorphoses" [in Hebrew]. In Yehuda Liebes, *God's Story,* 35–117.

———. *God's Story. Collected Essays on the Jewish Myth* [in Hebrew]. Jerusalem: Carmel, 2008.

———. *Mnemosyne. Translations of Classical Poetry* [in Hebrew]. Jerusalem: Carmel, 2011.

———. "The Work of the Chariot and the Work of Creation as Mystical Teachings in Philo of Alexandria." In *Scriptural Exegesis: The Shapes of Culture and the Religious Imagination,* ed. Deborah A. Green and Laura S. Lieber, 105–20. New York: Oxford University Press, 2009.

Liebeschuetz, J. H. W. G. *Continuity and Change in Roman Religion.* Oxford: Clarendon, 1979.

Lieu, Judith. *Marcion and the Making of a Heretic: God and Scripture in the Second Century.* New York: Cambridge University Press, 2015.

Lipka, Michael. *Roman Gods: A Conceptual Approach.* Leiden: Brill, 2009.

Lisi, F. L., ed. *Études Platoniciennes VII. Philon d'Alexandrie.* Paris: Belles Lettres, 2010.

Löhr, Winrich. "Editors and Commentators: Some Observations on the Craft of Second Century Theologians." In *Pascha Nostrum Christus,* ed. Pier Franco Beatrice and Bernard Pouderon, 65–84. Paris: Beauchesne, 2016.

———. "Logos." In *Reallexikon für Antike und Christentum,* ed. Theodor Klauser et al., vol. 2, 327–435. Stuttgart: Hiersemann, 2009.

Lona, Horacio E. *Die "Wahre Lehre" des Kelsos.* Freiburg: Herder, 2005.

Long, Anthony A. "Allegory in Philo and Etymology in Stoicism: A Plea for Drawing Distinctions." *SPhA* 9 (1997): 198–210.

———. "Roman Philosophy." In Sedley, ed., *Cambridge Companion,* 184–210.

———. "Stoic Readings of Homer." In Lamberton and Keaney, eds., *Homer's Ancient Readers,* 44–66.

———. *Stoic Studies.* Cambridge: Cambridge University Press, 1996.

Long, Anthony A., and David Sedley. *The Hellenistic Philosophers.* 2 vols. New York: Cambridge University Press, 1987.

Männlein-Robert, Irmgard. "Umrisse des Göttlichen." In *Platon und das Göttliche,* ed. D. Koch, I. Männlein-Robert, and N. Weidtmann, 112–38. Tübingen: Attempto, 2010.

Markschies, Christoph. *Das Antike Christentum.* Munich: Beck, 2006.

———. *Gnosis: An Introduction.* London: T&T Clark, 2003.

———. "The Price of Monotheism: Some New Observations on a Current Debate about Late Antiquity." In Mitchell and Van Nuffelen, eds., *One God,* 100–111.

———. *Valentinus Gnosticus?* Tübingen: Mohr Siebeck, 1992.

Martens, John W. *One God, One Law: Philo of Alexandria on the Mosaic and Greco-Roman Law.* Leiden: Brill, 2003.

Mason, Steve. "Flavius Josephus in Flavian Rome: Reading on and between the Lines." In *Flavian Rome: Culture, Image, Text,* ed. A. J. Boyle and William J. Dominik, 559–89. Leiden: Brill, 2003.

———. *A History of the Jewish War, A.D. 66–74.* New York: Cambridge University Press, 2016.

———. "Josephus as a Roman Historian." In Chapman and Rodgers, eds., *A Companion,* 89–107.

———. "Josephus' Autobiography." In Chapman and Rodgers, eds., *A Companion,* 59–74.

———. *Josephus Flavius: The Life. Translation and Commentary.* Leiden: Brill, 2004.

Mason, Steve, and Thomas A. Robinson. *Early Christian Reader.* Atlanta: SBL, 2013.

Massebieau, Louis. *Le classement des oeuvres de Philon.* Paris: Ernest Leroux, 1888.

Mattila, Sharon Lea. "Wisdom, Sense Perception, Nature and Philo's Gender Gradient." *HTR* 89 (1996): 103–29.

Mauch, Mercedes. *Senecas Frauenbild in den philosophischen Schriften.* Frankfurt: Peter Lang, 1997.

Meeks, Wayne A. *The First Urban Christians.* New Haven, CT: Yale University Press, 1983.

Meinel, Peter. *Seneca über seine Verbannung.* Bonn: Rudolf Habelt Verlag, 1972.

Mendelson, Alan. *Secular Education in Philo of Alexandria.* Cincinnati: Hebrew Union College, 1982.

Meredith, Anthony. "Porphyry and Julian against the Christians." *ANRW* II 23, 2 (1980): 1119–49.

Mheallaigh, Karen Ni. *Reading Fiction with Lucian.* Cambridge: Cambridge University Press, 2014.

Millar, Fergus. *A Study of Cassius Dio.* Oxford: Clarendon, 1964.

Mitchell, Stephen. "Further Thoughts on the Cult of Theos Hypsistos." In Mitchell and Van Nuffelen, eds., *One God,* 167–208.

Mitchell, Stephen, and Peter Van Nuffelen, eds. *One God: Pagan Monotheism in the Roman Empire.* Cambridge: Cambridge University Press, 2010.

Mohnike, Gottlob Chr. F. "Kleanthes der Stoiker." Greifswald: Mauritius, 1814.

Momigliano, Arnaldo. *Claudius: The Emperor and His Achievement.* Cambridge: Heffer, 1961.

———. *The Development of Greek Biography.* 2nd ed. Cambridge, MA: Harvard University Press, 1993.

Montanari, Franco. "L'Erudizione, la Filologia e la Grammatica." In *Lo Spazio letterario della Grecia Antica,* ed. Giuseppe Cambiano, et al., vol. 1. Rome: Salerno, 1993.

———. "Zenodotus, Aristarchus and the Exdosis of Homer." In *Editing Texts—Texte Edieren,* ed. Glenn W. Most, 1–21. Göttingen: Vandenhoeck & Ruprecht, 1998.

Montanari, Franco, and Paola Ascheri, eds. *Omero tremila anni dopo.* Rome: Edizioni di storia e letteratura, 2002.

Morford, Mark. *The Roman Philosophers.* New York: Routledge, 2002.

Morgan, Teresa. *Popular Morality in the Early Roman Empire.* Cambridge: Cambridge University Press, 2007.

———. *Roman Faith and Christian Faith.* Oxford: Oxford University Press, 2015.

Morris, Jenny. "The Jewish Philosopher Philo." In Emil Schürer, *The History of the Jewish People in the Age of Jesus Christ,* ed. Géza Vermès, Fergus Millar, and Martin Goodman, 809–89. Edinburgh: T&T Clark, 2014.

Moss, Candida R. *The Myth of Persecution.* New York: HarperOne, 2013.

Most, Glenn W., ed. *Historicization—Historisierung.* Göttingen: Vandenhoeck & Ruprecht, 2001.

———. "Philosophy and Religion." In Sedley, ed., *Cambridge Companion,* 300–322.

Murray, Gilbert. *Five Stages of Greek Religion.* 2nd ed. Garden City, NY: Doubleday, 1955.

Najman, Hindy. "Decalogue." In Collins and Harlow, eds., *Eerdmans Dictionary,* 526–28.

———. *Losing the Temple and Recovering the Future.* Cambridge: Cambridge University Press, 2014.

———. "A Written Copy of the Law of Nature: An Unthinkable Paradox?" *SPhA* 15 (2003): 55–63.

Nasrallah, Laura Salah. *Christian Responses to Roman Art and Architecture.* Cambridge: Cambridge University Press, 2010.

———. "Mapping the World: Justin, Tatian, Lucian and the Second Sophistic." *HTR* 98 (2005): 283–314.

———. "'Out of Love for Paul': History and Fiction and the Afterlife of the Apostle Paul." In *Early Christian and Jewish Narrative,* ed. Judith Perkins and Ilaria Ramelli, 73–96. Tübingen: Mohr Siebeck, 2015.

———. "The Rhetoric of Conversion and the Construction of Experience: The Case of Justin Martyr." *Studia Patristica* 40 (2006): 467–74.

Nesselrath, Heinz-Günther. "Das Museion und die grosse Bibliothek." In Georges et al., eds., *Alexandria,* 65–88.

Nesselrath, Heinz-Günther, Reinhard Feldmeier, and Rainer Hirsch-Luipold, eds. *Cornutus: Die Griechischen Götter.* Tübingen: Mohr Siebeck, 2009.

Neuschäfer, Bernhard. *Origenes als Philologe.* Basel: Friedrich Reinhardt Verlag, 1987.

Nicholas, Barry. *An Introduction to Roman Law.* Oxford: Oxford University Press, 1962.

Niebuhr, Karl-Wilhelm. "Die Spientia Salomonis im Kontext der hellenistisch-römischen Philosophie." In Niebuhr, ed., *Sapientia Salomonis,* 219–45.

———, ed. *Sapientia Salomonis.* Tübingen: Mohr Siebeck, 2015.

Niehoff, Maren R. "Alexandrian Judaism in 19th Century *Wissenschaft des Judentums:* Between Modernity and Christianity." In *Jüdische Geschichte in hellenistisch-römischer Zeit. Wege der Forschung: vom alten zum neuen Schürer,* ed. Aharon Oppenheimer, 9–28. Munich: Oldenbourg, 1999.

———. "Associative Thinking in Rabbinic Midrash: The Example of Abraham's and Sarah's Journey to Egypt" [in Hebrew]. *Tarbiz* 62 (1993): 339–61.

———. "Commentary Culture in the Land of Israel from an Alexandrian Perspective." *Dead Sea Discoveries* 19 (2012): 442–63.

———. "Desires Crossing Boundaries: Romance and History in Josephus' *Antiquities.*" In *Sibyls, Scriptures, and Scrolls: John Collins at Seventy,* ed. Joel Baden, Hindy Najman, and Eibert Tigchelaar, 1004–21. Leiden: Brill, 2016.

———. "Die Sapientia Salomonis und Philon—Repräsentaten derselben alexandrinisch-jüdischen Religionspartei?" In Niebuhr, ed., *Sapientia Salomonis,* 257–72.

———. "Eusebius as a Reader of Philo." *Adamantius* 21 (2015): 185–94.

———, ed. *Homer and the Bible in the Eyes of Ancient Interpreters.* Leiden: Brill, 2012.

———. "The Implied Audience of the Letter of James." In *New Approaches to the Study of Biblical Interpretation in Judaism of the Second Temple Period and in Early Christianity,* ed. Garry Anderson, Ruth A. Clements, and David Satran, 57–77. Leiden: Brill, 2013.

———. "A Jewish Critique of Christianity from Second Century Alexandria: Revisiting Celsus' Jew." *Journal of Early Christian Studies* 21 (2013): 151–75.

———. *Jewish Exegesis and Homeric Scholarship in Alexandria.* Cambridge: Cambridge University Press, 2011.

———, ed. *Journeys in the Roman East: Imagined and Real.* Tübingen: Mohr Siebeck, 2017.

———. "Justin's *Timaeus* in Light of Philo's." *SPhA* 28 (2016): 375–92.

———. "Mother and Maiden, Sister and Spouse: Sarah in Philonic Midrash." *HTR* 97 (2004): 413–44.

———. "'Not Study Is the Main Objective, but Action.' (*Pirqe Avot* 1:17). A Rabbinic Maxim in Greco-Roman Context." In *From Text to Context in Ancient Judaism: Studies in Honor of Steven Fraade,* ed. Michal Bar-Asher Siegal, Christine Hayes, and Tzvi Novik, 2017.

———. "Origen's Commentary on Genesis as a Key to Genesis Rabbah." In *Genesis Rabbah in Text and Context,* ed. Sarit Kattan Gribetz, David M. Grossberg, Martha Himmelfarb, and Peter Schäfer, 129–53. Tübingen: Mohr Siebeck, 2016.

———. "Parodies of Educational Journeys in Josephus, Justin and Lucian." In Niehoff, ed., *Journeys.*

———. "Philo and Plutarch on Homer." In Niehoff, ed., *Homer and the Bible,* 127–54.

———, ed. *Philo of Alexandria: Writings* [in Hebrew]. Vol. 5.1. Jerusalem: Bialik Institute and Israel Academy of Sciences and Humanities, 2012.

———. *Philo on Jewish Identity and Culture.* Tübingen: Mohr Siebeck, 2001.

———. "Philo's Contribution to Contemporary Alexandrian Metaphysics." In *Beyond Reception: Mutual Influences between Antique Religion, Judaism, and Early Christianity,* ed. David Brakke, Anders-Christian Jacobsen, and Jörg Ulrich, 35–55. Frankfurt: Peter Lang, 2006.

Nikiprowetzky, Valentin. *Le commentaire de l'écriture chez Philon d'Alexandrie.* Leiden: Brill, 1977.

Nünlist, René. *The Ancient Critic at Work.* Cambridge: Cambridge University Press, 2009.

Nünlist, René, and Angus M. Bowie, eds. *Narrators, Narratees, and Narratives in Ancient Greek Literature.* Leiden: Brill, 2004.

Nussbaum, Martha. "Stoic Laughter: A Reading of Seneca's Apocolocyntosis." In Bartsch and Wray, eds., *Seneca and the Self,* 84–112.

Oertelt, Friederike. *Herrscherideal und Herrscherkritik bei Philo von Alexandria.* Leiden: Brill, 2015.

Opsomer, Jan. "Plutarch and the Stoics." In Beck, ed., *Companion to Plutarch,* 88–103.

Osiek, Carolyn, and David L. Balch. *Families in the New Testament World.* Louisville, KY: Westminster John Knox, 1997.

Papadoyannakis, Yannis. "Instruction by Question and Answer: The Case of Late Antique and Byzantine Erotapokriseis." In *Greek Literature in Late Antiquity,* ed. Scott F. Johnson, 91–105. Aldershot: Ashgate, 2006.

Pauly, August Georg Wissowa, Wilhelm Kroll, Kurt Witte, Karl Mittelhaus, and Konrat Ziegler, eds. *Paulys Realencyclopädie der classischen Altertumswissenschaft: neue Bearbeitung.* Stuttgart: J. B. Metzler, 1894–1980.

Paz, Yakir. "From Scribes to Scholars" [in Hebrew]. PhD diss., Hebrew University, 2014.

Pearce, Sarah J. "King Moses: Notes on Philo's Portrait of Moses as an Ideal Leader in the Life of Moses." In *The Greek Strand in Islamic Political Thought,* ed. Emma Gannagé, 37–43. Beirut: Imprimerie Catholique, 2004.

———. "Philo of Alexandria on the Second Commandment." In *The Image and Its Prohibition in Jewish Antiquity,* ed. Sarah J. Pearce, 49–76. Oxford: Journal of Jewish Studies, 2013.

———. "Philo, On the Decalogue." In *Outside the Bible,* ed. Louis H. Feldman, James L. Kugel, and Lawrence H. Schiffman, 989–1031. Lincoln: University of Nebraska Press, 2013.

Pearson, Birger A. "Philo and Gnosticism." *ANRW* II 21, 1 (1984): 295–342.

Pelling, Christopher B. "The Moralism of Plutarch's Lives." In *Ethics and Rhetoric,* ed. Doreen Innes, Harry Hine, and Christopher Pelling, 205–20. Oxford: Oxford University Press, 1995.

———. "Plutarch." In Nünlist and Bowie, eds., *Narrators, Narratees,* 403–21.

―――. *Plutarch and History*. London: Classical Press of Wales, 2002.

Pépin, Jean. *La tradition de l'allégorie de Philon d'Alexandrie à Dante*. Paris: Études Augustiniennes, 1987.

Perkins, Judith. *Roman Imperial Identities in the Early Christian Era*. London: Routledge, 2009.

―――. *The Suffering Self: Pain and Narrative Representation in the Early Christian Era*. London: Routledge, 1995.

Pervo, Richard I. *Acts: A Commentary*. Minneapolis: Fortress, 2009.

Petrocheilos, Nikos. *Roman Attitudes to the Greeks*. Athens: National and Capodistrian University of Athens, 1974.

Petsalis-Diomidis, Alexia. *Truly beyond Wonders: Aelius Aristides and the Cult of Asklepios*. Oxford: Oxford University Press, 2010.

Pfeiffer, Rudolf. *History of Classical Scholarship*. Vol. 1. Oxford: Clarendon, 1968.

Pohlenz, Max. *Die Stoa*. Göttingen: Vandenhoeck & Ruprecht, 1949.

Pomeroy, Sarah B. *Plutarch's Advice to the Bride and Groom and a Consolation to His Wife*. New York: Oxford University Press, 1999.

―――. *Women in Hellenistic Egypt*. New York: Schocken Books, 1984.

Porter, James I. "Hermeneutic Lines and Circles: Aristarchos and Crates on the Exegesis of Homer." In Lamberton and Keaney, eds., *Homer's Ancient Readers*, 67–85.

Prost, François. "La psychologie de Panétius: réflexions sur l'évolution du Stoïcisme à Rome et la valeur du Témoignage de Cicéron." *Revue des Études Latines* 79 (2001): 37–53.

―――. *Les théories hellénistiques de la douleur*. Louvain: Peeters, 2004.

Pucci Ben Zeev, Miriam. *Jewish Rights in the Roman World*. Tübingen: Mohr Siebeck, 1998.

Purves, Alex C. "Ares." In Finkelberg, ed., *Homer Encyclopedia*, 1:81–82.

Radice, Roberto. "Observations on the Theory of the Ideas as Thoughts of God in Philo of Alexandria." In *Heirs of the Septuagint*, *SPhA* 3 (1991): 126–34.

―――. "Philo's Theology and Theory of Creation." In Kamesar, ed., *Cambridge Companion*, 124–45.

Rajak, Tessa. *Josephus*. London: Duckworth, 1983.

―――. *Translation and Survival*. Oxford: Oxford University Press, 2009.

Ramelli, Ilaria. *Hierocles the Stoic*. Atlanta: SBL, 2009.

Rawson, Beryl, ed. *Marriage, Divorce, and Children in Ancient Rome*. Oxford: Oxford University Press, 1991.

Reydams-Schils, Gretchen. "Authority and Agency in Stoicism." *GRBS* 51 (2011): 296–322.

―――. *Demiurge and Providence: Stoic and Platonist Readings of Plato's "Timaeus."* Turnhout: Brepols, 1999.

―――. *The Roman Stoics: Self, Responsibility, and Affection*. Chicago: University of Chicago Press, 2005.

———. "The Socratic Higher Ground." In Alesse, ed., *Philo,* 169–95.

Riddle, John M. *Contraception and Abortion from the Ancient World to the Renaissance.* Cambridge, MA: Harvard University Press, 1992.

Rives, John B. *Religion in the Roman Empire.* Oxford: Wiley-Blackwell, 2007.

Romney Wegner, Judith. "Philo's Portrayal of Women—Hebraic or Hellenic?" In *Women like This,* ed. Amy-Jill Levine, 41–66. Atlanta: Scholars Press, 1991.

Rösel, Martin. *Übersetzung als Vollendung der Auslegung.* Berlin: de Gruyter, 1994.

Rowlandson, Jane. *Women and Society in Greek and Roman Egypt: A Sourcebook.* Cambridge: Cambridge University Press, 1998.

Royse, James. "Some Observations on the Biblical Text of Philo's De Agricultura." *SPhA* 22 (2011): 111–29.

———. "The Text of Philo's Legum Allegoriae." *SPhA* 20 (2000): 1–28.

———. "The Works of Philo." In Kamesar, ed., *Cambridge Companion,* 32–64.

Runia, David T. "Confronting the Augean Stables: Royse's Fragmenta Spuria Philonica." *SPhA* 4 (1992): 78–86.

———. "Further Observations on the Structure of Philo's Allegorical Treatises." *VC* 41 (1987): 105–38.

———. "God and Man in Philo of Alexandria." *Journal of Theological Studies* 39 (1988): 48–75.

———. "Philo in Byzantium." *VC* 70 (2016): 259–81.

———. *Philo in Early Christian Literature: A Survey.* Minneapolis: Fortress, 1993.

———. "Philo of Alexandria." *Christentum* 27 (2015): 605–27.

———. *Philo of Alexandria and the "Timaeus" of Plato.* Leiden: Brill, 1986.

———. *Philo of Alexandria: On the Creation of the Cosmos according to Moses. Introduction, Translation and Commentary.* Leiden: Brill, 2011.

———. "Philo's *De Aeternitate Mundi*: The Problem of Interpretation." *VC* 35 (1981): 105–51.

———. "The Structure of Philo's Allegorical Treatises: A Review of Two Recent Studies and Some Additional Comments." *VC* 38 (1984): 209–56.

———. "The Theme of Flight and Exile in the Allegorical Thought-World of Philo of Alexandria." *SPhA* 21 (2009): 1–24.

———. "Was Philo a Middle Platonist? A Difficult Question Revisited." *SPhA* 5 (1993): 124–33.

———. "Why Philo of Alexandria Is an Important Writer and Thinker." In Inowlocki and Decharneux, eds., *Philon d'Alexandrie,* 13–33.

———. "Witness or Participant? Philo and the Neoplatonic Tradition." In *The Neoplatonic Tradition,* ed. Arie Johan Vanderjagt and Detlev Pätzold, 36–56. Cologne: Dinter, 1991.

Rüpke, Jörg. *Die Religion der Römer: Eine Einführung.* Munich: C. H. Beck, 2001.

———, ed. *The Individual in the Religions of the Ancient Mediterranean.* Oxford: Oxford University Press, 2013.

Russell, Donald A. "On Reading Plutarch's Lives." In Scardigli, ed., *Essays*, 75–94.

———. *Plutarch*. London: Duckworth, 1973.

Rutgers, Leonard Victor. *The Jews in Late Ancient Rome*. Leiden: Brill, 1995.

Rutherford, Ian. "Concord and Communitas: Greek Elements in Philo's Account of Jewish Pilgrimage. In Niehoff, ed., *Journeys in the Roman East*.

Ryu, Jang. *Knowledge of God in Philo of Alexandria*. Tübingen: Mohr Siebeck, 2015.

Salles, Catherine. *Lire à Rome*. 2nd ed. Paris: Belles Lettres, 2008.

Sanders, E. P., and Margaret Davies. *Studying the Synoptic Gospels*. London: SCM, 1989.

Sanders, Jack T. *The Jews in Luke-Acts*. Philadelphia: Fortress, 1987.

Scardigli, Barbara, ed. *Essays on Plutarch's Lives*. Oxford: Clarendon, 1995.

Scarpat, Giuseppe. *Il pensiero religioso di Seneca e l'ambiente ebraico e cristiano*. 2nd ed. Brescia: Paideia Editrice, 1983.

Schäfer, Peter. *Judeophobia*. Cambridge, MA: Harvard University Press, 1997.

———. *The Origins of Jewish Mysticism*. Tübingen: Mohr Siebeck, 2009.

———. *Zwei Götter im Himmel. Gottesvorstellungen in der jüdischen Antike*. Munich: C. H. Beck, 2017.

Schenkeveld, Dick M. "Strabo on Homer." *Mnemosyne* 29 (1976): 52–64.

Schimanowski, Gottfried, "Die jüdische Integration in die Oberschicht Alexandriens und die angebliche Apostasie des Tiberius Julius Alexander." In *Jewish Identity in the Greco-Roman World*, ed. Jörg Frey, Daniel R. Schwartz, and Stephanie Gripentrog, 111–36. Leiden: Brill, 2007.

Schironi, Francesca. "Alexandrian Scholarship." In Finkelberg, ed., *Homer Encyclopedia*, 1:30–32.

———. "Plato at Alexandria." *CQ* 55 (2005): 423–34.

———. "Theory into Practice: Aristotelian Principles in Aristarchan Philology." *Classical Philology* 104 (2009): 279–316.

Schmidt, M. "The Homer of the Scholia: What Is Explained to the Reader?" In Montanari and Ascheri, eds., *Omero tremila anni dopo*, 159–83.

Schmitz, Thomas A. "Plutarch and the Second Sophistic." In Beck, ed., *Companion to Plutarch*, 32–42.

Schofield, Malcolm. "Academic Epistemology." In Algra, ed., *Cambridge History*, 323–51.

———. "Stoic Ethics." In *The Cambridge Companion to the Stoics*, ed. Brad Inwood, 233–56. Cambridge: Cambridge University Press, 2003.

Scholem, Gershom. *Jewish Gnosticism, Merkabah Mysticism, and Talmudic Tradition*. New York: Jewish Theological Seminary of America, 1965.

———. *Major Trends in Jewish Mysticism*. New York: Schocken Books, 1948.

Schremer, Adiel. *Brothers Estranged*. Oxford: Oxford University Press, 2010.

———. *Male and Female He Created Them* [in Hebrew]. Jerusalem: Zalman Shazar Center, 2003.

Schüssler Fiorenza, Elisabeth. "A Feminist Critical Interpretation for Liberation: Martha and Mary: Luke 10:38–42." *Religion and Intellectual Life* 3 (1986): 21–35.

Schwabe, Moshe. "Introduction" [in Hebrew]. In *Writings of Philo of Alexandria: On the Creation of the World. Translation and Annotation*, XIII–XXXVI. Jerusalem: J. Yunovitch, 1931.

Schwartz, Daniel R. *Agrippa I.* Tübingen: Mohr Siebeck, 1990.

Schwartz, Joshua J. "Pilgrimage." In Collins and Harlow, eds., *Eerdmans Dictionary*, 1088–90.

Scramuzza, Vincent M. *The Emperor Claudius.* Cambridge, MA: Harvard University Press, 1940.

Sedley, David, ed. *The Cambridge Companion to Greek and Roman Philosophy.* Cambridge: Cambridge University Press, 2003.

———. "Cicero and the *Timaeus.*" In *Aristotle, Plato and Pythagoreanism in the First Century BC,* ed. Malcolm Schofield, 187–205. Cambridge: Cambridge University Press, 2013.

———. *Creationism and Its Critics in Antiquity.* Berkeley: University of California Press, 2007.

———. "The Ideal of Godlikeness." In *Plato 2: Ethics, Politics, Religion, and the Soul,* ed. Gail Fine, 309–28. Oxford: Oxford University Press, 1999.

———. *The Midwife of Platonism: Text and Subtext in Plato's Theaetetus.* Oxford: Clarendon, 2004.

———. "Plato's Auctoritas and the Rebirth of the Commentary Tradition." In *Philosophia Togata II,* ed. Jonathan Barnes and Miriam T. Griffin, 110–29. Oxford: Clarendon, 1997.

———. "Three Platonist Interpretations of the *Theaetetus.*" In *Form and Argument in Late Plato,* ed. Christopher Gill and Mary Margaret McCabe, 81–101. Oxford: Clarendon, 1996.

Segal, Ben-Zion, ed., *The Ten Commandments as Reflected in Tradition and Literature throughout the Ages* [in Hebrew]. Jerusalem: Magnes, 1985.

Segal, Michael. *The Book of Jubilees.* Leiden: Brill, 2007.

Seland, Torrey. *Reading Philo.* Grand Rapids, MI: Eerdmans, 2014.

Siegert, Folker. "The Philonian Fragment *De Deo.*" *SPhA* 10 (1998): 1–33.

Sievers, Joseph, and Gaia Lembi, eds. *Josephus and Jewish History in Flavian Rome and Beyond.* Leiden: Brill, 2005.

Sly, Dorothy. *Philo's Perception of Women.* Atlanta: Scholars Press, 1990.

Smallwood, E. Mary. *Philonis Alexandrini Legatio ad Gaium.* Leiden: Brill, 1961.

Smith, Mark S. *God in Translation: Deities in Cross-Cultural Discourse in the Biblical World.* Tübingen: Mohr Siebeck, 2008.

Sorabji, Richard. *Animal Minds and Human Morals.* Ithaca, NY: Cornell University Press, 1993.

———. *Emotion and Peace of Mind.* Oxford: Oxford University Press, 2000.

———. *Self: Ancient and Modern Insights about Individuality, Life, and Death*. Chicago: University of Chicago Press, 2006.

Spencer, F. Scott. *Salty Wives, Spirited Mothers, and Savvy Widows*. Grand Rapids, MI: Eerdmans, 2012.

Stadter, Philip A. *Plutarch and His Roman Readers*. Oxford: Oxford University Press, 2015.

———. "Plutarch and Rome." In Beck, ed., *Companion to Plutarch*, 13–31.

Starobinski-Safran, Esther. "Ex. 3.24 dans l'œuvre de Philon." In *Dieu et l'être: exégèses d'Exode 3, 14 et de Coran 20, 11–24*, ed. Paul Vignaux, 47–55. Paris: Études Augustiniennes, 1978.

Stein, Edmund. *Philo of Alexandria*. Warsaw: A. Y. Shtibel, 1939.

Stein, Siegfried. "The Influence of Symposia Literature on the Literary Form of the Pesah Haggadah." *JJS* 8 (1957): 13–44.

Stein-Hölkeskamp, Elke. *Das Römische Gastmahl*. Munich: Beck, 2005.

Steinmetz, Peter. "Allegorische Deutung und Allegorische Dichtung in der Alten Stoa." *Rheinisches Museum für Philologie* 129 (1986): 18–30.

Sterling, Gregory E. *Historiography and Self-Definition: Josephus, Luke-Acts, and Apologetic Historiography*. Leiden: Brill, 1992.

———. "The Interpreter of Moses: Philo of Alexandria and the Biblical Text." In *A Companion to Biblical Interpretation in Early Judaism*, ed. Matthias Henze, 415–34. Grand Rapids, MI: Eerdmans, 2012.

———. "A Man of Highest Repute": Did Josephus Know the Writings of Philo?" *SPhA* 25 (2013): 101–13.

———. "Philo." In Collins and Harlow, eds., *Eerdmans Dictionary*, 1063–70.

———. "Philo and the Logic of Apologetics: An Analysis of the Hypothetica." *SBL Seminar Papers* 29 (1990): 412–30.

———. "'Philo Has Not Been Used Half Enough': The Significance of Philo of Alexandria for the Study of the New Testament." *Perspectives in Religious Studies* 30 (2003): 251–69.

———. "Philo's *Quaestiones*: Prolegomena or Afterthought?" In Hay, ed., *Both Literal and Allegorical*, 99–123.

———. "Philo's School: The Social Setting of Ancient Commentaries." In *Sophisten in Hellenismus und Kaiserzeit: Orte, Methoden und Personen der Bildungsvermittlung*, ed. Beatrice Wyss, Rainer Hirsch-Luipold, and Solmeng-Jonas Hirschi. Tübingen: Mohr Siebeck, 2017.

———. "Platonizing Moses: Philo and Middle Platonism." *SPhA* 5 (1993): 96–111.

———. "'Prolific in Expression and Broad in Thought': Internal References to Philo's *Allegorical Commentary* and *Exposition of the Law*." *Euphrosyne* 40 (2012): 55–76.

———. "The School of Moses in Alexandria: An Attempt to Reconstruct the School of Philo." In *Second Temple Jewish Paideia in Context*, ed. Gabriele Boccaccini and Jason Zurawski. Berlin: de Gruyter, forthcoming.

———. "'The School of Sacred Laws': The Social Setting of Philo's Treatises." *VC* 53 (1999): 148–64.

———. "The Theft of Philosophy: Philo of Alexandria and Numenius of Apamea." *SPhA* 27 (2015): 71–85.

Stern, Menahem. *Greek and Latin Authors on Jews and Judaism.* 2 vols. Jerusalem: Israel Academy of Sciences and Humanities, 1974.

Stowers, Stanley Kent. *Letter Writing in Greco-Roman Antiquity.* Philadelphia: Westminster, 1986.

Striker, Gisela. *Essays on Hellenistic Epistemology and Ethics.* Cambridge: Cambridge University Press, 1996.

Stroumsa, Guy G. *Another Seed: Studies in Gnostic Mythology.* Leiden: Brill, 1984.

———. *The Making of the Abrahamic Religions in Late Antiquity.* Oxford: Oxford University Press, 2015.

———. *The Scriptural Universe of Ancient Christianity.* Cambridge, MA: Harvard University Press, 2016.

Svebakken, Hans. *Philo of Alexandria's Exposition on the Tenth Commandment.* Atlanta: SBL, 2012.

Swain, Simon. "Biography and Biographic in the Literature of the Roman Empire." In *Portraits,* ed. Mark J. Edwards and Simon Swain, 1–37. Oxford: Clarendon, 1997.

———. *Hellenism and Empire.* Oxford: Clarendon, 1996.

———. "Plutarch's Lives of Cicero, Cato and Brutus." *Hermes* 118 (1990): 192–203.

Tarrant, Harold. "The Date of the Anon. in *Theaetetum.*" *CQ* 33 (1983): 161–87.

———. "Logos and the Development of Middle Platonism." In *From the Old Academy to Later Neo-Platonism,* ed. Harold Tarrant, 197–204. Farnham: Ashgate, 2011.

———. *Scepticism or Platonism? The Philosophy of the Fourth Academy.* Cambridge: Cambridge University Press, 1985.

———. *Thrasyllan Platonism.* Ithaca, NY: Cornell University Press, 1993.

Taylor, Alfred E. *A Commentary on Plato's Timaeus.* Oxford: Clarendon, 1928.

Taylor, Joan E. *Jewish Women Philosophers of First-Century Alexandria.* Oxford: Oxford University Press, 2003.

Tcherikover, Victor, and Alexander Fuks. *Corpus Papyrorum Judaicarum.* 3 vols. Cambridge, MA: Harvard University Press, 1957–1964.

Terian, Abraham. "A Critical Introduction to Philo's Dialogues." *ANRW II* 21, 1–2. (1984): 272–94.

———. "The Priority of the *Quaestiones* among Philo's Exegetical Commentaries." In Hay, ed., *Both Literal and Allegorical,* 29–46.

Termini, Cristina. "Taxonomy of Biblical Law and Φιλοτεχνία in Philo of Alexandria: A Comparison with Josephus and Cicero." *SPhA* 16 (2004): 1–29.

Theiler, Willy. "Philo von Alexandria und der Beginn des kaiserzeitlichen Platonismus." In *Parusia,* ed. Johannes Hirschberger and Kurt Flasch, 199–219. Frankfurt: Minerva, 1965.

Thom, Johan C. *Cleanthes: Hymn to Zeus.* Tübingen: Mohr Siebeck, 2005.

Thorsteinsson, Runar M. *Roman Christianity and Roman Stoicism.* Oxford: Oxford University Press, 2010.

Tobin, Thomas H. "The Beginning of Philo's *Legum Allegoriae.*" *SPhA* 12 (2000): 29–43.

———. *The Creation of Man: Philo and the History of Interpretation.* Washington, DC: Catholic Biblical Association of America, 1983.

———. "Logos." In *Anchor Bible Dictionary,* 4:348–56. New York: Doubleday, 1992.

———. "Philo and the Allegorical Reinterpretation of Genesis." Lecture at the Israel Institute for Advanced Studies, March 2017.

———. *Timaios of Locri: On the Nature of the World and the Soul.* Chico, CA: Scholars Press, 1985.

Tov, Emanuel. "The Septuagint between Judaism and Christianity." In *The Septuagint and Christian Origins,* ed. Thomas Scott Caulley and Hermann Lichtenberger, 3–25. Tübingen: Mohr Siebeck, 2011.

———. "The Septuagint Translation of Genesis as the First Scripture Translation." In *In the Footsteps of Sherlock Holmes: Studies in the Biblical Text in Honour of Anneli Aejmelaus,* ed. Kristin De Troyer, T. Michael Law, and Marketta Liljenström, 47–64. Leuven: Peeters, 2014.

Treggiari, Susan. *Roman Marriage.* Oxford: Clarendon, 1991.

Turner, John Douglas, and Kevin Corrigan, eds. *Plato's Parmenides and Its Heritage.* Atlanta: SBL, 2010.

Urbach, Ephraim E. "The Place of the Ten Commandments in Ritual and Prayer" [in Hebrew]. In Segal, ed., *The Ten Commandments,* 127–46.

Uxkull-Gyllenband, Woldemar. *Plutarch und die Griechische Biographie.* Stuttgart: Verlag W. Kohlhammer, 1927.

Van den Hoek, Annevies. "Philo and Origen: A Descriptive Catalogue of Their Relationship." SPhA 12 (2000): 44–121.

Van der Broek, Roelef. *Gnostic Religion in Antiquity.* Cambridge: Cambridge University Press, 2013.

Van der Horst, Pieter W. *Chaeremon: Egyptian Priest and Stoic Philosopher.* Leiden: Brill, 1987.

———. *Philo's Flaccus.* Leiden: Brill, 2003.

VanderKam, James C. "Made to Order: Creation in Jubilees." In *Jewish and Christian Cosmogony in Late Antiquity,* ed. Lance Jenott and Sarit Kattan Gribetz, 23–38. Tübingen: Mohr Siebeck, 2013.

Van Hoof, Lieve. *Plutarch's Practical Ethics.* Oxford: Oxford University Press, 2010.

Van Nuffelen, Peter. *Rethinking the Gods.* Cambridge: Cambridge University Press, 2011.

———. "Varro's *Divine Antiquities:* Roman Religion as an Image of Truth." *Classical Philology* 105 (2010): 162–88.

Veyne, Paul. "The Roman Empire." In *A History of Private Life: Vol. 1. From Pagan Rome to Byzantium,* ed. Paul Veyne, 5–233. Cambridge, MA: Belknap, 1987.

Vlastos, Gregory. "Creation in the *Timaeus:* Is It a Fiction?" In *Studies in Plato's Metaphysics,* ed. Allen E. Reginald, 401–19. London: Routledge, 1965.

Vogt, Katja Maria. *Law, Reason, and the Cosmic City.* New York: Oxford University Press, 2008.

Von Arnim, Hans Friedrich August. *Stoicorum Veterum Fragmenta.* 4 vols. Leipzig: Teubne, 1903–1924.

Wahlgren, Staffan. *Sprachwandel im Griechisch der frühen römischen Kaiserzeit.* Göteborg: Ekblads, 1995.

Wallace-Hadrill, Andrew. *Suetonius.* New Haven, CT: Yale University Press, 1984.

Walter, Nikolaus. *Der Toraausleger Aristobulus.* Berlin: Akademie Verlag, 1964.

Wan, Sze-kar. "Philo's *Quaestiones et Solutiones in Genesim:* A Synoptic Approach." *SBL Seminar Papers* 32 (1993): 22–53.

Wardman, Alan. *Plutarch's Lives.* London: Paul Elek, 1974.

Watson, Francis. *Paul, Judaism, and the Gentiles.* Grand Rapids, MI: Eerdmans, 2007.

Weiman-Kelman, Levi, and Oded Mazor, eds. *HaSimha SheBalev: Prayer Book for the Pilgrimage Holidays* [in Hebrew]. Jerusalem: Council of Reform Rabbis, 2015.

Weinfeld, Moshe. "The Uniqueness of the Decalogue and Its Place in Jewish Tradition" [in Hebrew]. In Segal, ed., *The Ten Commandments,* 1–34.

Weisser, Sharon. "Éradication ou modération des passions?" PhD diss., Hebrew University and École Pratique des Hautes Études, 2012.

———. "Why Does Philo Criticize the Stoic Ideal of *Apatheia* in *On Abraham* 257? Philo and Consolatory Literature." *CQ* 62 (2012): 248–50.

Wendland, Paul. *Philos Schrift über die Vorsehung.* Berlin: Gaertner, 1892.

Werman, Cana, and Aharon Shemesh. "Halakha in the Dead Sea Scrolls." In *The Qumran Scrolls and Their World* [in Hebrew], ed. Menahem Kister, 409–34. Jerusalem: Yad Ben Zvi, 2009.

Whitmarsh, Tim. *Beyond the Second Sophistic.* Berkeley: University of California Press, 2013.

———. *Greek Literature and the Roman Empire.* Oxford: Oxford University Press, 2001.

———, ed. *Local Knowledge and Microidentities in the Imperial Greek World.* Cambridge: Cambridge University Press, 2010.

———. "Philostratus." In Nünlist and Bowie, eds., *Narrators, Narratees,* 423–39.

———. "Thinking Local." In Whitmarsh, ed., *Local Knowledge,* 1–16.

Whittaker, John. "How to Define the Rational Soul." In Lévy, ed., *Philon d'Alexandrie,* 229–53.

———. "Neopythagoreanism and the Transcendent Absolute." *Symbolae Osloenses* 48 (1973): 77–86.

Wilamowitz-Moellendorff, Ulrich von. "Plutarch as a Biographer." In Scardigli, ed., *Essays,* 75–94.

Williams, Michael A. *Rethinking "Gnosticism."* Princeton, NJ: Princeton University Press, 1996.

Wills, Lawrence M. "The Depiction of the Jews in Acts." *JBL* 110 (1991): 631–54.

Wilson, Robert McL. *The Gnostic Problem.* London: A. R. Mowbray, 1958.

Wilson, Walter T. *Philo of Alexandria: On the Virtues. Introduction, Translation, and Commentary.* Leiden: Brill, 2011.

Winston, David. *Logos and Mystical Theology in Philo of Alexandria.* Cincinnati: Hebrew Union College, 1985.

———. "Philo of Alexandria on the Rational and the Irrational Emotions." In *Passions and Moral Progress in Greco-Roman Thought,* ed. John T. Fitzgerald, 199–220. London: Routledge, 2008.

———. *The Wisdom of Solomon.* New York: Doubleday, 1979.

Winston, David, and John M. Dillon, eds. *Two Treatises of Philo of Alexandria.* Chico, CA: Scholars Press, 1983.

Winter, Bruce W. *Philo and Paul among the Sophists.* Grand Rapids, MI: Eerdmans, 2002.

Wolfson, Harry Austryn. *Philo.* Cambridge, MA: Harvard University Press, 1947.

Woodman, Anthony J. *Rhetoric in Classical Historiography.* London: Routledge, 1988.

Wright, Benjamin G. *The Letter of Aristeas.* Berlin: de Gruyter, 2015.

Yli-Karjanmaa, Sami. *Reincarnation in Philo of Alexandria.* Atlanta: SBL, 2015.

Zeitlin, Solomon. "Did Agrippa Write a Letter to Gaius Caligula?" *Jewish Quarterly Review* 56 (1965): 22–31.

Ziegler, Konrat. *Plutarchos von Chaironeia.* 2nd ed. Stuttgart: Druckenmöller, 1964.

Zohar, Noam. "The Figure of Abraham and the Voice of Sarah in Genesis Rabbah." In *The Faith of Abraham* [in Hebrew], ed. Moshe Hallamish, Hannah Kasher, and Yochanan Silman, 71–85. Ramat Gan: Bar-Ilan University Press, 2002.

General Index

Aaron, 231, 233

Abraham, 102, 126–27, 145, 180–81, 236, 239; biography, 121, 125; husband of Sarah, 136–38; Josephus's view of, 106; mystical experience, 192, 201, 221–22; rabbinic view of, 107; spiritual journey, 102–3, 126, 135, 179–80, 182, 192, 227

abstinence, 87, 115, 163

Adam, 138–39, 180, 201

adultery, 145–47, 157–59; Roman view of, 145–47, 159

Aeschylus, 36–37

Agrippa I, 122; connection to Gaius, 30–33; involvement in Alexandria, 29–33, 42, 120; letter to Gaius, 43–45

Albinus, 223

Alcibiades, 113, 129

Alexander of Aphrodisias, 78

Alexander the Alabarch, 3, 29–30

Alexander the Great, 84, 87, 129

Alexandria, 11–12, 15, 16, 28, 51, 210; Alexandrian citizenship, 42, 60; ethnic violence, 7, 31, 60; library, 15, 28; scholars in, 15, 65, 179, 199, 202–5

Allegorical Commentary, 8–9, 61, 65–66, 79, 85, 101, 126, 133, 149, 169, 175–82, 185–87, 192, 195–96, 211, 222, 230, 232; Alexandrian context of, 65–66, 108

allegory: Christian view of, 190; Stoic view of, 181

ambassador: Egyptian ambassadors in Rome, 86, 111; Greek ambassadors in Rome, 14, 86; Philo as an ambassador (*see under* Philo); Plutarch as an ambassador, 128

Ammonius, 168, 207, 216

anthropomorphism, 210, 211–12; Aristobulus's view of, 210; Platonic view of, 212–13

Antiochus of Ascalon, 18, 69, 195, 199

Antipater, 226

apatheia, 231–32

Apion: criticism of the Jews, 14, 18, 39, 67, 86, 110–11, 150, 151, 164, 169; responses to, 110–12, 150, 165, 169–70; Roman influences on, 18, 150; view of Egyptian politics, 12

Apollonius, 19–20, 129

apologetics, 16, 85, 129, 150–51, 164, 169–70, 187; in Josephus's work, 150–51; in Justin Martyr's work, 170; in Origen's work, 190–91

Appius Silanus, 53–54

Aquila, 141

Ares, 64–65

Aristarchus of Samothrace, 15, 174, 177, 181–82

Aristeas, 16, 152, 167

Aristobulus, 105, 152, 210

Aristophanes, 15, 139

Aristotelian tradition, 79, 97

Aristotle, 78–80, 114, 153, 178

Arius Didymus, 17, 96, 132, 137

Athena, 218

Attalus, 133–34

Augustus: family values, 134, 135, 137, 145–46, 159; ideal of good emperor, 55–56, 63–64; regarding Judaism, 60, 66, 67, 120, 163; religious role, 64, 119

Balbus, 73, 76, 166

Bartels, Felix, 193

Basilides, 189, 216, 223

Bauer, Walter, 186

Ben Sira, 104–5

Bible interpretation, 8–9, 61, 65–66, 85, 94, 109, 173–80, 182–83, 205–6, 218, 222; in Alexandria, 16, 65–66; Demetrius's view of, 16; Eusebius's view of, 78, 260n19; Justin Martyr's view of, 107

biography, 109–10, 112–17, 122–23, 125, 129; the Gospel of Luke, 130, 168; Philostratus's biography, 129–30; Plutarch's biographies, 67, 113, 128–29; Roman biographies, 112–13, 115, 122

Boethus of Sidon, 80

Bréhier, Émile, 217

Brutus, 84

Cain, 178, 187, 190, 198, 240

Calanus, 84

canonical text, 65–66, 68, 72, 85, 93–94, 196; of Alexandrian Jews, 16, 65–66; of Alexandrian scholars, 65; Christian view of, 190; of the Second Sophistic, 19–21; Stoic view of, 113–14

Carneades, 84

Cato, 84, 114, 234

Celsus, 107

Chaeremon, 86, 111

Chrysippus: criticism of, 80, 81, 93, 241; on the divine, 17, 98, 99, 228; on human superiority, 100; on nature, 157, 158, 233, 234, 235, 238; on passion, 157, 230

Cicero, 17, 88, 73, 79, 83, 113; on Aristotelian tradition, 78; on ethics, 83; on historiography, 113; on law, 96–97, 156, 159; on love, 134; on Platonism, 73, 74–75, 79, 99; on Stoicism, 73, 75, 83, 97, 99, 153, 161, 166, 230, 231–34

classical tradition, 87; in the Second Sophistic, 19–21

Claudius, 30, 40–42, 47–48, 54, 56–57, 120, 122; in Agrippa's letter, 43–44; Dio Cassius's and Suetonius's views of, 53–54; letter to the Alexandrian, 41–42; on religion, 63, 120, 168–69; Seneca's view of, 48–50; view of gender and family, 132, 136–37

Cleanthes, 98–99, 153, 158, 226, 238–40

Cleopatra, 11, 87, 131

Clitomachus, 69

Cohen, Leopold, 247

commentary, 8, 9, 61, 65–66, 79, 85, 94, 99–100, 124, 173, 175–77, 185–90, 195–96, 207; in Alexandria, 15–16, 65–66, 109, 174, 177, 194, 207; of Alexandrian Jews, 174–75, 185–86, 189; Christian view of, 189–90; in Greek culture, 108; in the land of Israel, 177; Roman view of, 177; Stoic view of, 113–14, 177

companionship. See marriage

Concordia, 134

conflagration, 78, 80–93, 98; Philo's view of, 78, 80, 93–94, 226–27

contemplation, 86–87, 102–3, 151

Cotta, 73–75, 99

creation, 77, 81, 86, 93–97, 99–105, 154–55, 157, 203–6, 215, 217–20, 224; Aristobulus's view of, 105; Aristotelian view of, 79, 97; Ben Sira's view of, 104–5; Christian and "Gnostic" views of, 106–8; Josephus's view of, 89, 106; Platonic view of, 79, 98, 107, 221; rabbinic view of, 107–8; Stoic view of, 95, 97–100; Tauros's view of, 78–79

Damis, 19–20, 129
Daphnaeus, 139
Decalogue, the. *See under* law
Demetrius, 16, 174–75, 180–82
demiurge, 97, 99–102, 104; Gnostic view of, 107; Josephus's view of, 89; Origen's view of, 108; in Platonism, 74, 79, 99–100, 108, 216, 228; in Stoicism, 98, 227–28
Democritus, 233
desire. *See* passion
Dillon, John, 79, 210
Dio Cassius: view of Claudius, 53–55; view of Gaius, 52–53, 55, 65
Diogenes Laertius, 49, 97–98, 226–27, 229–30, 233–34, 236–37, 239
Diogenes of Babylon, 80
Dionysius, 184
Domitian, 83
Donini, Pierluigi, 233
Drusus, 135–36

embassy to Gaius, 4, 39–40; Agrippa's letter, 43–45; Gaius in Philo's *Embassy*, 51–53, 56–57; influences on Philo, 11, 14, 89, 98, 109, 112–13, 140, 170; religious interpretation of, 39–44
Enoch, 126
Epictetus, 82–84, 164
epistemology, 197–200, 204, 212–14, 221–22; Platonic view of, 193–94, 197–98, 200; Stoic view of, 199
Esau, 85
Essenes, 85–86, 124

ethics, 110, 117–18, 123, 125–26, 148, 151–53, 156–57, 160, 165–66, 170, 195–98, 206–7, 231, 235, 241; Paul's view of, 154; Platonic view of, 231–32; Plutarch's view of, 128, 232, 241; Stoic view of, 96, 123–25, 153, 155–56, 229–32, 234, 236–38
Eudorus, 194, 204–5, 209
Eugnotus, 216
Eusebius, 1, 74, 78, 86, 247
Eve, 131, 138–39, 180, 202
exemplar, 115–16; in Philo's work, 35–36, 84, 112, 117–18, 121–28; in Plutarch's work, 128–29; in Seneca's work, 35–36, 114
exile, 81, 118; of Flaccus, 57–58; of Jews in Alexandria, 59–61; as a loss of political power, 61–62; according to Luke-Acts, 62–63; Marcellus's view of, 49; philosophical interpretation of, 58–59, 118; Plutarch's view of, 62; and religion, 58–61; Seneca's view of, 48–51, 57
Ezekiel the Tragedian, 36, 116

Fabricius, 159
family values, 143, 160–61; Augustus's view of, 134, 135, 137, 145–46, 159; Roman Stoic view of, 161
Feldman, Louis, 42
femininity, 131–36, 138–45, 160, 202–3; Christian view of, 140–41; Plutarch's view of, 139–40; Roman view of, 132–33, 135–36, 142–45, 147–48
Flaccus, 31–32, 109; in exile, 57–58; repentance of, 58–59; trial of, 26–27, 31–33, 57–58
flattery, 49–50, 52, 56
forefathers, 93–94, 102–3, 106, 110–11, 121, 128, 135
freedom of speech, 124; under Claudius, 49–51, 53–56; under Gaius, 51–52, 54–56, 124; Philo's view of, 54–55

freedom of spirit, 81–82, 84–86, 124, 215, 238; Cicero's view of, 83; Epictetus's view of, 83–84; Stoic view of, 83, 124, 163–64

Gaius Caligula, 33, 38–39, 48, 51–53, 58, 63–64, 109, 115, 124, 136, 166; in Agrippa's letter, 43–44; attitude toward Alexandria, 31–33, 109; in contrast to Claudius, 40–42; embassy to, 4, 34–35, 38–39; in relation to Ares, 64–65; Seneca's view of, 49; statue in Jerusalem, 35–37, 165; Suetonius's and Dio Cassius's views of, 52–53
gender issues. *See* femininity
Germanicus, 136
Glucker, John, 195
God, 9, 26, 33, 58–59, 65, 67, 75–77, 80, 83, 86, 93–95, 97–104, 126–27, 152, 165, 169, 183, 188, 195, 198–202, 206, 211–15, 222–23, 227–28, 232, 235–36, 239–40; Aristotelian view of, 97; early Christian view of, 90, 108; Epictetus's view of, 84; Gnostic view of, 11, 107; Josephus's view of, 105–6; in Luke-Acts, 67; Phythago-rean view of, 214; Platonic view of, 11, 15, 74–79, 93–94, 98–101, 194, 199, 212–14, 216; rabbinic view of, 107–8; Stoic view of, 74, 76, 80, 83, 98–99, 101–3, 166, 226, 228, 238
godlikeness, 193–94, 210, 239
Goodenough, Erwin, 55
Greek (language): Claudius's knowledge of, 51; Lucian knowledge of, 19; Seneca's knowledge of, 18
Greek renaissance. *See* Second Sophistic

Hagar, 136–38, 193
Hebrew (language), 4
Heine, Ronald, 249
Heinemann, Isaak, 247
Helvia, 142, 161

Hesiod, 211
historiography: Lucian's historiogra-phy, 28; Philo's historiography (*see under* Philo, writings of); Roman historiography, 13, 113, 115. *See also* Josephus, Flavius
Homer, 174, 211
Horace, 150
Hosea, 184
Hoshaya (Rabbi), 107–8, 244
human superiority, 70, 72, 85, 100; Cicero's view of, 73; Platonic view of, 73; Second Sophists' view of, 74; Stoic view of, 73, 100; Tiberius Alexander's view of, 71

identity: Christian, 13, 170; Greek, 12, 19; individual, 51, 114, 123; Jewish, 120, 167–69; of Philo, 13, 19, 38–40, 65
individuality, 51, 112–15, 123, 157–58, 165, 235, 238, 240; Stoic view of, 158, 194, 232, 234–37
intertextuality: in Alexandria, 181–82; in Philo's work, 182, 189, 222
Inwood, Brad, 233
Irenaeus, 223
irony, 27–28, 40, 43, 87; of Josephus, 27–28, 40; of Lucian, 28, 40; of the Second Sophists, 19, 177
Isaac, 85, 121, 127, 184, 201

Jacob, 85, 121, 182, 237
Jeremiah, 183
Jerusalem, 67–68, 166–67
Jerusalem Temple, 66–67, 165–70; Augustus's attitude toward, 66–67, 132; in the Gospel of Luke, 62, 168; Qumranic view of, 165; the statue of Gaius, 35–37, 43–45
Jesus, 168
Jethro, 118
Jewish culture: in Alexandria, 15–17, 210; intercultural dialogue, 16, 36, 168; in Rome, 15–17

Jewish religion: in Alexandria, 152; in contrast to political power, 62–63, 120, 168; as a cult, 66–67, 120; otherness of, 38–40, 149–50; as a philosophy, 60–61, 65–66, 77, 85–87, 89, 102, 106, 124, 149–54, 162–63, 167–69; in Rome, 65–66; roots in nature, 68, 96, 155, 162; theology, 94, 97; as an urban universal religion, 67–68, 120, 160–61

Joseph (father of Jesus), 141

Joseph (son of Jacob), 121–25, 134, 146–47, 175

Josephus, Flavius, 27–28, 30–31, 40, 89, 140, 142–43, 150; apologetics, 150–51, 164–65, 169; Claudius's letter, 42; irony, 27–28, 40, 89; about Jewish religion, 105; in Rome, 13, 134, 136; view of Agrippa I, 30–31; view of Philo, 1, 3, 29–30, 70, 150

Julia, 145

Julia Domna, 19, 129

Julian the Apostate, 108

Justin Martyr, 13, 41, 90, 106–7, 170, 243

Juvenal, 162

knowledge, 197–202, 204, 206, 211, 214, 235–36; Platonic view of, 193–94, 197, 200–203, 211, 216; Stoic view of, 199

Lampo, 26–27

Latin (language): Philo's knowledge of, 14, 18; Plutarch's knowledge of, 232–33

law: biblical law, 93–94, 96, 103, 106, 111, 149, 152, 154, 159, 162–64, 169–70; the Decalogue, 151–54, 156–61; law of nature, 96–97, 100, 105–6, 137, 156–59, 161–62, 170, 238–39; philosophy of law, 149–50, 154–55; Roman law, 96–97, 159–60

Leah, 134, 236

Lévy, Carlos, 225

Livia, 131–35, 138, 140, 147

Livy, 113

Logismos, 34–36, 38, 123, 203, 206; in Seneca's work, 35–36

Logos, 101, 209, 216–24; Gnostic view of, 223; in Platonism, 79, 221, 223

love, 134, 137–39, 146; Aristophanes's view of, 139; Josephus's view of, 134, 140; Plutarch's view of, 139–40; in Rome, 134

Lucian of Samosata: Greek identity, 12, 19; irony and historiography, 28, 40, 70, 177; on Rome, 40

Lucilius, 75

Luke, 13, 40–41, 65, 130, 140–41, 243

Lysimachus, 29, 70–71

Macro, 51–56, 119, 124; Dio Cassius's view of, 52–53, 55; Suetonius's view of, 52–53

Marc Antony, 11, 87

Marcellinus, Tullius, 116

Marcellus, 49

Marcia, 132

Marcion, 107

Marcus Aurelius, 75, 107

marriage, 134, 136–42, 146–47, 160; Christian view of, 140–41; Josephus's view of, 134–36, 140; Plutarch's view of, 139–40; in Rome, 134–36, 139, 141–42; Stoic view of, 137, 139

Mars, 64–65

martyrdom, 38, 40–41; Dio Cassius's view of, 54; Justin Martyr's view of, 41; in Luke-Acts, 40–41; Seneca's view of, 50–51

Mary, 141

Mason, Steve, 62

materialism, 226–28, 240, 289

matriarchs, 131, 133, 135, 202

Matthew, 141

Mediterranean routes, 29, 34, 45, 56, 67

Messalina, 53–55, 136

Messalinus, Valerius, 135

metropolis: Jerusalem as, 67–68; Rome as, 18, 65

Miriam, 143, 145, 240

Mnester, 55

Moderatus, 221

monotheism, 93–94, 99–103, 126, 157, 165–66, 206; Josephus's view of, 105–6; Origen's view of, 108; Platonic view of, 99–100, 216; rabbinic view of, 107–8; Stoic view of, 98–99, 238

morality. *See* ethics

Morris, Jenny, 247–48

Moses, 110–11, 112, 115–18, 123, 144, 215, 231; according to Apion, 110, 111, 112; as the author of the Torah, 94, 96, 175–79, 181–82, 185–86, 230; biography of, 112, 115, 118–19, 142; as the lawgiver of the Jews, 77, 96, 104, 111, 154–55; as a philosopher, 85, 93–94, 97, 104, 116, 130, 163, 180, 182, 195, 196, 211, 213, 228, 230; religious role, 94, 96, 119, 120, 165, 185, 189, 213, 215, 228, 239

motherhood, 141–43, 161

Museum, the (Alexandria), 15, 28, 51, 65, 174–75, 189

Musonius, 134, 137, 142–45, 147, 161

mysticism, 183–85, 189, 201–3, 222–23; Platonic view of, 193–94

nature, 26, 68, 96–97, 100, 118, 122–23, 137, 143, 155, 157, 160–62, 164, 239–40; Epicurean view of, 158; Roman view of, 159–60, 162; Stoic view of, 96–97, 100, 137, 142–43, 156–59, 161, 228, 234, 237, 240

Nazirite, 219

negative theology, 214, 223

Neo-Platonism. *See under* Platonism

Nepos, Cornelius, 113

Nero, 50, 168–69

Noah, 126

noble suffering. *See* suffering

Numenius, 216

oikeiosis, 233–36, 241

Origen, 10–11, 107–8, 189–90, 243–44, 249

orthodoxy, 186–87

Ovid, 134

Panaetius, 17, 80–81, 93–94, 99, 114, 225, 228

paradoxical philosophy, 81–83, 178; Cicero's view of, 83; Stoic view of, 82

parenthood, 141–42, 160–61; philosophers' view of, 142; Roman Stoic view of, 142, 161

passion, 156–57, 203, 205–6, 229–33, 237; Platonic view of, 157, 204–5; Stoic view of, 156–57, 229–30

patriarchs. *See* forefathers

Paul, 13, 62–63, 154, 243

Paulina, 134

Petronius, 150

Pharaoh, 117, 121, 127, 138, 141

Pharaoh's daughter, 114, 143–44

Philo: as an ambassador, 16, 34–41, 150, 224, 240; early career, 1–2, 8–10, 16, 94, 131–32, 147, 149, 152–53, 160, 173–75, 185–87, 199–200, 207, 209, 223–26, 233, 240–41; family, 29–30, 72; mature period, 4, 6, 8–9, 11, 15, 70–84, 95–96, 98, 109–10, 131, 147, 153, 156–57, 160, 165, 191, 199, 224, 233, 238, 240; upbringing, 3–4. *See also* political influences on Philo

Philo, writings of: apologetics, 16, 85, 110–11, 129, 150, 164, 169–70, 187–89; on the Bible, 8–9, 72, 85, 93–94, 109, 117, 122–24, 133, 173–78, 182–83, 205–6, 218; biography, 109–15, 122–23, 125–27; chronology, 4–6, 11, 41, 47, 245–46; commentary, 8, 9, 61, 65–66, 79, 85, 94, 99–100, 124, 173, 175–76; genre, 7, 27; historiography, 4, 8, 33–34, 84, 110, 115, 148; implied audience, 6–10, 27, 57, 61, 67, 70, 81, 85–86, 101, 106, 110–12, 124–25, 127–28, 149–51, 162–63, 169, 175–76, 180, 185, 187, 243; philosophical treatises, 6–7, 69–70, 93–94, 103; relation to the Second Sophistic, 19–22, 67, 70; theological inclination, 39, 43–44, 60, 85, 93, 97, 119–20, 182–85, 210–24

Philolaus, 214

Philo of Larissa, 18, 69

Philostratus, 19–20, 74, 129–30, 169

pilgrimage, 166–68; in the Gospel of Luke, 168

Plato: on creation, 78–80, 93–94, 101, 139, 228; on epistemology, 193–94, 197–98, 200–201, 203, 211; on God, 100, 212–13; on godlikeness, 194; 193–201, 204–8, 212, 215, 221, 228; on Greek culture, 87; interpretation of, 107, 138, 155, 193, 195, 196, 199, 207, 215, 221, 223, 228–29, 243; on love, 139; on politics, 119; reception in Rome, 70; as a role model, 116; on the soul, 74, 114, 146, 157, 204–7, 232; treatises of, 77–78, 90, 95, 98, 194

Platonism: in Alexandria, 15, 70, 74, 95, 107–8, 132, 194–95, 199–200, 213–14, 216, 221; Middle Platonism, 11, 74, 79; Neo-Platonism, 216, 243; in Philo's work, 9, 69–70, 72–79, 94–95, 98, 116, 132, 149, 180–81, 190, 192–93, 195–97, 200–206, 211–13, 220, 227–28, 236, 241; Phythagorean Platonism, 213–14

Pliny, 85

Plotinus, 216

Plutarch: biography, 113, 115, 128–29, 131; comparison to Philo, 21–22, 139, 232–33, 241; connection to Rome, 14; on exile, 62; Greek identity, 12, 21–22, 168; on marriage, 139, 143; philosophy of, 80, 88, 128, 216, 221,

227; as a Second Sophist, 19, 67, 74; on Stoicism, 226

political influences on Philo: Claudius, 40–42, 54–57, 59–62; embassy, 109, 150, 242

politics and political influence, 35, 37–38, 118–19, 121–22, 128, 186

Polybius, 48

polytheism, 63–65, 94; Origen's view of, 108; Stoic view of, 98

Porphyry, 74, 108, 174

Posidonius, 98, 155, 228

Potiphar's wife, 121, 123–25, 146

Priscilla, 141

Protagoras, 197–99, 235

Protogenes, 139

providence, 74–76, 78, 80, 82, 86, 93–94, 97, 100–103, 121, 188, 218–20; Josephus's view of, 89, 106; Phythagoreanism, 213–14, 218; Platonic view of, 74, 100; Plutarch's view of, 80; Stoic view of, 75–77, 80, 101–2

Pyrrhus, 159

Rachel, 134, 202

rationality, 123–24, 137, 146, 152, 155, 203, 205–6, 220–21, 235, 239; Platonic view of, 204–5; Stoic view of, 132, 145–46, 157–58, 230, 232, 234–35

rationality of animals, 70, 72, 85; Cicero's view of, 73; Platonic view of, 73; Second Sophists' view of, 74; Stoic view of, 73; Tiberius Alexander's view of, 71

reason. See rationality

Robinson, Tom, 62

Roman culture, 11–12, 14, 69–70, 133–34, 160–61; relation to early Christianity, 13, 62–63, 90, 140–41; relation to Greek culture, 12, 84, 86–87; relation to nature, 159–60, 162; Roman discourses, 70–84, 88, 95–96, 105–7, 114–15, 124, 132, 134, 144, 148, 158–59,

Roman culture (*continued*)
    161; Roman ethnography, 85, 127;
    Roman mythology, 64
Rome: comparison to Alexandria,
    15–17, 63, 70, 73, 80, 83–84; intel-
    lectual history, 17–18, 63, 65; Jewish
    culture in, 16; Jewish religion in,
    63–66; philosophy in, 69–70, 75, 83;
    religion in, 63–65, 67, 75, 119–20; as
    a theatrical farce, 40
Runia, David, 98, 217

Sallustius, 108, 113
Salonkultur, 6, 151
Sarah, 127, 131, 133–38, 143–46, 183–84, 187,
    193, 202
Saturn, 163
sea travel: in early Christian times, 29,
    67; Philo's view of, 29, 34, 45, 67; in
    Roman Empire, 29, 34, 45, 67
Second Sophistic, 12, 19–20, 70, 243;
    Philo's connection to, 19–22, 67, 70,
    168–69
Sedley, David, 193
self, 9, 26, 35–36, 59, 156, 192, 195; rabbinic
    view of, 89; in Roman Stoicism, 17,
    35–36, 59, 114–15, 123, 236–37
self-fashioning: in historical writings,
    38, 45–46, 112, 115; of Lucian, 28;
    of Philo as a dramatic author,
    36–38, 40–41, 43–44; of Philo as an
    enigmatic author, 1–2, 25, 34, 43–44;
    of Philo as an ironic author, 27–28,
    40, 43, 87; of Philo as a paradoxical
    thinker, 81; in Rome, 69–70
Seneca, 14, 17–18, 35–36, 135; in compari-
    son to Philo, 35, 57–59, 89; on family
    and gender, 142, 145, 147, 161; on
    Livia, 132; noble suffering, 40–41,
    49; philosophical writings, 35–36,
    48–51, 73, 75–77, 83, 87, 96, 101, 114,
    153, 155–56, 159, 162–63, 230–32; view
    of Claudius, 41–42, 48–51; view of

exile, 48–51, 57–59; view of Gaius,
    56–57
Septuagint, 116, 141, 177, 183, 213, 220
Severus Caecina, 135
Silanus, 52–53, 55; Dio Cassius's view of,
    52–53; Suetonius's view of, 52–53
Silas, 62
Socrates, 84, 116, 129, 193, 195, 197, 201,
    203
soul, 102–3, 149, 152, 157, 169, 180, 182–85,
    192–93, 195, 200–202, 204–6, 218–19,
    222, 228–29, 231; Justin Martyr's
    view of, 207–8; Platonist view of,
    114, 116, 146, 149, 196, 201, 204–7,
    229, 231; Stoic view of, 232
spirituality, 102–3, 149, 152, 157, 169, 180,
    182–85, 192–93, 195, 200, 206–7, 215,
    222, 228, 236; Justin Martyr's view
    of, 207–8; Platonist view of, 114,
    116, 146, 149, 196, 207; Stoic view
    of, 232
Sterling, Gregory, 247–49
Stobaeus, 230
Stoicism: in Alexandria, 15–16, 83; dif-
    ferences within the school, 226; in
    Philo's writing, 7–9, 16, 35–37, 56–57,
    64, 72–82, 85–86, 89, 93, 95, 97–98,
    100–103, 113–15, 123–25, 129, 137–39,
    142–43, 153–58, 161–63, 166, 170, 225,
    228, 230–32, 234, 237–39, 241, 259n15;
    in Rome, 17, 73–74, 76, 82–83, 95–96,
    98–99, 101, 115–16, 123, 142–43, 153,
    161, 163
Strabo, 84
Striker, Gisela, 158
Suetonius: view of Claudius, 53–54; view
    of Gaius, 52, 65
suffering, 38, 40–41, 49–51, 82
suicide, 84; Stoic view of, 83, 114
symposium: Christian, 90; Greek,
    86–87, 122, 125; Jewish, 86–89; Ro-
    man, 88
synagogues, 16, 60, 62, 65–66, 70, 163

Tacitus, 132, 134–35, 150, 162
Tarrant, Harold, 194
Tauros, 78–79
temple worship: Apollonius's view of, 169; Philostratus's view of, 169; Plutarch's view of, 168–69. *See also* Jerusalem Temple
Ten Commandments. *See* law: the Decalogue
Theaetetus, 95, 193–95, 199–201, 207
Themistocles, 113
theodicy. *See* providence
Theodotus, 6
theology. *See* transcendent theology
Therapeutae, 86–87
Thrasyllus, 79, 221
Tiberius, 44, 57, 109, 132, 221
Tiberius Julius Alexander, 6, 29, 71–73, 74, 85, 88, 122
Timaeus, 74, 77–79, 90, 95, 97–99, 105, 107–8, 204, 220, 228
Tobin, Thomas, 247–49
transcendent theology, 26, 95, 97–98, 101, 104–5, 180, 195–96, 199, 209–10, 213, 215–16, 221, 223, 236; in Alexandria, 195, 199; Aristobulus's view of, 105;

Gnostic view of, 107, 215–16; Platonic view of, 74, 98, 180, 194, 196, 210, 214–16; Stoic view of, 102
Tsipora, 143–45
Turia, 137
tyranny, criticism of, 54–57, 84; by Dio Cassius, 52–54; by Seneca, 56–57

Valentine, 189, 216, 223
Valerius Maximus, 88
Varro, 63–64, 67, 119–20, 166
virtue, 82, 86, 110–11, 118–19, 125–26, 195, 238–39; Stoic view of, 82, 153, 158, 234, 236–37

Whittaker, John, 213–14
Winston, David, 210

Xanthians, 84
Xenophon, 87

Zeno, 81, 85, 96, 98, 114, 156, 158, 226–30, 234, 239
Zenodotus, 177
Zeus, 37, 98–99, 218, 238

Index of Ancient Sources

Boldface page numbers indicate where sources are cited.

Aristobulus
In Eusebius, *P.E.*, 8.10.2-3, **210**

Cicero
Ac., 1.6, **97**
Leg., 1.15-19, **96-97**
N.D., 3.28, **99**
N.D., 3.79, **75**

Claudius
Letter to the Alexandrians, CPJ no. 153,
    2.41, **42**

Comm. Theaet.
52.30-39, **202-3**
53.57-54, **202-3**

Dio Cassius
60.3.6, **53**
60.14.1, **54**
60.14.3, **53**
60.16.4, **54**
60.16.7, **54**
60.28.4, **55**

Diogenes Laertius
6.49, **49**
7.85-87, **233-34**
7.87, **239**
7.89, **238**
7.101-7, **236-37**
7.135-48, **227**

Eudorus
in Stob. *Ecl*, 2.66, **194**, **210**

Eusebius
P.E., 7.12.14, **78**

Josephus, Flavius
C.Ap, 2.21, **164**
C.Ap, 2.192, **106**
J.A., 1.155, **106**
J.A., 18.259-60, **1**

Lucian
Ver. Hist., 1.4, **28**
Ver. Hist., 2.20, **177**

Musonius
12.2-4, **147**

New Testament
Luke, 2:49, **168**
Rom, 13:8-10, **154**

Origen
C.C., 4.79, **108**
C.C., 7.42-44, **108**
PArch, 4.15, **190**

Philo
Abr., 4, **126**
Abr., 54, **125**
Abr., 70, **102**
Abr., 93, **133**
Abr., 95, **127**
Abr., 245, **135**
Abr., 246, **134**
Abr., 247, **133**
Abr., 248-49, **136-37**

Aet., 19, **85**
Aet., 76-77, **80**
Alex., 1.2, **129**
All., 1.1, **248**
All., 1.8-15, **218**
All., 1.16, **218-219**
All., 1.17, **219**
All., 1.19-20, **219**
All., 1.21, **220**
All., 1.43, **190**
All., 1.85, **179**
All., 1.86-87, **179**
All., 1.101, **177**
All., 1.105, **180**
All., 2.7-8, **199**
All., 2.38, **202**
All., 2.69, **199**
All., 3.100-103, **215**
All., 3.104-6, **215**
All., 3.115, **204**
All., 3.131, **232**
All., 3.137, **229**
All., 3.139, **229**
All., 3.156-57, **203**
All., 3.206, **214**
All., 3.223, **205**
Cher., 49-50, **183**
Conf., 14, **176**
Conf., 190-91, **176**
Congr., 74, **200**
Cont., 43, **87**
Cont., 64, **87**
Cont., 77, **87-88**
Dec., 69, **103**
Dec., 81, **223**
Dec., 142, **156**
Dec., 143, **157**
Det., 32, **177**
Det., 81, **179**
Det., 160, **94, 213**
Deus, 53-54, **212**
Deus, 55-56, **212**
Flacc., 6, **26**

Flacc., 32-40, **31**
Flacc., 46, **67**
Flacc., 103, **32**
Flacc., 104, **33**
Flacc., 109, **58**
Flacc., 121-23, **60**
Flacc., 131, **26-27**
Flacc., 158–59, **58**
Flacc., 163–64, **58**
Flacc., 183, **58**
Flacc., 184, **58**
Fug., 63, **95, 193**
Fug., 82, **196**
Fug., 85, **197**
Fug., 97, **222**
Her., 246, **199**
Her., 247, **201**
Her., 259, **201**
Jos., 4, **122**
Jos., 40, **146**
Jos., 43, **146**
Jos., 166, **122**
Legat., 1, **26**
Legat., 6, **65**
Legat., 32, **51**
Legat., 39-40, **54**
Legat., 41, **52**
Legat., 43-51, **56**
Legat., 74, **56**
Legat., 86, **63-64**
Legat., 112-13, **64-65**
Legat., 143-51, **63-64**
Legat., 157, **66**
Legat., 179, **33**
Legat., 180, **36**
Legat., 182-84, **34**
Legat., 186-88, **37**
Legat., 189-90, **37**
Legat., 194, **37**
Legat., 195-96, **38**
Legat., 261, **43**
Legat., 266-69, **44**
Legat., 349, **38**

Philo (*continued*)

Legat., 353-63, **39**

Legat., 362, **39**

Migr., 1-13, **192**

Migr., 13, **182**

Migr., 34, **192**

Migr., 39-42, **199**

Migr., 90, **149**

Migr., 128, **239**

Migr., 177, **179**

Migr., 179-82, **228**

Mos.,1.1, **111**

Mos., 1.7, **140**

Mos., 1.40, **117**

Mos., 1.51, **115**

Mos., 1.54, **117, 144**

Mos., 14.17, **144**

Mut., 140, **184**

Opif., 2, **154-55**

Opif., 3, **96, 155**

Opif., 7-11, **97**

Opif., 16, **217**

Opif., 20, **217**

Opif., 127, **14**

Opif., 152, **138**

Opif., 171-72, **100**

Plant., 26, **183**

Plant., 29, **184**

Plant., 49, **239**

Post., 1-9, **178**

Post., 1-12, **190**

Post., 12-20, **235**

Post., 32, **177**

Post., 35-37, **198**

Post., 49, **178**

Post., 51, **178**

Prob., 19, **83-84**

Prob., 57, **85**

Prob., 60, **82**

Prob., 61, **238**

Prob., 75, **86**

Prob., 88, **86**

Prob., 118-20, **84**

Prov., 2.1, **74-75**

Prov., 2.10, **75**

Prov., 2.35-47, **76**

QG, 1.21, **188**

QG, 3.8, **186**

QG, 4.243, **186**

Sobr., 16, **181**

Sobr., 17, **180**

Somn., 1.184, **214**

Somn., 1.233, **212**

Spec., 1.41, **104**

Spec., 2.66-69, **163**

Spec., 3.1-3, **7**

Spec., 3.137-43, **163**

Philostratus

Apol., 2.4, **19-20**

Plato

Soph., 246a-c, **197, 211**

Theaet., 150b-51c, **201**

Theaet., 186d, **197**

Tim., 27A-29E, **100**

Plutarch

Cat. Mai., 12.5, **84**

Cat. Mai., 22.1-23.1, **84**

Galba, 2.3, **128**

Is. and Os., 54, **221**

Quest. Conv., 1.1.1-5, **88**

Stoic. rep., 12, **241**

Seneca

Apoc., 8.2, **54**

Brev. Vit., 13.1, **66**

Clem., 2.2.2, **50**

Cons. Helv., 4.1-2, **49**

Cons. Helv., 8.6, **49**

Cons. Helv., 11.7, **49**

Cons. Helv., 15.4, **142**

Ira, 2.1.1-2.3.2, **230-31**

Prov., 1.1, **75**

Septuagint (LXX)
Gen, 2:4-5, **220**
Exod, 3:14, **213**
Ps, 36:4, **184**

Stobaeus
2.88, **230-31**

Suetonius
Claud., 25.4, **47**

Torah
Deut, 30:20, **235**
Exod, 2:17, **144**
Exod, 3:14, **94**

Exod, 20:17, **156**
Gen, 1:21, **182**
Gen, 1:26, **206**
Gen, 2:4-5, **220**
Gen, 4:9, **187**
Gen, 12:1, **61**
Gen, 12:4, **239**
Gen, 18:22, **236**
Gen, 21:6, **184**
Gen, 30:1, **202**
Gen, 39:7, **146**
Hos, 14:8-9, **184**
Jer, 3:4, **183**